T0315087

AMERICAN BIG BUSINESS
IN BRITAIN AND GERMANY

AMERICAN BIG BUSINESS IN BRITAIN AND GERMANY

A Comparative History of Two
"Special Relationships" in the
20th Century

Volker R. Berghahn

PRINCETON UNIVERSITY PRESS
PRINCETON AND OXFORD

In the United Kingdom: Princeton University Press, 6 Oxford
Street, Woodstock, Oxfordshire OX20 1TW

press.princeton.edu

Jacket art: Sascha Berghahn. Reprinted with permission of
Sascha Berghahn.

Library of Congress Cataloging-in-Publication Data

Berghahn, Volker R. (Volker Rolf), 1938–
    American big business in Britain and Germany : a compara-
tive history of two "special relationships" in the twentieth
century / Volker R. Berghahn.
        pages cm
Includes index.
    ISBN 978-0-691-16109-9 (cloth : alk. paper)   1. United
States—Foreign economic relations—Great Britain. 2. Great
Britain—Foreign economic relations—United States. 3. United
States—Foreign economic relations—Germany. 4. Germany—
Foreign economic relations—United States. 5. Corporations,
American—Great Britain—History—20th century. 6. Corpora-
tions, American—Germany—History—20th century. 7. Big
business—United States—History—20th century. 8. United
States—Commerce—Europe—History—20th century.
9. Europe—Commerce—United States—History—20th
century.   I. Title.
    HF1456.5.E8B47 2014
    338.8'89730410904—dc23

                                        2013047538

British Library Cataloging-in-Publication Data is available

This book has been composed in Palatino

Printed on acid-free paper. ∞

Printed in the United States of America

10 9 8 7 6 5 4 3 2 1

For Marion, Sasch, Viv, and Mel

CONTENTS

//

Introduction

    1. A Long Book in a Nutshell   1

    2. Conceptualizing "Americanization" and the "American Century"   2

    3. The Anglo-American "Special Relationship"   5

    4. The German-American "Special Relationship"   8

    5. Sources   11

    6. Transatlantic History and Its Global Dimensions   12

    7. The Trials and Tribulations of Venturing into a Foreign Economy   14

I   The North Atlantic Business Triangle and the Constellation of 1900–1901

    1. International Relations Around 1900   22

    2. Assessing the Old and the New Century   23

    3. Political and Economic Relations in the Age of Late-Nineteenth-Century Imperialism   27

    4. Frank Vanderlip's and William Stead's Views of Anglo-American Relations   30

    5. American Perceptions of the Wilhelmine Industrial System   37

    6. Trying to Understand the Peculiarities of the German Political System   45

    7. The Cultural Difficulties of Operating in Foreign Markets   49

II   Cooperation, Peaceful Competition, and the Specter of War, 1902–1914

    1. Introduction   57

    2. American Foreign Direct Investments in Britain and Germany   58

    3. Facing British and German Competition and Cooperation   63

    4. Prince Heinrich's Mission and German-American Relations in the New Century   70

    5. American Big Business in Britain and Germany at Mid-Decade   73

    6. The Threat of Deteriorating Political Relations   75

    7. Comparing the Peculiarities of the American and German Industrial Systems   79

    8. American Big Business and the Question of Political Participation   84

    9. American and European Businessmen and the Specter of a Major War   88

III From the Outbreak of War in July 1914 to the Genoa
     Conference, 1922

 1. *The Military-Political Origins of World War I* 105
 2. *The International Business Community and the Outbreak of War
    in 1914* 108
 3. *The Ambiguities of American Neutrality* 113
 4. *The American Economy and the Moves to Enter the War* 116
 5. *The American Entry into the War and the Dilemmas of Peacemaking* 123
 6. *American Big Business and European Reconstruction* 126
 7. *The Idea of an International Loan for European Reconstruction and Its
    Failure* 131
 8. *The State of the American, British, and French Economies in the Early 1920s* 134
 9. *American Big Business and the Postwar Crisis in Germany* 137
 10. *American Big Business, Washington, and the Question of
    European Loans* 139
 11. *The Origins of the Washington System in the Far East* 142
 12. *Britain's Rival Attempt to Spearhead a European Recovery Plan* 144

IV The North Atlantic Triangle: Economic Reconstruction
     and Collapse, 1923–1933

 1. *Introduction* 160
 2. *German Reparations and the Harding Administration* 161
 3. *American Big Business and the Crisis of 1923* 165
 4. *Political Stabilization through the Locarno Pact* 168
 5. *The American Business Community and the Dawes Plan* 170
 6. *American Big Business and the British Economy* 179
 7. *American Investments in Weimar Germany and Their Risks* 187
 8. *The Problem of International Cartels, Trusts, and Cooperations* 195
 9. *The Instabilities of Weimar Politics and American Business Optimism* 201
 10. *Parker Gilbert's Pessimism and American Business Gullibility* 206
 11. *America's Domestic Boom and the "Wild" Years of 1925–1929* 211
 12. *The Great Slump and Its Consequences in International Politics* 214

V Nazi Germany, Appeasement, and Anglo-American Big
     Business, 1933–1941

 1. *Introduction* 227
 2. *Hitler's Ideology of Conquest and Ultimate War Aims* 229
 3. *Hitler's Foreign Policy in the 1930s* 232
 4. *The Underestimation of Hitler and British Appeasement* 236
 5. *American Foreign Policy in the 1930s* 239
 6. *American Big Business and the Roosevelt Administration* 243
 7. *Stimulating American Industrial Production* 245

8. American Views of the Hitler Dictatorship 250

9. Hitler and German Industry 255

10. Doing Business in Nazi Germany 257

11. The U.S. Auto Industry and Mass Motorization 260

12. British and American Business and the Preservation of Peace 266

13. IBM in Germany 272

VI   British and German Business and Politics under the *Pax Americana*, 1941–1957

1. Hitler's Quest for Victory in the East 286

2. Planning for Victory and Henry Luce's "American Century" 288

3. Cartels and the "German Question" 293

4. The Role of American Big Business in Postwar Planning 299

5. The Start of the Cold War and Anglo-American Relations in Occupied Germany 301

6. The Politics of Decartelization 307

7. The Response of West German Industry to America's Recasting Efforts 313

8. Britain and the Difficulties of Economic Reconstruction 317

9. The Origins of the European Coal and Steel Community 323

10. American Big Business and Otto A. Friedrich 326

11. Modernizing Phoenix A.G. and Erhard's Anti-Cartel Bill 329

12. The Reluctant Modernization of British Industry 332

13. America and the Suez Crisis 339

Conclusions 355

Acknowledgments 365

Index 367

American Big Business
in Britain and Germany

Introduction

//

1. A Long Book in a Nutshell

This book is an attempt to examine three interrelated problems that not only historians but also social scientists have been grappling with at the beginning of the twenty-first century. The first one is how to deal conceptually and empirically with the role of the United States as a major socioeconomic, political-military, and cultural power since its emergence on the international stage at around 1900, and hence with the meaning and significance of "Americanization" and the resistance and adaptation to its impact by nations that came under its spell.

Second, there is the notion of the "special relationship" that America is said to have had with Britain during the period covered by this study. Its existence or nonexistence has been analyzed in most accounts of diplomatic as well as economic relations between the two countries. Some of them have even included the term in the title.[1] However and perhaps at first glance rather more puzzlingly, this book is also concerned with yet another "special relationship," that is, the one with Germany and in particular with its business community during more or less exactly the same period. As both Britain's and Germany's "special relationship" with the United States had a major influence on European history and on international affairs more generally in the first half of the twentieth century, the third approach adopted in this book is to discuss the evolution of this transatlantic triangle in comparative perspective.

Finally, this is not business history in a strict sense concerned with case studies of individual firms. Rather this work constantly asks questions about the *interaction* between existing political and economic power structures within and between the United States, Britain, and

Germany. In this context, it is also worth pointing out up front that this book contains a good deal of evidence that socioeconomic networks among corporations and their leaders established around 1900 or even before proved quite stable over many decades and notwithstanding considerable political upheavals. This means also that quite a few striking continuities in attitudes and practices emerge from the sources found within the broader time frame of sixty to seventy years adopted here, for example, with respect to industrial training or the stress on high-quality manufacturing in the German case, or the emphasis on teamwork in the American one, and, third, the persistence of Oxbridge-educated business and political elites in Britain. There are also continuities with respect to the growing interest in the "mind," not just of one's own workers and managers, but also that of foreign businessmen, socialized into their own national cultures. However, this does not mean that I take a static view of history. After all, there were plenty of ruptures between 1900 and 1957. In this respect, this book is, next to socioeconomic transformations, particularly interested in *generational* change.

2. Conceptualizing "Americanization" and the "American Century"

In 1902, the influential British journalist William T. Stead published a book with the title *The Americanisation of the World*; it attracted a good deal of attention at the time and has been frequently cited since then, especially in the past three decades or so when the concept of "Americanization" came to be used more widely in the social and historical sciences.[2] Some forty years after Stead's volume, Henry Luce, the owner and publisher of *Life*, wrote an article in that magazine titled "The American Century"; like Stead's title, this work has also generated plenty of public and scholarly discussion.[3] It even looks as if the debate on these two concepts has been heating up in the current century, as the question is being raised by international relations experts and others if the "Americanization of the world" and the "American century," if they ever existed, lasted for merely a "half-century." Thomas McCormick even went so far as to postulate this when he titled his book *America's Half-Century: United States Foreign Policy in the Cold War and After*, while Mary Nolan, highlighting the interaction between the two regions, has spoken most recently of a "Transatlantic Century." Finally, there is David Ellwood's recent book, *The Shock of America. Europe and the Challenge of the Century*. However, he defines his work as "a *political* history" and does not take an explicitly economic and big business approach. Furthermore, like Nolan, he undertakes a more wide-ranging comparison involving a whole range of European countries and thus goes beyond the North Atlantic triangle chosen here.[4]

The chapters that follow represent my attempt to wrestle with the viability of those two concepts, though they are not driven by the ambition to examine the Americanization of the *world*. Rather I am concerned with the European-American relationship in the twentieth century and in particular with the role of the United States as an industrial power in relation to Britain and Germany. However, this book is not a political-diplomatic or intellectual-cultural study of the triangle. Rather it approaches its themes primarily from an economic perspective, though not from that of quantitative economic history. The hard statistical "facts" of transatlantic relations, to be found in the relevant literature, form the foundation upon which the following analysis has been built. Some of them are woven into the text where they reinforce the qualitative arguments put forward in the central chapters, and in chapters IV to VI in particular, all of which revolve around problems of both comparative political economy and business culture.

In other words, the main text deals with tangible experiences that shaped patterns of action; with perceptions, mentalities and practices of economic and political elites that were also informed by positive and negative stereotypes and myths; and with international communication and the circulation of knowledge about another society among those elites and American businessmen in particular. In this sense it starts from the self-description of the *European Journal of Political Economy* whose articles are devoted to "theoretical and empirical research on economic phenomena within a scope that encompasses collective decision-making, political behavior, and the role of institutions," but also aims to enlarge this scope to problems of sociocultural traditions, ingrained attitudes and perceptions of Self and the Other among economic and political elites. This approach is in turn put here into a comparative framework concerned also with *mutual* perceptions and a focus not merely on the coevolution of practices, but also cultural pioneering innovation and copying.[5]

As mentioned above, much recent research on the "Americanization of the world" and the "American century" has focused on how American economic, political, and cultural power and influence affected Europe and other parts of the globe. The shelves of libraries are filled with studies on how the United States was received and what positive and negative responses it generated among foreign recipients.[6] The most important result that emerged from this scholarship is that the United States did not rumble into other countries like a steamroller that flattened all indigenous socioeconomic, political, and cultural traditions and practices. On the contrary, it is now generally accepted that, while there was enthusiasm for "America" on the part of some groups, there was rejection and resistance by others—until the more influential trends either asserted themselves or compromises were forged that combined or mediated previously divergent positions.

Support for, or resistance to, what was offered from across the Atlantic in the twentieth century has been observed and examined for various European, but also non-European societies, resulting in the more general conclusion that there occurred a blending in varying degrees between what had existed before and what was imported from the United States. In other words, there is by now an extensive literature that looks at interrelations and interactions with the United States from a *European* perspective. With exceptions, these studies have tended to move away from a dichotomous class model toward the study of elites within mass production and mass consumption societies.

It is only when we turn the telescope of historical investigation around and train it on the attitudes and practices of American big business elites toward Europe that considerable gaps in our knowledge come to light. At first glance, this may seem surprising. After all, if the United States was the original source of an "Americanization" process in an "American century," it would have made sense to ask how these elites perceived the world and their European business partners and/or competitors as well as the political systems and societies within which they began to operate and how this in turn informed their attitudes and practices. The overall direction of this book is therefore "eastward" across the Atlantic, and businessmen (and it was almost exclusively men) are at the center in order to complement the existing literature on political-military and cultural "Americanization." In this respect, the book is less interested in the question of the more long-term shifts in the patterns of transatlantic interactions before 1900. To be sure, there were times when the movement of people and influences was more from east to west. But after 1900 the currents were more, though not exclusively, in the opposite direction, when transfers of technology, but also of ideas and practices in the fields of industry, marketing, and finance, are being considered. To the best of my knowledge, this is attempted here for the first time and with respect to two European societies.

The dilemma I faced was how I could possibly get a handle on the veritable mountains of published and unpublished materials that I knew were available on "American big business in Britain and Germany." One solution to this would have been to undertake a microscopic study that dealt with the topic for a very limited period of a few years, and would do so in depth by examining as many American enterprises operating in Europe as I could lay my hands on. The solution adopted here goes for a medium-range time frame of several decades. The hope is that, though knowing that I could not be comprehensive, I would nevertheless be able to uncover significant continuities as well as major structural and attitudinal shifts. It also seemed that this design would enable me to avoid a mere diachronic tunnel vision and allow me to connect the development of American business with synchronic events in politics in all three societies. To me this synchronicity was particularly important, as I was covering a period that experienced two world wars, the Great Depression of the 1930s, the rise of a Bolshevik and fascist dictatorships, and finally the Cold War and decolonization. The question was how all this affected American big business and its perceptions and practices with respect to the economies and politics of twentieth-century Europe, and those of Britain and Germany in particular.

3. The Anglo-American "Special Relationship"

While this agenda amounts to an expansion of the scope of this book, the title and subtitle point to a restriction, that is, the question of "special relationships." For over a hundred years this concept has been very durable in international politics and the popular imagination. It was part of the political vocabulary and of public debate in both the United States and Britain around 1900, when, unlike in the eighteenth and early nineteenth centuries, it had predominantly positive connotations. In fact, it was deemed to exist not only as a lofty goal of diplomacy, but also as something that had a solid foundation of trust and close cooperation in political affairs and commercial exchange between the two countries.[7]

The idea of a "special relationship" also seemed plausible at this time to many politicians, businesspeople, journalists, and academics because the distribution of power and influence between Britain and the United States was, at least on the surface, still fairly evenly balanced. On the one hand, there was Britain, the hegemonic power of the nineteenth century, whose military and economic influence, while weakening, was still impressive enough to make London a major center in international business and politics. On the other hand, there was the United States—a nation that had transformed itself in the final decades of the nineteenth century from a society of rural and small-town immigrants and farmers to one with big cities and giant corporations engaged in modern industrial production.[8]

By 1900 there was little doubt that this massive continent in the New World would be a major player in international politics and the world economy of the twentieth century. Recognizing the dramatic ascendancy of what was once a rebellious colony of the British Empire, the political and economic elites of Britain decided that it would be unwise, to try to block America's advance and to confront it head-on in whatever international disputes might arise. It was much better to seek cooperation and to appease the Americans. After the turn of the century, the balance of industrial and financial power continued to shift further in favor of the United States. As will become clear in the next chapter, Stead's *Americanisation of the World* was, its title notwithstanding, in fact about the Anglo-American relationship.[9]

However, it would be wrong to assume, at least for the period up to 1914, that Britain regularly ate humble pie when it came to relations with Washington. On the contrary, the two countries were also rivals and competitors, especially in the field of trade and commerce. World War I then mitigated these tensions and created strong affinities in the struggle against Austria-Hungary and, even more so, against Germany. But the world conflict also greatly weakened Britain's political and economic clout around the world, while the United States together with Japan emerged as the actual winners. London's dependency on America became even more marked. In this sense, the wartime "special relationship" may be said to have continued beyond 1918. But it weakened as Britain tried to reassert itself in the world of finance and industry, while American big business labored to push both sectors into the second rank.[10] The collapse of the world economy in 1929 then constituted a severe blow to the economic prowess of both countries, though perhaps less to Britain than to America.

With the rise of fascism in Europe and of Nazi Germany in particular, the political and economic elites of Britain and the United States once more began to move more closely together, leading by 1940 to a reconstitution of the "special relationship" that was to prove vital to the survival of Britain in the face of Hitler's wars of military aggression and expansionism.[11] At the same time, World War II, even more than World War I, proved an enormous drain on Britain's wealth, forcing London to continue the transformation and partial dismantling of the Empire, but also its partial maintenance. After all, it had been the main pillar of its erstwhile political and economic strength. No less distressing from a British perspective was the fact that the United States emerged from the war and the defeat of the Axis countries as the power that came to occupy the same hegemonic position in the West that Britain had once enjoyed in the nineteenth century. Worse, it would now use this power to undermine for good and more successfully than in the 1920s the foundations of the "special relationship" that Winston Churchill thought he had forged with Franklin D. Roosevelt in 1940–41.[12]

As will be shown later, British wartime negotiators in Washington were deeply angered by the often blunt ways in which the Americans pursued their peace aim of establishing a liberal-capitalist Open Door multilateral world trading system without protectionist imperial blocs. This meant that they were not only working for the obliteration of the autarkic empires that the Germans, Japanese, and Italians were erecting in the early 1940s. They also tried to undermine sterling as a major currency and pillar of the City's influence that was now being challenged by nationalist independence movements in India and other parts of the once so powerful British Empire and Commonwealth. In this sense, the "Pax Anglo-Americana" that Ursula Lehmkuhl has written about was but a weak extension of the wartime "special relationship" that was meant to work mainly outside Europe and whose precariousness was revealed in the 1950s.[13] These were rather more the years when the interests and strategies of London and Washington once again diverged, as evidenced not only in Washington's encouragement of the integration of continental Western Europe but also at the time of the Suez Crisis of 1956. It was at this point that the Americans firmly told the British government to stop their military action, jointly staged with France and Israel, against Nasser's Egypt. The age of old-fashioned European colonialism was, in the eyes of the Washington administration, definitely over.[14]

While little was left of the "special relationship" during the 1960s and 1970s, it revived after Ronald Reagan and Margaret Thatcher had come to power in the 1980s. But the imbalance of political and economic influence between the two countries had by then become so glaring that it was visible to all. Britain was militarily so weak that she would not have been able to reconquer the Falkland Islands from the Argentine invaders, had it not been for major logistical support from Washington. Meanwhile the British economy had experienced a further decline. The upswing of the 1950s that came with the larger postwar boom in the West could not be sustained. A further shift came when Thatcher copied "Reaganomics" and tried to build a "special relationship" with respect not to manufacturing industry, but to banking and finance. Anglo-American business relations came to be dominated by the nostrums of privatization and deregulation that the neoclassical macroeconomists at Chicago and elsewhere had meanwhile persuaded Washington and Wall Street to adopt.

Finally, there is the debate on "varieties of capitalism" to be considered. It began among political economists during the 1990s, when an "Anglo-Saxon" model of running a modern economy was juxtaposed with a "Rhenish" and also a "Scandinavian" model.[15] But on closer inspection the former was in effect an American model that the Thatcherites practiced even more dogmatically than Reagan. After Thatcher's successful destruction of the British manufacturing sector, there still remained something "special" about the Anglo-American relationship if one focuses on the cooperation between Wall Street and the City during the past twenty-five years. But looking at it in political terms, it collapsed at the time of Reagan's invasion of Grenada and the disagreements over German reunification after the collapse of the Soviet Bloc in 1989 when Thatcher opposed the strategy of Reagan's successor.[16] After this, Washington adopted a unilateralist foreign policy, believing it no longer needed European partners to deal with the problems of the world.[17] The "special relationship" became a pure myth when Tony Blair decided to throw Britain's support behind president George W. Bush's war in Iraq. The British prime minister may have believed that he had resuscitated the British-American "special relationship" in 2002. But from all that has become known about the ways the Bush administration treated him, the metaphor that Blair had become Bush's "poodle" is more accurate.[18] During Prime Minister David Cameron's visit to Washington in April 2012 there were again invocations on the British side of the "special relationship" that no one in the United States and in the business community in particular took seriously.[19]

4. The German-American "Special Relationship"

This book tries to live up to a basic methodological point that Jürgen Kocka and others have made, that is, that genuine comparison needs a *tertium comparationis*.[20] This third element is provided here by reference to Germany. However, it is not an equally balanced triangular one, but an "asymmetrical comparison" that starts from its American center of gravity and its relations with Britain and Germany. The third Anglo-German angle emerges more indirectly from this asymmetry, but, it is hoped, emerges clearly enough; for this book not only is concerned with the American impact on two European societies and economies, but also tries to discover why the British industrial system in the end lost out against the German one as well.

So, what about the German-American relationship in the twentieth century? In 1980, Hans W. Gatzke published a book titled *Germany and the United States. A "Special Relationship"?*[21] While the question mark and the quotation marks are significant, the concept itself is evidently taken from the above-mentioned British-American debate. On closer inspection, it becomes clear that Gatzke is ultimately more concerned with interpreting the peculiarities of modern German history rather than offering a finely balanced German-American comparison. As he puts it,[22] "To blame what happened between 1930 or 1933 and 1945 on an unfortunate combination of uncontrollable circumstances which were taken advantage of by an unscrupulous maniac, would absolve the majority of contemporary Germans from guilt for the Nazi nightmare. But this would also be a gross oversimplification, as untenable as the opposite thesis, that the Third Reich was but the culmination of German history since Bismarck, or Frederick the Great, or Luther. . . . Yet anyone familiar with Germany's past knows that certain trends in the nineteenth century, although not leading directly to Nazism, were akin and pointed the way to it."

Accordingly, Gatzke's book—notwithstanding its title—is best seen as a contribution to the long debate on the German "special path" (*Sonderweg*), a notion that has preoccupied American and European historians of Germany ever since 1945, if not since 1933. In terms of the meaning of "special relationship" adopted in this study, it is better to quote from Edwin O. Reischauer's foreword to Gatzke's volume:[23]

> Germany is without doubt one of the most important countries in the world and its relations with the United States are of particular relevance. The German people constitute the largest ethnic group in Europe west of the Russians. By the early twentieth century they had provided the United States with about a quarter of its population. The two great World Wars that focused around Germany drew the United States deeply into international affairs and threatened to bring down the whole edifice of Western civilization. Twice our bitter enemies, the Germans have at other times had relations of cordiality with the United States. Today [in 1980] West Germany alone ranks fourth in productive power in the world and is among the two or three staunchest and most important allies the United States has.

He added, "The story of modern Germany and its relations with the United States thus is a complex one. Germany has swung wildly between great successes and terrible failures. The relations between the two countries have gone through the same sort of rapid and violent fluctuations. Neither modern German history nor German-American relations are easy to analyze or describe in clear coherent fashion." While Reischauer's verdict poses a daunting challenge to any historian, it highlights not only the complexities that this book has to grapple with, but also the ups and downs and ambivalences in this second "special relationship" that will be subjected to an asymmetrical comparison in subsequent chapters.

As far as I can see, this kind of study has not been attempted before with respect to the three *business* worlds. In this sense, it goes beyond a more traditional investigation into British-German-American relations that is based primarily on diplomatic and other official government documents. My handicap is that my approach has not been particularly popular in history departments in North America and Europe in recent decades. Sociocultural topics and a history "from the bottom up" had greater appeal, at the center of which were often relatively small and less organized groups, individuals and people, such as women and minorities, that had remained "invisible" in previous decades.

These genres of historical writing have undeniably enriched the discipline in terms of both its research agendas and its capacity to offer more appealing teaching material than business history. But what fell by the wayside in the process was work with an economic focus. It is not that economic historians vanished; they are to be found in economics departments, and in many cases this move was made quite some time ago when diplomatic and political historians showed little interest in economic questions. Nor did it help that, within economics departments, economic historians increasingly came under the pressure to adopt quantitative methods that had begun to sweep the board in economics. In short, history and economic history had been going their separate ways.

In an attempt to overcome this rift, some "mainstream" history departments have again been trying to build bridges to economic and business historians in economics departments and business schools, partly stimulated perhaps by the rediscovery that macroeconomic problems are shaping our lives more profoundly than historians of memory or identity have realized. This book represents an attempt to contribute to this bridge-building effort.[24] This also applies to the secondary literature where greater reliance on what has been written across the aisle would aid cross-fertilization. Still, as has been mentioned above, the book is qualitative rather than quantitative in its approach. The shifts in the balance of German-American "special relations" ran countercyclically to the shifts in Anglo-American business relations. While the latter saw an overall decline from around 1900 onward, they experienced an uplift during the two world wars.[25] The opposite trend can be observed with respect to German-American business relations. They grew stronger between 1900 and 1912, but deteriorated from 1913 until the early 1920s. There was another stabilizing upswing in the mid-twenties,[26] before the relationship went downhill again after the Nazi seizure of power, demonstrating at the same time how difficult it is to study international big business relations without taking account of surrounding political environments, in this case relations between Berlin and Washington that ended up in another clash of arms.[27]

And yet this second deep estrangement was not the end of the road for German-American business relations. Big business came back after 1945, forging a relationship that was even stronger than that of the mid-twenties. The other point about these ups and downs in American businessmen's "special relationship" with industrial Germany is that they were not merely guided by a coolly calculated interest in the bottom line. Just as the protagonists of the Anglo-American "special relationship" stressed deep-rooted affinities that, whatever their differences, were supposedly holding the two nations together, parallel feelings existed with the German business community, notwithstanding the repeated difficulties that had intervened between them in the first half of the twentieth century.

It is my contention that the second reversal in the American-British-German triangle became most tangible in 1956–57. For it was during the Suez Crisis that the United States told Britain quite categorically that if London did not stop the invasion of Egypt, Washington, while not intervening militarily, would ruin the British currency and economy. The age of old-style colonialism and protective tariff blocs, which both before and after 1945 had repeatedly clashed with the American conception of the Open Door, was over. The British should accept that they were no longer a first-rank power. No less significant, 1956–57 was also the moment when Washington and its business community could look back with satisfaction on the reconstituted relationship with West Germany. The reconstruction, but also the *recasting* of the economy had been achieved. The Law for Securing Competition had been ratified. Industry had been wrenched out of its long-standing anticompetitive cartel tradition and a larger European market had been created within which a parliamentary-democratic Federal Republic could deploy its industries as a dynamo of an American-style, Western European civilian mass production and mass consumption capitalism.

5. Sources

For a study that aims to cover several decades of Anglo-American-German business relations and politics, it has not been possible to scour hundreds of company archives for evidence of the changing quality in the relationships of the many enterprises that did business in Europe. Where the quality of published research is very good, I am relying on secondary sources and the archival material quoted in them. In addition, I have used newspapers and magazines. These sources contain many references that provide not merely statistical evidence but also statements and speeches by American businesspeople and politicians. Even before 1914, it was the practice of American newspapermen to look up the passenger lists of the big ocean liners that arrived in New York from Europe virtually every day. They waited by the quayside to ask returning businessmen to give them impressions of the European countries they had visited. The rich private papers of a few bankers and industrialists represent a third and very illuminating source. Their correspondences and diary notes will be used to open windows to the worlds of industry, finance, and politics in which they operated both at home and abroad. Given their positions in commerce and finance, they often had access to information that was more private and often different from what American diplomats were able to gather in Berlin or London. While some of these businessmen operated in relatively small companies, this book is not about the role of family firms that have attracted more research again in recent years. Rather it is the big American corporations whose policies and attitudes are at the center. It is only at the end that the question of the relative dynamism and innovative drive of smaller firms will briefly be taken up.

In this connection, the question will have to be raised whether those sources were more reliable or how far they, too, fell victim to misinformation and propaganda that government agencies circulated. There is also the problem of how far they may have suffered from "cognitive dissonance" (Leon Festinger), that is, saw only what they wanted to see or what fitted into their long-held preconceptions and prejudices. Through their business connections and often also family contacts, they may have acquired a greater familiarity with the foreign society that they visited than ordinary travelers. But the question remains how far this enabled them, especially in times of crisis, to look behind the public facade of words and images that they heard and saw. And because these crises were time and again about politics rather than economics, this study is not merely about commerce and industry, but in many ways also about political developments that interfered with economic relations just as the latter influenced the former. The German-American "special relationship" is on the whole less well researched than the Anglo-American one, partly because German business historians have for a long time concentrated on domestic developments and have been reluctant to include the question of an "Americanization" of German industry in their work. Still, on the whole I have tried to keep a balance.

6. Transatlantic History and Its Global Dimensions

It is against the background of these considerations that this section of the Introduction begins with a study, published in German in 2000, that is not an economic history in the strict sense. It is nevertheless of interest here because it advances an important transnational argument that reaches beyond the Anglo-German-American comparison. Ute Mehnert's *Deutschland, Amerika und die "Gelbe Gefahr"* is—as she puts it—a "diplomatic history" at whose core is the debate relating to the catchword of the "Yellow Peril" at the turn of the twentieth century.[28] Her main interest is in the "question of the origins of the global international system of states that provided an expanded sphere of action to the foreign policies of the European great powers and the U.S." Against Paul Kennedy,[29] who placed America "at the periphery of a European-centric international system," Mehnert wants to highlight "the growing importance of the U.S. in the world economy and its increasing political engagement in areas beyond the Western Hemisphere."[30] In other words, she puts at the center of her analysis the United States as an Atlantic as well as a Pacific power. Furthermore, she is critical of Reiner Pommerin's *Kaiser und Amerika*.[31] He argued with respect to German policy toward the United States after 1905–6 that the kaiser and his advisors had been aiming to reduce conflict potentials and concentrated on Europe instead of continuing to pursue German *Weltpolitik* they had promulgated in the late 1890s. This is why Pommerin believed that Berlin had failed to appreciate the significance of the two new players on the international stage before 1914, that is, the United States and Japan.

This interpretation, Mehnert continues, shifted "German-American relations to an isolated plain and reduced expansionist clashes of interest to sham conflicts that were primarily due to misunderstandings and political miscalculations."[32] However, if one includes the presence of the "Japanese Danger" as a factor in German and American policy making, the analysis is moved in "another direction." Indeed, "the integration of the ['Yellow Peril'] catchword into the foreign policy conceptions and decision-making processes of both powers" explains that the United States and Germany "continually oriented their political calculations toward a global international system." This, Mehnert concluded, means that both powers had a "clear awareness of the interaction between the power constellations in the Atlantic and the Pacific space"—an important aspect of chapter III, where the attempt will be made to connect the history of the transpacific "Washington System" of 1922 to early post-1918 developments in European-American relations.

While Mehnert's study thus adds the indispensable transpacific angle, along came Magnus Brechtgen in 2006 with a major book on what he called the crucial *Scharnierzeit* (hinge period) of 1885–1907 in world politics in order to raise the question of whether there was nevertheless a center of gravity in this grand planetary panorama.[33] Although he was primarily interested in "personality networks and international politics," he located this center of gravity in the British-German-American economic triangle. In comparison to the capacities of France, Russia, and other European states to project their economic and political might abroad were markedly weaker than those of the triad. His analysis enabled Brechtgen to break away from the Eurocentrism that had still informed Kennedy's work, to expand it to the Atlantic region and to take up a position *between* Kennedy and Mehnert's globalism. No less important, he shows on the basis of the statistical material that he put together that the United States had become the strongest economic player in the British-German-American triangle. Indeed, as Sebastian Conrad has argued when writing on "regimes of territorialisation and the globalization of the national," this was not the age of the decline, but rather of the "globalization of the nation state" and in particular of those states that by virtue of their military and economic capabilities occupied the top spots in the international hierarchy.[34]

Pre-1914-era readers are asked to refer to the array of pertinent tables in Brechtgen and Conrad. They form the foundation of the argument in this study that a triad of the United States, Britain, and Germany had constituted itself by 1900. By 1913 the total industrial potential of these three countries amounted to 60.4 percent of the world total, with Britain being the weakening power and America and Germany moving into the first and second ranks.[35] Small wonder that American businessmen increasingly turned their attention toward Central Europe as a competitor and partner. Moreover, the merger movement and the creation of huge corporations had continued in both countries. However, there emerged an important difference: in the wake of the passage of the Sherman Act in 1890, the United States was pushed in the direction of *oligopolistic competition;*[36]; German industrialists, by contrast, reinforced their system of *protectionist cartels and syndicates* that they had begun to build during the Great Depression in the 1870s and 1880s.[37] Apart from these structural differences that became a topic of discussion in the United States for the first time before 1914 and will be dealt with in chapters II and III, there were other factors that American industrialists and bankers had to consider when they contemplated cooperation or investments in the German monarchy.

7. The Trials and Tribulations of Venturing into a Foreign Economy

It is safe to assume that American investments in Europe were market seeking and strategic asset seeking rather than resource seeking and that as capitalist entrepreneurs they always had to pay attention to the bottom line as they calculated the opportunities and pitfalls of expanding their business into a foreign market. In an attempt to systematize international economic behavior, John Dunning has spoken of entrepreneurial calculations relating to ownership advantages, locational advantages, and internalization advantages.[38] Such calculations were also on the mind of American travelers who sailed to Britain and Germany before 1914 to explore foreign direct investments (FDI), defined not merely as the establishment of production facilities in another country, but also as investments in local agencies, sales offices, partnerships, and participations. Inevitably, they also studied domestic politics.

However, since before 1914 American businessmen rarely went to Germany or Britain to build their own factories, Kenichi Ohmae's phase model seems to offer the most convincing approach to understanding the steps that foreign investors took. Once a decision had been taken to enter a foreign market, most companies would initially rely on native representatives who are familiar with both the product and with local market conditions. The layout would be small in the expectation that turnover would be modest. The next step would be to assess, after initial successes, whether the opening of a company-owned sales office would be more cost-effective than a foreign agent. The investments required for this step were also likely to be low, even if they included warehousing and services. The next and usually most expensive phase would be to move further functions abroad, including research and development (R&D) and ultimately production. At this stage, local legal, tax, and social security systems as well as labor relations would assume a prominent place in the overall calculation. Obviously, having to close down an agency or a sales office that proved uneconomical or politically compromising was much less costly than having to shut down a factory.[39]

It is clear that for each and every phase a variety of local factors had to be considered and a business judgment had to be made. Like every investment in the domestic economy, FDI also carried risks that were mostly even higher than those in the home market. Advantages had to be carefully weighed against transaction costs and the costs of failure. Given the ups and downs that the world economy had seen in the nineteenth century, American businessmen looking at Britain or Germany before 1914, while hoping for larger sales, wanted to avoid losses. But it was not just a matter of calculating *economic* risk. Christopher Kobrak and Per Hansen have recently again raised the question of *political* risk and taken the emergence of dictatorships in the 1930s as their testing ground.[40] In chapter V, we shall have to discuss how American big business was faced with major dilemmas after Hitler had come to power in Germany in January 1933 and embarked upon a massive rearmament program with increasing controls and regimentation of what was in principle still a capitalist economy, and one in which companies such as Ford and General Motors had made major investments.

Yet, the problem of political risk posed itself not merely in the face of the Nazi dictatorship in the 1930s, but already before 1914. The Hohenzollern monarchy under Wilhelm II was not, to be sure, a brutal and murderous totalitarian regime; but it was nonetheless authoritarian and centralized in its decision-making structure, especially in the field of foreign policy. Under the Reich Constitution, the emperor was not only the commander-in-chief in wartime; it was his constitutional right to decide single-handedly whether to go to war or to keep the peace. He was also in charge of foreign policy making in times of peace. The national parliament, the Reichstag, had but limited powers in this field and—no less significant—over the military budget in particular. Wilhelm II had surrounded himself with political and, above all, military advisors who jealously guarded not only the monarchy's constitutional rights, but also their own influence and privileges. Other elite groups, and German businessmen in particular, had little informal input, never mind an official voice.

In light of these realities, American businessmen also had to calculate a measure of political risk when they entered the German market even before 1914. The central point to be made here is therefore that FDI involved a number of factors that could not be calculated precisely. The situation required qualitative judgments and a good or an uneasy feeling about the contacts that American businesspeople began to establish in Germany to explore a foreign market or to negotiate with a prospective agent, manager of a proposed sales office, or even a director of a factory who had been tapped to run it. A sense of trust and an at least rudimentary familiarity with the other society and its business culture, societal traditions, and elite as well as popular attitudes were vital. This applied in principle also to Britain, which, although it had a parliamentary system, still relied upon a relatively small elite to run its foreign policy. At the same time, political risk was smaller there, partly because from the late 1890s the country was anxious to promote an Anglo-American rapprochement and partly because Germany's increasingly erratic and aggressive political behavior around the globe led Washington to interact more closely with London.

All this meant that there were affinities that gave the potential investor a feeling of comfort. Family ties or long-standing friendships, the value of none of which could be quantified, had to be included in the decision-making process. It is also important to remember that information was much less complete and more imperfect than it is today, even if transparency continues to be a major problem to this day. One final point has to be made in the context of American FDI assessment and decision making. As John Dunning and Sarianna Lundan have reiterated in the second and very detailed edition of *Multinational Enterprises and the Global Economy*, such enterprises undertook FDI for "extremely varied" reasons so that "no satisfactory *general* answer" can be given.[41] Moreover, in comparison to the often very sophisticated methods by which today's big corporations evaluate FDI opportunities, FDI before 1914 was much more haphazard and ad hoc. In this respect business decision making was perhaps comparable to diplomatic maneuvering before 1914. As will be seen in chapter III, there was little systematic research and no drawing up of "scenarios." Often it was just hunches that were based on trust and mistrust of the partner or competitor.

We began, by reference to the "Americanization" debate, with setting out the larger framework of international relations in which subsequent chapters will be configured. American elites disposed of a general foundation that could help them in their assessment of opportunities and risks as they reached out to their counterparts in Britain and Germany. As capitalists familiar with their firms' balance sheets, there was no doubt a certain amount of cool calculation with respect to the advantages and disadvantages of FDI and to whether to export via an agency or a sales office or whether to build an internalized production facility abroad. They were, however, also aware of the limits of such assessments and appreciated the uncertainties inherent in a locality that they were looking at. They knew about the economic future of Britain and Germany only in broadest outline and were generally aware of the risks of all operations abroad, including political risks relating to Britain's and Germany's domestic developments.

There were times when they underestimated these risks and got burnt; or they were too pessimistic about the future and left opportunities unexploited. In terms of what I have called the "special relationship" with Britain and Germany, the Germans—to put it mildly— would give American political and business elites plenty of issues to worry about. The United States fought that country in two world wars and had to deal successively with an autocratic monarchy, a volatile Weimar Republic, a Nazi dictatorship, and finally an initially devastated post-1949 Federal Republic. Yet, with Germany time and again developing a more dynamic industrial economy, their relations with Britain improved only when the ones with Germany were bad or very bad. Overall, the Anglo-American "special relationship," except in wartime, was on a downward slope during the decades covered by this book. Meanwhile, the relationship with Germany recovered after World War I and, after another slump and world war in the 1930s and 1940s, became very strong in the 1950s. This may seem ironic or paradoxical, but it presents a basic line of investigation through which the relevant empirical material will be examined in subsequent chapters.

Notes to the Introduction

1. See, e.g., Wm. Roger Louis and Hedley Bull, eds., *The "Special Relationship." Anglo-American Relations since 1945* (Oxford, 1986); C. J. Bartlett, *"Special Relationship": A Political History of Anglo-American Relations since 1945* (London, 1992); John Dickie, *"Special" No More. Anglo-American Relations: Rhetoric and Reality* (London, 1994); Alan P. Dobson, *The Politics of the Anglo-American Economic Special Relationship, 1940–1987* (New York, 1988); Iestyn Adams, *Brothers across the Ocean: British Foreign Policy and the Origins of the Anglo-American "Special Relationship," 1900–1915* (London, 2005).

2. W[illiam] T. Stead, *The Americanisation of the World* (London, 1902). The original English or American spelling of titles and quotes in this book has been retained. On the subsequent scholarly debate, see, e.g., Harm G. Schröter, *Americanization of the European Economy* (Dordrecht, 2005); Volker R. Berghahn, "The Debate on 'Americanization' among Economic and Cultural Historians," *Cold War History* 10, no. 1 (February 2010): 107–30, with a discussion of changing conceptualizations and a bibliography of relevant books and articles.

3. Henry Luce, "The American Century," *Life*, 17 February 1941, 61–65. For background, see Alan Brinkley, *The Publisher. Henry Luce and the American Century* (New York, 2010); Alfred Eckes and Thomas Zeller, *Globalization and the American Century* (Cambridge, 2003); Peter J. Taylor and David Slater, eds., *The American Century. Consensus and Coercion in the Projection of American Power* (Oxford, 1999).

4. Thomas J. McCormick, *America's Half-Century: United States Foreign Policy in the Cold War and After* (Baltimore, 1989); Mary Nolan, *The Transatlantic Century: Europe and the United States, 1890–2010* (New York, 2012); David W. Ellwood, *The Shock of America. Europe and the Challenge of the Century* (Oxford, 2012). On the globalization perspective, see Kevin O'Rourke, *Globalization and History. The Evolution of the Nineteenth-Century Atlantic Economy* (Cambridge, MA, 1999); Jürgen Osterhammel and Niels P. Petersson, *Globalization. A Short History* (Princeton, 2005).

5. See, e.g., Jörn Leonhard, *Bellizismus und Nation. Kriegsdeutung und Nationsbestimmung in Europa und den Vereinigten Staaten, 1750–1914* (Munich, 2008), 13–14; Cushing Strout, *The American Image of the Old World* (New York, 1963); Ragnhild Fiebig-von Hase and Ursula Lehmkuhl, eds., *Enemy Images in American History* (Oxford, 1997), with a range of relevant articles. See also Robert Jervis, *Perception and Misperception in International Politics* (Princeton, 1976), and Knud Krakau, "Einführende Überlegungen zur Entstehung und Wirkung von Bildern, die sich Nationen von sich und anderen machen," in Willi P. Adams and Knud Krakau, eds., *Deutschland und Amerika. Perzeption und historische Realität* (Berlin, 1985), 9–15. On the concept of coevolution, see, e.g., Richard R. Nelson, *Technology, Institutions, and Economic Growth* (Cambridge, MA, 2005).

Simon N. Hellmich, Bielefeld, is completing a study using this approach with respect to the coevolution of production regimes, technologies, and labor market institutions in the United States between 1897 and 1933.

6. See Schröter, *Americanization of the European Economy* (note 2), with a discussion of disciplinary approaches. See also, e.g., Alexander Stephan, ed., *Americanization and Anti-Americanism* (New York, 2005); Jan C. Behrends and Arpad von Klimo, eds., *Antiamerikanismus im 20. Jahrhundert. Studien zu Ost- und Westeuropa* (Bonn, 2005); Marie-Laure Djelic, *Exporting the American Model: The Transformation of European Business* (Oxford, 1998); Paul Hollander, *Understanding Anti-Americanism. Its Origins and Impact at Home and Abroad* (Chicago, 2004); Matthias Kipping and Ove Bjarnar, eds., *The Americanisation of European Business* (London, 1998); Rob Kroes, ed., *If You've Seen One, You've Seen the Mall: European and American Mass Culture* (Urbana, IL, 1996); Jean F. Revel, *Anti-Americanism* (San Francisco, 2003); Jonathan Zeitlin and Gary Herrigel, eds., *Americanization and Its Limits* (Oxford, 2000).

7. See, e.g., Bradford Perkins, *The Great Rapprochement* (New York, 1968); Lionel M. Gelber, *The Rise of Anglo-American Friendship* (Hamden, CT, 1966); Charles S. Campbell, Jr., *Anglo-American Understanding, 1898–1903* (Baltimore, 1957); Richard H. Heindel, *The American Impact on Great Britain 1898–1914. A Study of the United States in World History* (New York, 1968).

8. Patrick O'Brien and Armand Cleese, eds., *Two Hegemonies. Britain, 1846–1914, and the United States, 1941–2001* (Aldershot, 2002), with several contributions on British economic decline and America's rise; Laurence James, *The Rise and Fall of the British Empire* (London, 1994); Piers Brendon, *The Decline and Fall of the British Empire, 1781–1997* (New York, 2008); Max Beloff, *Imperial Sunset* (London, 1969); Egbert Klautke, *Unbegrenzte Möglichkeiten* (Stuttgart, 2003); Ernest R. May, *Imperial Democracy. The Emergence of America as a Great Power* (New York, 1961); Derek H. Aldcroft, ed., *The Development of British Industry and Foreign Competition, 1875–1914* (Toronto, 1968); Sidney Pollard, *Britain's Prime and Britain's Decline. The British Economy, 1870–1914* (New York, 1989); Pollard, *The Development of the British Economy, 1914–1950* (London, 1952); Frank Ninkovich, *Global Dawn. The Cultural Foundations of American Internationalism, 1865–1890* (Cambridge, MA, 2009); Michael Hunt, *The American Ascendancy* (Chapel Hill, NC, 2007).

9. See also the contemporaneous analyses by John Dos Passos, *The Anglo-Saxon Century and the Unification of the English-Speaking People* (New York, 1903), and Brooks Adams, *America's Economic Supremacy* (New York, 1900). Adams's book is a collection of essays, published between 1898 and 1900 in journals such as *Forum* and *McClure's Magazine*. As reflected in some of the essay titles ("England's Decadence in the West Indies"; "The Decay of England"), he is very critical of Britain, arguing that "the most important and absorbing phenomenon of our time is the condition of Britain" (vi). He continued that if she cannot maintain her energy, her supremacy would "pass from her, either toward the east or west." To him all indications pointed westward toward the United States achieving supremacy (192).

10. See chapter III.

11. Best enshrined in the Atlantic Charter of 1941. See, e.g., Douglas Brinkley and David R. Facey-Crowther, eds., *The Atlantic Charter* (New York, 1994); Theodore A. Wilson, *The First Summit. Roosevelt and Churchill at Placentia Bay* (Lawrence, KS, 1991).

12. See chapter V.

13. See Ursula Lehmkuhl, *Pax Anglo-Americana. Machtstrukturelle Grundlagen anglo-amerikanischer Asien- und Fernostpolitik* (Munich, 1999).

14. See chapter VI.

15. Michel Albert, *Capitalism Against Capitalism* (London, 1999); Peter A. Hall and David Soskice, eds., *Varieties of Capitalism* (Oxford, 2001); Volker R. Berghahn and Sigurt Vitols, eds., *Gibt es einen deutschen Kapitalismus?* (Frankfurt, 2006).

16. See, e.g., Mary Sarotte, *1989: The Struggle to Create a Post-Cold War Europe* (Princeton, 2009).

17. See, e.g., Francis Fukuyama, *End of History and the Last Man* (New York, 1993).

18. See, e.g., Glen Ruffle, "America Still Britain's Best Buddy," *European Journal*, March 2011, 2, and the contrarian view by Alex Massie, "What Special Relationship?," *Foreign Policy*, 25 May 2011.

19. Kathleen Burk, *Old World, New World* (New York, 2008), 659, came up with the following overall verdict: "Fundamentally when the occasion demanded it, there re-emerged the early twentieth-century assumption that, different from each other they were in their cultures, interests and ability to project power, they were, nevertheless, more alike than any other two powers on the globe. And the instinctive feeling persists: there is a true love-hate Anglo-American special relationship." See also A. E. Campbell, *Great Britain and the United States, 1895–1903* (London, 1960); Patrick Cohrs, *Unfinished Peace after World War I* (Cambridge, 2006); Niklas H. Rossbach, *Heath, Nixon and the Rebirth of the Special Relationship. Britain, the U.S. and the EEC, 1969–1974* (New York, 2010); Richard Aldous, *Reagan and Thatcher. The Difficult Relationship* (New York, 2012).

20. See Jürgen Kocka and Heinz-Gerhard Haupt, *Comparative and Transnational History* (New York, 2009). See also Franco Amatori and Andrea Colli, *Business History: Complexities and Comparisons* (New York, 2011).

21. Hans W. Gatzke, *Germany and the United States. A "Special Relationship"?* (Cambridge, MA, 1980).

22. Gatzke's words on the dust jacket of his book.

23. Ibid., vii.

24. See, e.g., Volker R. Berghahn, "A Plea for a Rapprochement between History and Economic History," *Bulletin of the German Historical Institute Washington*, no. 40 (Spring 2007): 1–8.

25. See chapter III. See also Detlef Junker, *The Manichaean Trap. American Perceptions of the German Empire, 1871–1945* (Washington, DC, 1995).

26. See chapter IV.

27. See chapter V.

28. Ute Mehnert, *Deutschland, Amerika und die "Gelbe Gefahr"* (Stuttgart, 1995).

29. Paul M. Kennedy, *The Rise and Fall of the Great Powers* (New York, 1987).

30. Mehnert, *Deutschland* (note 28), 12.

31. Reiner Pommerin, *Kaiser und Amerika* (Cologne, 1986).

32. Mehnert, *Deutschland* (note 28), 16.

33. Magnus Brechtgen, *Scharnierzeit, 1895–1907. Persönlichkeitsnetze und Internationale Politik in den Deutsch-British-Amerikanischen Beziehungen vor dem Ersten Weltkrieg* (Mainz, 2006).

34. Sebastian Conrad, *Globalisation and the Nation in Imperial Germany* (Cambridge, 2010), esp. 380.

35. Brechtgen, *Scharnierzeit, 1895–1907* (note 33), 47. See also Stephen N. Broadberry, "How Did the United States and Germany Overtake Britain? A Sectoral Analysis of Comparative Productivity Levels, 1870–1990," *Journal of Economic History* 58, no. 2 (June 1998): 375–407; Broadberry, "Economic Growth and the United States since 1870. A Quantitative Economic Analysis Incorporating Institutional Factors," in David Coates, ed., *Varieties of Capitalism—Varieties of Approaches* (Houndmills, 2005), 85–105.

36. See Robert Himmelberg, ed., *The Rise of Big Business and the Beginnings of Antitrust and Railroad Regulation, 1870–1900* (New York, 1994), and Himmelberg, *The Monopoly Issue and Antitrust, 1900–1915* (New York, 1994), both with a large number of relevant articles that had been published elsewhere over the years; Theodore P. Kovaleff, ed., *The Antitrust Impulse*, vol. 1 (Armonk, NY, 1994); R. B. Heflebower, "Monopoly and Competition in the United States of America," in Edward H. Chamberlin, ed., *Monopoly and Competition and Their Regulation* (New York, 1954), 110–39.

37. See Volker Hentschel, *Wirtschaft und Wirtschaftspolitik im wilhelminischen Deutschland* (Stuttgart, 1978).

38. See John Dunning, *Multinational Enterprises and the Global Economy* (Wokingham, 1993); Geoffrey Jones, ed., *Transnational Corporations. A Historical Perspective* (New York, 1993).

39. For a fuller discussion of Dunning and Oehmae, see Antje Hagen, *Deutsche Direktinvestitionen in Grossbritannien, 1871–1918* (Stuttgart, 1997), 32ff.

40. See Christopher Kobrak and Per Hansen, eds., *European Business, Dictatorship and Political Risk, 1920–1945* (New York, 2004).

41. John Dunning and Sarianna M. Lundan, *Multinational Enterprises and the Global Economy*, 2nd ed. (Cheltenham, 2008), 8, 295.

I

//

The North Atlantic Business Triangle and the Constellation of 1900–1901

1. International Relations Around 1900

Against the background of the analytical framework within which the American-British-German business and political relationship will be seen in this book, the year 1900 offers a good starting point, and for three reasons. To begin with, this was the year when both the Europeans and the Americans were looking back on the nineteenth century that had just ended and ahead to the twentieth. Germany and the United States did so in an overall mood of optimism, believing that, generally speaking, their future would be as bright as the previous decades had been. Britain by contrast was less certain.

Second, it was a phase in international politics when American relations with both Britain and Germany had come under strain while those between Britain and Germany were negatively affected by differences of opinion over the Boer War and the growing suspicion in London that Emperor Wilhelm II was preparing to challenge the Royal Navy when he decided to expand his battle fleet.[1] Finally, tensions had arisen between all three powers over the higher protective tariffs that the United States as well as Germany had introduced or were on the verge of imposing.[2] Meanwhile Britain continued to adhere to its traditional Free Trade policies, although this, too, had come under pressure both from parts of British industry and from Conservative Party protectionists rallying around Joseph Chamberlain. Finally, there were the problems created by U.S. president Theodore Roosevelt's imperial ambitions and his conduct of the Spanish-American War as well as the Anglo-American and German-American conflicts over Venezuela.[3]

2. Assessing the Old and the New Century

Starting with the question of moods at New Year 1900, what did the newspapers in the three countries have to say at the very end of December 1899 or in the first days of the new century?[4] As was to be expected, there were joyous public and private celebrations. At midnight, the church bells were ringing. In the port cities ships blew their horns. Many citizens attended religious services or watched the midnight fireworks. While it is important to bear in mind the continuing huge differentials in wealth and income, middle-class families who had become wealthy or well-to-do during the past century, looked back on it with a sense of gratitude and pride. Those who had remained stuck in the poverty trap of working-class life may not have been quite so cheerful. Still, many of them, too, were full of hope that the new century would bring improvements to their material position, more social justice, and greater participation in politics and cultural life.

On the whole, the German press reflected this optimistic mood. Reviews looked back as far as the early years of the nineteenth century with its defeats and humiliations by Napoleon and juxtaposed them to Germany's rise to great power status after the victory over France in 1870 and the unification of the country a year later. Next to such political successes, the liberal *Frankfurter Zeitung*, in its edition of 30 December 1899, also celebrated the century's achievements in science and technology.[5] What had marked the past century was not so much the noise of the great battles of the Napoleonic Wars but the "thundering of the railroad train that was rushing through a tunnel cut through the massive granite of a snowy mountain, the whistling of steam engines, the singing sounds of the breeze along telegraph wires, and the strange noise with which an electric streetcar, attached to an overhead cable, comes along." On the following day, the same paper carried a full-page leader article that focused on the political gains.[6] At the top was mentioned "the founding of a huge German Reich in the heart of Europe" that had contributed to the promotion of world peace. Despite "the frequent wars of recent years . . . the idea of peace had made great strides." Wars, the paper believed, were "special cases," and wars between the great powers were now "almost unthinkable because the inputs are too high in comparison to the gains that can be expected." Germany was exhorted to use its "growing power always in a spirit of justice for the benefit of all humankind so that the word of the medieval poet may come true," that is, that "the world may be healed through the German spirit."

There is also an illuminating poll that the *Berliner Illustrirte Zeitung* published under the heading of "Balance-Sheet of the Century."[7] The paper had undertaken a survey to identify the most important people of the past century. Among the statesmen, Otto von Bismarck assumed first place. Among the military leaders, Napoleon I came out slightly ahead of Helmuth von Moltke the Elder, who had defeated France in 1870. Among women, the feminist Bertha von Suttner and the writer George Sand took the second and third ranks behind Queen Louise of Prussia. Thomas Edison was judged to be the greatest inventor, and the railroads emerged as a major innovation for the benefit of all.

The "social question" was also a recurrent theme covered in other German newspapers. Whatever progress had been made in the transition from an agricultural society to an industrial-urban one, further social reforms were deemed necessary in the new century. The *Frankfurter Zeitung* argued that "the better the conditions of the total working populations of Germany, and the more informed and enlightened they were and the more freely they were able to move, the more insistently Germany will be able to appear on the world market and in world politics."[8]

However, it was precisely such self-confident comments in the middle-class press that filled the conservative papers with unease. Thus the *Neue Preussische Kreuz-Zeitung* of 31 December 1899 began its review with an attack against the parliamentary movements of the pre-1848 period and the liberal revolutions that followed.[9] They pointed to the Prussian Constitutional Conflict of the 1860s that had barely been won by Bismarck. Even after the founding of the German Empire in 1871 major efforts still had to be made to consolidate the Bismarckian state at home and abroad. However great these successes had been, in the eyes of the *Kreuz-Zeitung* editors the "giant edifice of the new Reich" was now being persistently beleaguered from all sides by forces that were driven by a "burning hatred." The article added, "Though driven by divergent motives" international movements were aiming to "destroy this edifice." Worse, "the party [i.e., the Social Democrat Party, SPD] that openly professes to favor general revolution" had become the largest party thanks to universal manhood suffrage. It had allegedly become so powerful that "no-one except the Conservatives is around anymore to counter it." The paper still believed that there was much good to be expected from the future. However, if party disunity and the lack of a reliable nationalism could not be overcome, "the course of our political and economic development would over time again be retarded."

At the other end of the political spectrum, the Social Democrat *Vorwärts* also had some critical things to say, though it ultimately came to an optimistic conclusion.[10] The labor movement's cause had made "great progress." At the same time it was undeniable that the economic and social contrasts were getting sharper. Resistance against "capitalism" was rising, but in turn this "capitalism was resorting to ever more brutal means to overcome this resistance." Next to domestic politics, the Left targeted Germany's foreign and colonial policies that it dubbed "the last chimera of declining capitalism." The Social Democrats would never support such policies, the more so since the government demanded further financial sacrifices from the general population for the expansion of a navy that would always remain inferior to that of Britain and France.

While capitalism was the main target of the labor movement, on the Right the *Alldeutsche Blätter* articulated quite radical political demands of a different sort.[11] They believed that Germany faced a momentous decision in the new century. The question was "if we want to sink back to the level of a power that is at most second rank, or do we want to become [a nation] for which Providence has endowed the German people with the richest gifts," that is, to be an "*Edelvolk*, a *Herrenvolk* chosen to become the bearers of culture for all of mankind."

Turning to the British press at the turn of the century, the liberal *Manchester Guardian* of 1 January 1900 asked what label might be put on the nineteenth century with its famous men such as Darwin and Helmholtz, Browning and Tolstoy, Gladstone and Bismarck.[12] The writer came up with the dualism of "science and democracy," but then added that the optimism of the French Revolutionary period about democracy had evaporated and that Germany's predominance in the sciences was more likely to set the sciences back rather than to open up new possibilities.

In the pages of the conservative London *Times* little optimism could be found in its edition of 30 December 1899, in which the state of international politics was analyzed.[13] One reason for this was that the British Empire was still mired in a war in South Africa. Accordingly, news about the Boer War continued to make the headlines in its issue of 1 January 1900.[14] There followed reports on the situation in other parts of the world, among which Anglo-German relations were given extra space. In any case, Britain was thought to have reached a "turning point" that confronted the country with two "important tasks." Whether the nation would live up to these tasks would largely define its future as a great power and a dominant people. The first task was to end the war in South Africa as soon as possible. After this, a thorough stock taking would have to be initiated. As far as Britain's economic situation was concerned, the paper had no more than a few positive things to say about some parts of the Empire. Other papers similarly reflected this sense of decline that some of them wanted to reverse with the help of a national efficiency campaign that the Fabian Society and other organizations were rooting for. But this campaign was probably also inspired by the American rationalization and Scientific Management movement, to be discussed later.

If we now turn to the United States, the *Chicago Daily Tribune* felt some sympathy for the British in their gloomy mood and concluded that, with "pessimism" being the "prevailing note," the British "are the severest critics of their own shortcomings" and look at themselves "with stark naked candor."[15] In examining the German situation, the *New York Times* carried a longer analysis on 1 January 1900 that it had commissioned from James C. Monaghan, the United States consul in Chemnitz in industrial Saxony. He focused on the prosperity of the Hohenzollern monarchy and the opportunities it offered to American business.[16] He gave a long list of American products that he believed would do particularly well in Germany and whose successes and failures will be examined in greater detail in chapter II.

A general mood of confidence in the future also pervaded other American papers. The *Washington Post* took the view that "he, who 100 years ago" had offered an "optimistic horoscope" would have been ridiculed.[17] Now the only real danger was that the country might overstretch itself and begin to suffer from exhaustion. Nevertheless, there was an important mission to be fulfilled in the new century that was to be geared not merely to economic success but also to the need to upgrade morality. After all, "all our progress in the way of luxury and knowledge and purely personal refinement has not been attended by a corresponding elevation and purification of our morals, our humanity, and our altruism." If this could be achieved, "the housing of the poor is likely to be still further improved, partly by greater municipal purity and partly by virtue of the new political doctrine." At the same time, "the health of the people will be improved by still greater advances in the sciences of medicine and surgery." No less important, "the commercial morality will improve by the popular control which will come with the development of people's law, as well as by the recognition of the everlasting truth that honesty is always the best policy." Finally, "the political state of man will improve by the still further recognition of the falseness of all forms of arrogated authority, and by the recognition of man's natural right to rule himself." The author ended with the belief that "the century of humanity will witness great progress in the attitude of the people towards international affairs."

3. Political and Economic Relations in the Age of Late-Nineteenth-Century Imperialism

Against the backdrop of these press comments and of the experience of the nineteenth century that they tried to capture, positive visions of the future tended to predominate; but the papers also contained evidence of the conflicts that were smoldering within the societies of Britain, Germany, and the United States. Although the basic domestic and foreign issues were similar in all three, it appears that these conflicts were particularly virulent in Wilhelmine Germany. As they increased toward 1914, they had by 1910–11 become a source of concern within the American business community, while around 1900 the focus was more on the conflicts that were brewing closer to home. Here the crisis in the Caribbean is of interest because it took both Britain and Germany into what the Americans, under the Monroe Doctrine, considered very much their sphere of influence and "backyard."[18] From 1895, Venezuela had become one of the points where London had been trying to gain a foothold. Anglo-American tensions reached a climax in 1899, which then cleared the path for a settlement when London realized that it was not worth their while to upset Washington in that part of the world. The Germans, rather less sensitive and farsighted, took until 1902 to come to the same conclusion, following their attempt to obtain a base in Venezuela.[19] They failed to appreciate that America's Monroe Doctrine was not just a general claim by Washington to a sphere of influence in Latin America. It was also that the U.S. administration had become more determined than ever to assert its claims after their victory in the Spanish-American war in 1898 that had pushed the Spaniards out of the region.

It had also been irritating to the two European powers that in the late 1890s the United States had begun to pursue an expansionist policy across the Pacific into Asia. Again by 1898, the Philippines, Guam, Hawaii, and a number of other Pacific islands had come under American rule. Farther to the south, in Samoa, it was the Germans who had begun, from the mid-1880s, to expand and to clash with British and American interests. The resulting disputes were finally resolved in 1899 when the Samoan Islands were divided between Washington and Berlin, with Britain being compensated with other Pacific territories.[20] There is no need to go into the details of these international conflicts in this age when all three powers were quite blatantly imperialist. The point is that these disputes were largely settled around the turn of the century, with the German-American crisis over Venezuela finally ending by 1903.

Although the imperialist and naval rivalries between the three powers in the Caribbean and the Pacific are not to be underestimated in their
influence upon the general climate of transatlantic relations, it seems
that, in taking the American perspective, the conflicts over tariffs had a
more profound impact on mutual perceptions and attitudes among industrialists and bankers. In the 1880s the Republicans had raised again
the issue of higher tariffs to protect "infant industries" in the United
States. The free-trading Democrats had responded by ratifying the
Mills Bill that contained a number of modest reductions. While there
were many factors other than tariffs that subsequently contributed to
defeating the Democrats at the polls, the new Republican majority in
Congress "took care of the industrial contributions to the campaign" by
increasing tariffs to new heights.[21]

Worse from the point of view of Britain and Germany, "by raising already high duties even higher, the new tariff not only protected
domestic industries, but made it virtually impossible for foreigners
to compete." Accordingly, the Europeans began to complain quite
bitterly, including the British whose government had continued its
low-tariff policy despite waves of protectionist pressure back home.
In 1880, Parliament had passed the Merchandise Marks Act requir-
ing imported goods to reveal their country of origin. It was the beginning of the "Made in Germany" stamp on imports from Germany
that, ironically, later became of mark of high quality. In other words,
legislation that was intended to promote the purchase of domestic
products had the opposite effect on the British consumer, who now
demanded German goods.

Later there were various "Buy British" campaigns as well as the new
Patent Law of 1907 that complicated the sale of foreign goods. Still,
the important point is that Britain in principle never abandoned its
long-standing Free Trade tradition, and foreign products continued to
flow into the country even when they vitally threatened some domestic
industries. In the early years of the twentieth century, Joseph Chamberlain had become the leader of a tariff reform movement within the
Conservative Party. He proposed a general raising of tariff walls, but
then to knock holes into them to let cheap agricultural produce into
the country. The hope was that this would keep the price of basic items
of food consumption low for the benefit of the laboring classes. But
in the 1906 national elections the Conservative platform was resound-
ingly defeated. Coming to power were the Liberals, who had promised
to impose, instead of tariffs, higher taxes on the wealthy with which to
finance social reforms and welfare benefits for the "masses."[22]

The tariff solution that Chamberlain offered to Britain was the opposite of what the German government, also under pressure to raise

protective tariffs, introduced in the Reichstag in 1901–2. There the pressure came not from industry but from the powerful large-scale estate owners who wanted to reverse the low tariff policies introduced in 1893–94 at the insistence of German industry that was looking for favorable trade treaties with other nations for its exports. Since the Prussian agrarians in particular had never stopped complaining about their being bankrupted by imports of cheap grain from the Russian Ukraine and the American Midwest, Reich Chancellor Bernhard von Bülow, in an effort to support Germany's "ailing" agriculture, had proposed higher agricultural tariffs.[23] Industrial tariffs were to remain low in an effort to obtain advantageous trade agreements with other nations that were coming up for renewal.

After hard-fought political battles, Bülow finally got his way: agricultural tariffs went up, though not as high as the agrarians had demanded. While the relatively low industrial tariffs pleased German exporters, the negative consequence of higher agricultural tariffs was that the price for bread and other basic items of mass consumption increased. The German lower classes were promptly hit by higher prices for food and the "small pleasures of the working man," that is, beer and tobacco. Embittered by these policies, they voted in even larger numbers for the Social Democrats in the 1903 national elections, that is, for the party that the *Kreuz-Zeitung*, but also other right-wing voices, had identified as constituting a most dangerous force for the continued stability of the conservative Prusso-German monarchy.[24]

Looking at the world situation through the eyes of the American business community, which, through mergers and the general growth of the U.S. economy, had become more and more powerful, the situation around the turn of the century therefore looked quite favorable. The nineteenth century had generally been an era of progress and increased prosperity. While there was still plenty of room for an expansion of the domestic market, entrepreneurs were confident that they were also ready to compete abroad. This confidence was reinforced by the sense that they had at their disposal new and very competitive forms of rationalized production and also of the marketing of their products.

Germany, which had undergone a similarly rapid process of industrialization and urbanization as America, also seemed to offer good prospects for American exports. Consequently, many of them began to book a cabin on one of those many fast ocean liners that plowed the North Atlantic back and forth between Southampton, Le Havre, and Bremerhaven. By comparison to those prospects, the risks arising from disputes over colonial claims and possessions and over higher tariffs looked relatively small.

4. Frank Vanderlip's and William Stead's
Views of Anglo-American Relations

Whereas these observations of the European-American constellation in the early years of the twentieth century have been mined from contemporary newspapers and the secondary literature, we also have for this period a particularly rich archival source that allows a close glimpse at American businessmen's perceptions of the European-American economic and political relationship. These documents are to be found in the papers of Frank Vanderlip, who, having grown up in Illinois, after a career as financial editor of the *Chicago Tribune* and at the Treasury Department in Washington, had joined the National City Bank of New York (NCB) in 1901 and rose to a position of great influence on Wall Street and in the world international banking more generally.[25] Vanderlip's papers proved invaluable throughout this study of British-German-American business and political relations.

Soon after assuming his post at the NCB, he undertook an extensive tour of Europe to inform himself about the economic situation and the business climate across the Atlantic. His notes and those of his assistant whom he took with him are as detailed as they are jumbled. They cover conversations and impressions gained in Russia, Sweden, Italy, Austria-Hungary, Germany, and Britain. While the material on the first four countries is interesting in its own right, it can be ignored here because none of these nations were, at least at this early point, a major focus of American attention. Most of the observations pertain to Britain and Germany, the two powers that are also at the center of this study.

To start off with the British case, Vanderlip's verdict emerges firmly and clearly: time and again, the theme of relative decline comes up. Thus he highlights the conservatism of British entrepreneurs. They are, he notes, slow to write off machinery and hence reluctant to replace it with more modern equipment from across the Atlantic. Citing the example of the rejection of an American-made hoisting machine, he concludes that the British would not accept it, even if it hoisted faster.[26] He added, "Here we find the celebrated British prejudice with a vengeance." Later he commented that Britain "is woefully deficient in technical schools," except in training facilities of the textile industry, one of the oldest developments of the First Industrial Revolution that were still being deemed "equal to any in the world."[27]

Moving from poorly educated British workers to their living conditions, Vanderlip discusses alcoholism and class divisions. He observed,[28] "I cannot help thinking that England must learn a lesson from Germany and the United States, and in her search for a remedy for her labor troubles must do more to establish schools for technical education." He believed that employers live in fear of trade unions and concluded that the country "cannot compete with Germany and the United States unless her trade unions change their policy and endeavor to make English workmen, both skilled and unskilled, the best and fastest in the world." Thus, "if we search for the real cause of England's decay, I think we shall not blame the laborer so much as we do the so-called upper classes. The real responsibility for the selfish ignorance of the working men, in my opinion, lies with those people who have insisted that the poorer classes do not need an education. We find in England as well as in Russia men who think that popular education is 'a dangerous thing'" and that more than a basic education would turn workers into socialists. To Vanderlip, British workers were products of this kind of environment who had no confidence in their employers. In short, the treatment of workers was better under American superintendents and managers. In the end and coming back to his initial point, the American banker conceded that, even if British manufacturers were slower in taking up improvements, there was nevertheless also visible change in that country.

It is against the background of such observations that the publication of the above-mentioned book of 1902 by Stead, the influential British journalist, becomes plausible.[29] Because of its title, this study has frequently been cited to mark the moment when the "Americanisation of the World," or at least of Western Europe, did indeed set in. But the study was only one of several that, significantly enough, appeared around this time on the subject of the rise of the United States. Although the concept of "Americanization" is useful for making sense of the European-American relationship after the turn of the century and is therefore also deployed in this study of the "special relationships" with industrial Britain and industrial Germany, the core of Stead's argument is in fact about something else. It amounted to a plea to form a reunion between Britain and the United States. It confirmed the sense of weakness felt by the hegemonic power of the nineteenth century that was now falling behind. It also buttresses the earlier point that rather than resisting the rise of American economic and political power, the British wanted cooperation with the Americans in a modern "Americanized" version of the union that had existed up to the late eighteenth century, but had then fallen apart in the rebellion of the New England colonies against their British masters. It is an example of a book of which more than the title should be read.

Stead introduces his vision of the "special relationship" with a fanfare:[30] "The advent of the United States of America as the greatest of world-Powers is the greatest political, social, and commercial phenomenon of our times. For some years past we have all been more or less dimly conscious of its significance. It is only when we look at the manifold manifestations of the exuberant energy of the United States and the world-wide influence which they are exerting upon the world in general and the British empire in particular, that we realise how comparatively insignificant are all other events of our time." Arguing that what he had to say was "of transcendent importance" to his countrymen, he continued, ". . . we are confronted by the necessity of taking one of those momentous decisions which decide the destiny of our country." For "we have an opportunity—probably the last which is to be offered to us—of retaining our place as the first of world-Powers. If we neglect it, we shall descend slowly but irresistibly to the position of Holland and of Belgium."

However, if "we substitute for the insular patriotism of our nation the broader patriotism of the race, and frankly throw in our lot with the Americans to appreciate the great ideal of Race Union, we shall enter upon a new era of power and prosperity the like of which the race has never realized since the world began." Ultimately, this would mean that "we must reconcile ourselves as best we can to accept a secondary position in a world in which we have hitherto played a leading role." But in doing so, "we shall continue on a wider scale to carry out the providential mission which has been entrusted to the English-speaking Race, whose United States will be able to secure the peace of the World."

Accordingly, the first part of Stead's book is devoted to the English-speaking world. He admitted that the slogan of the "Americanisation of the World" generates "some resentment in Great Britain," especially among those who believe that this world "is to be Anglicized." But such feelings, Stead asserted, are groundless. After all, when the Americans try to refashion the world in their image, they were doing so "substantially [in] the image of ourselves." Americans have "sprung from our loins" and were hence part of the "family." Stead then proceeded to the constitutional question of how the Empire might be approximated "to the Republic or the Republic to the Empire."[31] What would be the balance between the two? Ultimately and again given the common heritage, he did not find any major obstacles to producing a viable constitutional solution.

Having examined in the next section "the Americanisation of Ireland" and other parts of the Empire, the author proceeded to the question of the Americanization of Continental Europe.[32] He found that there is considerable enthusiasm for it. But it is a different matter, he argued, "with the sovereigns and nobles who represent feudalism and the old world monarchical and aristocratic ideas which have at their European centre the Courts of Berlin and Vienna." On the other hand, Belgium, Holland, and Scandinavia, "while monarchical in form, are republican in essence." In his view, the Russian monarchy presented a particularly serious obstacle. Nevertheless, "the centre of resistance to American principles in Europe lies in Berlin," with Wilhelm II in the lead:[33] "There is something pathetic in the heroic pose of the German Emperor resisting the American flood. It is Canute over again, but the Kaiser has not planted himself on the shore, passively to wait [for] the rising tide in order to rebuke the flattery of his courtiers; he takes his stand where land and water meet and, with drawn sword, defies the advancing tide."

And yet "he himself is driven to Americanise, even when he is resisting Americanisation." The reason for this is to be found in the socio-economic reality of the *Kaiserreich*: "There are no more Americanised cities in Europe than Hamburg and Berlin." For "they are American in the rapidity of their growth, American in their nervous energy, American in their quick appropriation of the facilities for rapid transport." Pinpointing affinities, he continued that "Americans find themselves much more at home, notwithstanding the differences of language, in the feverish concentrated energy of the life of Hamburg and of Berlin than in the more staid and conservative cities of Liverpool and London. The German manufacturer, the German shipbuilder, the German engineer, are quick to seize and use the latest American machines."

While these were very shrewd observations that will be confirmed by the evidence to be presented in subsequent chapters of this book, Stead also considered the effects of German emigration to the United States:[34] "German-Americans, like the Irish-Americans, are passionately patriotic, with a dual patriotism. They are intensely Republican; the hyphenated American, as he is called, has shown a readiness to shed his blood and sacrifice himself in the service of his adopted country equal to that of any native born of the States." The dilemma of the German Americans, however, was that the kaiser wanted them to identify Germany and Wilhelm II, even though they "have escaped beyond the glamour of his personality." And yet, he continued his "desperate but unavailing war." For "in resisting the Americanisation of Germany, his first aim has naturally been to prevent the Americanisation of the Germans who leave Germany." In his effort "to arrest this process of the thorough Americanisation, appropriation, and from his point of view the absolute effacement of German citizens, the Emperor has sought to deflect the tide of German emigration to German colonies which he has acquired and which he has subsidised regardless of expense in various parts of the world."

With the focus on his analysis still on the kaiser and his ambitions in ways that had a good deal of truth to them and will have to be examined more critically and in greater detail in this study in chapter II,

Stead had finally reached the crucial point of his argument that was designed to buttress his quest for a British-American reunion. For a Briton, worried about the future of his country, this was also the link to the anti-British elements of the kaiser's *Weltpolitik*, proclaimed with much posturing just before the turn of the century: "The dependence of Germany for her daily bread on shipments from over-seas contributed greatly to strengthen the Kaiser's decision to double the German navy." Stead also saw this decision against the background of "the three-fold defeat of British arms in South Africa" that "had severely shaken our prestige." From all that is known about the expansion of the German navy, Stead was no doubt correct that it was "aimed against Great Britain." As will be seen later, such views on Wilhelmine *Weltpolitik* pinpointed quite uncannily key elements of the kaiser's global strategy, whose navy was in the first instance being built against Britain but also contained a long-term anti-American calculation. No less important, chapter V will reveal rings of this vision of twentieth-century power politics in Hitler's struggle for world domination with the United States.

Suspicions of a German design that was ultimately anti-American finally came to the surface in July 1901, when, as Stead wrote, "M[onsieur] Pierre de Ségur was entertained by the Kaiser, along with other French tourists, on board [his yacht] *Hohenzollern*" during his annual Norwegian cruise.[35] It was only several months later, in November 1901, that the Frenchman published his interview, creating a sensation in the United States and causing deep embarrassment to the German Foreign Office. The German ambassador to Washington put out an official denial that "all talk that his Majesty . . . desires to bring the European nations together in a challenge of America's progress in the commercial world is without foundation." On the contrary, the ambassador added, "My sovereign has the most frank admiration for America's progress and the most cordial and friendly feelings for the United States." But the damage had been done and the seeds of the kaiser's hypocrisy had been sown. What, asked the *New York Herald*, would the reaction of the German press have been if U.S. president Theodore Roosevelt, himself no soft-spoken advocate of American imperialism, had dropped a remark in front of a group of French tourists that he favored a general boycott of German imports because he rejected certain forms of German business behavior.

If Stead was therefore rightly suspicious about the larger foreign policy vision of Wilhelm II against both Britain and America, by 1902 the British political and naval elites had come to share them. After the turn of the century, it became less and less of a secret that naval minister Alfred von Tirpitz was preparing the German navy to become a lever of

German *Weltpolitik* at the power-political negotiating table. However, should this lever not work and the Royal Navy try to confront the Tirpitzian navy in a do-or-die battle in the North Sea, the latter was to be strong enough to inflict a devastating defeat on British naval power.[36] For this battle the Imperial Navy was by 1902–3 systematically being expanded. At the same time and no less preposterously, the admiralty in Berlin was also drawing up operations plans for a war against the U.S. Navy. In other words, Wilhelm II was fanning resentments against both the old hegemonic power, Britain, that he believed stood in the way of his own colonial ambitions, as well as against American claims to supremacy that were being articulated with considerable noise in Latin America and the Far East by Roosevelt. Both aims contained a vital commercial and industrial element that large sections of the German business community in their dynamism shared in their mood of early-twentieth-century self-confidence. However, by the end of the decade, with German foreign policy suffering repeated setbacks due to British-American increasing efforts at containment, German businessmen, like their British and American counterparts and partners, became increasingly nervous about Wilhelmine *Weltpolitik* leading to a catastrophic world war, as it eventually did in July 1914. This triangular constellation and the perceptions of German power politics therefore also help explain why Stead's primary concern was to highlight the political and economic tensions between Germany and America, on the one hand, and to extol the reunion of the English-speaking world.[37]

Meanwhile in Berlin, Stead reported, the German Industrial Union had also raised its voice through its secretary general: "He declared that the time had come for some Bismarck to rise up and assemble the nations of Europe and throttle the American peril." As a liberal Free Trader and Liberal reformer that he evidently was, he then pointed to the domestic consequences of a quest for self-sufficiency: "Although the Governments of the Old World may compel their subjects to pay higher prices for goods which the Americans, if left unhindered, would supply more cheaply, they will thereby increase discontent and dissatisfaction which will facilitate the Americanisation of Europe. For the higher the tariff, the dearer will be food. Dear food means misery in the home. Misery in the home means discontent in the electorate, means the increase of the motive force which will seek steadily to revolutionise the Old World governments on what may be more or less accurately described as American principles."

And so, after a further diversion into the situation of the Ottoman Empire, a discussion of the Monroe Doctrine, and the potentialities of developing Latin America in a joint British-American venture, Stead returned to his initial appeal. Having summarized once more the reasons for the commercial and industrial success of the United States, among them being the American tradition of democratic education and lavish spending on the over six hundred universities and colleges that existed in America, the choice for Britain was clear on political and cultural grounds. There were also the "incentives to increased productive power" that could be appropriated by Britain.

Here, though, Stead came back once more to a handicap that was, in his view, very unfortunate:[38] "The difficulty about machinery [that] arises largely from the English prejudice in favour of good solid machines which, if once built, will last for a long time." By contrast, "the American deliberately puts in flimsy machinery which will wear out, as he calculates that by the time he has got all the work out of his machine that it will stand, new improvements will have been invented which necessitate in any case the purchase of new machinery." In other words, British business conservatism and reluctance to invest in new technology contributed in Stead's view to why British industry not only was falling behind the innovative American businessmen but, implicitly also behind the energetic Germans. Furthermore, there was the difference between British and American workers and their attitudes: "The American workman who suggests an improvement in the machinery he is working, is encouraged and rewarded," whereas "in England he is too often told to mind his own business."

The conclusion that Stead drew from all this was the same that he had set out at the beginning of his book. Britons faced two alternatives:[39] "If they decide to merge the existence of the British Empire in the United States of the English-speaking World, they may continue for all time to be an integral part of the greatest of all World-Powers, supreme on sea and unassailable on land, permanently delivered from all fear of hostile attack and capable of wielding irresistible influence in all parts of this planet." The other choice was "the acceptance of our supersession by the United States as the centre of gravity in the English-speaking world, the loss, one by one, of our great colonies and our ultimate reduction to the status of an English-speaking Belgium." For Stead the choice was, of course, clear: "Unification of the race by the only means which are still available." With "unification under the Union Jack having become an impossibility by our own mistakes, why should we not seek unification under the Stars and Stripes?"

It was from this platform that he finally mapped out the "steps towards Reunion," the details of which can be skipped here. However, there is Stead's telling quotation from an editorial in New York's *Evening Journal*:[40] "The nations of Europe, and especially the English, wonder at the success of the American people. If any Englishman wants to know why the American race can beat the English race in the struggle for industrial precedence, let him stand at the Delaware-Lackawanna station in Hoboken from seven until nine in the morning as the suburban trains come in" to witness how "the American succeeds because he is under high pressure always, because he is determined to make speed, even at the risk of bursting the boiler and wrecking the machine."

It should have become sufficiently clear why, following American perceptions of British business practices that are to be found in Vanderlip's travel logs of his trips to Europe in 1901 and also the *Americanisation of the World* written by a Briton who, aware of his country's decline, advocated an Anglo-American reunion deserve close scrutiny in order for us to grasp the larger international constellation of 1900–1901. Stead also spent considerable time examining the views of the German emperor and his Anglophobia as well as his anti-Americanism that even in this early period could no longer be kept completely under wraps (as Tirpitz had been hoping to when he designed his naval challenge). He and Wilhelm II expected that its scope would not become immediately obvious to Germany's presumptive rivals in the twentieth century. The role of Kaiser in this picture will come up again in the next chapter. For the moment the question is whether and how far Stead's critical assessment of German policy was shared by the American business community. For this we return, as a first step, to the material to be found in the Vanderlip Papers before broadening our analysis to the evolution of the actual economic relations between the two countries—relations that have to be seen in comparison to the British commercial position within the Atlantic region.

5. American Perceptions of the Wilhelmine Industrial System

If the American press had shown much optimism about the country's future at the turn of the century, the self-confidence of Vanderlip, the Wall Street banker, and the socioeconomic milieu in which he moved was no less telling. Thus his notes of his 1901 European travels contain the following sentence:[41] "It is no doubt a comfortable reflection for Americans to assume themselves that, although the Germans may copy machinery and their methods, American genius will always keep this country far in advance of her competitors." He then added the caveat that it was of course "a mistake to suppose that all industries advance at the same rate [since] improvement is active now in one industry and now in another."

Later on he made a similar argument, but added a comparison with respect to education:[42] "The natural endowments of the American business man are far greater than that [*sic*] of his German competitor and, if to these natural endowments can be super-added a training similar to that which is received in the great business schools of Germany, the American business man can remain indefinitely in the lead." As will be seen, it was not just Vanderlip who was thinking about education, commercial as well as technical. At one point Vanderlip referred to the Charlottenburg Polytechnic Institute in Berlin and similar institutions in Dresden, Munich, and other cities: "The young men who emerge from the German schools are eagerly siezed [*sic*] by the great manufacturing houses." Fortunately, MIT, Worchester Polytechnic, the Lowell Institute, and the Case School of Applied Science had been established in the United States, to which the banker added the following differentiation: "Foreign critics admit that American mechanical engineers are far in advance of any that Europe can produce. In chemical engineering, however, we have done little or nothing, and here the Germans have almost monopolized the field." But there were also the institutes of management education, such as the Wharton School at the University of Pennsylvania. Founded some twenty-two years earlier, it "has given the courses outlined in the field of general instruction of the German Business School during that entire period." The universities of Illinois, Wisconsin, and California had also made "considerable progress in the same direction."

There was, as Vanderlip noted (perhaps also thinking of his above-mentioned criticism of the Oxbridge system), some resistance "from advocates of old classical studies" whose quest was "to turn out cultured gentlemen rather than efficient industrial agents."[43] But the American business community should not feel irritated by this and was doing what it can "to further the cause of higher commercial education." After all, the world of industry and commerce was too complex "to be understood by men who are trained in the old-fashioned school of business apprenticeship." A thorough professional training was needed.

Proceeding to a discussion of the blue-collar workforce, Vanderlip had some critical words about a democratic education.[44] America, the banker urged, should build up "a great system of primary education, such as that through which the German working man is passed." Moreover, primary schools should be linked to a system of intermediate technical education to produce highly skilled workers. It was of course true that American industry had created a more composite pattern of labor consisting of many "different races" and including "all grades of intelligence and skill." This is where the United States had benefitted from European immigration, and with demand for labor continuing, there was, in Vanderlip's view, no reason to fear those immigrants. Surely, "the history of emigration is a record of industrial progress" in Europe, too. Thus, "the industrial awakening of Germany during the last quarter century shows clearly the effect of domestic prosperity upon emigration." If German emigration had been declining, it was not least because German workers had been finding opportunities back home.

Comparing the German worker with his British colleague, he was "in many respects superior to the English."[45] Universal military service and three years in the armed forces had made him "more temperate," physically and morally improved, clean and with regular work habits. He had also received a thorough elementary education and was less questioning of his foremen. With evident approval, Vanderlip pointed to the German insurance system and sanitary conditions. Indeed, many things were done for the German worker by the state that were left to the individual to provide for in the United States. On the other hand, the Wall Street banker found that upward mobility in Germany was low. Comparing the efficiency of workmanship and production standards, he thought that it was difficult to make comparisons between Germany and the United States, though he was confident that American products were competitive enough. Nevertheless, "it does become the United States, until that inferiority has been wiped out, [not] to boast very much of what they can accomplish in the markets of the world."

Offering a number of specific examples, Vanderlip mentioned printing and engraving as an area of American inferiority, adding that "most of our chemicals apparatus comes from Germany and nearly all of our fine chemicals."[46] Practically all of America's "analine dyes are imported." The story was similar with respect to cotton goods, earthenware, shoes, paper, and artists' supplies, all of which were cheaper but also inferior to those produced in (Continental) Europe. Although many Americans believed that the country was the world's leader in iron and steelmaking, it was sad for Vanderlip to have to say that "in many particulars our iron and steel production is much less advanced" than that of its competitors. In "crude iron and steel," it was true, American superiority was tangible due to the availability of cheap raw materials from inside the country and labor-saving devices as well as the effect of higher wages. The Europeans had even more to learn from the United States in the area of finished iron and steel, machine tools, agricultural implements, cash registers, and typewriters. On the other hand, in "no branch of iron and steel production, outside of machine tools, do we exceed the Germans" who were also very good "in everything in the use of metal."

Accordingly, Vanderlip urged his colleagues to visit the "great Krupp establishment at Essen, which is, by the way, the greatest of its kind in the world."[47] There the visitor would be "at once impressed with what appears to be a superfluity of men" who, "with possibly one exception," produce the best crucible steel in the world." Because the American equivalent was not of the same Krupp standard, "the Krupp people are able to do business in this country in spite of the [high] tariff." As will also emerge in chapter II, for many of these articles the United States simply had to have "this steel and no tariff can keep it out." As far as engines were concerned, it was true that "the master patents on the steam engines are mainly English" but in "the improvement and development of these master patents the Germans have done quite as much as we have." Indeed, "in the case of engines, broadly speaking, all that is known in the United States came from Europe." This also applied to the American turbines to be displayed at the St. Louis Exhibition that were based on British patents. Similarly, all American knowledge "of the utilization of blast furnaces and gases came from Germany and France, and it has only been a year since the matter of super-heating and re-heating steam, by which the efficiency of the steam engine is greatly increased and which has long been practiced abroad has been seriously taken up in the United States."

These, Vanderlip concluded, "are the facts and I leave it to my readers to judge the truth of the opinions which were expressed by" the Germans he had met on his trip.[48] He admitted that as a result of his conversations, his "enthusiasm over the achievements of the United States in the world's markets was greatly tempered and qualified." After his visit, he had begun "to see that foreigners have some justification for the irritation which they so frequently express over what they term the 'bumptiousness' of the Americans." They were just paying too "little attention to the foreign market." So, for American business, operating behind high tariff walls, to praise its excellence was "little less than offensive" to European ears.

Continuing in a self-critical vein, he also commented on the use of the American flag by enterprises overseas.[49] To be sure, "some American houses abroad, whose goods, by the way, are above reproach, such as [those of] the Westinghouse Company and the Frazer and Chalmers Company, machine manufacturing, and Babcock & Wilson, [the] boiler makers, make no such mistake." But there were others who proudly and naively waived their American patriotism straight into the faces of their foreign competitors and customers. Vanderlip then gave another illustration of how "Americans are not able to utilize in a foreign market the advantages which they actually have" by reference to "the introduction of machine tools into Germany."[50] These exports had "secured a place because of their excellence." This, he observed, "goes without saying in Germany." But to make the Germans aware that "these high-grade American machines" were a must-have "was due largely to two resident Germans, Schuckert and S[c]hütte."

Vanderlip then added a story to the Schütte case that nicely illustrates the cautious ways in which American FDI unfolded around the turn of the century. It is also a good case in point relating to the conceptual work of Dunning and Ohmae discussed in the Introduction. Schütte, the American banker had learned on his trip to Germany, had taken up the introduction of American machine tools "as a result of visiting the World's Fair at Chicago in 1893."[51] He returned so impressed "with the excellence of our output" that from 1894 onward he "undertook to represent American machine houses" helping them to make "a great deal of money in this business." What Schütte, probably quite rightly, stressed in his conversation with Vanderlip was a cultural point, that is, that his firm was " 'able to push American machine tools through our knowledge of German conditions and through our knowledge of the country.' "

Of course, it was never wise for American firms entering foreign markets to sell shoddy products. But Vanderlip also learned from Schütte another basic point, namely "that American exporters, even when they have superior articles to sell, display very little intelligence in getting a market." The American banker agreed that there was much room for improvement. Rather than stressing "cheapness and rapid execution," excellence and thoroughness of workmanship should be highlighted, certainly when it came to Germany where the notion of *Qualitätsarbeit* had meanwhile come to be seen as being an asset.[52] In fact, as far as the manufacture of motor cars was concerned, this was thought to be an Achilles' heel of American workmanship. Thus in 1903, the journal *Der Motorwagen*, referring to Daimler-Benz's attitude toward quality production, printed the following comparison between German and American practices: "Here [we do things] meticulously and thoroughly; over there [in America it is] skimping and rushing." And very telling also the related verdict concerning European-American differences with respect to mass production and social stratification: "Over here we are still a long way from the American situation where every Mr. Jones owns a car. With us the automobile is for the most part a vehicle for the better-off classes."[53]

In line with such sociocultural differences and in light of the popularity of American machine tools that had also been in evidence at the Paris World Exposition in 1900, Vanderlip had furthermore come across one particularly serious disadvantage stemming from the export of superior American machine tools:[54] At the Union Electrical Works in Berlin "I found a shop which will rank with the best in the United States."

There was "every appliance for economical production and most of the machines are of American make." Similarly, the Niles Tool Works also had "a branch in Germany filled up with American machinery and directed by American superintendents and foremen," though this personnel policy was, Vanderlip noted, an exception. More alarming to him was that, while the "export of machinery and tools to Germany and to a less[er] extent to England and Switzerland" was large, they were also used to copy these imports in an effort to make themselves "independent of us."

Accordingly, Vanderlip had found out from European observers that "the European manufacturers everywhere are studying American methods and are adopting them as rapidly" as their economies were expanding.[55] America was said to have "done the pioneer work in developing the use of labor-saving machinery." In this sense, the Europeans were reaping "the fruits of our labors." The banker was "inclined to agree with these European observers" and felt confirmed by his visits to the Union Electrical Works and other establishments in Berlin where a remarkable shift had occurred. As one of his German interlocutors told him, "ten years ago, I should have found . . . in such shops as they existed English tools for the most part." However, as he looked around the shop, "I saw only German tools, enormous lathes, slotters, boring machines, traveling cranes, and all the paraphernalia that go to make up a manufacturing plant." He continued, "German shops are being rapidly equipped with the most approved labor-saving devices," and this also applied to "the arrangement of the plant."

It was clear that the Germans had taken many ideas home from their visits to the United States, especially following the Paris Exposition where the American pavilion had attracted many visitors and where the interest in American steel-cutting machinery was particularly strong.[56] Taylorism and shop-floor organization had by this time and in addition to technology also attracted considerable attention. But it is also significant in terms of larger argument pursued in this book that Britain was falling behind. As Vanderlip reported,[57] "English manufacturers are slower" in taking up improvements. Still, even there "a great change" was in evidence, as they, too, were looking toward the United States.

The cultural difficulties the Americans had with FDI implementation notwithstanding, American corporations, as the next chapter will confirm in more detail, did establish branches in Europe, and companies such as Niles Tools, Westinghouse, and others fitted them "exclusively on American lines."[58] Vanderlip learned that "more than one hundred of these branch houses have been established within the last few years." No less important, "they cannot fail to exercise the most profound influence on improving European machinery." The Germans were particularly keen "to seize upon anything of value in our methods of factory management."[59] At the Union Electrical Works in Berlin, "for example, great emphasis is put upon the system of control; foremen are scattered about on raised platforms and the supervision is constant and energetic."

The story of "one of the managing directors of this company" was probably not untypical about what was going on. He had, as Vanderlip learned, been "in Paris in 1900" where he "met Mr. Francis E. Drake, director of machinery and electricity for the Commissioner General of the Paris Exhibition." Drake hailed from New England and had "a great faculty for industrial organization."[60] Vanderlip's German interlocutor was so impressed with Drake that he invited "him to come to Berlin and look after his shop" and to make suggestions "regarding shop methods, system of time keeping and reporting of costs." In other words, what the American visitor was observing in Berlin was the copying not only of American technology, but also of factory rationalization—a key point to be borne in mind also in later chapters all the way to the post-1945 period, indeed whenever questions of technology transfer came up, with the exception of "intellectual reparations" from Germany to the United States, especially after the two world wars.

Finally, there is a detailed summary of another conversation that the American banker had with "a typical German, a man of probably less than fifty years; and, though German in appearance, he has American characteristics and a thorough appreciation of American methods of doing business."[61] To Vanderlip he "exemplified this most strongly in the conduct of his business, surrounding himself with American superintendents, filling his shops with American tools and adopting at every opportunity American business methods." It was therefore not surprising that this man "showed great friendliness toward America" and indicated at the same time "that by aid of this friendliness to America he was able to be a more useful and patriotic son of the [German] Fatherland," for he was improving his methods and making his factories better able to compete in the markets "of the world." In the course of their wide-ranging conversation the two also "broached the subject of industrial combinations." Evidently thinking of mergers but also of cartels and syndicates, his host had developed a concept "which certainly is as comprehensive as any which has been produced from the brain of an American industrial promoter."

In any case, Vanderlip's interlocutor believed "that the propitious moment had arrived for a world combination of electrical interests." He thought that German companies "could be brought into the line" while assuming that British companies "could be absorbed." He then suggested that "if the two leading American companies could be brought together," a giant combination could be effected. Its advantage would be "in addition to all those benefits which come with a combination of interests of any single industrial line, such as economization of management," a set of further special economies in the electrical field "which he considered by far the most attractive industrial field in which to work a worldwide combination." In addition economies in R&D would also "result in many new discoveries." He also mentioned how this would resolve patent protection problems—a thorny issue to be discussed in chapter II.[62]

Apparently in an attempt to interest the American banking community in this project, the German businessman pointed out that the European electrical industry was waiting for American FDI and capital. He also thought that a number of products could also be developed "by specialization" within this combination "at very low cost," while they would be expensive if they had to be made in small quantities. All these were no doubt alluring vistas in a particularly dynamic branch of manufacturing industry, and this was apparently also why Vanderlip recorded this meeting so extensively. In justifying his long account, he added that "to my mind it illustrates better than any other incident that has come under my observation the quality of the German business man's mind." He believed "that he is in no respect inferior to his American competitor." On the contrary, "to begin with, he is better educated." Moreover, he "is likely to know two languages besides his own" and "will usually speak English and French with facility," often in addition to "one or two others."

There could be no doubt that these Germans were well informed about global business, commercial geography, foreign tariffs, and "methods of doing business." They also had enjoyed an excellent training in finance, economics, and frequently also jurisprudence. No less noteworthy to Vanderlip was that "in the matter of training business men, the Germans are far ahead of us." They appreciated "that business is a science, that the laws of business are definite and exact [and that] the methods of business can be reduced to a definite form." These Germans also realize the need for "an accurate knowledge of the facts of the business world." They also appreciated that "the principles which govern the conduct of business" were "of the very greatest pecuniary value." Returning to an earlier cultural point, Vanderlip also noted that "since the German business man must carry on extensive operations in foreign countries, a knowledge of the language of those countries is an indispensable part of his equipment."

Reinforcing his earlier observations about the educational system, he reported that a thorough training was being given at "institutions

which are known as Handel's Realschule [sic] and Handel's Hoch-
schule [sic]."[63] Ordinary clerks would have gone to the equivalent of the
American high school, whereas the curricula at higher business schools
provided a good theoretical training, also in the sense of transmitting
a facility to handle commercial facts, thereby facilitating a faster entry
into the practical world of business. It was obvious to Vanderlip that
an educated manager would be far ahead of his less educated competitor. He would have an independent mind and an exact, inquiring,
and searching spirit that was also required of the German scientist, as
Vanderlip's research into the curricula and interdisciplinary teaching
had revealed. It was against this backdrop that he also made the above-
mentioned comparisons with American business school education. His
final verdict, "It has been commonly supposed in the United States that
the innate conservatism of the European manufacturer would prevent
him [from] adopting American methods and machinery until they had
already been discarded by [the] Americans." This attitude might be
true of many Britons; but "the best German business man with whom I
had the opportunity to become acquainted is little if any inferior to the
business man of the United States." Again, these observations should
be compared to the American traveler's verdict on the British situation
so that once again it is the comparison by a contemporary observer that
offers fresh insights.

6. Trying to Understand the Peculiarities
of the German Political System

Moving from German economic relations to politics, Vanderlip, like
Stead, first took up the question of the role of the kaiser before broach-
ing larger constitutional issues. Despite the anti-American and anti-
British statements that Wilhelm II had been making around the turn
of the century of which Vanderlip seems to have been aware, he did
not paint the monarch as a reactionary. Apparently, his German interlocutors had talked more about the monarch's role in domestic
politics at this time when the agricultural tariff debate was gathering steam. Accordingly, the American banker wrote that "the German
Emperor has aroused the wrath of the Prussian squirearchy by the
marked attention and the special favors which he has given to the
leading business men and bankers of the German Empire."[64] With
Wilhelm II having come out with rambling and undiplomatic statements about business and about relations with the two Anglo-Saxon
powers, it made sense for Vanderlip to immerse himself in politics
during his trip.

He confirmed that "in Europe . . . outside of Great Britain, the government has very much more potent influence than in the United States,
operating in all directions in which it is active in this country and extending its influence into many fields with which influence the United
States is not concerned." The drawback of this was that "every country
of Europe, with the possible exception of Great Britain, is in a continual
state of political excitement over questions which sometimes threaten
the very foundations of government and bring almost to a standstill the
activities of trade and commerce." To Vanderlip, Austria-Hungary was
a good example of this political instability.

With reference to Germany, he mentioned the disputes over tariffs.[65]
Thus, the lowering of tariffs in 1893 had stimulated higher industrial
exports and imports but had caused extreme difficulty to a continuation of a liberal commercial policy "owing to the attitude of the agrarians."[66] Being close to the court, the latter had an influence on the Reich
government that was "out of proportion to their numbers." The progress that industry and commerce had been making was "distasteful to
the landlord," and they were indeed being left behind by the former. As
Vanderlip wrote, the agrarians had also opposed the building of railroads and canals on which cheaper foreign grain could be transported
to the urban centers further inland.[67]

Moreover, the electoral system was skewed in favor of the rural and
provincial parts so that the cities did not have a fair parliamentary representation in the federal states where restrictive class- and tax-based
voting systems continued to be in force.[68] Other handicaps existed at the
Reich level with its universal manhood electoral system. There a vote in
a city counted for less, as many electoral districts had not been adjusted
to the rising numbers of people who, during the period of rapid industrialization and urbanization, had moved from the countryside into the
cities in droves. While the restrictive suffrage systems in the federal
states undermined the working-class vote, it had, after the lapse of Bismarck's Anti-Socialist Laws in 1890, regained its weight. The SPD was
the main beneficiary.[69] Thus, in the Reichstag elections of 1903, the SPD
had added short of one million additional votes compared to 1898 and
had gained a total of eighty-one seats, up from fifty-six in 1898. Small
wonder that it was not just the agrarian *Kreuz-Zeitung* that had warned
of an escalating threat from the Left. Employers were similarly growing fearful of a party that attracted larger and larger numbers of industrial workers and contained reformist elements as well as more radical
voices wedded to orthodox Marxist views of modern industrial societies, with the latter talking about an impending socialist revolution.

Having undertaken a further analysis of the German Empire's internal problems that resulted from both the peculiarities of its monarchical

government and its party system, Vanderlip concluded very percep-tively:[70] "The present melancholy situation has a significance which is not merely transitory, but which is of decisive importance to the future of Germany as a world power." With Bülow having yielded, at least partially, to the agrarians by increasing agricultural tariffs, Germany had been led "into a situation which is fraught with serious menace to her prosperity." The SPD was dead opposed to the resultant price increases of foodstuffs that hit its working-class constituencies most. Vanderlip's verdict "that the passage of this [tariff] bill seemed to mark the final surrender of the German people to the Prussian Squires" was perhaps what he had heard from some pessimistic businessmen on his visits to Berlin and other places. No doubt there were the negative consequences of rising food prices due to higher agricultural tariffs. At the same time his conclusion also reflected quite well what American businessmen thought about the political power structure of the Ger-man monarchy:[71] The passage of the tariff was "in truth a singular spec-tacle which is here represented in the entire German people abjectly surrendering to a class of decadent landholders, the extent of whose extortionate demands is measured only by their stupid rapacity."

Examining further the structure of Wilhelmine government, Vander-lip focused on its other authoritarian features, arguing, rather generally, though not incorrectly, that the Reichstag had only nominal authority. However, his claim that there was "no freedom of the press" and that other freedoms were also restricted was less accurate.[72] He also men-tioned the restrictive three-class voting system in Prussia, the largest state in Germany, and continued,[73] "The ruling classes believe that the lower classes are unfitted for government, that the direction of public business belongs by right to the upper classes and that they are de-termined to repress not only agitation but even discussion." Vanderlip acknowledged the existence of trade unions, among which the Social Democrat ones had some 680,000 members around 1900, followed by the Hirsch-Duncker "yellow" unions with 92,000 and the Catholic unions with 77,000 members.[74] The latter two had gained some recog-nition from the employers, but there was no general legislation per-mitting unionization and collective bargaining, as Vanderlip seems to have thought. However, he added, this time correctly, this "privilege is often nullified by the action of the authority" that tended to intervene whenever there were strikes and these certainly happened in growing numbers up to 1914.[75] Although he noted that some statements of the SPD were hostile to business, in discussing its aims Vanderlip, again not quite accurately, recorded as their main aim "that the German na-tion should be transformed into a liberal constitutional monarchy, with a responsible government and a free people."[76]

Vanderlip's account of his German tour ended with a report on a conversation he had had in Hamburg with a businessman involved in the export business who complained about America's high tariffs.[77] He believed that this conversation illustrated "in a striking way the influence which the economic policy of the United States may exert upon the counter-politics of European nations." While the Hamburgian was hoping for reciprocity, Vanderlip, with his better understanding of American politics, could not but end his notes by saying that this argument, however plausible, had no chance of being accepted by the majority of Congress in Washington.

There are a number of other papers documenting Vanderlip's conversations of 1901, this time with prominent bankers and apparently recorded by an assistant.[78] Having first contacted Arthur Gwinner of Deutsche Bank, who was in poor health and could not receive him, and then spoken, apparently only briefly, with Franz von Mendelssohn, he saw Franz Urbig of the Disconto-Gesellschaft. This conversation revolved partly around "the organization of the steel trust and similar combinations" that he "regarded with great concern" and "filled foreign manufacturers with fear," because "such combinations were quite impossible in Europe."[79] The "tremendous scale, on which they could operate, it was feared, meant cheaper and cheaper production." But there was always also the question of Britain's industrial and financial muscle in the background, and so the two bankers, with an eye on the City, talked about the weakening of sterling and their impression "that England is now rapidly losing her position of prominence in the Exchange market."

The next in line was Urbig's colleague "Director Schoeller," who wanted to know "whether or not I intended to make any arrangement here in Berlin for the purchase of a bank in the interest of the National City."[80] Asking him to elaborate, Vanderlip was told that a direct purchase would be difficult, except for smaller banks. Also since German banks had close links with industry, acquisition might be thought undesirable for that reason. After learning that both the Bleichroeder and Mendelssohn banks were definitely not for sale, a third option— Schoeller remarked—would be to establish an institution from scratch. But this would raise the question of who would run it, since first-class personnel was scarce. On the question of acquiring British banks, Schoeller believed, that this would be easier than an acquisition in Germany. But there was a rub:[81] "If you bought an established [British] bank and retained men of high position and standing as Directors, you would find that those men would not be subservient to your wishes in the management of the institution." Schoeller's experience with British boards had been "that you cannot control them if they are composed of men of independent means and established positions. You would find them too influenced by politics." If, on the other hand, Vanderlip would replace a British board by "mere figure-heads, you at once lose the confidence of the [British] business community, and your opinion will be seriously hampered."

Whether this was a genuinely confidential advice on Britain or just a scare tactic, these arguments gave Schoeller the opportunity to suggest a closer relationship between Disconto-Gesellschaft and NCB.[82] He expressed a readiness to come to the United States for further discussions on this idea, but then added a mild complaint about cooperation between the two institutions until now: "We have at times taken large risks and the final statement of accounts" had merely shown an "extremely small profit." NCB had certainly driven "a very sharp trade in the exchange market." It was not that Schoeller was looking "for anything like the old times when we used to make one per cent." But despite considerable risk-taking on Disconto's part, they were not pleased by the low closing profit. By contrast, the sale of a German loan worth 80 million marks such as the one a "year ago was the sort of business we would like to do." There was, Schoeller thought, no reason to believe that this could not be done again.

The German banker then came to the crucial point: Vanderlip, he said, could not "hope to get a fair share in an undertaking here for so long as you are ostensibly connected with a half-dozen institutions and really connected to none." By contrast, NCB would get its fair share in a participation, "if you formed a close relation[ship] with a single institution and let that relation[ship] be practically exclusive both ways." Promising his own absolute confidence, integrity, and fair play, Schoeller was apparently hoping that Vanderlip would take the bait.

7. The Cultural Difficulties of Operating in Foreign Markets

Vanderlip's account ended with a report on a conversation that he had had with a Mr. Magee of the Union Electricitäts-Gesellschaft on German-American trade relations and the cultural problem of operating in a foreign market.[83] Magee, though "a thorough American in his ideas," had lived in Germany long enough to be very familiar with the local milieu and promptly complained, as Vanderlip had also heard from other sources, that Americans did not know how to secure a market share in another country. American manufacturers were receiving "inquiries perhaps from German importers." But the answers they got were "almost in the nature of a repulse." Thus the Americans would send back "a circular—printed in English—with a statement of their terms—cash—and practically no tangible information regarding the capacity or shipping weight of the article." Consequently, "they fail to secure trade." And "if they were to give their measurements in terms the Germans understand—the metric system—with payment terms somewhat more flexible than a flat-footed demand for cash and show samples, they could undoubtedly build up their trade that would be valuable."

So, according to Magee, American businessmen still had a lot to learn. Nor was it enough to send over a representative who would see the American consul or ambassador, but would otherwise be clueless about how to go about establishing a business. Magee also pointed out that Americans also had no knowledge of German speak and tended to be unfamiliar with the local geography. He warned that the situation would improve only when "we realize the necessity for personal contact with the countries which we wish to reach."

The final section of the record of Vanderlip's talk with Magee was devoted to German science. The latter had nothing but praise for German abilities in the field, especially as far as "their habit of stimulating and encouraging independent investigation" was concerned. This is where, he believed, the Germans were ahead of the Americans. Of course, the latter had achieved a number of "brilliant breakthroughs." In most cases, however, "the great discoveries of the world have come, as a rule, as a result of patient effort and study," and this is what the Germans were good at. Americans, on the other hand, were, in Magee's view, "more superficial" and often had no time to look at a problem from all sides, probing it "deeply like the Germans." Referring to imports of American machine tools, he observed that when the country realized that it had to enter international competition, it abandoned ambitions to manufacture machinery at home and just bought American technology.

When Vanderlip asked Magee how Germany "saw the great prosperity of America and her tremendous strides in the way of commercial development," he was told "that this was not viewed with great alarm in Germany."[84] Only when it came to iron and steel was there "a little" uneasiness because it would no doubt inflict some injury on German steel companies, especially "on account of the formation of the steel trust," which, if it exported its products to Germany, would hurt some German steel firms "that are not now on any too firm a basis."

Having analyzed Stead's book and Vanderlip's extensive notes, what did this chapter try to achieve? It was designed to set the stage for the triangular relationship among the United States, Britain, and Germany. The examination of contemporary newspapers around New Year

1900 gave a first impression of the sociopolitical and economic climate in the three countries and of how they looked back on the nineteenth century and forward into the new one. Although it is true that Stead and Vanderlip are but two sources, they are nevertheless very significant not merely in their rich detail. They also provided first answers to the questions that are underlying this book and that were set out in the Introduction relating to the encounter of three divergent business and political cultures and the complexities of transatlantic trade and FDI decision making. The impressions that Vanderlip brought back to the United States from Britain and Germany were in many ways also those that other travelers were gathering in Europe. They represented information, but also stereotypes and incomplete knowledge that they had picked up beforehand in the American business community or from the press. Many of them were corrected during their travels.

As we have noted above and will see again in later chapters, misperceptions tended to be more glaring when it came to the dynamics of politics in another nation than to grasp how a foreign economy ticked. Still, while the details of the constitutional arrangements may have been more difficult to see through, by 1914 American businessmen had learned how the German monarchical system differed from that of the American republic and also that of Britain and how this affected mutual relations.

The preceding analysis of Stead's book not only tried to correct the assumption that this book was about the "Americanisation of the World," whose myths and realities we shall have to trace in subsequent chapters. On closer inspection, this book was in effect a plea for forging a "special relationship" between the United States and Britain that would secure not only American hegemony but that of the English-speaking peoples. In Stead's vision of the new century, the Germans and especially Wilhelm II appeared as the spoilsports who were assumed to be pursuing anti-American alliance plans that, on closer inspection, were aimed at the future positions of both Britain *and* the United States within the international system.

If the Vanderlip Papers are any guide, many German businessmen did not share the kaiser's and Tirpitz's resentments and preposterous ambitions. They may have been quietly fearful of American economic power, as reflected in some of Vanderlip's notes. Occasionally, the hostile views of the kaiser and right-wing politicians were echoed by German university professors. Thus, Ekkehard Wenger and Leonard Knoll were reported in the British *Financial Times* to be urging to "launch a de-Americanisation process without delay" before the country "becomes more deeply embroiled" in the United States.[85] They saw America as a "country of crisis, unsound economic activity and pathological overcompensation of fair-weather captains." German entrepreneurs and bankers by contrast were by and large keen to connect and do business with the Americans, just as the British remained their very good customers. All sides were unhappy with policies that hampered contact, such as tariffs or diplomatic blunders. American businessmen also came to believe that the economic power of Britain was weakening, while that of Germany, like that of the United States, was rising. Both countries were thought to have dynamic industries that could learn from each other and with which closer economic ties seemed logical and desirable.

The next chapter will look in more detail at German-American business relations up to 1914, when, in American eyes, these were not yet particularly "special." This issue only appeared on the horizon in a negative sense when political factors, that is, international diplomacy and the arms race, began to affect commercial affairs. This is why international politics and the problem of political risk will always have to be borne in mind as we move toward World War I. It was at that point that the British-American relationship became more what Stead had hoped for, that is, "special" in a positive sense, while the relationship between Germany and America moved into a peculiarly negative "special" mode.

Notes to Chapter I

1. On Anglo-German tensions in the late 1890s and the building of the kaiser's navy, see Jonathan Steinberg, *Yesterday's Deterrent* (London, 1965); Patrick J. Kelly, *Tirpitz and the Imperial German Navy* (Bloomington, IN, 2011); Peter Winzen, *Reichskanzler Bernhard Fürst von Bülow* (Göttingen, 2003).

2. On German and American tariff politics, see Cornelius Torp, *Die Herausforderung der Globalisierung. Wirtschaft und Politik in Deutschland, 1860–1914* (Göttingen, 2005); F. W. Taussig, *The Tariff History of the United States* (New York, 1964); T. E. Terrill, *The Tariff, Politics, and American Foreign Policy, 1974–1901* (Westport, CT, 1973).

3. On the Spanish-American War and Venezuela, see Holger H. Herwig, *Germany's Vision of Empire in Venezuela, 1871–1914* (Princeton, 1886); Ragnhild Fiebig-von Hase, *Lateinamerika als Konfliktherd der deutsch-amerikanischen Beziehungen, 1890–1903*, 2 vols. (Göttingen, 1986).

4. For an excellent analysis of these days with a more detailed evaluation not only of the actual celebrations but also of speeches, sermons, poems, and photos, see Michael Salewski, " 'Neujahr 1900.' Die Säkularwende in zeitgenössischer Sicht," *Archiv für Kulturgeschichte* 53, no. 2 (1971): 335–81. See also the reports on events in New York and Berlin in the *New York Times* (*NYT*), 31 January 1900. See also Ute Frevert, ed., *Das neue Jahrhundert* (Göttingen, 2000).

5. *Frankfurter Zeitung*, 30 December 1899.

6. *Frankfurter Zeitung*, 31 December 1899.

7. Quoted in Hans Dollinger, ed., *Das Kaiserreich* (Munich, 1966), 296.

8. *Frankfurter Zeitung*, 31 December 1899.

9. *Neue Preussische Kreuz-Zeitung*, 31 December 1899.

10. *Der Vorwärts*, 31 December 1899 (suppl. 1).

11. Quoted in Salewski, "'Neujahr 1900'" (note 4), 355.

12. *Manchester Guardian*, 1 January 1900.

13. *The Times*, 30 December 1899.

14. *The Times*, 1 January 1900.

15. *Chicago Daily Tribune*, 30 December 1899.

16. *New York Times* (*NYT*), 1 January 1900.

17. *Washington Post*, 1 January 1900.

18. See Dexter Perkins, *A History of the Monroe Doctrine* (London, 1960).

19. See the literature listed in note 3.

20. See, e.g., Paul M. Kennedy, *Samoan Tangle* (Dublin, 1974).

21. Leon F. Litwack and Winthrop D. Jordan, *The United States: Becoming a World Power*, vol. 2, 6th ed. (Englewood Cliffs, NJ, 1987), 462.

22. See Michael Balfour, *Britain and Joseph Chamberlain* (London, 1981).

23. See Torp, *Die Herausforderung* (note 2), esp. 211ff.; Derek M. Bleyberg, "Government and Legislative Process in Wilhelmine Germany. The Reorganisation of the Tariff Laws under Reich Chancellor von Bülow, 1897–1902" (PhD thesis, University of East Anglia, 1979).

24. See Peter-Christian Witt, *Die Finanzpolitik des Deutschen Reiches von 1903 bis 1913* (Lübeck-Hamburg, 1970), 58ff. See also note 9 above.

25. Columbia University Archive (CUA), Vanderlip Papers, D-4, folder I. Vanderlip was born in Aurora, Illinois, and became an apprentice in a machine shop at age sixteen. He then worked as a reporter for a local paper until he moved first to Chicago to join an investors' bureau and eventually assumed the position of financial editor of the *Chicago Tribune*. Subsequently he became private secretary to Lyman Gage during his time as secretary of the treasury in Washington, where he then rose to the position of assistant secretary of the treasury. He went to NCB as one of its vice-presidents in 1901. When James Stillman, the NCB president, was elected a chairman of the board, Vanderlip became president. See *WSJ*, 4 June 1919. Stillman had two daughters who were married to two sons of William Rockefeller. The Rockefeller family was the largest stockholder in NCB before 1918, and the bank therefore also had a major connection with Standard Oil. See Carl P. Parrini, *Heir to Empire. United States Economic Diplomacy, 1916–1923* (Pittsburgh, 1969), 58. See also chapter III, pp. 126f.

26. CUA, Vanderlip Papers, Vanderlip's handwritten notes, D-4, "23 and 24," pp. 19–20, p. 29. This observation relates to the larger argument that Martin Wiener advanced in the 1980s in his *English Culture and the Decline of the Industrial Spirit* (Cambridge, 1981), passim, i.e., that the English elites never felt comfortable with industrial production and management. It is also a theme that is running through the rest of this book, which is based on actual observations

by American businesspeople all the way into the post-1945 period and in contrast to German entrepreneurial attitudes. For a retrospective on this debate, see Bruce Collins and Keith Robbins, *British Culture and Economic Decline* (London, 1990). See also chapter VI and the Conclusion for the post-1945 period.

27. CUA, Vanderlip Papers,, Diary 1901, 12–13.

28. CUA, Vanderlip Papers,, handwritten notes "23 and 24," 40.

29. William T. Stead, *The Americanisation of the World* (London, 1902). On European and American attitudes toward Britain and its culture in the eighteenth and nineteenth centuries, see also Ian Buruma, *Anglomania* (New York, 1998). Stead died onboard *The Titanic* when it went down in the Atlantic in April 1912 after hitting an iceberg. See also Frederick Whyte, *The Life of William T. Stead*, 2 vols. (New York, 1925).

30. Stead, *Americanisation* (note 29), 5, also for the following quotes up to 7.

31. Ibid. 14–64.

32. Ibid., 65ff. and especially the passages on Germany, 67–68.

33. Ibid., 65.

34. Ibid. 67–68, also for the following quotes on the kaiser. See also the biography by John C. G. Röhl, *Wilhelm II* (Munich, 2008).

35. Stead, *Americanisation* (note 29), 70. See also Röhl, *Wilhelm II* (note 34), 251–52.

36. Volker Berghahn, *Der Tirpitz-Plan* (Düsseldorf, 1971), 173ff. On German naval operations plans against the United States, see Holger H. Herwig, *Politics of Frustration. The United States and German Naval Planning, 1889–1941* (Boston, 1976).

37. Stead, *Americanisation* (note 29), 70–71. also for the following quotes.

38. Ibid., 149ff. up to 152.

39. Ibid., pp.154–55.

40. Ibid., 164.

41. CUA, Vanderlip Papers, D-4, "23 and 24," 17.

42. Ibid., 28.

43. Ibid., 29.

44. Ibid., 54 and 29ff.

45. Ibid., 42–43.

46. Ibid., 46ff.

47. Ibid., 48–49. On Krupp and America, see also below p. 63.

48. CUA, Vanderlip Papers, D-4, "23 and 24," 49. The mention of his "readers" refers to the fact that some of these notes were published as articles, although I was unable to determine where.

49. Ibid., 50.

50. Ibid., 51.

51. Ibid. See also below p. 42, 75. On the world exhibitions and their economic and cultural significance, see, e.g., Robert Rydell, *All the World's a Fair. Vision of Empire at American International Expositions, 1876–1916* (Chicago, 1984); Robert Wilson, *Great Exhibitions. The World Fairs* (Melbourne, 2007).

52. CUA, Vanderlip Papers, D-4, "23 and 24," 52. On German *Qualitätsarbeit*, which established itself as a principle in the late nineteenth century after Ger-

man goods had been deemed shoddy and cheap in earlier decades, see, e.g., Anson Rabinbach, *Human Motor* (New York, 1990).

53. Quoted in Anita Kugler, "Von der Werkstatt zum Fliessband," *Geschichte und Gesellschaft* 13 (1987): 304–39, esp. 315–16.

54. CUA, Vanderlip Papers, D-4, "23 and 24," 15–16.

55. Ibid., 16.

56. Ibid., 17. On the importance of the World Exhibition at Paris in 1900 and the interest shown by Europeans in the American pavilion and the machinery on display there, see Richard D. Mandell, *Paris 1900. The Great World's Fair* (Toronto, 1967).

57. CUA, Vanderlip Papers, D-4, "23 and 24," 16.

58. Ibid., 17.

59. Ibid.

60. This is a key point to keep in mind for later chapters. It was made many years ago by Heinz Hartmann, *Amerikanische Firmen in Deutschland* (Cologne, 1963): It is not just technologies that are transferred to another industrial system but also the ways in which the introduction of new machinery influenced the organization of labor and factory layout. See also John Dunning and Sarianna Lundan, *Multinational Enterprises and the Global Economy*, 2nd ed. (Cheltenham, 2008), 362ff.; Hubert Bonin and Ferry de Goey, eds., *American Firms in Europe, 1880–1980. Strategy, Identity, Perception and Performance* (Geneva, 2009). Hence also the European interest in Taylorism and Scientific Management and later in Fordism. See, e.g., Mary Nolan, *Visions of Modernity* (New York, 1994). On the rise of Taylorism and Scientific Management in the United States, see, e.g., Harry Braverman, *Labor and Monopoly Capital* (New York, 1974), esp. chaps. 4 and 5; Samuel Haber, *Efficiency and Uplift* (Chicago, 1984); Robert Kanigel, *The One Best Way* (New York, 1977); Lyndall Urwick, *Life and Work of Frederick Winslow Taylor* (London, 1957). See also below pp. 64ff and pp. 261f. on Fordism.

61. CUA, Vanderlip Papers, D-4, "23 and 24," 22ff., also for the following.

62. See pp. 28, 165, 306ff.

63. CUA, Vanderlip Papers, D-4, "23 and 24," 26–27. On the German systems of these commercial training institutions, see Heinz-Dieter Meyer, "Handelshochschulen and American Business Schools. German Business Education, 1879–1933, in Comparative Perspective" (paper, Cross Fertilisation of Learning through Foundations conference, Brussels, 27–28 June 1996). On the German system of education more generally, see, e.g., James C. Albisetti, *Secondary School Reform in Imperial Germany* (Princeton, 1983); Marjorie Lamberti, *Society and Elementary Schools in Imperial Germany* (Oxford, 1989); Charles McClelland, *State, Society and Universities in Germany* (Cambridge, MA, 1980); K. A. Schleunes, *Schooling and Society* (Oxford, 1991); Konrad H. Jarausch, *The Transformation of Higher Learning, 1860–1930* (Stuttgart, 1982).

64. CUA, Vanderlip Papers, D-4, "23 and 24," 21.

65. Ibid. On the tensions between the kaiser and Prussia's agrarian conservatives, see, e.g., Hannelore Horn, *Kampf um den Bau des Mittellandkanals* (Cologne, 1964); Eckart Kehr, *Schlachtflottenbau und Parteipolitik, 1894–1901* (Berlin, 1930).

66. CUA, Vanderlip Papers, D-4, "23 and 24," 57–58.

67. On these tariffs, see John A. Nichols, *Germany after Bismarck. The Caprivi Era, 1890–1894* (Cambridge, MA, 1958); Torp, *Die Herausforderung* (note 2), 179ff. On the canal issue, see the literature cited in note 65 above.

68. For details, see, e.g., Margaret Anderson, *Practicing Democracy* (Princeton, 2000); Thomas Kühne, *Dreiklassenwahlrecht und Wahlkultur in Preussen 1867–1914* (Düsseldorf, 1994); Jonathan Sperber, *The Kaiser's Voters* (Cambridge, 1997); Stanley Suval, *Electoral Politics in Wilhelmine Germany* (Chapel Hill, NC, 1985).

69. See, e.g., Willy L. Guttsman, *The German Social Democratic Party, 1875–1933* (London, 1981); Vernon Lidtke, *The Outlawed Party* (Princeton, 1966); Lidtke, *The Alternative Culture* (Oxford, 1985).

70. CUA, Vanderlip Papers, D-4, "23 and 24," 76.

71. Ibid., 77ff. also for the following quotes.

72. On the question of press freedom and censorship, see, e.g., Peter Jelavich, *Munich and Theatrical Modernism* (Cambridge, MA, 1985).

73. CUA, Vanderlip Papers, D-4, "23 and 24," 80.

74. On German trade unions and their memberships, see John A. Moses, *Trade Unionism in Germany from Bismarck to Hitler* (London, 1982); Eric D. Brose, *Christian Labor and the Politics of Frustration in Imperial Germany* (Washington, DC, 1985).

75. On strikes and the police, see, e.g., Klaus Saul, *Staat, Industrie, Arbeiterbewegung im Kaiserreich, 1903–1914* (Gütersloh, 1974).

76. CUA, Vanderlip Papers, D-4, "23 and 24," 82.

77. Ibid., 85.

78. CUA, Vanderlip Papers, D-4, folder II, notes on Vanderlip's trip to Berlin, 6 May 1901, 175.

79. Ibid., 176.

80. Ibid., 178.

81. Ibid., 177.

82. Ibid., 178.

83. Ibid.

84. Ibid. See also below, pp. 63ff.

85. *Financial Times*, 8 April 1908.

I I

///

Cooperation, Peaceful Competition, and the Specter of War, 1902–1914

1. Introduction

The previous chapter examined British-American and German-American economic and political relations at the turn of the century on the basis of William Stead's appeal to reunite the English-speaking world. It also dealt with the information and impressions that Frank Vanderlip, a well-known and perceptive Wall Street banker, had gathered on his trips to Britain and Germany in 1901. The aim of this chapter is to trace how American business relations with the two major industrial powers of Europe developed up to 1914. As will be seen, the economic ties with Britain had been weakening for several years, but then saw a re-strengthening as the political threat of a major war loomed larger and larger on the horizon. The Anglo-American relationship became close and in this sense "special" at the outbreak of hostilities between Britain and Germany in August 1914. Meanwhile German-American economic relations, which, despite many political difficulties, had been intensifying after the turn of the century, became antagonistic in the summer of 1914, even if it took until April 1917 for Washington formally to enter the world conflict on the Allied side against Berlin and Vienna.

Like Vanderlip, other American businessmen on their trips to Europe not only talked about FDI in Britain and Germany, but also practiced it. The first part of this chapter will look at a variety of companies and their activities and experiences in both Britain and Germany, with the latter emerging as the main partner but also as a competitor. The second half will then highlight issues that arose not so much at the local and commercial levels, but increasingly at the level of international politics, thus raising the problem of how much risk the American business community trading with Europe was prepared to accept.

At the Paris World Exposition, American machines and machine tools had attracted a lot of attention, and, as Fritz Blaich has shown, this did indeed become a branch of industry in which the United States were particularly successful abroad. Included in this category was not just heavy industrial and agricultural equipment, but also such manufactured products as sewing machines and typewriters.[1] Although the Prussian landowners were claiming to be in dire straits, agriculture was in fact still expanding. A growing German population had to be fed and farmers were looking for labor-saving machinery, as exploited land laborers migrated to urban centers in search of better-paying jobs in industry.[2] American firms had been thriving back home thanks to the opening of the agricultural Midwest. They had also led the way in building complex mechanical implements. Consequently, fresh export opportunities to Britain as well as Germany offered themselves. In the first six months of 1900 alone Germany "imported some 21,700 tons of agricultural machinery of which 16.200 came from the United States."[3]

2. American Foreign Direct Investments in Britain and Germany

International Harvester (IH) exported its sophisticated and versatile products after its position back home had been strengthened by the great merger movement in the final decades of the nineteenth century. Promoted by J.P. Morgan Bank, the Deering and McCormick families, after years of fierce competition, finally came together in August 1902 to form IH, with capital of $120 million.[4] Looking at the photos of IH binders, reapers, corn harvesters, and other farm machinery, it is not surprising that IH's products were greatly in demand in North America and Europe and that the company became very active in marketing its products overseas. More and more agencies were founded, followed by the building of factories, first in Canada. By 1905 a plant had opened at Norrköping in Sweden. A few years later and next to Britain and France, production began in Neuss on the Rhine. In 1908 IH had added tractors to its product range and "in the next few years, the 'Titan' and 'Mogul' [tractor] trademarks became household words across America and in the far corners of the world." In short, the Americans not only were technologically more advanced and had a wide choice of popular products but also were quite daring with respect to their investments. Recognizing the potential for business, they were no longer content with agencies or sales offices, but also began to manufacture their models abroad.

Next to IH, Singer Sewing Machines of New York became another company that was very successful in Europe.[5] Having become one of the largest sewing machine manufacturers in the world, it had made its debut in Germany as early as 1861 when the Hamburgian merchant Gustav Wieler took its products on commission. From 1865 Singer built up its own sales organization. Demand for the new household machines increased competition from a number of firms that, interestingly enough, tried to promote themselves as protagonists of American technological refinement and reliability, such as the "Hamburg-Amerikanische Nähmaschinen-Fabrik." Keen to expand overseas, Singer also learned early on about the vagaries of selling patents internationally. Thus a French company refused to pay the agreed royalties and also took on the sale of machines by Singer's competitors. The Americans were unable to obtain accurate sales figures from this company. These troubles with agents help explain why by 1885 the corporation built factories in Glasgow and soon also others in Germany and Austria.

In the first half year of 1900, Germany imported some 906 tons of sewing machines, some 786 tons of which were American. This success "was intimately connected with the firm's dynamic and successful investment in overseas marketing," including a system of hire-purchase. But there was also plenty of German competition.[6] By 1912, there were some two dozen companies, some of which had moved into specialized niches, for example, in the field of industrial sewing machines. Pfaff was particularly adept at holding its own against the American giant and at adopting American methods of rationalized production. While Singer came to see Germany as its main market, its competitors soon occupied the second rank in sewing machines on the world market, exporting between 60 and 70 percent of their products. However, being at the top also meant incurring hostility from domestic producers, with their lobbies charging that Singer was threatening some fifty thousand German jobs.

One company that decided to compete with the Americans was Dürkopp AG, which advertised its machines as "Singer Machines"—a method apparently permissible under German law. It specialized, in, inter alia, machines to sew buttonholes. But this company also diversified into another lucrative industry: bicycles.[7] This boom started in the mid-1880s, but began to decline again between 1898 and 1902, when motorcycles and automobiles came along that required more complex

machinery and organization. This was the hour of Adam Opel at Rüsselsheim near Frankfurt, which was bought by General Motors in the
1920s.[8]

With the rise of the white-collar employee and "white-blouse" professions began the story of office equipment and appliances, such as
typewriters, data processors, and cash registers. Government as well
as private bureaucracies increasingly converted their operations from
scribes to office machines. The success of the Union Typewriter Company (UTC) and International Business Machines (IBM) must be seen
in this context.[9] National Cash Register Company (NCR) of Ohio had
achieved a virtual monopoly position in the United States by 1912. This
was yet another firm that relied not merely on ingenious technology
but also on aggressive marketing, convinced that successful salesmen
were not born but trained. After a good start in Britain, NCR turned
to Germany in the late 1890s. Its Berlin headquarters became the hub
for its European sales and service network. By 1903 NCR also had factories that assembled cash registers from imported parts. Significantly
enough, the company was also sensitive to local feelings in ways that
Vanderlip had suggested in his report by assuming names in indigenous languages. Thus, in 1908 NCR in Germany became Nationale
Registrier-Kassen GmbH (NRK). Overall, it is not difficult to see why
modern American equipment attracted European buyers.[10] The Americans stimulated technological innovation as well as fierce competition.

While Singer was prepared to take the risky plunge into manufacturing overseas quite early, other American companies waited longer.
Among them was Merganthaler Linotype, which, like NCR, viewed
FDI in Germany as particularly promising.[11] They made their move in
1909 and established Merganthaler Setzmaschinen G.m.b.H., set up as
an agency controlled from the United States and affiliated with German or British firms. Apparently it ran into many difficulties. When the
Kayser glove-making company went to Saxony, it encountered stiff
opposition from local entrepreneurs. Nor did business go well for the
Button Company. American importers of shoe-manufacturing machines and machine-made shoes also had a difficult time when traditional shoemakers resisted the shift into mass production. Undeterred,
the United Shoe Machinery Co. of Boston established a subsidiary in
Frankfurt as early as October 1900 and a new factory three years later.
As Richard Heindel put it, American machine-made shoes were in demand because of their "lightness, elegance, finish, and quarter and half
sizes."[12] The *New York Times* (*NYT*) added on 5 January 1902 with reference to Germany, "An American three-dollar shoe would find an unlimited market here" and also "cheap jewelry" as well as other articles
for mass consumption. Tobacco had become one of the inexpensive

"pleasures of the little man" at a time when cigarette manufacture also underwent a process of mechanization, after cigar making had relied primarily on hand-rolled brands. When the Duke family of North Carolina ventured into the British market to set up British-American Tobacco (BAT), the local tobacco industry formed the International Tobacco Company (ITC) in 1902. Subsequently, BAT tried to corner the German market by investing in the Jazmatzi cigarette company, again against local opposition.[13]

Cigarettes were but one manifestation of an expanding market in consumer goods. While basic items of food consumption were still primarily sold through small retailers, by the turn of the century the department store had also appeared on the scene, often growing out of an initially much smaller venture. In Germany Wertheim and Tietz were among the pioneers. The American Woolworth Corp. saw opportunities in large-scale retailing of inexpensive consumer goods and opened its stores in Britain and Germany.[14] After a trip to Europe in 1913, F. W. Woolworth proudly announced that the number of his "Thri'-Penny" and "Six Penny" stores had doubled in Britain from just a year ago.

Demand for sophisticated machinery shot up both in the United States and in Europe once a safe elevator technology had been developed. Before this, buildings in cities like New York had no more than five floors for reasons of safety and physical maneuverability. Now these "walk-ups" could be complemented by higher and more lucrative office and residential buildings. Otis became one of the leading companies in this field "with factories in Britain, Germany, France and Canada by 1914."[15] In heavy textile machinery, the Germans continued to rely on British firms and their older patented technologies. But probably because technological innovation in Britain had begun to stall, fresh opportunities arose for American companies. Barber & Coleman of Rockford, Illinois, founded a subsidiary in Munich in May 1908 for its specialized weaving machine products, with Germany's cotton weavers being its main customers in Europe.

Finally, heavy machine tools for the iron and steel, stone, and wood industries have to be considered.[16] American firms had a reputation of being particularly modern. Imitators were therefore keen to advertise the modernity of their products by reference to the United States. Here, too, British firms had been losing their dominant position to the Americans, whom the Germans now used as their model. Still, it took them some time to make the transition from factories that manufactured all sorts of machinery adapted to the American system of standardized volume production and to develop American-style machines in which worn-out or broken parts could be easily and quickly replaced. What also contributed to the early transition to this system in the United

States was its relative lack of skilled workers, while Europe retained workers who had been trained as experienced craftsmen working in small workshops.

American principles and practices of work organization were closely studied by entrepreneurs when they began to visit machine tool firms in the industrial centers of the United States.[17] By 1914, the Ludwig Loewe Company in Berlin whose founder had shrewdly put into practice what he had seen across the Atlantic had become the "biggest machine tool factory in Europe that produced according to the American system."[18] Others, such as the R.J. Reinecker Company of Chemnitz in Saxony, had moved from mere imitation to technological innovation of its own. The firm also placed much emphasis on sales and marketing, and its service department could guarantee swift repairs in case one of its machines had broken down. Their reliance on highly skilled labor also allowed the Germans to stress quality and reliability, as they became keen competitors with American firms on the world market.[19]

Sooner or later American machine tool companies faced the question of whether to confine themselves to sales offices or to found a new indigenous company with primarily local money. The Niles Werkzeugmaschinenfabrik of Berlin is an example to the latter type of engagement, with less than one-tenth of its shares coming from the Niles Tools parent in Hamilton, Ohio.[20] The rest of the capital was put up by four German banks as well as Ludwig Loewe and Allgemeine Electricitäts-Gesellschaft (AEG). More than that, Niles Tools did not contribute actual capital but blueprints and patents from its Hamilton headquarters. For many years, the German company did not do well. It was only in 1912 that it registered a small profit for the first time. The dividend a year later was a mere 4 percent. The Gavin Machine Company of New York, having found its export business to be profitable in the 1890s, took up actual production in Germany. It had a capital stock of 2.5 million marks, most of which was raised in the country with the help of Berliner Bank, while some 700,000 marks came from the American parent.

Developments in the machine tool business reflected a growing interest of American big business in Britain and Germany, but machinery exports were probably outdone by the ambitions of the American and German steel industries. Vanderlip had already observed this during his trip to Germany and had also commented on the anxieties that the big American steelmakers had triggered, as British, German and American producers began to eye each other suspiciously.[21] The great merger movement in the United States at the end of the nineteenth century had led to the formation of giants such as U.S. Steel.[22] Given the large capital layouts that steelmaking required, exports through local specialized agencies or their own sales offices became the general pattern. Still, the emergence of trusts across the Atlantic greatly concerned British and German heavy industry. This became one of major sources of talk about an "American danger" and an "American invasion."[23] The topic was in turn picked up by politicians, journalists, and academics. In 1902 Vanderlip published an essay titled "The American Commercial Invasion of Europe."[24] Similar words began to be used at this time with reference to the overwhelming power of the Standard Oil Company. The campaign against it peaked in the years before 1914.

3. Facing British and German
Competition and Cooperation

The only German steelmaker that felt confident enough to challenge U.S. Steel and to venture into the American market was Krupp of Essen, with its specialized steels. As the *WSJ* put it in July 1903:[25] "[I]n deciding to inaugurate at this time a vigorous competition for American business in bridge and structural building of all sorts in which iron and steel enter into construction will be followed with interest." The paper added, "The first contest of importance in which the Krupp Company will be in open competition with the American Bridge Co. of the United States Steel Corporation will be in the bids for a new Manhattan bridge across the East river." But it was felt that Krupp's competition "ought not to prove especially hurtful, as the advantages the home companies enjoy are great. . . . The entrance of the Krupp Company as a competitor may result in close bidding, but the chances are that a relatively insignificant percentage of contracts only will go to the foreign firm." And indeed, it was difficult to outdo the Americans. By 1911, U.S. Steel alone had some 218,000 employees and exported 13 percent of its production. As early as 1900, the United States was well ahead in total steel production, with 10.3 million metric tons per annum, followed by Germany with 6.4 and Britain with 4.9. By 1914 American production had reached 23.8 million, as against Germany's 13.1 and Britain's 7.9.

This was also the time when American and German steel companies stepped up their competition in Britain, where indigenous steelmaking was falling behind. The estimates for 1903 were that the country would import some 1.3 million tons of foreign steel, "of which Germany will furnish not less than 900,000 tons."[26] There was also the complaint that German steel exporters were given preferential freight rates when shipping their products via the Reich's state-owned railroad system.[27] But this did not deter the Americans from planning to undersell the Germans, to be achieved not only through the advantages that American steelmakers had over Germany thanks to their access to cheap raw materials back home, but also through their lower freight rates. The newly negotiated rates on steel rails and steel products intended for export would, it was hoped, enable U.S. Steel to secure more business from England in competition with Germany.[28]

It is not clear how successful the "invasion" by Krupp was in the longer term. One motive for the challenge seems to have been that Krupp's special steels were very much in demand, so that even the high American import tariffs did not pose a major obstacle.[29] There was always also another calculation of the Europeans, that is, to learn more about American technology and factory organization. In August 1902 the Germans had sent a group of experts to study U.S. Steel.[30] By 1904 there was talk of cooperation, though apparently it never materialized. One reason for this may have been that by 1905 the naval arms race was accelerating with the decision, first by Britain, but imitated by Wilhelm II and soon by all navies, to build dreadnought-class battle ships with heavier armor and bigger guns.[31] With the hardening of steel improving all the time, companies became more and more secretive about their R&D. Moreover, increased armament orders at home diminished the incentive to export steel.

It was a different matter with automobiles. Both in Britain and Germany car and truck manufacture was very fragmented and geared to the production of quite limited numbers in small workshops, often made to order and to greatly varying specifications.[32] The end product tended to be a luxury car whose superior workmanship contrasted with the poorer quality of the much cheaper American-made automobiles. The dismissive and arrogant though very telling comment in one of the 1903 issues of *Der Motorwagen* has already been quoted.[33] This criticism was exacerbated by the other comment from the same source that strikingly encapsulated an important difference between the societies of the more democratically organized New World and Old Europe that was more rigidly stratified by socioeconomic class and status. It is a contrast that should be remembered as constituting the *basso continuo* of this book, until the impact of economic and cultural "Americanization" along Fordist lines became very tangible in the 1950s.

Given the great fortunes that were being accumulated in the United States by 1900, European carmakers did have opportunities for exporting their expensive custom-made vehicles. At the same time, American exports to Western Europe saw sizeable increases by 1912–13, as motorization got under way. These developments made the observations and comparisons by Adam Opel, "one of Germany's most prominent motor-car manufacturers," all the more significant when he remarked after his return from a trip to the United States in December 1909 that "Europeans have no conception of the magnitude of automobile traffic in New York which is rapidly driving horses to oblivion."[34] But his "chief impression of Industrial America" was that "mighty" as the country was, "she was no longer ahead of Germany." This was in marked contrast to what he had felt after his return from a trip in 1893, when he had "realized how hopelessly behind Germany was." As he added self-confidently after his 1909 visit, "During the intervening sixteen years . . . we have caught up all along the line. Things are no longer done in America on any bigger scale than here. Our industrial business systems are on the same high level." There may be, he concluded, more cars "in New York and other great cities," but he "found America poorly provided with the good roads and magnificent highways which make the [German] Fatherland the motorists' paradise."

Closely related to the rise, first of bicycles and then of motorbikes and automobiles was the tire industry. Paul Erker has analyzed in a pioneering study of the history of American, British, and German rubber corporations how US Rubber, B.F. Goodrich, and other firms expanded into powerful trusts that began to explore European markets for their exports. By 1908, Goodrich had founded its own B.F. Goodrich & Co. AG in Frankfurt. In 1913 it had some twenty-one sales offices and seventy-six dealerships outside the United States. With motorization in France ahead of Germany, the company opened a factory at Colombes near Paris in 1910 with a capacity of two hundred tires per day. The idea was to supply the British and German markets from the French base. Between 1913 and 1916, the value of American tire exports grew fivefold. Still, the power of the major European manufacturers was not to be underestimated. Competition was fierce, with Britain and its major manufacturer, Dunlop, losing ground. As early as 1900, the trade journal *Gummi-Zeitung* had written,[35] "The most important competitor with which Germany will have to reckon in the future is, without any doubt, America, especially since the British [rubber] industry cannot keep up anymore."

Like Krupp and Adam Opel, German rubber firms, and the Continental Gummi AG of Hanover in particular, had enough confidence to attempt forays into the American market.[36] In 1903, it opened a subsidiary in New York, and Willy Tischbein of its management board sailed to the United States in an effort to persuade American carmakers to equip their new vehicles with Continental tires. The firm also concluded a license agreement with the Reverse Rubber Company for production of its tires, supported by German technical personnel and bearing its brand name. With the American tariff at 45 percent, it was a method to achieve an at least partial reduction of the advantages that domestic producers enjoyed against their foreign competitors. Continental's strategy seems to have borne fruit until 1907–8. Thereafter opportunities declined due to the concentrated economic power that American corporations had by then acquired. Doing business in America also became unprofitable due to the continued imposition of high American tariffs. Revere Rubber was therefore given the right to manufacture tires with Continental's name for another eight years. But well before that date US Rubber had bought up Revere. Ultimately, Continental suffered the same fate as the British pioneer Dunlop before it: tires bearing the brand name remained on the market. The original company had disappeared.

If Opel, as quoted above, had been bragging a bit too much about the size of the German automobile market, there was one branch of industry, that is, electrical engineering, in which the Germans could rightly compare themselves to the Americans. The other industry was chemicals and pharmaceuticals, in which, as Vanderlip had conceded in chapter I, they had taken the lead.

Thus both Siemens and AEG had undergone a rapid expansion in the second half of the nineteenth century for which they had raised millions of marks in new capital and signed cooperation agreements with complementary enterprises. AEG, founded by Emil Rathenau originally as "German Edison" and headquartered in Berlin, tried to gain control of Schuckert in Nuremberg with the help of a group of Berlin banks.[37] Schuckert successfully resisted and as a specialist in low-tension electrical equipment became Siemens & Schuckert in 1903, with Siemens's high-tension branch trading as Siemens & Halske. AEG combined with the Union Elektricitäts-Gesellschaft, which owned a number of Thomson-Houston patents for Germany and neighboring countries. The technical manager at Union was Mr. Magee, whom, as has been mentioned in chapter I, Frank Vanderlip had met on his trip to Berlin.[38] As the *NYT* reported in December 1902, the management of AEG and Union was "identical, though the companies [remained] nominally . . . separate."[39] During the 1901–2 recession, AEG had made "various efforts . . . to organize a combination after the method practiced in America." It formed an alliance with the Swiss firm of Brown, Boveri & Cie. and signed a patents exchange agreement with General Electric (GE) in 1903. Meanwhile Siemens had come to occupy the second place in Britain behind Westinghouse.

Given this expansion, Germany became a major importer of American copper.[40] Confident that the German electrical industry had "a big future," the two German companies not only were each other's main rivals but also competed vigorously with GE that had also seen a great increase of its business.[41] Its orders in the first quarter of 1903 had risen by 16.4 percent over the end of the previous year. In subsequent years Siemens and AEG achieved a size that was about the same as GE's and Westinghouse's in the United States, leading the German economic historian Harm Schröter to conclude that in electrical engineering competition was even stiffer than in chemicals.[42]

As to the latter, American corporations, such as Dow and DuPont, were in fact struggling to keep up with the Germans both in the development of new products and the marketing of these around the world. This also applied to Britain, where before 1914 there existed four big corporations: Brunner, Mond & Co., United Alkali, Crossfields & Lever Bros., and Nobel. Germany had meanwhile seen the rise of such key corporations as Badische Anilin und Soda-Fabriken (BASF), Bayer, Agfa, Hoechst, Casella, and Kalle, all of them occupying a special niche in this branch of industry. There is no space here to deal with the history of all six of them.[43] BASF may serve as a good illustration of the interactions that developed with Britain and the United States in a rapidly expanding international market. This company, based at Mannheim-Ludwigshafen on the Rhine in southwestern Germany, had first emerged as a leader in the coal-tar dye industry. It soon added Alizarin dyes and was to become an early model of "science-based" manufacturing. By the late nineteenth century, BASF had branch factories in several European countries and, "conscious of its own considerable strength," had embarked upon a "course of intense competition" with American and British firms while seeking cooperation with Bayer and Agfa in Germany.[44] The "Little I.G." (Interessengemeinschaft) was formed in 1905 to become the mighty I.G. Farben in the 1920s.

One of its most important scientific breakthroughs came shortly before World War I with the development of the process of nitrogen fixation from the air. The great interest that this discovery generated became apparent at the New York International Congress of Applied Chemistry in September 1912 when BASF's "August Bernthsen spoke to an overflowing lecture hall (1,300 people were in attendance) on the technologies of fixing atmospheric nitrogen."[45] The hope was that this invention would solve "one of the world's critical problems, the growing demand for nitrate fertilizers." It should be added that the process proved no less vital to Germany during World War I for the manufacture of explosives after the importation of Chilean guano had been stopped by the British naval blockade. Without this prewar development, Germany would have been unable to produce grenades and other explosives to continue the war.[46]

As to the pre-1914 period, it is not difficult to see that BASF's laboratories, just as those of Bayer and other chemical firms, secured Germany a very strong position vis-à-vis their American and British competitors and encouraged them not merely to have agencies but also to build factories abroad. As Schröter put it,[47] "Before the First World War, not only the European but the world market for organic chemicals was in German hands." However, foreign companies, he continued, were on the Germans' heels "to make themselves independent of German chemical supplies." In the United States in particular competition forced several firms "to establish branch factories in order to retain their business." While circumventing the high American tariffs was probably another reason for adopting this particular FDI strategy, BASF also found that "those making aniline colors" had "less to fear, as it will take some time before Americans learn the secrets of their manufacture."[48]

If the American firms examined so far were involved with Britain and Germany as exporters of industrial equipment and consumer goods, there is one last area of commercial activity that should not be ignored in an analysis of the Atlantic trade triangle: shipping. This was another area in which competition among the three countries was stiff, if only because it was a very lucrative business that also carried plenty of national prestige with it. While virtually all American exports made their way across to Europe in freighters, it was also almost daily that one of the huge ocean liners docked in New York or left the city as the main U.S. transatlantic gateway. Given that it took about a week to reach Europe, travelers usually left for several weeks, sometimes even for several months, with businessmen regularly among them.

They had a choice among American, British, French, and German liners, all of which tried to outbid each other with regard to speed, service, and luxury, now that the traffic in impoverished migrants from Europe who were looking for a better life in North America was declining. Older steamers that had taken poor immigrants to the United States were refitted and huge ultrafast liners came off the shipyards. The British 46,000 BRT *Titanic* immediately springs to mind.[49] But the Germans were never far behind when they launched the 52,000 BRT *Europa* and the even more luxurious *Imperator*. On the German side, there was the HAPAG (Hamburg-Amerika-Paketfahrt-Actien-Gesellschaft), which, from 1886 onward, blossomed under Albert Ballin. Its main competitor at home was Norddeutscher Lloyd (NGL) of Bremen, which by 1900 was ordering new steamships and "raising its ocean fleet to ninety-three vessels, the largest number under the control of any one company in the world."[50] Cunard was arguably the most important British shipper. The company was part of an elaborate network of commercial firms and banks that in 1911 employed over 130,000 people in London alone. On the other side of the Atlantic, the International Mercantile Marine Company (IMMC), founded in the United States in 1901 with strong financial backing by J.P. Morgan, eventually combined with smaller companies such as the White Star and Red Star Lines as well as Atlantic Transport.

Given this array of the great shipping companies, it is not surprising that attempts were made to cooperate and divide up the market. Apparently with the aim of strengthening IMMC, Morgan approached the two German companies to constitute a "community of interests."[51] The idea was to regulate the number of journeys, with Mondays and the winter being periods of low passenger demand. There was also the question of which European ports were to be serviced, again in order to reduce competition. While Ballin was interested in an agreement without harm to the Morgan group, it was no secret that the German-American combination was really aimed at Cunard and British shipping. HAPAG, NGL, and IMMC eventually formed a cartel. But Cunard quickly proved to be a "very dangerous and energetic competitor" that unleashed a "war" in regard to passenger rates. When the first Annual Report of IMMC came out in 1904, the advantages of the combination were not at all clear and the question was how long it would continue to hang together. It finally failed by 1905, but the two German companies remained optimistic about their own prospects and now cooperated among themselves. By 1914, Ballin's empire employed some 25,500 people in all parts of the world and paid high dividends to its shareholders.[52]

However, from 1908 onward there was the threat of the skyrocketing building costs of those luxury liners, also because the Anglo-German naval arms race kept escalating with the construction of bigger and bigger battleships. There was growing nervousness about a major war, and Ballin could be found among those businessmen on both sides of the Atlantic who became increasingly cautious about making huge investments, the more so—as will be seen later in this chapter—since credit became also more expensive and tight, especially in Germany.[53]

Although many liners that sailed from New York to Europe stopped at Southampton in Britain, the hope of the German companies was that their American passengers would go on to Bremerhaven and then spend time in Germany. Consequently, it was not just American businessmen whom they tried to woo but also wealthy tourists who wanted to see Berlin, the Rhine Valley, or southern Germany. With the world economy experiencing repeated recessions, there were times of worry that the tourists would stay away. But when they came, hotels did their best to meet their every wish and expectation and there was much transnational learning and adaptation in this industry.[54] Interior design was changed to satisfy American tastes, including those of well-educated, wealthy, and young American ladies who arrived at the reception desk without a male chaperone and at first caused confusion and embarrassment until hotels got used to welcoming them as guests rather than suspecting them of being high-class prostitutes. Many of the more expensive international hotels upgraded their amenities to American standards, while retaining an atmosphere of "refined" European living.

Most American business travelers and tourists took home with them a favorable impression of London and Berlin during their visits. But in this age of quite intense patriotism and nationalism, they also left with certain images and stereotypes of the European host countries that they had previously encountered or read about in books, magazines, and newspapers back home. Although American businessmen also had other and perhaps more reliable sources of information about the countries they visited, members of the New York business community also got their news from the local press, and the *NYT* and the *WSJ* in particular, both of which reported regularly on German and British affairs. Furthermore they had many opportunities to swap impressions with their colleagues at luncheons, receptions, and dinners that were an indispensable part of their professional lives. Finally, the many family ties provided channels of information spanning the Atlantic.

4. Prince Heinrich's Mission and German-American Relations in the New Century

One of the widely reported occasions to mix with those who had contacts with Germany was the visit of Prince Heinrich of Prussia, the brother of Wilhelm II. His mission was to improve German-American relations, which had been disturbed by the tariff debates in the Reichstag with their strong expressions of anti-American feelings, especially on the part of the agrarian Conservatives. There were also the tensions over Venezuela and the suspicions that the plans and speeches of the kaiser had aroused about his ambitious *Weltpolitik*.[55] Finally, there were the publications by Stead and others that pleaded for a closer Anglo-American "union." The *NYT* repeatedly reported on the kaiser's "friendly talk" that was clearly related to his and his advisors' quest to demonstrate Germany's peaceful intentions.[56] The idea was to avoid international tensions while the covert naval building program was passing through the "danger zone" that—Tirpitz feared—might lead to an attempt by the Royal Navy to destroy the German fleet in a surprise attack before his building plan had been completed.[57]

Ragnhild Fiebig-von Hase has examined the peculiar relationship between Wilhelm II and Theodore Roosevelt as well as the visit by Prince Heinrich.[58] She does not diminish the significance of the kind of personal diplomacy that the kaiser initiated in the "belief that he could manipulate the [U.S.] President by personal favours and by honouring him with medals and gifts." But she also shows that Roosevelt remained suspicious of the monarch's motives and of his "jumpiness," as he called it. He considered him "unstable [and] crazy for notoriety—not to be trusted. Not a man to rely on at all—with a saving sense of the danger of war and a strong inclination to bully up to the verge of war." Although he also knew how to flatter Wilhelm II, he had no sympathy with "certain Americans who seem to be wholly unable to withstand contact with royalty" and who "have been profoundly affected by meeting the German Emperor and having him courteous to them." When the two men met in Berlin in May 1910 after Roosevelt had left office, he was disappointed.[59] But with regard to his view of Wilhelm II as a man who would shrink from unleashing a war, he was misled just as other visitors were. In 1914, Wilhelm II was one of the key persons to push Europe and the world over the brink.

It is against this background of the kaiser's hypocrisy that the visit of his brother Prince Heinrich to the United States has to be seen. The trip created some anxiety in the German Foreign Office, which feared that Heinrich would be as prone to diplomatic gaffes as Wilhelm II. Reich Chancellor Bülow therefore advised Heinrich to "keep your eyes open and your mouth shut."[60] It is doubtful that the visit was a great success in Roosevelt's eyes. But in New York, he was wined and dined by the German business community and those who had business interests in Germany. The *NYT* gave a good deal of space to these encounters, also in Boston, and published the dinner menus and guest lists among which many very prominent names could be found. At Harvard, the prince was given an honorary law doctorate. But there was some embarrassment not about the smaller gifts that he carried with him, but about where to put up a big one in the shape of a statue of Frederick II (the Great) of Prussia. Wilhelm II, overjoyed by the friendly reception of Heinrich, sent it to Washington a few months later, oblivious that Americans were proud republicans. After lengthy negotiations the monarch finally found a home in November 1904 in a rather inconspicuous place: the grounds of the Army War College at the Washington Barracks Reservation.

The prince's visit was hardly over when rumors started in the American press about the anti-American and anti-British naval aims that Alfred Mahan, the influential American strategic thinker, and others were by then also writing about. What they did not fully appreciate when speculating about German aims was that the discussions of a European combination were not confined to court circles in Berlin.[61] They also appeared in the German press, and on 17 August 1902, the *NYT* published a report on the views of an influential economist, Professor August

Sartorius von Waltershausen, headlined by the paper "Proposed Alliance to Fight American Trade."[62] In it the author called for a customs union between Germany and Austria-Hungary and economic cooperation in Europe. The article also quoted remarks by the late king of Saxony to the effect that the "Americans will certainly make us trouble. Now we are suffering under their tariff and finally they will crush our industry."

We have already encountered not merely American self-confidence after the turn of the century, but also the anxieties that their assertiveness produced in Europe.[63] The point is that in this unsettled and unsettling situation, the kaiser came to play an ambivalent role.[64] On the one hand, he continued to be prone to make spontaneous undiplomatic remarks that raised suspicions abroad about his foreign policy objectives. The ways in which he intervened in the debates on the building of "his" battle fleet caused acute embarrassment in the Reich Navy Office and the Foreign Ministry. German diplomats in particular were often very unhappy about the unruly and tactless monarch and set up an elaborate system of preventing his utterances from becoming public. On the other hand and maybe precisely to counteract these negative images, Wilhelm's civilian advisors persuaded him to make remarks in which he posed as a man of peace and peaceful trade. Accordingly, the kaiser was also wheeled out on other occasions to calm foreign nerves about Germany being an unpredictable player in international affairs.[65] As will be seen below, another maneuver of this kind was started in the wake of the 1905 Moroccan Crisis and the tensions that it had generated.

But whatever anxieties arose around 1900 in Germany and Britain relating to American economic power, there were many counterforces that did not share the pessimistic views of Sartorius and others. They were keen to expand existing relationships and trade. One manifestation of this was moves in January 1903 to found an American Chamber of Commerce in Berlin.[66] It was also a recognition of the growing need for information on Germany that the *NYT* introduced a special column titled "German Money and Trade." Another new journal devoted to German-American affairs was the *Columbian*, on which the *NYT* reported the following:[67] "To establish a commercial embassy in Berlin for the purposes of championing American interests in Germany, Joseph Bruckner, managing editor of The Illinois Staats Zeitung [*sic*], today resigned and within a month will sail for the German capital. In connection with the commercial embassy he will publish, in both English and German languages, a weekly paper" with this title. The publication "will try to create a demand for American goods. Mr. Bruckner's scheme is indorsed by many leading businessmen in this country." In

Germany books and articles were also published at this time that cast commercial relations in a positive light.

For the next several years, economic relations and mutual business perceptions saw further improvement and a growing involvement of American companies in the German and British economies and rising shares in the global production of goods. By 1913 these shares, in terms of world production, had grown to 35.8 percent for the United States and to 15.7 percent for Germany, while the share of Britain had fallen back from 19.5 percent in 1900 to 14.0 percent in the year before World War I.[68] Although American interest in exports to Europe remained underdeveloped because of a still expanding home market, it was clear that Germany had become a major economic partner, with Britain losing its earlier pride of place.

5. American Big Business in Britain and Germany at Mid-Decade

A long letter to Frank Vanderlip on 1 October 1903 offers good insight into how the American-German-British business relationship was being assessed by a friend and colleague after a trip to Europe where he had spent close to nine months and visited all major iron- and steel-makers in Germany, Britain, Switzerland, and Belgium as well as a few in France, Italy, and Sweden. Godfrey Carden began by reporting that in the previous year order books of the "machinery houses" had been so full that going to the World's Fair in St. Louis had little attraction for them.[69] But now the same companies "are keenly interested in exhibition space in the hope of increased trade."

In Britain he had encountered some talk about the need for protection, with only a few companies not favoring it, such as the Swan Hunter shipyards, with Cunard as its customer, and Fowlers Ltd., a manufacturer of agricultural equipment and tractor engines. He concluded, "The United Kingdom is demanding protection against American goods and German goods, but more particularly against American goods." Carden also noted that "England today is woefully deficient in technical schools" and had "nothing to compare with the great Charlottenburg Polytechnic Institute" in Berlin as well as those in Hanover, Chemnitz, and Switzerland's Zürich, "which is practically a German school." As far as the British market was concerned, "we are technically abreast of the Germans in many lines, but not in all." If there was a lack of orders, it was because of American "ignorance." There was also "chauvinism and an absolute disregard for the advice of those in a position to know." The traveler then listed a number of other shortcomings, such as displays of the American flag. There was, he felt, simply a "lack of appreciation of the susceptibilities of the people." Results could only be expected if "we . . . know something about the people with whom we are dealing." Thus, Westinghouse should be known as " 'British Westinghouse.' " As long as American business remained insensitive, "England needs no protective tariff against us; her prejudice alone will suffice."

Turning to his experiences in Germany, he had visited over 350 machine tool factories, mainly in the Rhineland. There he had found the most modern workshop sanitary appliances he had seen anywhere in the world. He added that there may be a number of American companies that are equal, "but, as a whole, the Germans have paid more attention to a permanent layout of their plants than we have, and it is in keeping with their traditional national character."

He continued that ten years ago German factories would have had mostly British tools. Now they were all German, with a few exceptions in older workshops. Carden also saw a small number of American machine tools as "a silent tribute to the excellence of our output." If American tools had been acquired, he continued, it was due to two Germans, one of whom had been at the Chicago World's Fair in 1893 and both of whom then took up representing American firms. They now had branches in Berlin, Stockholm, and other places and had done well. But however proud Carden may have been of American machinery and tools, "after inspecting the German plants" he had "returned in a much meeker spirit." More significantly, this sense did not just apply to this industry: "There is very little in which we excel the Germans. They are our great competitors and in reaching out for the world's trade, it is the German[s] we must expect to encounter at every step."

Discussing electrical engineering, "the Germans are pretty nearly equals," while Swiss firms such as Oerlikon and Brown Boveri & Cie "are just a little in advance of us." When it came to "chemistry and kindred products," though, "the Germans lead the world." Apparently, he felt that this was to some extent due to work habits. "In Germany the directors are generally at their office at half past eight, and they too are away for about two hours, say from 1 to 3 [p.m.] Their rule is to continue at their desks until 7 or 7.30," with dinner at 8 p.m. Workers normally started at 6.30 a.m., with a thirty-minute break at 11, one hour at 1 p.m., and thirty minutes at 4 p.m. At Krupp strikes were unknown and employees received 5 percent on their deposits. Some 20 percent of the workforce had been with the company "for more than fifteen years. Think of it!" By contrast, the British had been talking freely about their labor problems, of which they had plenty.

Finally, in Berlin he had met the managing director "of the great agricultural firm [of] Eckert that . . . was more than able to hold its own against American agricultural implements owing to the fact that they did not hesitate to take orders and made machines according to local ideas and notions, instead of offering standard implements which latter was the practice of American representatives." Carden's letter concluded with observations on German politics and the position of "unreconciled" minorities such as the Poles.

Comparing this document both to the activities of American firms in Britain and Germany and to the fears that American industrial prowess generated in both countries, Carden's report confirms what has been said earlier on about the ambivalent feelings that all three business communities harbored about each other. Whereas the British tended to be admired for their past achievements, the Germans looked more interesting as potential partners as well as competitors and were given considerable credit for what they were doing.

The attractions that this created were also reflected in the interest that Americans and Germans took in their respective systems of education and industrial and commercial training. Especially after the Paris World Exposition of 1900, a growing number of British and German businessmen had been traveling to the industrial centers of the United States in Pennsylvania, Ohio, Illinois, and Michigan to inspect installations and technologies as well as factory organization.[70] They learned about Scientific Management, and some of them even succeeded in getting an interview with Frederick Taylor, the apostle of rationalized production. Conversely, American businessmen and academics went to Germany to study its systems of education. It is well known how German ideas about graduate education in universities and *Technische Hochschulen* were transferred to Johns Hopkins University and other institutions of higher learning.[71] But there was also the secondary and postsecondary training sector. Vanderlip had gathered information about *Fachschulen* and *Fachhochschulen* during his visit in 1901. In 1902 and 1903 the *NYT* published several articles on German education and training of skilled workers and commercial clerks.

6. The Threat of Deteriorating Political Relations

However, while politics had interfered only intermittently with the building of more stable and amicable relations, the years 1904 and 1905 witnessed the first in a sequence of diplomatic developments that, ever so slowly, began to undermine the efforts of the American business community to establish peaceful trade relations with their two major European partners.[72] Increasingly suspicious of the relentless buildup of the German navy with its focus on battleships, which were evidently to be deployed against the Royal Navy in a climate of growing Anglophobia among nationalist groups in Germany, London began to abandon its traditional policy of disengagement from politics on the European Continent and to sign the Entente Cordiale with France in 1904. While this was by no means a strong alliance, it nevertheless had a disquieting effect on German foreign policy makers. After all, France had concluded a formal alliance with Russia in 1894. As the Entente Cordiale became more cordial due to Germany's assertive *Weltpolitik*, the Prusso-German general staff began to worry that the country might find itself in a war on two fronts, with Austria-Hungary, a multiethnic empire, as its only reliable ally that was itself in a precarious state, as it struggled with a growing Slavic nationalism on the Balkans.

These German concerns about the country's changing political position in Europe became a key consideration in Berlin's response to the Entente Cordiale. Wilhelm II decided to challenge Paris over its possessions and claims in northwestern Africa to include Morocco in its sphere of influence.[73] And so, he went on a cruise to the south, in the course of which he briefly landed in Tangiers, announcing grandly that Germany was prepared to protect Moroccan independence. When Paris protested against the visit, Berlin called for an international conference. The Germans expected that France would find itself isolated at this conference and be forced into a humiliating retreat. Indirectly, the German demand for a conference was also set up to test the cohesion of the Entente Cordiale and, if possible, to drive a wedge between Britain and France. As it turned out London backed Paris, and the conference that finally took place at Algeciras in January 1906 virtually turned the tables on Germany. In the end, only Austria-Hungary supported Berlin's objectives, with Italy and Russia joining the Franco-British camp. Washington also became involved in the negotiations.[74] While Roosevelt did his best to pose as the disinterested mediator, it was clear that he had little sympathy for what everyone perceived to be Germany's aggressive purposes and discreetly sided with the French. When it was all over, he, being an accomplished politician, congratulated the Germans on their masterful diplomacy, reaffirmed his feelings of friendship, and advocated closer links between the two countries.

The fallout from the First Moroccan Crisis was considerable. It created further unease about the aims of Germany also in the United States. From the outside, the country now appeared not only as a bustling industrial power at the heart of Europe, but also as an increasingly unpredictable one. Worse, it was led by a seemingly erratic monarch who, under the constitution, was in charge of German foreign policy making and had the constitutional right, without having to ask the national assembly or any other institution, whether the country should go to war or stay at peace. The fears that this generated were now added to British suspicions of the kaiser's naval plans. This, in turn, produced an arms race when the Royal Navy built the *Dreadnought*, a much more powerful battleship that made most of the older fleet obsolete.[75] No less important, by joining the race in dreadnoughts, Tirpitz, the kaiser's naval minister, turned what was hitherto a more covert buildup into an open competition that the Royal Navy was determined to win.

It was not that Germany could not have kept up with the annual building tempo that London adopted in 1907–8 for lack of shipbuilding technology and capacity. Rather it became increasingly difficult for the Imperial government to raise the funds for this much more expensive navy than what Tirpitz had originally budgeted to reassure the members of the Federal Council, the representation of the various states of Germany, the deputies in the Reichstag, and the tax-paying public.[76] In the late 1890s, the Reich Navy Office had made supposedly careful financial calculations that would enable the kaiser to expand the navy from the steadily growing tax revenues that the treasury had been expecting to collect from a manifestly very prosperous country. But this calculation had merely been based on the construction of an additional *number* of battleships. It had not included any figures for much bigger and hence costlier dreadnoughts. This question was now raised for the government and the politicians who would have to vote to pay for these unexpected cost overruns and in turn unleashed huge conflicts between different social classes and political parties over who was to shoulder the additional tax burdens.

The problem found a relatively simple solution in Britain, where the Liberals had been returned to power in the 1906 elections with the promise that they would keep the country powerful internationally and at the same time introduce welfare benefits and social insurance for the average Briton. Lord Haldane, a member of the Liberal Cabinet in London, put this as follows on 8 August 1908:[77] "We should boldly take our stand on the facts and proclaim a policy of taking, mainly by direct taxation, such a toll from the increase and growth of this wealth as will enable us to provide for the increasing cost of social reform, national defense, and a margin in aid of the sinking fund." He added, "The more boldly such a proposition is put, the more attractive, I think, it will prove. It will commend itself to many timid people as a bulwark against the nationalization of wealth." Germany's conservatives adopted exactly the opposite strategy by increasing indirect taxes and blocking attempts to raise higher direct taxes.

Unlike in Britain where, thanks also to the electoral system, the government always had a clear majority to get its legislation passed, the

German political system was too fragmented and complex to facilitate
a tax policy as proposed by Haldane. With the monarch at the top, the
executive looked very centralized, and it most certainly was, according
to the Reich Constitution, in matters of war and peace. But in domestic
politics, and taxation in particular, no legislation could reach the statute book, unless it had the approval of both the Federal Council and
the Reichstag.[78] Especially the "ailing" agrarian Conservatives resisted
higher taxes on wealth, inheritance, and property. This increased social
and political tensions at home when the burdens were being shifted to
higher indirect taxes on consumption and hence onto the shoulders of
the majority of the working population. In fact, for reasons to be examined toward the end of this chapter, this led by 1913–14 to a financial
crisis. This crisis in turn made the political and military decision makers around the monarch all the more prone to cut the Gordian double
knot of Germany's international isolation and the impasse in domestic
politics by launching a war before it was, in the eyes of the key political
and military decision makers, "too late," with enormous repercussions
for Europe and the rest of the world.

Albert Ballin, the Hamburgian shipping magnate, had access to the
kaiser. He was, like his American and British counterparts, also a man
who had a vital and personal business interest in peaceful trade, good
relations with the two Anglo-Saxon powers, and the avoidance of a
major war. When hearing about the stepped-up naval arms race and
its diplomatic and fiscal implications, he warned Bülow in July 1908
against continuing on the path of challenging British naval power. As
he put it simply, but very farsightedly,[79] "We just cannot afford a race in
dreadnoughts against the much wealthier British."

I have spent some time discussing the political-diplomatic and
military-strategic developments of the years 1904–8, not only to draw
attention to the close and ever-present link between economy and politics as a factor that must always be borne in mind when analyzing international business communities. It was also to explain why—as in
1901–2—the kaiser was again moved into the limelight to profess Germany's entirely peaceful intentions. He did this first by receiving a
number of prominent businessmen.[80] Thus, he talked to Thomas Edison, who on his return to New York stated that he thought Wilhelm II
was a promoter of peace and had a good sense of the importance of
business. To be sure, Edison's optimism was rooted, as he explained,
in the conviction that wars between great powers were relics of the
past—a pious hope that (as will be seen in a moment) was more widely
held in American business circles.

Second, Wilhelm II gave a number of interviews—always a risky
business for him, if we recall his conversation with Pierre de Ségur in

1901.[81] While the audiences that he granted seem to have had some effect on American perceptions of Germany, his newspaper interviews tended to undermine them when they were published. Still, overall it was in effect the broader drift of international politics in the years before 1914 that had a negative impact not only on British foreign policy making, but also on German-American relations, as a consequence of which Washington moved closer to the British side. It was in these years that American businessmen also became more aware of the structural differences between their own economic and political system and the German one.

7. Comparing the Peculiarities of the American and German Industrial Systems

One of these differences related to what might best be called the economic-constitutional order with respect to the organization and institutional arrangements of industry and finance within the capitalist marketplace. As to the American side, the introduction in 1890 of the Sherman ("Antitrust") Act became a crucial turning point.[82] It banned and even criminalized the creation of monopoly positions by one enterprise as well as cartels (anticompetitive horizontal agreements between independent firms on prices, production quotas, etc.) and syndicates (anticompetitive agreements to combine sales in a single organization). Obliging American business to compete, Sherman did not prevent a further concentration of American industry and the emergence of powerful trusts. But it also pushed business in the direction of *oligopolistic* competition that left enough space and niches for smaller enterprises as well.

The origins of this piece of congressional legislation reveal much about the American political economy and the dynamic relationship between big business and Washington in the late nineteenth century. By the 1880s, economic power in America was becoming increasingly concentrated and some entrepreneurs were accumulating huge fortunes. No less important, some of them were found to be colluding by forming "pools," that is, "horizontal combinations of competitors joining forces to create large, regionally dominant systems that, today, would be called cartels."[83] Among sections of the population (and hence among voters) there arose a growing suspicion that entrepreneurial power was being abused to the detriment of the "sovereign people," just as Americans had continued to be wary of concentrations of *political* power after the removal of the autocratic King George II during the war of independence. Significantly, by the 1880s an "Anti-Monopoly Party" had constituted itself and competed in the 1884 presidential elections. In 1888, U.S. president Grover Cleveland felt obliged in his Message to Congress to warn that pools and monopolies were becoming the "master[s]" of the people. The Republican and Democratic Parties quickly joined the bandwagon of populist pressure from below.

By the late 1880s, the Republican Party platform proclaimed its opposition to "monopolies" and tried to win over voters by promising legislation to "prevent the execution of all schemes to oppress the people."[84] Not to be left behind in this popularity contest, the Democrats began to assert that "the interests of the people" were being "betrayed" by economic and commercial conglomerates "which, while enriching the few that combine, rob the body of our citizens." By 1890 and with the courts taking up similarly hostile positions, a stream of petitions, submitted to Congress, finally moved Senator John Sherman of Ohio to draft a bill that became the famous Sherman Antitrust Act. After some thirteen federal states had already introduced antitrust regulations before 1890, the House of Representatives approved the bill by a vote of 242 to none, with 85 abstentions.[85] The Senate concurred, with only one nay vote. The significance of this ban on cartels and monopolies for the subsequent development of American capitalism can hardly be overestimated, also in comparison to developments in Europe, and especially in Germany and Britain.

The Sherman Act was "unfriendly" to virtually all types of monopoly. Since in an era of rising living standards voters were also consumers, the aim was to protect them "from unreasonable price increases." It was the beginning of the shift from a *mass production* capitalism to a *mass consumption* capitalism that first emerged in the United States, while taking much longer to strike roots in Germany and also in Britain. The rise of this particular capitalism and its market organization represent an American-European story that also forms an important thread running through this book from the pre-1914 period through two world wars all the way to the 1950s.[86]

While the Sherman Act slowly established itself in the United States, the economic constitution and market organization of German industry developed in the opposite direction toward the formation of cartels and syndicates. The origins of this tradition go back to the so-called Great Depression that, though perceived as such by the business community, economic historians today regard as a period of retarded growth.[87] Still, the experience of harder times in Germany led to a rise in protectionism. Responding to pressure of agricultural and industrial lobbies, Reich Chancellor Otto von Bismarck in 1879 surrounded the domestic market with higher tariff walls that he successively raised in the 1880s, shielding both industry and agriculture from the harsh winds of foreign competition. Meanwhile, in a further move toward protectionism, individual firms began to conclude horizontal agreements among themselves to fix prices and coordinate output. Next to these cartels, they also founded joint sales syndicates.

Initially cartels were deemed to be "children of an emergency situation."[88] It was assumed that they would disappear once the depression was over and the mechanisms of the market and of market competition again provided the basic elements of business activity and forward planning. Yet, even though the world economy experienced another upswing from 1895 onward, Germany's cartels persisted and even multiplied. Some branches were particularly successful at coordinating their production and marketing. The drawback of the system was that cartels had to adapt their prices to the least efficient members, and these, protected by the agreement, had no strong incentive to modernize and increase their productivity with the aim of enabling the entire cartel to lower its prices. In the final analysis, the producer orientation of this system worked to the advantage of the manufacturer and to the detriment of the consumer, who did not experience the benefits of price competition and the prospect of lower prices in the open marketplace. The trend was toward the abolition of economic competition, just as political competition was hampered by the monarchical constitution and the restrictive voting systems practiced by the federal states. Thus, Prussia had a three-class voting system that its agrarian conservatives defended tooth and nail because it guaranteed—very unfairly—that a third of the seats in the Diet went to a small upper-class minority.[89]

While there was repeated pressure to introduce anti-cartel legislation, neither the Reich government nor the major political parties were interested in ratifying a law similar to the Sherman Act. In the end, the judiciary took up the problem of economic competition. In contrast to the United States, where the courts upheld and the Justice Department enforced the Sherman Act, the Reich Court rendered an opinion that declared cartel agreements to be permissible and binding under private law.[90] In other words, it sanctioned discriminatory cartel practices against nonmembers. The threat of litigation also facilitated bringing nonconformist members to heel. Hans Pohl and other scholars have rightly argued that the opinion that the Reich Court handed down confirmed the restrictive practices of the previous decades and moved German industry toward a market organization that differed markedly from that of the United States.[91]

Examining the evolution of the organization of German industry before 1914, Volker Hentschel concluded that cartels solidified into an "ideology."[92] The system became deeply ingrained in the behavior of many German businessmen. Their attitudes were buttressed by a majority of the country's economists and jurists who also thought that a protectionist producer capitalism was preferable to one that promoted price competition for the benefit of the consumer. Businessmen who believed that in matters of competition Germany should move in the same direction as America remained in a minority. The struggle between the two camps in Germany continued in the 1920s and was won by the "cartelists" in the 1930s, until the Americans came along after 1945 and pushed—as will be seen in chapter VI—West German industry into Sherman-style oligopolistic competition and a consumer-oriented competitive market economy.

These differences in the organization of German and American industry had become sufficiently marked by 1910, if not before, to catch the eye of the American business community.[93] Partly because the Justice Department took the enforcement of the Sherman Act seriously, leading, for example, to a lawsuit against the giant Standard Oil Company, the proliferation of German cartels became a topic of interest in the United States. After all, cartels were also directed against foreign competitors, who could be excluded from a German cartel with its superior pricing and marketing power.

In this connection it is instructive what the Vanderlip Papers contain on the subject of American antitrust. In a correspondence with Dr. Ferdinand Baumgarten in the summer of 1904, the banker pointed to a shift in the use of the term "trust," arguing that "in its original form it hardly exists in America any longer."[94] The term was now being used "rather loosely . . . to include any great industrial organization, but perhaps more particularly such an organization as is built up of [the] corporate merger of a number of smaller corporations." Of course, such mergers were now bound by the Sherman Act that had banned cartels and also mergers that resulted in a monopoly position by one firm. Where the principles of (oligopolistic) competition were being preserved, Vanderlip expressed the belief "that the trust system is to be considered progressive from a political point of view, and that it works out toward better economic results." He added that "on the whole I am inclined to think that the trust movement lowers prices." Since "the shrewdest managers of trusts in America believe that the only sound principle upon which these great organizations can stand is the demonstrative ability" to sell more cheaply.

However, in the following year, if not before, there arose, as in the 1880s, a "clamor against combinations and . . . the danger that there may be most ill advised legislation in some of the states."[95] There appeared, Vanderlip continued, "to be an energetic attitude in Chicago to prosecute the beef people under the Sherman Act." But soon it was not the big slaughterhouses and meatpacking corporations of Chicago that attracted the attention of the politicians and lawyers. This time it was the question of Standard Oil's monopoly position. By 1910, the pressure to move against this corporation had become so strong that U.S. president Taft (during a conversation that he had with Vanderlip) expressed his determination to enforce antitrust laws. He added that it depended on the size of a company, and if it became too big, it could "be stopped under the Sherman Act Anti-Trust Law and ought to be stopped for the welfare of the country."[96] Taft was "perfectly confident that the Supreme Court decisions in the tobacco and Standard Oil cases will be substantially in favor of the Government." Subsequently, the two cases were winding their way through the courts and therefore not only unleashed a debate about a breakup of Standard Oil, but also drew attention to European developments and the German cartel system in particular.

Articles on the subject appeared in the New York press. On 16 August 1912, the *NYT* carried an item on "German and American Ways with Trusts" that began with the following words:[97] "We published yesterday, in our London cable dispatches, the report of the British Consul General in Düsseldorf stating in general terms that Germany regards its trusts [i.e., cartels] as aids to prosperity and not as enemies of the people." In the view of German entrepreneurs the making of high profits was being favored because it aided capital formation, whereas "here [in the United States] the idea is that profits are theft, the capitalists are wealthy malefactors who ought to expiate their crimes in jail, and that profits ought to be forbidden or, better yet, divided." However blunt these words were, the article as a whole discussed the still unsettled state of American antitrust and highlighted some of the advantages that the German system provided to producers. At the same time, it stressed that the process had not yet reached its final stage: "Our counsels on this subject are still too hectic. The electorate still tends to listen too much to appeals to Passion and prejudice, and refuse to listen to the facts." Certainly "the abuses of the trust system have been reduced in a manner little appreciated and assisted not at all by the loudest shouters into the ear of the people." A few weeks later, on 15 September 1912, "economic expert" Dr. Samuel P. Orth explained in the same paper "How They Handle the Trust Problem in Germany."[98] Having examined, inter alia, the German "Steel Syndicate," the author felt in the end that he had "said enough to show that the attitude of the [Reich] government is one of solicitude for the investor. Its point of view is that of industry, not of consumption."

With awareness of very different approaches to competition and implicitly also to international economic and political affairs between the

United States and Germany growing, earlier affinities that the American business community had felt with their German counterparts began to weaken. Conversely, attitudes toward Britain became friendlier, also because the country did not take the distinctly German path into proliferating cartelization. This was partly due to the antiprotectionist Free Trade policies that, as has been mentioned, the country upheld even as its industrial prowess declined. The Liberals, who had come to power in 1906, were firmly wedded to Free Trade. The protectionism of Joseph Chamberlain and the Conservatives was soundly defeated. Faced with growing American and German competition, there was a tendency in some industries to resort to self-protection by forming domestic cartels. It was a tradition that continued through the interwar period, and it was only after 1945 that Britain, like Germany, moved toward a market organization similar to that of the United States. But cartelization in Britain was never as thoroughgoing as in Germany, where the system became ubiquitous in the 1930s, though British protectionism against foreign companies increased throughout the Empire and Commonwealth as a structure that granted preferential tariffs to those inside the club.

8. American Big Business and the Question of Political Participation

The rapprochement between the United States and Britain also occurred in matters of constitutional politics, while the rifts in German-American and Anglo-German relations owing to their divergent political orders widened. At the most basic level there was the difference between a Republic with a (by no means flawless) democratic system, on the one side, and a Hohenzollern *semi-autocratic* monarchy, on the other, with Britain's *constitutional* monarchy somewhere in between. As in the case of the origins of the Sherman Act, it is worthwhile to look at the roots of this American democratic republicanism and compare it to what historians have more generally defined as "Prusso-German constitutionalism."

The United States was among the first countries to allow mass participation in politics through the ballot box. During the early period of the American polity, following its successful war of secession from England, ownership of property was the key qualification for obtaining the vote that was furthermore restricted to white men. But as Chilton Williamson has put it, between the late 1780s and the first half of the nineteenth century a gradual shift took place from "property to democracy" so that by the 1860s most federal states had "universal white manhood suffrage or its rough equivalent."[99] The age of property taxes and deference to the status quo was coming to an end. Popular politics had come to stay. As Sean Wilentz added, recent historiography has described this political development "in terms of a market revolution."[100]

Indeed, as Alexis de Tocqueville had observed long ago, the first modification of voting qualifications was bound to have something like a snowball effect: each extension increased the strength of democratic participation and with it came further demands to be even more inclusive. Moreover, it became very difficult to abolish the right to vote once it had been introduced. In this sense, it was only logical that with the end of slavery the passage of the Fourteenth and Fifteenth Amendments gave the right to vote, at least in theory, to all adult black males. The concomitant emergence of political parties promoted the development of a representative system based on competition in the *political* marketplace. Because parties fought to win elections, they worked hard to mobilize the white population by campaigning for the reduction or elimination of existing property requirements. By the 1830s, all this had led to a situation in which (white) Americans had become "very enthusiastic about voting." Turnout was on average around 75 percent.[101] After the Civil War and up to the turn of the century it rose to 82 percent and more in the North. To be sure, the gains that African Americans had made in the 1870s were gradually lost when racist restrictions were introduced against black men, especially in the South, and intimidation and electoral fraud were rampant. So, no attempt is being made here to minimize the glaring injustices of segregation. Still, the basic principle of suffrage had established itself, even if it took well into the twentieth century for a universal system covering all adults, male and female, to become something of a reality. It is against this background that the struggle over the Sherman Act and over the securing of competition in the *economic* marketplace, that has been discussed above, must be seen.

Meanwhile the German constitution underwent a significantly different development that became an issue of considerable concern also to the American and British business communities in the years before 1914. Although various of Germany's federal states retained electoral systems in which the right to vote was restricted and based on property or income qualifications, Bismarck, then the minister president of Prussia and from 1871 chancellor of the newly founded Reich, introduced the universal manhood suffrage in one fell swoop, first in the North German Confederation of 1867 and then in the Reich as a whole in 1871.[102] This occurred in the context of the formation of political parties that, at election time and soon all year round, would compete for the favor of male voters from different strata of society.

Theodore Hamerow, in a still very important article, has examined the calculations that led the founder of the German Empire to grant what was perceived at the time as a revolutionary concession to the "masses."[103] In Bismarck's eyes, the middle-class Liberals were his main opponents who, in the Prussian Constitutional Conflict of 1862–66, had been rooting for representative government and a shift in the power structure away from the monarch toward the Diet. By introducing the universal manhood suffrage in a society that was then still predominantly agrarian, Bismarck hoped to mobilize the mass of peasant voters as a conservative monarchist counterweight to those liberal middle-class politicians who appreciated that the agrarian sector was unlikely to support them in their quest for participation in politics. With a few exceptions, this commercial and professional bourgeoisie was therefore not interested in a *universal* suffrage; in their majority they wanted to parliamentarize the Prusso(-German) political system and retain a restrictive suffrage that weakened the powers of the monarch and that of the "masses." In the vision of the Liberals, the autocratic Prussian monarchy was to be transformed into a constitutional one with a restrictive voting system that favored the middle classes.[104] To many of them, the British constitutional monarchy was the model where Parliament was the power center.[105]

The Liberals failed in this quest in 1870–71. Bismarck succeeded in ending the political crisis of the previous years and in blocking a power shift from the crown to the Diet and later to the Reichstag. This outcome had far-reaching consequences for the subsequent constitutional development of the country. The containment of the Liberals in the 1860s enabled the chancellor in 1871, in the wake of his military victory over France, to shape a Reich Constitution that preserved the powers of the kaiser and the federal princes. The monarch was not subject to the will of the people. He continued to appoint and dismiss "His" chancellor and "state secretaries," as the heads of ministerial departments were called. The emperor was also the supreme commander of the armed forces and in charge of the nation's defense and foreign policy.[106]

As Germany underwent a rapid demographic and economic change in the following decades, the question of a stronger political participation in the country's power structure was bound to come up. After the turn of the century, if not before, parliamentarization became a key issue of political transformation and pressure for reform. But Imperial Germany did not find itself on a trajectory of parliamentary-constitutional government. The only major party that now demanded it persistently was the reformist wing of the Social Democrats. Meanwhile the other parties either were increasingly reluctant to pursue parliamentarization or had become too weak to be able to marshal a larger supporting bloc of votes in the Reichstag for it. With international and domestic conflicts escalating before 1914, the majority in the national parliament became more interested in stabilizing the existing constitutional order than in parliamentarizing it and thereby opening it up to the participation of the Social Democrats, who were gaining more and more votes under the Reich's system of universal manhood suffrage, but continued to be excluded from decision making. As we have seen, Germany was suffering major foreign policy setbacks from 1904 onward and an arms race for which Wilhelm II and his advisors, holding vast constitutional powers in the military and foreign policy-making field, were ultimately responsible. Domestic politics also began to deteriorate, as the monarchy and the agrarian Conservatives time and again impeded reform and a more equitable distribution of tax burdens.

Instead, the country saw the formation of increasingly solid blocs of right-wing and center-right party coalitions. Germany became a nation of *political* cartels (comparable to the *economic* cartels that have been discussed above), that is, horizontal alliances concluded to curb the competition of the Social Democrats at the polls.[107] By 1912, the latter party had become the largest in the Reichstag, whose demands for fundamental constitutional and social reforms deeply worried both its competitors and an increasingly reactionary government. A rallying (*Sammlung*) of the antisocialist forces became the watchword, even if it proved difficult to forge durable alliances between them. As the country approached 1914, German domestic politics faced increasing gridlock. The added influence of right-wing nationalist extraparliamentary associations, such as the Navy League, the Army League, and the Pan-Germans, exacerbated a growing dogmatism at a time of general tensions both at home and abroad. By 1914, the political system was faced with an urgent need of constitutional reform, but such a reform would by then have been tantamount to a constitutional revolution, and neither the crown nor the nonsocialist parties were prepared to contemplate it. Instead they stubbornly asserted that all was well politically, even though it clearly no longer was.

The progressive political polarization inside Germany was promoted by an ever more radical nationalism and attempts to divert internal tensions to the outside through an assertive foreign policy, also as a means of rallying the right-wing parties against the "unpatriotic" Social Democrats. It is this aggressiveness that was increasingly registered by Germany's neighbors as "militarism," defined as both the growing dominance of the military considerations in the shaping of foreign policy and as a gradual percolation of military values and attitudes of hierarchy and obedience into a society led by an autocratic monarch. In July 1911 *WSJ* still differentiated between American perceptions of a German political system that was "militarist-feudalist," on the one hand, and a German society that was one "of education, enlightenment or progress."[108] This kind of criticism, to be sure, could also be heard on the Social Democrat Left where it gave rise to fears of a great cataclysm to come. August Bebel, the leader of the SPD, came to be haunted by this scenario when he wrote in 1910:[109] "To reform Prussia is impossible; it will remain the State of the [agrarian] *Junker* it is at present, or go to pieces altogether. . . . I am convinced we are on the eve of the most dreadful war Europe has ever seen. Things cannot go on as at present; the burden of military expenditure is crushing people and the Kaiser and his government are fully alive to the fact. Everything works for a great crisis in Germany."

As political-constitutional questions moved more into the foreground of Anglo-American-German relations from the mid-decade onward, the affinities with Britain's parliamentary monarchy also grew stronger. True, Westminster was not a republic and the Cabinet was constituted by the majority party in Parliament rather than by a president who had been elected by a popular vote. While the British constitutional system therefore continued display monarchical and aristocratic elements, it lacked the unrepresentative centralization of political and military powers of the Prusso-German system of government. As American businessmen became more aware of these differences and their implications for the distribution of political power in London and Berlin, it is not surprising that they would veer toward the former during the last years before 1914, when politics and nationalist saber rattling increasingly disturbed peaceful commercial exchange.[110]

9. American and European Businessmen and the Specter of a Major War

It is against this larger international backdrop that a book by Norman Angell, a British businessman, must be seen. His analysis, *The Great Illusion. A Study of the Relation of Military Power in Nations to Their Economic and Social Advantage*, originally published under the title *Europe's Optical Illusion* in 1909, became a best seller a year later in the English-speaking world and was translated into other European languages.[111] It was a very wide-ranging analysis, but its basic point was simple, that is, that the statesmen and peoples of Europe would be living under an illusion if they thought that territorial conquest would pay off in the new century. Given the interdependence of industry, finance, and commerce, a nation, even if militarily victorious, would find its economic life after a major war no less badly damaged than its defeated opponent. In other words, according to Angell, militarism and territorial expansionism no longer offered any benefits.

This was not how Germany's nationalists and the military leadership saw the international picture. One piece of evidence of this, dating from 1911, is the unleashing of the Second Moroccan Crisis.[112] The renewed confrontation with France was deliberately prepared in the German Foreign Office as another attempt to weaken the Entente Cordiale that had meanwhile been expanded to the Triple Entente in 1907 among France, Britain, and Russia. This trilateral accord was perceived in Berlin as an encirclement of the two Central European monarchies and led the German Foreign Office to attempt to break the Franco-British link by reviving the earlier dispute over Morocco. The plan was to gain a diplomatic success against France that would have the added advantage of strengthening the monarchy and the right-wing parties in the upcoming national elections of 1912.

However, this strategy, once implemented, quickly turned into a humiliating double defeat. As in 1905, Britain threw its weight behind France, this time even more strongly when David Lloyd George made a fiery speech at London's Mansion House. After this Berlin decided to beat the retreat, but then found that the policy had also backfired at home. In the March 1912 national elections, the Social Democrats became the largest party in the Reichstag, making the cobbling together of antisocialist coalitions even more difficult. Pressured by the nationalist associations, the Reich government now responded by introducing an armaments bill in 1912 that expanded the army and tacitly admitted that Tirpitz's naval race against Britain had, for all practical purposes, been lost. The erstwhile arms race at sea now continued on land, with France and Russia reacting by enlarging their land forces in turn.[113]

The Germans promptly followed suit again by introducing another bill in 1913. While there were enough right-wing votes in the Reichstag to get both bills passed because they were propagandized as a defense of the fatherland, the question of how to pay for them led to a huge political wrangle among the parties. Reich Chancellor Theobald von Bethmann Hollweg realized that there would be an even greater rebellion at the polls if the military increases were paid for by once again by raising indirect taxes that would hit the working classes. Apart from a variety of higher duties and smaller tax levies, his budget proposal therefore also contained a one-off "defense contribution" that was in effect a direct tax on wealth.[114] The bill was fiercely resisted by the Right, also because, if approved, it could be used as a precedent for the levying of higher Reich income taxes in the future. Appreciating this potential, the SPD voted for this one-off direct tax, while the frantic agrarians and their allies inside and outside the government warned of this being the first step toward a "confiscatory tax" system as a prelude to an even more radical democratic revolution and the end of the status quo.

The American and British business communities watched all these developments with alarm.[115] They did not have to read Norman Angell's book to realize that this arms race escalating into a major war would be extremely disruptive to international trade and inflict severe losses on all participant nations. In light of the kaiser's aggressive Anglophobia and anti-American prejudice, distrust mounted. It had become very hard to believe that Wilhelm II was a man of peace. Those few Americans who had been hoodwinked earlier on by his charm and had praised his internationalism now regretted their gullibility.

It was no less nerve-racking to German commerce and banking. They were in constant touch with one another, and many even had family ties. They knew how to read the statistics of the Reich Finance Ministry, and it was no secret to them that the German Empire was suffering from financial overstretch. Short of money to fund their armaments programs and embryonic social security schemes as well as the capital needs of industry, commerce, and agriculture, both public and private sectors were in search of credit on the international markets.[116] As tensions mounted, they found that the French were less and less willing to support any of the capital needs of German industry and agriculture. When they approached the American banking community, it proved similarly reluctant to provide loans.[117] Money became even tighter on both sides of the Atlantic when the world economy seemed to be dipping into another recession in 1913–14. This meant that Germany increased its public as well as private debt loads further. The repayment of loans was put on the shoulders of the next generation, and fiscal policy became ever more irresponsible. In short, the paralysis of the political system was beginning to spill over into the economy.

Some of this is neatly reflected in Vanderlip's correspondence. For 1906–7 there are a number of letters that discuss collaborations and joint projects with the Europeans. As late as October 1911, he regretted that his bank had not participated in the placing of Prussian Treasury Notes on the American market and pleaded for closer cooperation:[118] "That we should not have relations in Berlin which would have kept us informed of the situation and enabled us to have done this business is to me a great disappointment. It is exactly the sort of thing that we ought to be doing." Indeed, "we could readily have taken the whole issue and replaced it in an hour."

But then, as he wrote in November, "independent information I have from Berlin . . . is . . . very pessimistic."[119] Yet, Vanderlip could not believe "that the obligation of the Prussian Government, maturing within the next nine months, is not perfectly good." On the contrary, he was "entirely confident that the market here will take 100,000,000 on a 4 per cent basis." Nevertheless, he now had "a feeling that the

European conditions are so complicated that we cannot count with confidence on continued low money after the first of the year." The American banker added that Melville Stone was "extremely pessimistic with regard to the German-English-French situation and holding the belief that the Russo-Japanese alliance with regard to Chinese affairs may also become a disturbing factor." All this made him "feel like running very strong indeed." It was no doubt reassuring that in February 1912, NCB had "about eight million of loans in London on call and an equal amount [was] just maturing in Berlin." Also, the bond accounts contained mostly "short-term stuff." Long-term commitments were no longer deemed to be safe.

By March 1912, Vanderlip hoped that there would be another upturn, if the political situation both at home and in Europe cleared up.[120] And yet, there were many "pitfalls in the way." Certainly, "all Europe would find its cash reserves pitifully inadequate in the event of the breaking of a storm." He thought that "few Americans have begun to grasp that awful significance to the whole world of a general European war." Even his own imagination would be "quite inadequate to picture what it would mean."

Some of Vanderlip's colleagues seem to have shared Angell's view that war between the great powers would be so ruinous that no rational person would want to start one. But gloom and pessimism was now also spreading in New York. As Vanderlip put it to Robert Benson in London,[121] "We are beginning to learn here how extremely close to the edge of the precipice you all came a few months ago." He was hoping that "something better" could be worked out, "although I must admit that I fail to see how the military and naval expenses can go on unlimitedly without a crash of some sort, military, political or financial, inevitably ensuing. Our own political problems are pigmies compared to those of Europe, though they are serious enough." The trouble was that "there are a thousand sticks of dynamite in the way . . . and while we may avoid explosions—and I begin to have some feeling that we will—it is idle to feel any great amount of security about the outlook."

Always on the lookout for positive signs, Vanderlip wrote in the middle of February 1912 (rather naively, considering the power structure of the *Kaiserreich*) that the "socialistic victories in Germany have undoubtedly given the war spirit there a back-set."[122] A month later, he received a very pessimistic assessment from Lord Revelstoke at the Baring Bank in Britain about what a war would mean for business.[123] His response was: "We are only beginning to understand what a happy state we used to be in when we knew nothing of foreign politics and when business concerned itself very little with domestic policy questions unless they happened to touch the money standard or the tariff.

We have certainly gotten out of that Arcadian situation so far as domestic politics are concerned, but the changes in European politics [still] have very little concern for the average [American] business man."

When Vanderlip learned a few days later that German banks were "again in the market for money at a high rate," that is, at about 6 percent "from the larger banks there for a 30-day mark loan," he took "some pains to learn what the German situation is."[124] He could get no better judgment than "that these high rates are the result of the Reichstag . . . insisting upon the commercial banks carrying large reserves." To him this looked more like a conservative policy on the part of the Reichstag than an alarming sign of an impending war. Nevertheless, he wanted to err on the side of caution and make no more than "very moderate loans to Germany" and otherwise not do "much in that direction."

By the summer 1912, Vanderlip was in touch with his colleague Jacob Schiff of Kuhn, Loeb & Co. in an effort "to get a fairly clear idea of the amount of foreign credits we have in the shape of loans or otherwise, especially to Germany."[125] Schiff had strong family and business ties with Germany. On the positive side, German banks, he continued, probably in light of what had learned from his colleague, "have liquidated large amounts of their holdings of industrial stocks," while "America's international position has been greatly improved as a result of the large amount of aid we gave to German banks last winter and spring." He had also heard "frequent comments of a favorable nature in London in this connection." At the same time, he felt some apprehension about the Viennese banks, "while in France financial circles have apparently not recovered yet from the shock they had a year ago in regard to the prospect of war" during the Moroccan Crisis. Consequently, "there was much hoarding at that time and apparently the funds locked up then have not entirely found their way back into active channels, for there is no disposition to go into new enterprises or absorb foreign securities."

This nervousness did not diminish over the next year. On 29 November 1912, Vanderlip wrote to Stillman that if war came, "I suppose nothing is all right anywhere in a financial way."[126] Two months later, he noted that "there is something of a chill all through the banking situation in the West and the banks are drawing in on their credits and taking extra precautions as to their reserves."[127] He was not completely alarmist, but certainly felt that "the elements for expansion are not here." On 8 March 1913, he confessed that he had "rarely felt so pessimistic about the outlook," even if NCB was doing well. He could discover nothing comforting in the European situation:[128] "The growth of the warlike spirit, the increased expenditures in large military bases, all point to an inevitable calamity some day and whether that day is next spring, or some other time, it must surely come." The United States and Britain were in a similar position with respect to industrial activity, "and the strain on bank credits," Vanderlip believed, was "very severe."[129]

That month he received another letter from Poniatowski in Paris and found his "discussion of the European situation . . . highly enlightening."[130] Although there had been "considerable anxiety as to future developments in Europe" in the United States, "the note of optimism which you sound marks, I hope, the inception of better conditions." He also thought Poniatowski's "explanation of the increasing armaments in Germany and the attitude of France . . . very encouraging." And yet Vanderlip could not see much "to justify any marked feeling of relief at the present time." Thus "the drawing of gold" had been "disquieting" to him. Meanwhile American domestic business was still "very large" and so were its needs for credit.

He then drew Poniatowski's attention to the fact that "Germany's reserves [were] showing an alarming condition and its splendid banking and currency systems [were] hardly adequate to meet the strain." Despite some criticisms he had about French "hoarding of gold," in the end he did not "really feel that we are going to have any serious trouble, but I do believe that it is necessary to keep a watchful eye on the financial barometer." With the future being so uncertain, Vanderlip's own political and economic barometer also continued to go up and down. In May 1913 he thought that, apart from the development of the economy back home that was showing signs of weakness in the steel and railroad sectors, only "the prospect of a settlement of the European war difficulties and a better condition there" offered some hope.[131]

By June, the banker was reporting to Stillman on the extreme pessimism of Wall Street. This pessimism was not as great in the rest of the country, though there was also a "strongly conservative attitude" developing there.[132] To no small degree this pessimism was "due to the European situation." He felt "that the situation in Germany may become very critical."[133] As a result of the Balkan wars, losses there would be "extremely large" and "apparently no one will help Germany's financing of Austria." He expected further pressure on the German market and understood "that Berlin merchants in good credit have been paying eight per cent for some time." While in August 1913, the U.S. money market had "continued to grow easier," Poniatowski had reported that the French were very pessimistic about the future political outlook.[134] After the Second Balkan War in the fall of 1913 had posed another threat to international peace, the situation became somewhat calmer in early 1914.

And yet Vanderlip thought "that the outlook is as full of difficulties as it was three months ago, except of course that we have got these very easy money conditions the world over."[135] They would, he continued, enable NCB "to do the immediate financing that is necessary." But at the end of March 1914, and despite the bank "making lots of money," the "general business conditions" were in his view still "on the whole dull."[136] In May his intuition was again somewhat more optimistic, and in the following month he learned that U.S. Steel was doing foreign business to the tune of $100 million per year. To be sure, contemporaries did not know the future, and this obviously explains the constant vacillations of businessmen at this time. But their uneasiness at the evolution of political events is palpable enough, and while the focus of this last section has been on American, British, and French businessmen's sentiments, the mood in the German community was also growing more and more apprehensive, as will be seen when the July Crisis of 1914 is discussed at the beginning of the next chapter.

At the end of June 1914, Archduke Ferdinand, the heir to the Habsburg throne, and his wife were assassinated by Serbian nationalists at Sarajevo, setting in motion a chain of events that ended in World War I four weeks later.[137] While the details of the decision-making processes in Berlin, Vienna, and St. Petersburg continue to be researched and debated among historians, it is clear that a decisive push came from Berlin. In the end, the kaiser and his advisors were concerned not to preserve peace, but to make certain that the German population thought that their country went to war because of alleged Russian aggression. Hence the German ultimatum to withdraw the Russian mobilization order of 31 July 1914, and when this did not happen, Wilhelm II reacted on the following day by signing the German order.

Notes to Chapter II

1. On Paris 1900, see the literature in chapter I, note 56, also with reference to the interest that American machine tools generated at the World Exhibition. On machine tools, see also Fritz Blaich, *Amerikanische Firmen in Deutschland, 1890–1918. US Direktinvestitionen im deutschen Maschinenbau* (Wiesbaden, 1984); *NYT*, 9 April 1902; *NYT*, 4 January 1903; *NYT*, 8 September 1907 (with a piece on German imitation). On the situation in the British engineering industry, see S. J. Nicholas, "The American Export Invasion of Britain: The Case of the Engineering Industry, 1870–1914," *Technology and Culture* 21, no. 4 (1980): 570–88; Eric Dorn Brose, *Technology and Science in the Industrializing Nations, 1500–1914* (Atlantic Highlands, NJ, 1998), esp. 81ff. ("The Relative Decline of England").

2. See chapter I, pp. 28f. See also Alfred Vagts, *Deutschland und die Vereinigten Staaten in der Weltpolitik* (New York, 1935), 1:1ff., 121ff.

3. Quoted in *Wall Street Journal (WSJ)*, 28 August 1900.

4. For a most instructive analysis of the rise of IH, see Hubert Kiesewetter, "'Mein Vater ist mit seinen McCormick Ma(s)chinen sehr zufrieden.'

Verkaufsstrategien eines internationalen Unternehmens in Deutschland," *Zeitschrift für Unternehmensgeschichte* 34, no. 2 (1989): 91–123. See also Blaich, *Amerikanische Firmen* (note 1), 63ff.; C. H. Wendel, *150 Years of International Harvester* (Sarasota, FL, 1981), 29ff., also for the following. See also *NYT*, 8 February 1902; *NYT*, 8 January 1903; *WSJ*, 10 March 1910 (on plants in Neuss and Lille, northern France). Regular reports on good business in Europe appeared in *WSJ*, 3 September 1910; *WSJ*, 26 October 1910; *WSJ*, 17 February 1913, with an item that business had further expanded and was very profitable in Germany.

5. On Singer also for the following, see Blaich, *Amerikanische Firmen* (note 1), 24ff.; ibid., 36ff., on the establishment of production facilities; Geoffrey Jones, *The Evolution of International Business* (London, 1996), 113ff.; *NYT*, 4 January 1903. One of the plants was in Wittenberge on the Elbe River near Hamburg, producing sewing machines under the brand name of Veritas.

6. Blaich, *Amerikanische Firmen* (note 1), pp.38ff.; Jones, *Evolution* (note 5) with the quote on 100. On divergent FDI strategies, see John H. Dunning and Sarianna M. Lundan, *Multinational Enterprises and the Global Economy*, 2nd ed. (Cheltenham, 2008), esp. pt. III. Also relevant and very interesting is the analysis of the socioeconomic impact of (Singer) sewing machines and their marketing by Karin Hausen, "Technical Progress and Women's Labour in the Nineteenth Century. The Social History of the Sewing Machine," in Georg G. Iggers, ed., *The Social History of Politics* (Leamington Spa, 1985), 259–81. See also Judith Coffin, "Credit, Consumption, and Images of Women's Desires: Selling the Sewing Machine in Late Nineteenth-Century France," *French Historical Studies* 18 (1994): 749–83.

7. On the temporary boom in bicycles, see Richard H. Heindel, *The American Impact on Great Britain, 1898–1914. A Study of the United States in World History* (New York, 1968), 144.

8. See the more detailed discussion of the rise of the automobile industry, see below, pp. 260ff.

9. On these companies, see Jones, *Evolution* (note 5), 104; Blaich, *Amerikanische Firmen* (note 1), 40ff.; *NYT*, 8 June 1902; *NYT*, 4 January 1903; relating to office furniture: *NYT*, 8 September 1907. On IBM during the interwar period, see chapter V, pp. 272ff.

10. See chapter I, pp. 37ff.; Blaich, *Amerikanische Firmen* (note 1), 44ff.

11. On Merganthaler, see Blaich, *Amerikanische Firmen* (note 1), 76ff.; *NYT*, 21 October 1909; *WSJ*, 22 July 1910; *WSJ*, 20 October 1910; *WSJ*, 15 November 1911.

12. On Kayser's problems, see *WSJ*, 21 August 1912; *NYT*, 17 August 1912; *NYT*, 18 August 1912. On the general situation in Saxony, see *NYT*, 26 October 1902; *NYT*, 3 January 1904; *NYT*, 28 April 1911. Shoes: Thus the description of Heindel, *American Impact* (note 7), 143. See also Vagts, *Deutschland* (note 2), 1: 348; *NYT*, 5 December 1902; *NYT*, 15 March 1908.

13. See *NYT*, 1 January 1903; *NYT*, 15 April 1903; *NYT*, 6 December 1903; *NYT*, 1 July 1913; *WSJ*, 24 September 1913. For a fuller analysis of German reactions to American penetration of the European market, see Fritz Blaich, *Der Trustkampf (1901–1915)* (Berlin, 1975), 46ff. and 80ff. (on activities to contain the Americans). On the British side, see Heindel, *American Impact* (note 7), 148.

14. On the "invasion" of Woolworth, see *WSJ*, 29 August 1913. The rise of more splendidly built department stores is another interesting chapter of European-American business relations because it is an example that some developments occurred in parallel in the two regions. See, e.g., Geoffrey Crossick and Serge Jaumin, *Cathedrals of Consumption. The European Department Store, 1850–1939* (Aldershot, 1999); on Britain: William Lancaster, *The Department Store. A Social History* (London, 1995); on Germany: Klaus Strohmeyer, *Warenhäuser* (Göttingen, 1979); on the United States: Susan Porter Benson, *Counter Cultures* (Urbana, IL, 1986). Woolworth's had a different business model in that it catered to the lower classes, whereas Tietz and other stores were more upmarket. Still, the latter attracted customers from all social strata, if only to go window shopping or to admire the palatial interiors and glittering decorations, especially during holiday seasons. See David Hamlin, *Work and Play* (Ann Arbor, 2007), esp. chaps. 3 and 5. See also the report on Tietz in *NYT*, 26 April 1914, with references to an increased Americanism. Overall, department stores must be seen in the context of the rise of consumer culture and the impact of mass production and Fordism. Henry Ford was one of the first to pass some of the gains of factory rationalization and mass production on to the consumers by lowering prices. This strategy opened the door to more lower-income customers to acquire consumer durables, triggering in the case of Ford and the car industry mass motorization. See chapter II, pp. 79ff., also on the organizational differences between American and German industry (Sherman Act vs. cartels) and the middle position that Britain occupied in this respect: see below pp. 83f.

15. On Otis: Blaich, *Amerikanische Firmen* (note 1), 85ff. Growth in demand in Germany was strong enough for Otis to add to its large plant there. See *WSJ*, 3 August 1912.

16. Jones, *Evolution* (note 5), 104. See also *WSJ*, 3 August 1912.

17. On standardization, Scientific Management, and Taylorism, see the literature cited in chapter I, note 60.

18. Blaich, *Amerikanische Firmen* (note 1), 15–16.

19. On *Qualitätsarbeit*, see chapter I, p. 41. On the connections with the education system, see also chapter I, p. 45. On American attempts to learn from the German system, see above, p. 75.

20. On the Niles Company, see Blaich, *Amerikanische Firmen* (note 1), 20ff. This is an interesting case of mixed capitalization. See Dunning and Lundan, *Multinational Enterprises* (note 6), 295ff. On American FDI in machines and machine tools, see *WSJ*, 26 March 1904. On German FDI in Britain, see Antje Hagen, *Deutsche Direktinvestitionen in Grossbritannien, 1871–1918* (Stuttgart, 1997), 142, 232ff.

21. See above, chapter I, pp. 37ff.

22. On the merger movement, see Naomi Lamoreaux, *The Great Merger Movement in American Business, 1895–1904* (Cambridge, 1988).

23. On the widespread discussions relating to American economic power and the wavering between fear and optimism in Britain, see *NYT*, 26 March 1900; *NYT*, 23 April 1900; *NYT*, 21 May 1900. Similarly in Germany: *NYT*, 27 December 1900; *NYT*, 20 January 1900. Reiner Pommerin, *Kaiser und Amerika* (Cologne, 1986), 115, 207; Vagts, *Deutschland* (note 2), 1:237ff.

24. It appeared in a German translation under the title *Amerikas Eindringen in das europäische Wirtschaftsgebiet* (Berlin, 1902), and reached its second impression in 1903. See also Vanderlip's remarks in chapter I, pp. 42ff., and as reported by *NYT*, 12 April 1903; *NYT*, 19 October 1904. On Standard Oil, see *NYT*, 3 May 1902. By 1912, concerns about the corporation's grip on the crude oil and petroleum market had become so great on both sides of the Atlantic that it was sued in the United States and eventually broken up. See Jones, *Evolution* (note 5), 65; Hagen, *Deutsche Direktinvestitionen* (note 20), 264ff. see also below pp. 73ff., 82f. On the opposition and reporting on the case in Germany, see *NYT*, 23 February 1910; *NYT*, 21 July 1912; *NYT*, 15 October 1912; *NYT*, 22 October 1912; *NYT*, 15 November 1912; *NYT*, 20 November 1912; *NYT*, 28 May 1913; *NYT*, 28 February 1914; *NYT*, 14 March 1914; *NYT*, 29 March 1914; *WSJ*, 15 March 1911; *WSJ*, 5 August 1912; *WSJ*, 8 May 1914. See also Alison Frank, "The Petroleum War 1910: Standard Oil, Austria, and the Limits of the Multinational Corporation," *American Historical Review* 114, no. 1 (February 2009): 16–41; Vagts, *Deutschland* (note 2), 1:237ff.

25. *WSJ*, 30 July 1903. On the 1911 boom, see *WSJ*, 1 June 1911. Among the few German firms that, like Krupp, ventured into the American market with FDI was the chocolate manufacturer Stollwerck. See the fine study by Angelika Epple, *Das Unternehmen Stollwerck. Eine Mikrogeschichte der Globalisierung* (Frankfurt, 2010).

26. See above, pp. 58ff. See also, *NYT*, 30 August 1903; *NYT*, 7 September 1903; William T. Hogan, *Economic History of the Iron and Steel Industry in the United States* (Lexington, MA, 1971).

27. On the question of freight rates, see Werner Abelshauser, "Staat, Infrastruktur und regionaler Wohlstandsausgleich im Preussen der Hochindustrialisierung," in Fritz Blaich, ed., *Staatliche Umverteilungspolitik in historischer Perspektive* (Berlin, 1980), 9–58.

28. See *NYT*, 17 April 1902.

29. Ten years later, there was still a sense that the Europeans were ten years behind. See *WSJ*, 1 June 1911.

30. *NYT*, 29 August 1902.

31. See Arthur Marder, *From Dreadnought to Scapa Flow. The Royal Navy in the Fisher Era, 1904–1919* (London, 1974); Volker R. Berghahn, *Der Tirpitz-Plan* (Düsseldorf, 1971), 419ff. On the U.S. Navy, see Holger H. Herwig, *The Politics of Frustration. The United States in German Naval Planning, 1889–1941* (Boston, 1976).

32. See Jones, *Evolution* (note 5), 115. When Benjamin Briscoe of the U.S. Motor Company toured Europe for six weeks in 1910, he returned with the feeling that business was very satisfactory. *WSJ*, 29 November 1910. However, in light of the prosperity that the United States experienced in this period, there was a demand for expensive European cars that grew toward 1914. See *NYT*, 29 December 1907; *NYT*, 9 June 1912; *NYT*, 18 May 1913.

33. See above, p. 41. See also Hagen, *Deutsche Direktinvestitionen* (note 20) 187ff.; Elfriede Grunow-Osswald, *Die Internationalisierung eines Konzerns. Daimler-Benz, 1890–1997* (Königswinter, 2006). Paul Erker, *Vom nationalen zum globalen Wettbewerb. Die deutsche und amerikanische Reifenindustrie im 19. und 20.*

Jahrhundert (Paderborn, 2005), 113, came across the intriguing self-definition of German automobiles as "Qualitäts-Repräsentationswagen."

34. Quoted in *NYT*, 12 December 1909.

35. Erker, *Vom nationalen* (note 33), with the quote on U.S. companies on 182; Hagen, *Deutsche Direktinvestitionen* (note 20), 206ff.

36. Erker, *Vom nationalen* (note 33), 92ff. See also Erker, *Wachsen im Wettbewerb. Eine Zeitgeschichte der Continental A.G.* (Düsseldorf, 1996).

37. On AEG and the Rathenaus, see, e.g., Henry Rogge, *Fabrikwelt um die Jahrhunderwende am Beispiel AEG Maschinenfabrik in Berlin-Wedding* (Cologne, 1983); Peter Strunk, *AEG. Aufstieg und Niedergang einer Industrielegende* (Berlin, 1999); Ernst Schulin, *Walther Rathenau. Repräsentant, Kritiker und Opfer* (Göttingen, 1979); Christian Schölzel, *Walther Rathenau. Eine Biographie* (Paderborn, 2006). On Siemens, see, e.g., Wilfried Feldenkirchen, *Von der Werkstatt zum Weltunternehmen* (Munich, 1997); Feldenkirchen, *Werner von Siemens. Erfinder und internationaler Unternehmer* (Munich, 1992/1996); Herbert Goetzeler and Lothar Schoen, *Wilhelm und Carl Friedrich von Siemens. Die zweite Unternehmer-Generation* (Stuttgart, 1986); Jürgen Kocka, *Unternehmensverwaltung und Angestelltenschaft am Beispiel Siemens, 1847–1914* (Stuttgart, 1969); Martin Lutz, *Carl von Siemens* (Munich, 2013). See also Peter Herkner, "Financial Strategies and Adaptation to Foreign Markets. The German Electrotechnical Industry and its Multinational Activities," in Alice Teichova et al., eds., *Multinational Enterprise in Historical Perspective* (New York, 1980), 145–59. On the British electrical industries and their problems and German FDI, see Hagen, *Deutsche Direktinvestitionen* (note 20), 107, 113, 121, 132. On opticals, ibid., 169, 179.

38. See above, pp. 49ff.

39. *NYT*, 23 December 1902.

40. On copper consumption figures, see *WSJ*, 7 November 1911. At that time, Germany consumed one-quarter of world production, with AEG and Siemens being the main users and a large percentage being imported from the United States. See *WSJ*, 21 February 1911. Consumption was also rising in Britain, where Westinghouse established a factory. See *WSJ*, 26 March 1904; Robert Jones and Oliver Marriott, *Anatomy of a Merger. A History of G.E., A.E.I., and English Electric* (London, 1970).

41. On GE, see John W. Hammond, *Men and Volts. The Story of General Electric* (New York, 1941). The company does not seem to have established European branches but preferred affiliations. According to *WSJ* (12 February 1913), two out of the five largest corporations were German. See also the sales figures for 1911 for AEG, GE, Siemens & Halske, and Westinghouse in *WSJ*, 27 January 1912. Around 1904 relations between the latter two firms were deemed to be very friendly.

42. Harm Schröter, "The German Question, the Unification of Europe, and the European Market Strategies of Germany's Chemical and Electrical Industries, 1902–1992," *Business History Review* 67 (Autumn 1993): 375.

43. See Ludwig F. Haber, *The Chemical Industry, 1900–1930* (Oxford, 1971); Paul M. Hohenberg, *Chemicals in Western Europe, 1850–1914* (Chicago, 1968); Ernst Homburg et al., eds., *The Chemical Industry in Europe, 1850–1914* (Dordrecht, 1998); Anthony S. Travis, *The Rainbow Makers. The Origins of the Synthetic*

Dyestuffs Industry in Western Europe (Bethlehem, PA, 1993). On Du Pont, see Graham D. Taylor, *Du Pont and the International Chemical Industry* (Boston, 1984). On Britain, see William J. Reader, *Imperial Chemical Industries* (Oxford, 1971). On Bayer, see Anne Nieberding, *Unternehmenskultur im Kaiserreich* (Munich, 2007). On BASF, see Wolfgang von Hippel, "Becoming a Global Corporation—BASF from 1865 to 1900," in Werner Abelshauser et al., *German Industry and Global Enterprise. BASF: The History of a Company* (Cambridge, 2004), 5–114, quotes on 51.

44. Von Hippel, "Becoming a Global Corporation" (note 43), 92.

45. Jeffrey A. Johnson, "The Power of Synthesis (1900–1925)," in Abelshauser et al., *German Industry* (note 43), 151. Before 1914 BASF was among the largest chemical corporations in the world, with 9,200 employees. Ibid., 157. See also *WSJ*, 2 August 1913, on the prosperity of the German chemical industry.

46. On the munitions crisis during the world war, see Jeffrey A. Johnson, *The Kaiser's Chemists. Science and Modernization in Imperial Germany* (Chapel Hill, NC, 1990).

47. Schröter, "German Question" (note 42), 375.

48. *NYT*, 1 January 1900. On the call to make the United States independent of Germany in potash production, see *WSJ*, 18 March 1911. On American feelings about German chemicals in the hour of defeat and the subsequent relationship between these industries, see chapter III, pp. 137f., and chapter IV, pp. 197ff.

49. The White Star Line's *Titanic*, which had been built by IMMC, on 15 April 1912 had a fatal collision with an iceberg in the North Atlantic in which over fifteen hundred lives were lost. On the launching of the two German ships, see Susanne Wiborg, "Mit Volldampf der Zeit voraus," *Die Zeit*, 17 July 2003.

50. *NYT*, 1 January 1900.

51. Werner Link, *Die amerikanische Stabilisierungspolitik in Deutschland, 1921–1932* (Düsseldorf, 1970), 67.

52. On Ballin, see Lamar Cecil, *Albert Ballin* (Princeton, 1967); Gerhard A. Ritter, "Der Kaiser und sein Reeder. Albert Ballin, die HAPAG und das Verhältnis von Wirtschaft und Politik im Kaiserreich und in den ersten Jahren der Weimarer Republik," *Zeitschrift für Unternehmensgeschichte* 42, no. 2 (1997): 137–62; Hella Kemper, "Auf hoher See," *ZEITGeschichte*, 4/10, 38–39. See also Vagts, *Deutschland* (note 2), 1:395ff.; *WSJ*, 17 July 1913, on the great reputation that he and HAPAG enjoyed at the time. By 1914, the company's total BRT had reached 1.3 million. In 1913 the total number of passengers sailing on its ships was 464,000.

53. On developments in shipping, see *NYT*, 21 November 1901; *NYT*, 23 April 1902; *NYT*, 22 May 1902; *NYT*, 27 May 1902. On Cunard's "war" and the fate of those combinations, see Ritter, "Der Kaiser" (note 52), 145ff.; *NYT*, 27 June 1903; *NYT*, 10 July 1904; *NYT*, 14 April 1905. See also Paul Overzier, *Der englisch-amerikanische Schiffahrtstrust* (Berlin, 1912).

54. See, e.g., Charles Endy, "Travel and World Power: Americans in Europe, 1890–1917," *Diplomatic History* 22, no. 4 (1998): 565–94. Habbo Knoch's study of luxury hotels is scheduled to appear by 2013.

55. See the very detailed analysis by Clara Schieber, *The Transformation of American Sentiment toward Germany, 1870–1914* (Boston, 1923), with an extensive evaluation of the American press from different regions of the country. There was also the signing in October 1901 of the Hay-Pauncefote Canal Treaty between the two countries. See A. M. Campbell, *Great Britain and the United States, 1895–1903* (London, 1960), 48ff. On the kaiser's interventions at this time, see Ragnhild Fiebig-von Hase, " 'The Uses of Friendship.' The 'Personal Regime' of Wilhelm II and Theodore Roosevelt, 1901–1909," in Annika Mombauer and Wilhelm Deist, eds., *The Kaiser* (Cambridge, 2003), 143–75.

56. *NYT*, 20 December 1902.

57. Jonathan Steinberg, "The Copenhagen Complex," *Journal of Contemporary History* 1, no. 3 (July 1966): 23–46.

58. Fiebig-von Hase, " 'Uses of Friendship' " (note 55), 150, 152.

59. Ibid., 154.

60. The visit of Prince Heinrich is mentioned in a number of studies. See ibid., 161ff., with Bülow's advice. It is extensively discussed in Schieber, *Transformation* (note 55), 239ff., including the negative and positive reports that appeared in the American press. Quote in Fiebig-von Hase, " 'Uses of Friendship' " (note 55), 161.

61. Thus the kaiser began to talk about this idea that may be seen as a counter to the Anglo-American talk about a union. See *WSJ*, 12 January 1904; *NYT*, 23 April 1901; *NYT*, 27 May 1901; *NYT*, 23 October 1901; *NYT*, 7 December 1903.

62. *NYT*, 17 August 1902.

63. On American confidence and anti-Americanism, see, e.g., *NYT*, 7 January 1900; *NYT*, 21 January 1901; *NYT*, 22 January 1901.

64. On the kaiser's foreign policy, see Christopher Clark, *Wilhelm II* (Stuttgart, 2000), 166ff.

65. Ibid., 210ff.

66. *NYT*, 30 January 1903; *NYT*, 22 February 1903; *NYT* 29 March 1903; *NYT* 20 April 1904.

67. *NYT*, 1 May 1901.

68. See Magnus Brechtgen, *Scharnierzeit, 1895–1907* (Mainz, 2006), 49. See also the Introduction and chapter I, pp. 23ff.

69. CUA, Vanderlip Papers, D-4, 1901, folder I, Godfrey L. Carden to Vanderlip, 1 October 1901, 1–11, also for the following. On the relatively weaker British trading position, see also *NYT*, 4 October 1903.

70. See Mary Nolan, *Visions of Modernity. American Business and the Modernization of Germany* (Oxford, 1994), 17–57.

71. Johns Hopkins University was one of the first American institutions of higher learning to introduce the German system of graduate training, in the late nineteenth century. But the discussion soon extended to secondary education and training. See, e.g., *NYT*, 3 August 1902; *NYT*, 8 April 1903. Interesting also are the articles in *WSJ*, 20 May 1905, pleading for mutual learning in this area. See also *WSJ*, 2 June 1905; *WSJ*, 12 October 1905, referencing a speech that Frank Vanderlip had made on this topic. Also *WSJ*, 14 April 1906, with an article titled "Business Lessons from Germany."

72. The shift in British foreign policy first occurred in the Far East with the conclusion of an Anglo-Japanese accord. See G. W. Monger, *The End of Isolation* (London, 1963). On the Entente Cordiale, see, e.g., Christopher Andrew, *Theophile Delcassé and the Making of the Entente Cordiale, 1898–1905* (London, 1968).

73. On the origins and evolution of this crisis see, e.g., E. N. Anderson, *The First Moroccan Crisis, 1904–1906* (New York, 1928).

74. On the resolution of the crisis and also on Roosevelt's mediating role in it, see Fiebig-von Hase, "'Uses of Friendship'" (note 55), 171ff. After the crisis had subsided, the American business press stressed once more that there were no feelings of hostility and that Germany was, as before, an important trading partner: *WSJ*, 27 January 1906; *WSJ*, 20 September 1906. To be sure, it was also a competitive relationship: *WSJ*, 10 October 1907.

75. See Marder, *From Dreadnought to Scapa Flow* (note 31); Berghahn, *Der Tirpitz-Plan* (note 31).

76. On the enormous complexities of the German system of tax collection, see Peter-Christian Witt, *Die Finanzpolitik des Deutschen Reiches von 1903–1913* (Lübeck, 1970), pts. I and II.

77. Quoted in H. V. Emy, *Liberals, Radicals and Social Politics, 1892–1914* (Cambridge, 1973), 201.

78. Witt, *Die Finanzpolitik* (note 76), pts. III and IV.

79. Quoted in Volker R. Berghahn, *Germany and the Approach of War in 1914* (Basingstoke, 1973), 90.

80. Roosevelt, as quoted above, was quite right in criticizing prominent Americans (to whom the kaiser was graciously giving an audience) of being too gullible and taken in by royalty. This certainly applied to Thomas Edison, who called Wilhelm II Germany's "greatest asset" who ruled a country that Edison admired for having great theorists and scientists, but then thought that they were inferior to the United States in technical savvy and application. In the field of inventions, he added, probably thinking of himself, America was holding all the trumps. See *WSJ*, 26. September 1911, in which he gave his impressions of a tour of Europe. There was also Andrew Carnegie, who considered the kaiser a great ruler, but—himself concerned about the preservation of peace in an increasingly dangerous world—played down the threat of war. See *WSJ*, 1 September 1906; *NYT*, 29 October 1911. Finally, there was P. C. Penfield, who, in an article in the *American Review of Reviews* and at the height of the Berlin-engineered Second Moroccan Crisis, called Wilhelm II the "Trade Lord of Europe." *WSJ*, 22 July 1911. In *WSJ* (17 September 1913), the monarch was called the "greatest businessman in Germany." See also the quest to maintain good business relations as reflected in the columns of *WSJ*, 21 January 1911, with the remark that "Germany is hardly a foreign country to the Yankee." The paper added that the achievements of the German businessman were "largely mental and his best asset is a certain way of thinking"—a sentiment that is also to be found in other articles at this time. See *WSJ*, 19 July 1911, with a reference to the importance of knowing foreign languages and to the skills of German workers who had undergone army service. On this latter point, see Ute Frevert, *Nation*

in Barracks (New York, 2004), who discusses the preparation for factory work through the disciplining effect of military service.

81. On the totally "undiplomatic" interviews that Wilhelm II gave in 1907/8, evidently oblivious to the fuss over his conversations with Ségur, see John Röhl, *Wilhelm II. Der Weg in den Abgrund, 1900–1941* (Munich, 2008), 251.

82. See, e.g., Robert F. Himmelberg, *Business and Government in America since 1870* (Hamden, CT, 1994); R. B. Heflebower, "Monopoly and Competition in the United States of America," in Edward H. Chamberlin, ed., *Monopoly and Competition and Their Regulation* (New York, 1954), 110–39; Tony Freyer, *Regulating Big Business. Antitrust in Great Britain and America, 1880–1990* (Cambridge, 1992); Charles Postel, *The Populist Impulse* (Oxford, 2007); Richard Hofstadter, "What Happened to the Antitrust Movement. Notes on the Evolution of an American Creed," in E. F. Cheit, ed., *The Business Establishment* (New York, 1964).

83. Eleanor M. Fox and Lawrence A. Sullivan, "The Good and Bad Trust Dichotomy. A Short History of a Legal Idea," in Theodore Kovaleff, ed., *The Anti-Trust Impulse* (Armonk, NY, 1994), 1:80. See also the introduction by Kovaleff, 1:3–18.

84. Quoted in ibid., 1:8.

85. Fox and Sullivan, "Good and Bad" (note 83), 87.

86. See below, especially chapter VI, pp. 293ff., 307ff., 329ff.

87. See Hans Rosenberg, *Grosse Depression und Bismarckzeit* (Berlin, 1967).

88. Quoted in Hans Pohl's introduction to Pohl, ed., *Kartelle und Kartellgesetzgebung in Praxis und Rechtsprechung vom 19. Jahrhundert bis zur Gegenwart* (Stuttgart, 1985), 12.

89. See Thomas Kühne, *Dreiklassenwahlrecht und Wahlkultur in Preussen, 1867–1914* (Düsseldorf, 1994).

90. See Jeffrey Fear, "German Capitalism," in Thomas K. McCraw, ed., *Creating Modern Capitalism* (Cambridge, MA, 1997), 135–219, esp. 149, with a longer quotation from the Reich Court's decision. To *WSJ* (23 September 1911) the court ruling represented an instance of German collectivism that the paper contrasted with American individualism.

91. Pohl, *Kartelle und Kartellgesetzgebung* (note 88).

92. Volker Hentschel, *Wirtschaft und Wirtschaftspolitik im Wilhelminischen Deutschland* (Stuttgart, 1978), 99–100.

93. See, e.g., *NYT*, 23 February 1910; *NYT*, 21 July 1912; *NYT*, 15 October 1912; *NYT*, 22 October 1912; *NYT*, 20 November 1912; *NYT*, 28 May 1913; *NYT*, 28 February 1914; *NYT*, 14 March 1914; *NYT*, 29 March 1914. See also *WSJ*, which first began to report on German cartelization on 15 April 1905. A year later *WSJ* (30 May 1906) discussed the disadvantages of cartels to the average consumer. Further reports on discriminations against deviant companies, protectionism, and the maintenance of high prices are in *WSJ*, 4 April 1908; *WSJ*, 20 August 1910; *WSJ*, 4 February 1911. But in connection with the lawsuits that the Justice Department launched against certain firms, most notably Standard Oil, there was also opposition to the Sherman Act. See *WSJ*, 8 October 1911; *WSJ*, 4 November 1911; *WSJ*, 14 December 1911. See also Steve Coll, *Private Empire* (London, 2012).

94. CUA, Vanderlip Papers, B-1-1, Vanderlip to Dr. Ferdinand Baumgarten, 8 August 1904. The letter was written onboard the *Kaiser Wilhelm II* on his trip to Europe that was to take him to Budapest.

95. Ibid., Vanderlip to Stillman, 22 February 1905

96. CUA, Vanderlip Papers, B-1-3, Vanderlip to Stillman, 11 February 1910.

97. *NYT*, 16 August 1912.

98. *NYT*, 15 September 1912.

99. See Volker Berghahn, "Industrial Capitalism and Universal Suffrage: German, American, and British Paths into the Twentieth Century," in Detlev Schulze et al., eds., *Rechtsstaat statt Revolution, Verrechtlichung statt Demokratie?* (Münster, 2010), 1:361–80.

100. Sean Wilentz, "Property and Power. Suffrage Reform in the United States, 1787–1860," in D. W. Rogers, ed., *Voting and the Spirit of American Democracy* (Urbana, IL, 1992), 31–41, here 32.

101. Rogers, *Voting* (note 100), 3.

102. See Hans-Ulrich Wehler, *The German Empire* (Leamington Spa, 1985), 52ff.

103. Theodore S. Hamerow, "The Origins of Mass Politics in Germany, 1866–1867," in Imanuel Geiss et al., eds., *Deutschland in der Weltpolitik des 19. und 20. Jahrhunderts* (Düsseldorf, 1973), 105–20. See also Margaret Anderson, *Practicing Democracy. Elections and Political Culture in Imperial Germany* (Princeton, 2000).

104. Elmar Hucko, ed., *The Democratic Tradition. Four German Constitutions* (Leamington Spa, 1987), 119–45.

105. For a summary of this research and ongoing debates with relevant literature, see Berghahn, "Industrial Capitalism" (note 99), 361–64.

106. See Wehler, *German Empire* (note 102), 52ff.

107. See, e.g., Dirk Stegmann, *Bismarcks Erben* (Cologne, 1970); Gustav Schmidt, "Innenpolitische Blockbildungen in Deutschland am Vorabend des Ersten Weltkrieges," *Das Parlament (Beilage)*, 13 May 1972, 3ff.

108. *WSJ*, 25 July 1911. On German militarism, see Stig Förster, *Der doppelte Militarismus* (Wiesbaden, 1985); Nicholas Stargardt, *The German Idea of Militarism. Radical and Socialist Critics, 1866–1914* (Cambridge, 1994).

109. Quoted in Berghahn, "Industrial Capitalism" (note 99), iii.

110. For a contemporary American view, see, e.g., *WSJ*, 4 February 1912.

111. Norman Angell, *The Great Illusion. A Study of the Relation of Military Power in Nations to Their Economic and Social Advantage* (London, 1911). See also *WSJ*, 12 March 1913, warning of German militarism and arguing that military expenditure is unproductive. See also *WSJ*, 13 March 1913; *WSJ*, 15 March 1913; *WSJ*, 18 March 1913, pointing out that fewer armaments would mean lower taxes. See also *WSJ*, 22 April 1913, raising the issue of growing tax burdens and their distribution and setting an Old Germany against a New Germany. As to the threat of war, the paper (12 November 1912) stated clearly that a big war would be a "calamity"; *WSJ*, 13 November 1912, making the same point.

112. On the Second Moroccan Crisis, see Fritz Fischer, *Krieg der Illusionen* (Düsseldorf, 1969), 117ff.

113. On the situation in 1912, see ibid., 145ff.

114. On the debates surrounding the tax bill of 1913, see Witt, *Die Finanzpolitik* (note 76). See also *WSJ*, 31 March 1913.

115. See, e.g., *WSJ*, 12 November 1912, reporting on the tensions in the Balkans; *WSJ*, 18 March 1913, making the rearmament programs responsible for war scares.

116. On the deteriorating state of Germany's finances at the Reich and also local level, see Witt, *Die Finanzpolitik* (note 76) and Rudolf Kroboth, *Die Finanzpolitik des Deutschen Reiches, 1909–1913/14* (Frankfurt, 1986), with special attention to German money and capital markets. See also Boris Barth, *Die deutsche Hochfinanz und die Imperialismen* (Munich, 1995); Marc Flandreau et al., eds., *International Financial History in the Twentieth Century* (Cambridge, 2003).

117. In light of Germany's financial position and the difficulties of raising taxes, *WSJ* repeatedly commented on this aspect of German politics and economics. After the Second Moroccan Crisis, American banks had made loans to the tune of $29 million, and the paper referred proudly to the country's lending power. A few months later (*WSJ*, 21 February 1912), loans to the Reich and to Prussia had reached over $100 million. The fact that money had become even tighter a year later did not yet cause alarm, but German borrowing now left no doubt that there was a shortage of capital at home. This, *WSJ* (13 March 1913) warned, invited a crisis, though the American business community apparently still downplayed the possibility of a recession.

118. CUA, Vanderlip Papers, B-1-4, Vanderlip to Stillman, 27 October 1911.

119. Ibid., Vanderlip to Stillman, 24 November 1911.

120. Ibid., Vanderlip to Robert Benson, 2 March 1912.

121. Ibid.

122. Ibid., Vanderlip to Stillman, 17 February 1912.

123. Ibid., Vanderlip to Lord Revelstoke, 16 March 1912.

124. Ibid., Vanderlip to Stillman, 26 March 1912.

125. Ibid., Vanderlip to Jacob Schiff, 12 August 1912.

126. Ibid., 29 November 1912.

127. Ibid., B-1-5, Vanderlip to Stillman, 4 January 1913.

128. Ibid., Vanderlip to Stillman, 8 March 1913.

129. Ibid.

130. Ibid., Vanderlip to Poniatowski, 20 March 1913.

131. Ibid., Vanderlip to Stillman, 2 May 1913.

132. Ibid., Vanderlip to Stillman, 6 June 1913.

133. Ibid., Vanderlip to Stillman, 28 August 1913.

134. Ibid., Vanderlip to Stillman, 29 August 1913.

135. Ibid., Vanderlip to Stillman, 12 February 1914.

136. Ibid., Vanderlip to Stillman, 28 March 1914.

137. See, e.g., Fischer, *Krieg der Illusionen* (note 112), 663ff.

III

//

From the Outbreak of War in July 1914 to the Genoa Conference, 1922

1. The Military-Political Origins of World War I

Decades of research into the immediate origins of World War I have resulted in the generally accepted view that a small group of political and military decision makers in Berlin and Vienna deliberately escalated into a major war the smaller regional conflicts in the Balkans that had been going on for many years. In July 1914 they became a threat to the rest of the world, following the assassinations of the heir to the Austro-Hungarian throne, Archduke Ferdinand, and his wife by Serb nationalists at Sarajevo.

While there is still some debate on the role of Tsarist Russia in this picture, it seems fairly certain that, except for the two emperors and their advisors in Berlin and Vienna, no other men (and they were all men) were directly responsible for the ultimate mismanagement of the crisis. Not involved in this process were the ordinary men in the belligerent countries who, from the first days of August onward, were sent to the front, where a staggering nine million of them died up to 1918. Worse, the decision makers in Berlin and Vienna, knowing that the "masses" were unlikely to support a war of aggression, hoodwinked their populations into believing that they were being mobilized for the defense of their fatherland. As Admiral Karl Alexander von Müller, the chief of the Naval Cabinet and an insider at the court in Berlin, put it so cynically in his diary on 1 August 1914, "Brilliant mood. The government has succeeded very well in making us appear as the attacked."[1]

From all that is known, businessmen did not participate in the decision making either. On the contrary, they were desperately hoping that peace would prevail. We saw this in the previous chapter with respect to the British and American worries about a major war. But this was also true of many German businessmen. Albert Ballin, who had a personal relationship with Wilhelm II, is a good case in point. As will emerge in a moment, he, although powerless when it came to having a direct input into decision making in Berlin, tried his best but was ignored.

Meanwhile Germany's recruits went to the front, just as the recruits of the other nations of Europe did, believing that—as we now know correctly—they had in fact been attacked by the Central Powers. Grossly underestimating the dynamics of modern warfare among industrialized great powers in the twentieth century, they all thought that it would be a short war and that they would be home again by Christmas 1914. Their slaughter in the trenches of the Western Front or in the war of movement in the east between Russia and the two Central European monarchies was to last over four years and cost a minimum of twenty million lives.

As to the motives of the military and political advisors around Wilhelm II and Franz Joseph II, the emperor of the Habsburg Empire, there continues to be a division of views among academic historians. On the one hand, there are those who argue that the decision makers in Berlin in particular wanted to use the Sarajevo murders for the unleashing of an all-out war against France and Russia, while they hoped that Britain would stay out of the conflict.[2] Other historians have insisted that in early July the German and Austro-Hungarian leaderships merely opted for a "punishment" of Serbia by Vienna, after which they planned to call an international conference that would curb Serbian ambitions on the Balkans and restabilize the Habsburg Empire.[3] However, this local-war strategy that, as Bethmann Hollweg acknowledged at the start of July, was very risky, finally collapsed when on 25 July Russia appeared on the scene as the protector of Serbia, indicating that it would not permit a humiliation of its Slavic client state. By this time the German military, which had spent the previous weeks on vacation, had returned to Berlin to learn about the shipwreck of Bethmann's localization strategy and insisted that there was no alternative to waging a war against France and Russia.

It is also important that they expected to win this war quickly under a plan that Helmuth von Moltke, the chief of the general staff in Berlin, had refined on the basis of an idea developed by his predecessor Alfred von Schlieffen:[4] Moltke wanted to invade France and Belgium first and, expecting a swift victory in the west, then send his troops eastward to defeat the Russians, whose mobilization would not be completed until after the German conquest of Paris. In a way, this was the German generals' solution to the problem of war between industrial nations in the twentieth century: while Norman Angell and the business community believed war to be unthinkable because of the catastrophic consequences for all countries involved, Moltke thought that a major conflict was still winnable, provided it started in 1914 and was conducted as a lightning war that lasted no more than a few weeks.[5]

As to the possibility that Britain might enter the conflict on the Franco-Russian side, the German generals did not take it seriously. The British Cabinet was expected to remain neutral, and should it decide to intervene, it would take time to raise an army and to prepare it for battle since the country did not have the draft.[6] In other words, the war in the west would by then have been won by the Germans, just as the campaign in the east was assumed to end with a subsequent early victory over Russia.

Whatever their differences about how to interpret the beginning of the crisis in early July 1914, most historians are agreed that Moltke's strategic gamble contained a strong dose of preventive war calculations. Apart from viewing developments inside Germany and the rise of the Social Democrats with alarm, he and his colleagues assumed that, following the loss of the naval arms race against Britain in 1911–12, the country would also find itself in a militarily inferior position once the French and Russian rearmament programs had been completed by 1915–16. There is a very telling statement that foreign secretary Gottlieb von Jagow recorded after a meeting with Moltke in March 1914:[7] "The prospects for the future weighed heavily upon him. Russia would have finished arming in 2 to 3 years. The military superiority of our enemies' military power would be so great then that he did not know how he could deal with it. Now we would still be more or less a match for it. In his view there was no alternative but to fight a preventive war so as to beat the enemy while we could still emerge fairly well from the struggle. The Chief of the General Staff therefore put it to me that our policy should be geared to bringing about an early war."

This argument was apparently also adopted by the kaiser at this time. On 21 June Max Warburg, the banker, met Wilhelm II at a banquet in Hamburg, at which he found the latter in a very agitated state about Russia's armaments and railroad building in the western parts of the Tsarist Empire. He then rambled on about war breaking out by 1916 and that in light of Russian and French military superiority at that point, it would be better for Germany to start a war soon rather than to wait until it was too late. Gloomy thoughts about the future of the

Habsburg Empire also circulated throughout 1914 in Vienna, where Moltke's opposite number, Franz Conrad von Hötzendorf, was among the advocates of a strike before the military balance had shifted against the Central Powers.

2. The International Business Community and the Outbreak of War in 1914

Countless historians of politics and diplomacy have meticulously analyzed the moves that the European governments, and those in Berlin and Vienna in particular, made during the last weeks, days, and hours of peace. A fair amount is by now also known about popular responses to the threat and eventual outbreak of World War I. Much less has been written on the business communities of Europe and those of Britain, the United States, and Germany in particular. Unlike the monarchs of Austria-Hungary and Germany they had no constitutional powers to declare war and hence had no direct part in Berlin's and Vienna's decision to unleash a major war. The question therefore is this: what role did these communities play in the summer of 1914? This question is best approached from three different angles: (1) What were the basic attitudes toward a great power conflict at this point? (2) What were the reactions of the markets and the general public, once the possibility of war appeared on the horizon and then became a reality in August 1914? (3) What actions, if any, did businessmen take to try to prevent a catastrophe?

As to the first issue, a good deal of evidence has already been presented in chapter II to show that businessmen in Europe and the United States feared a clash of arms among the great powers in the years before 1914. They accurately predicted the enormous disruptions that it would bring to the world economy and trade between the major industrial nations and had been warning of this since 1909–10, if not long before. Warburg made this point again in a different way when—as mentioned above—he saw Wilhelm II on 21 June 1914. Trying to counter the latter's hawkish mood, he remarked that Germany "was growing stronger with every year of peace, [while] our enemies are getting weaker. Waiting could only be to the country's advantage."[8] In making this point, he was evidently thinking of the country's economic success and considered an informal commercial penetration of its neighbors preferable to formal conquest and military occupation.[9]

Warnings about the disruptive consequences of war appeared in the press and in personal statements by other businessmen in July 1914.[10]

On 28 July, the day of the Austro-Hungarian attack in Serbia, the *WSJ* wrote,[11] "The whole world is engaged in business as never before. Industrial Germany in thirty years has far outrun military Germany. . . . Throughout the civilized world, villages have become mill centers; towns have become cities; empires have succeeded states, and the Empire in the modern world is commercial and not martial." On 1 August, J.P. Morgan raised his influential voice by warning,[12] "Alarming as the news is from Europe, I am still hoping that there will not be a general war. While the gravity of the present situation can hardly be exaggerated, there is still the opportunity for a sobering second-thought of the people of Europe to prevail over their first impulses. If the delicate situation can be held in abeyance for a few days, I should expect a rising tide of protest from the people who are to pay for war with their blood and their property." He continued, "It is idle to say that America will not be hurt by a general European war. The wholesale waste of capital involved in such a catastrophe would result in a distribution of the losses the world over, but the loss here would be infinitesimal compared with the losses to the countries immediately involved."

Frank Vanderlip of NCB, too, believed that something unprecedented might happen if there was war. After all, "the world is so much more closely related financially than it ever was before and the commitments of every character are on so much larger [a] scale that the light of past experience is of very little use."[13] He felt that the crisis might be "cleared up in a few days" or "it might break into a flame that might involve all the large powers and then there would be financial chaos." Indeed, the stock markets around the world had begun to react to the looming crisis at the end of July. On 1 August, the *WSJ* reported that "with the exception of the Chicago Board of Trade, every exchange in America and practically everyone in Europe" had closed on the previous day.[14] As early as 27 July the Russian national bank had suspended its gold convertibility.

Meanwhile in London, the Bank of England had increased its bank rate first from 3 to 4 percent and on 31 July to 8 percent, a day later even to 10 percent. The immediate effect was a run on banks by savers and the closing of the stock markets. Bond prices and consols had also begun to fall. As Prime Minister Herbert H. Asquith recorded in his diary,[15] "The City . . . is in a terrible state of depression and paralysis. . . . The prospect is very black." On 27 July Lord Rothschild had noted in London that everyone in the City talked about nothing else "but the European situation and the consequences that might arise if serious steps were not taken to prevent a European conflagration."[16] After the Austro-Hungarian invasion of Serbia, he added on 30 July,[17] "Clumsy as Austria may have been, it would be ultra-criminal if *millions of lives* were sacrificed in order to sanctify the theory of murder, a brutal murder which the Servians [sic] have committed."

Panic also occurred in France. The Paris branch of the Rothschilds advised the sale of large quantities of consols. By 28 July, German banks began "to withdraw deposits and [to] round up positions."[18] Deposit banks holdings shrank by some 20 percent and by early August the Reichsbank's discount rate had gone up to 6 percent. Attempts to prevent disaster must also be seen against the background of popular demonstrations in major German cities warning Austria-Hungary against attacking Serbia. Jean Jaurès, the leader of the French socialists, called for an emergency congress of the Second International to be held in Brussels to mobilize the working-class movements of Europe against the impending slaughter of its members and the rest of Europe's young men.[19] But it was too late to organize this kind of resistance, and on 31 July Jaurès was assassinated by a nationalist fanatic.

As to the third issue of whether businessmen proactively tried to stop the slide into war, there is the verdict by historian Alfred Vagts.[20] Writing in the 1930s, he charged the German business community with too much deference, if not even cowardice, for not having used their good connections to Wilhelm II more decisively to avert what they, just as their colleagues in Britain, France, and America, acknowledged would be a catastrophe. As Vagts put it rather sarcastically, "there were the elites of politicians and bureaucrats, against whose noble work capital was, in its majority interest, too cowardly to stand up."

There is also Ballin's retrospective self-reproach for not having intervened more forcefully with the kaiser. He added that he had lacked the courage to do so and, not knowing of Moltke's role, later refused to meet Jagow, accusing him that he "must carry the terrible responsibility for the stage-management of this war which is costing Germany generations of splendid people and is throwing it back 100 years."[21] In December 1915 he told the Reich chancellor that he "rejected all [of] Bethmann's protestations and excuses [about the unleashing of the war] as fairy tales that he should be ashamed to tell."[22] He added, "I have spent my entire life building up something which has been of immense value to the German Reich, and then you come along with a couple of others and destroy it all." He considered this conflict the most stupid war "that world history has ever seen," and when Germany was defeated in 1918 and with his shipping empire in tatters, he, after several attempts to end the war and advocating the abdication of Wilhelm II, became so depressed that he committed suicide on 9 November.[23]

Yet, Vagts's criticism and Ballin's self-reproach seem to go too far. Bankers in particular did try to get the decision makers to think twice about the wisdom of their plans. On 31 July, Rothschild endeavored to persuade the London *Times* to tone down its defiant language against Germany and contacted his cousins in Paris as well as Paul Schwabach in Berlin. The former were supposed to influence French president Raymond Poincaré to ask the Tsarist government to hold back as "the calamity [of a war] would be greater than anything ever seen or known before."[24] He was of course also thinking of the large investments and loans that the French had put into Russia, their alliance partner since the mid-1890s.

Ballin went even further when, encouraged by Jagow, he sailed to Britain, believing that he was on a mission to prevent war altogether.[25] But the German Foreign Ministry, totally in the dark about Britain's attitude, was apparently more interested in finding out, if she would stay out of the conflict. While in London, Ballin met with Foreign Secretary Sir Edward Grey, as well as with Lord Morley, Lord Haldane, and Winston Churchill. He came away with the impression—later disputed by the British and also erroneous, as events were to demonstrate—that Britain would stay out. It is possible that Ballin was so anxious to stop the outbreak of war that he believed in the success of his larger quest and did not realize that he was being used by Jagow for Berlin's much narrower calculations of keeping Britain neutral, while Moltke launched his attack against Belgium, Luxemburg, and France in the west.

The more fundamental reason for the failure of the business community to stop the conflict at the end of July was that it was aristocrats, not businessmen, who held the political power in matters of foreign policy and above all the right to declare war. They were said to live in different universes, as not even the arms manufacturers, such as Skoda, wanted a major war.[26] And this also applied to the power structure in Berlin, buttressed as it was by the exclusive privilege of the monarch, enshrined in the Reich Constitution, to decide on whether to wage war or stay at peace.

What all this added up to was that, just as the demonstrations by workers in different German cities, organized to warn Austria-Hungary against an invasion of Serbia, or Jaurès's attempt to rally the Second International proved futile, businessmen maneuvered similarly helplessly in the face of the powers held by the German and Austro-Hungarian military and their supreme commanders, Wilhelm II and Franz Joseph I. Not surprisingly, Vanderlip was among those who expected catastrophe. Writing to his wife on 30 July he was "still hopeful that the result will not be a general conflagration."[27] Nevertheless, he judged to situation to be "undoubtedly very critical." In another letter to her of 4 August, the day when Britain entered the war and the Wilson administration decided to remain neutral, Vanderlip added,[28] "In the quiet of the country, so far away from the actual stress of the moment, you cannot possibly have any conception of what has happened to the world. Civilization has broken down, and there is the most absolute derangement of our affairs."

Consequently, he was now on duty by day and by night, although he also felt that "we have things as well in hand as they can be in a cyclone which is still raging." This, he thought, was due "largely to the fact that the country is by no means awake to the extent of the calamity. We are having to think along lines and about things that men, who are now alive, never thought before." It struck him "as if it would take some Jules Verne plot of a changed law of nature, or some equally impossible premise and then figure out what consequences would flow from that." However, this time it was not Verne's "fiction; it is very real and substantial." A week later, he told Lucy Evan Chew,[29] "It is of course very hard to predict with any degree of certainty what the outcome of affairs in Europe will be, but it looks to me as though Paris would have far from the artistic atmosphere for a long time to come."

Meanwhile, on 3 August, *WSJ* had ventured a firmer prediction that focused on the consequences that the kaiser's decision had for Germany:[30] "Already the German mercantile marine is tying itself up in neutral ports, while the thrifty British vessels are doing the business. It is said that the German naval officers were daily raising their glasses to 'the Day' [of the great battle at sea with Britain]. It is by no means improbable that Germany, with everything to lose and little enough to gain, will in a short time be praying desperately for the night." Indeed, Ballin's HAPAG was the first victim of Wilhelm's decision to wage a major war. Some 50 percent of his employees were called up. Another four thousand who were employed at the HAPAG offices around the world were interned as enemy aliens. There were also the huge material losses. The ships that happened to be in German ports became what Lamar Cecil termed a "moth ball fleet . . . permanently [stationed] on the Elbe" river.[31]

Others that happened to be in British or French ports around the world were immediately sequestered; those in the ports of neutral countries, and of the United States in particular, sought refuge from capture by the Royal Navy until, following the American entry into the war in April 1917, they were used to transport Allied soldiers to the Western Front. North German Lloyd's ships suffered the same fate. Just before the outbreak of war two HAPAG and two NGL liners with some 4,100 passengers onboard were sailing in the Atlantic and were apparently caught by the British blockade. Meanwhile an embargo had been imposed on a dozen HAPAG steamers with a total tonnage of 155,000, while the tonnage of the nine NGL steamers held in American ports amounted to 123,000.

There is also the curious story of the *Kronprinzessin Cecelia* that illustrates the confusion that broke out with the imposition of the British blockade.[32] In late July, she was on her voyage to Europe. Among her cargo were $10 million in gold bars for Britain and France. Portsmouth and Cherbourg were to be her first stops before she was to sail on to Germany. The skipper was then told to go straight to Hamburg for fear that she might be seized in Portsmouth. The Germans also wanted to get hold of the gold. But when there was no further news from her, it was assumed that she had been captured with her precious cargo by the Royal Navy—until the vessel turned up unexpectedly in Bar Harbor, Maine, on 4 August. Passengers reported that they were taken on a rather scary escape at full speed in dense fog from the waters west of the Scilly Islands back to the United States. Having continued her journey in American waters from Bar Harbor to New York, the gold was handed over to the Guarantee Trust against the promise that it would be returned to the original shippers. This seems to have happened after the requisite documents were found in *Kronprinzessin Cecelia*'s mail bags. Vanderlip was one of the bankers who felt greatly relieved by this outcome. The NCB share of the gold amounted to one-fifth, that is, some $2 million. They gave a further boost to its reserves that had already gone up by 25 percent thanks to the inflow of monies from abroad.

If German shipping was very badly hit, hundreds of commercial and manufacturing firms involved in international trade lost their overseas investments and the goods that were in transit to Germany or had been waiting to be exported to destinations overseas. Inbound goods were seized by the Royal Navy and its tight blockade in the North Sea. Imports to Germany were held up in the ports of neutrals. In 1913 Germany had foreign investments to the tune of 230 million pounds sterling, over 50 percent of which was outside Europe. In short, if the outbreak of war constituted an unprecedented challenge to British, American, and French finance and industry, the impact on the German economy was nothing less than catastrophic. The *WSJ* reported on 8 August that Britain had severed the cables that ran from New York to Germany via the Azores.[33] As Vanderlip confirmed in a letter to his wife of 11 August, the country had by then been "wholly cut off from any sort of communication."[34]

3. The Ambiguities of
American Neutrality

With a general war looming, J.P. Morgan had been confident on 1 August "that the whole American people will co-operate to restore normal conditions throughout this country at the earliest possible moment."[35] And indeed, once the first shock had been overcome, the situation in the United States began to stabilize. As Vanderlip wrote to his wife on 11 August, things were certainly going well at NCB "although down in my heart are some apprehensions of the very gravest character."[36] He thought it "possible that we will pull through everything without any more serious trouble than we have had." After all, he and his colleagues had "been very fore-handed and intelligent in managing the whole situation." Meanwhile "the country happily is keeping asleep so that everyone is keeping his head." Nevertheless, as he wrote in another letter of 21 August to William Sloan at Colorado College, some markets remained closed, at least "for the present," and there was little trading in securities.[37]

Thenceforth the problems facing the United States were not so much economic as they were political, and this in turn was related to the ethnic makeup of American society. The Wilson administration was realistic enough to expect the population to wake up to the enormity of the conflict across the Atlantic sooner or later. But the president also knew that, while there was an outburst of anti-German feeling over the treatment of Belgium and a basic Anglophilia among the East Coast elites, many of whose families had emigrated from Britain, over 20 percent of the population hailed from the German-speaking lands and were, initially at least, pro-German. In light of Britain's troubles in Ireland, Irish Americans were also hostile to the Allies, and overall it is important to emphasize that pro-British sentiments did not imply a strong popular demand to intervene on the side of the Allies.

To avoid internal cultural-political divisions, but also for economic reasons, Washington tried hard to maintain strict neutrality between the two warring blocs. The economic consideration was that the country was in a very advantageous position to supply the belligerents with agricultural produce, raw materials, and industrial goods. These exports had to be financed and, while many prewar contacts had existed with the German banking community, they had now been disrupted. Meanwhile the links with the Allies and with the London City in particular had grown closer even before the war began. Increasingly, the British-American relationship became "special" in a positive way while that with Germany went downhill.

However, this Anglo-American closeness was being undermined by the actions of the Royal Navy. Under international law, trade between neutrals was to continue. Anxious to block all supplies to Germany, including those that had initially been destined for neutral Dutch ports, Britain began to search all American vessels for contraband and to seize those goods that were deemed to have Germany as their final destination. Thus, Standard Oil of New Jersey found on 3 August 1914 that, as oil would be regarded as contraband, the company would be "unable to ship any oil whatever for the time being, as it is liable to seizure no matter what flag the vessel carrying the oil" was flying.[38] Worse, the carrying of contraband, the attempt to run a blockade, or the rendering of any "unneutral service" also made "neutral merchant ships liable to confiscation." The 1909 London Naval Conference had attempted to constitute a prize court that would adjudicate disputes. But Britain had refused to accept an international solution so that "the nation making the capture of a neutral merchant ship" was free to handle cases in its own national prize court. Consequently, and much to the irritation of the Americans, Britain interpreted the prize law very narrowly. Protests led to some temporary wavering on the part of London. Still, the practice of searching American ships continued, casting a shadow over Anglo-American relations.[39]

In the meantime, the Germans had discovered that their high seas fleet of battleships with which Tirpitz had been planning since the turn of the century to out-build the Royal Navy and, if necessary, to defeat it in a major battle in the North Sea, was not strong enough to seek an all-or-nothing confrontation. The kaiser now embarked upon a massive submarine building program. These U-boats soon began to hunt and sink British vessels in the Atlantic on their way to deliver war-essential supplies to British ports. Again, there were specific procedures under international law to be observed. A ship stopped by a German submarine had to be ordered to evacuate its crew to the lifeboats before it was torpedoed and sunk. Since submarines could accommodate only a few evacuees, the lifeboats were left to fend for themselves on the high seas.

The first British response to this tactic was to arm merchant ships with light guns against which a surfaced submarine had insufficient armor. Consequently, the Germans began to torpedo British vessels without warning from a submerged position. It did not take long for this practice also to be used against ocean liners with even greater loss of life, including citizens from neutral countries and from the United States in particular. The resulting diplomatic tensions between Washington and Berlin reached a first climax in the summer of 1915 when the ocean liner *Lusitania* was torpedoed. Some 1,200 passengers lost their lives, among them 124 Americans. Soon thereafter the passengers of the *Arabia* suffered the same fate.[40]

While the Imperial Navy insisted that submarine warfare was a foolproof strategy for starving and defeating Britain, Theobald von Bethmann-Hollweg, fearful of an American entry into the war, succeeded in imposing restraints on submarine warfare. The Germans also tried to break the blockade by building large submarines to be deployed not to attack merchant shipping in the Atlantic, but to get valuable contraband cargo from the United States to Germany. Although this enterprise never got beyond its embryonic stage, there is nevertheless the intriguing case of the submarine *Deutschland* that in July 1916 suddenly surfaced in the mouth of the Delaware River, causing a public sensation and much diplomatic activity.[41] German motives for this mission remained obscure since the skipper and other Germans refused to reveal what kinds of goods the submarine had come to load. But it may be that the Reich government also wanted to test American neutrality during this period of slightly improved relations.

All this came to an end when Bethmann lost his internal battle in Berlin against the military in February 1917. With an extremely bloody war continuing on land without a German victory in sight, the admirals once more gained the upper hand over the civilian government in Berlin, claiming that with a resumption of unrestricted submarine warfare the Imperial Navy could sink enough tonnage per month over several months to bring the British to their knees. After this it did not take long for further losses of American lives to occur. Moreover, the infamous Zimmermann Telegram, intercepted by the British and passed on to Washington, revealed that Berlin was trying to forge an alliance with Mexico with the aim of encouraging that country to start a war for the reconquest of Texas, Arizona, and New Mexico.[42] Wilson, who had only a few months earlier made major efforts to get negotiations for a "peace without victory" started among the European combatants, angrily abandoned these initiatives and on 6 April 1917 got Congress to support a declaration of war on Germany.

These developments affected not only American popular attitudes toward Britain and Germany, but also the policies of industry, commerce, and finance. This was the period when British-American relations, the tensions over the seizure of contraband notwithstanding, became closer and closer, culminating in the American entry into the war on the Allied side. It was also the phase when German-American relations got progressively worse.

4. The American Economy and the Moves To Enter the War

Upon entering the war, the United States became a very close ally of Britain. What London needed most was more food, raw materials, and credit. Although the country's manufacturing industries had declined in comparison to those of Germany and America for several decades, there was enough capacity and know-how in the Midlands and

the English North as well as in Scotland to churn out military hardware, now in ever greater demand to supply what had become a war
of attrition in northern France.[43] With men desperately needed in the
trenches, women took their place to produce shells and guns and other
vital equipment. The United States shipped the raw materials. No less
important, Britain, with its predominantly urban populations, needed
cereals that British agriculture could not supply in sufficient quantities,
even though many fields and meadows that had lain fallow or been
used for meat, wool, und dairy production were now being plowed up
for grain growing. America offered foodstuffs as well as farm implements, horses, and fertilizers.

Against unlimited German submarine warfare, now in full force,
the two allies refined the convoy system. The more extensive laying of
antisubmarine mine barriers also made the German effort ever more
dangerous. Germany's naval strategists had calculated that a loss of
600,000 BRT per month would bring the British to sue for peace.[44] By
June 1917, this target had been surpassed with the loss of 352 Allied
ships and a total of 669,218 BRT. Yet, the country refused to collapse, indicating that this particular path to a German victory was reaching a cul-
de-sac. Instead of hunger spreading in the British Isles, mass starvation
came to Germany due to the Allied blockade and German agriculture's
inability to produce more food, except for a growing black market.

American deliveries to the Allies had to be financed. Before 1917,
Washington's neutrality had prevented the granting of government
credits. The Allies had to rely on the American private sector, which remained cautious as long as Washington was unprepared to underwrite
such credits. There was also resistance among those connected with
the German-American business community. For other bankers whose
sympathies lay with Britain, it was clear from the start that Britain and
France had to be given credits. With the panic and turmoil of August
1914 subsiding, Wall Street had entered into negotiations with London
and Paris. As early as 6 August, the *WSJ* wrote that "there is every reason to foresee, beyond a short period of suspense, a great boom in business in this country, created through no effort of our own."[45]

Once again, the notes and letters of Vanderlip provide a window to
how the European situation was perceived in American business circles and to the practices that they adopted. In September 1914, he was
convinced that American exports could be built up over time, even if
"we can hardly hope that it will be equal to the losses that are already
upon us as a result of the destruction of some of the great European
markets."[46] During the same month, International Harvester, which
had made major investments in Europe, announced that it would not
be paying out dividends because of "the tie-up in its foreign credits."

The situation was very different back home. From Chicago to the West and Northwest there was "some considerable semblance of prosperity owing to the high prices for grain and the great crop" of that year. The American economy, Vanderlip added, will "save the world financially," just as it was "the only thing that will save Europe from utter ruin."

One of the consequences of America's favorable position was that large sums of money were "flowing toward New York," while much of industry was running on overtime.[47] And yet, all this did not cause Vanderlip, the ever cautious banker, to have "foolish ideas about New York becoming the financial center of the world." As long as the United States remained a debtor nation as it had been before the war, "we are a long ways short of that." However, he had no doubt that "with the complete disorganization of the world's exchanges, we are going to play a very important part" in the larger picture. It was also reassuring to him that NCB had "a position in this field of great prominence"—until after the war when the United States had become a creditor nation and Wall Street and many big corporations began to aim at being number one in the world.

The shift became visible as early as 1915. If the United States had been running a trade deficit before 1914, the balance of trade was now turning into a surplus. Up to October 1913 American exports to Germany amounted to $48 million, as against imports from that country to the tune of $15 million. The ratios with respect to Britain in October 1913 were $71 million in exports as against $20 million in imports from there. By October 1914 trade with Germany had declined very steeply as a result of the war and British blockade, whereas exports to Britain had increased by $1 million over the previous October. According to Vanderlip, this also had the effect that "we will be able . . . to absorb our own securities held abroad and thus decrease our indebtedness here."[48]

And yet worries about the future and how it might affect the American economy never disappeared. When Lloyd George announced that in 1915 the Allies would be spending $10 billion on top of what the war had already been costing up to the end of 1914, Vanderlip felt "that we are getting into figures that are astronomical rather than financial."[49] It was difficult for him "to attempt to grasp what the ultimate significance of such a creation of obligations is going to mean to the world." He added that it was "idle for any human mind to try to predict just what all this is going to mean economically." The only counsel he had in those circumstances was to adhere to an "extreme conservatism." A week later, he wrote that "the tragedy" in Europe was "so great that it must, of course, be profoundly depressing, and there is no chance to forget it."[50]

So, notwithstanding the tensions over contraband seizures by the Royal Navy, the American business community began to move more closely toward their British counterparts. In December 1914 there had still been some impatience because the latter expected, not explicit American neutrality, but strict partisanship. By April 1915 Vanderlip's pro-British sympathies were palpable:[51] "The English people have handled the situation masterfully," though he wondered "if anybody could really handle it." He continued, "The prevailing sentiment in this country is, of course [!], all pro-allies, and nobody has any doubt of the final outcome" and "a marked success for the armies or for the English navies would be productive of about as much real satisfaction in this country as in England." In the meantime, "the horror of the war" was also growing in the United States, with everybody feeling "a deep grief in the situation and a sense of uncertainty. . . . We hope that soon there will be a brighter hue to the general outlook and prospects for peace."

Only a few weeks later came the shock of the sinking of the *Lusitania* that inevitably stoked anti-German feelings. Yet Vanderlip was not the only one in the American business community who was still "determined to keep out of the war."[52] Indeed, it seemed "hardly probable that anything within reason can be done which will arouse us into a war fever." In this respect Wilson's policies, he added, "really represent the country, for there is utmost aversion in everyone's mind to our becoming a belligerent either in Europe, the Orient, or Mexico." At the same time, he reassured Sir Felix Schuster in London on 1 June 1915:[53] "The United States will be found firmly and courageously on the side of civilization, no matter what such a stand may involve us in." And so Vanderlip and other businessmen vacillated between gloom and hope for a bright future, especially for their own country. On 11 June 1915, he mentioned the "feeling of relief" around the country at Wilson's moderate reaction to the *Lusitania* crisis because "no one wants war."[54] Any earlier blue-eyed notions about the war had disappeared, for "when it becomes a contest of machine shops and chemical laboratories, whatever romance there might have been in it, fades away," even among young men. Indeed, "we are today much further from the probability of becoming involved than we have been in a long time before." Of course, "some untoward action [may] change all this at any time."

Two weeks later, Vanderlip was more jubilant:[55] "What a wonderful opportunity America really has to take a great place in world finance with this ability to expand credits!" The Americans may be an insular people, and there were certainly plenty of opportunities to develop the domestic market. Nevertheless, "the next great commercial period in America . . . is likely to be a period of expanding foreign relationships."

If there was any problem, it was cultural, that is, a lack of training, temperament, and initiative.

With international trade no longer being what it was before 1914, the field of finance and foreign exchange became a major focus of activity, and here—although Vanderlip was "personally very pessimistic about the outlook for long-term bonds"—there emerged a trend toward not only expansion but also concentration.[56] Given the high degree of fragmentation of the American banking system, NCB and other big institutions began to realize that business as well as government were bound to become more centralized and coordinated. This trend was making rapid strides in all spheres of life from 1915 onward under the exigencies of war in Europe and the conflict's slow "totalization."[57] Government, business, and trade unions moved more closely together, leading everywhere to the creation of war boards. The further hope was of course that this cooperation and coordination would increase efficiencies and yield productivity gains in industry.

All this meant with respect to banking that, with the American economy doing so well, the private-sector loan business remained as alluring as it was risky. To be sure, Latin America and Scandinavia were less problematical in this respect. Russia, by contrast, was a different matter, where International Harvester still saw business opportunities in 1915. But Russia had never been deemed a safe business proposition, and in light of the lengthening of the war, American business soon began to retreat from the crumbling Tsarist Empire. At the same time there were the strained finances of Britain and France. For the moment, Britain had shouldered the main burden "of supplying credit to pay for the huge purchases being made" in the United States, which in turn created "extremely serious" fresh problems.[58] Vanderlip became so worried about all these pressures that he even began to wonder about the viability of capitalist system as a whole. He added that "here in America, of course, we are having no touch of that, but in a way our commercialism is hardened and men calculate the duration of the war in figuring out possible profits and gamble in war stocks with great recklessness."

To the New York banker this was one reason why "there is the strongest disposition to keep America out of the struggle" in "recognition of our utter unpreparedness" and with it "a growing disposition to rectify this in some measure."[59] And yet, he doubted that this would lead to a more fundamental "regeneration of the spirit" or to get in some other way "an adequate compensation which we must ultimately pay for this destruction of life and wealth that half the world is engaged in." He confessed that he was "depressed over the situation in world affairs." To him it seemed "like waking up and finding that a horrible nightmare turns out to be a terrible reality." One aspect of this was that the intensifying interaction with Britain and France was still vexed by problems.

As he put it in a very long letter to Prince Poniatowski, his long-time correspondent in Paris, while it was right "that England did the wisest possible thing in arranging for her purchases to be made through a single channel on this side" and that it was proper for France at first to approach the same source in its discussions of "financial ways and means," "this house [i.e., J.P. Morgan] felt that this primary approach placed it in a leading position for future discussions."[60] Having admitted, also in later remarks, to some typical Wall Street rivalries and Morgan's position within the system, he also agreed that there was not "the greatest cooperation on the part of our unorganized financial resources." In fact Vanderlip expressed disappointment in not "obtaining on this side the financial cooperation to which any consideration of historic friendship and personal interest ought to have led." By way of explanation, he referred to the large debts that the United States still had abroad from earlier years. The country had made "strenuous efforts to pay our foreign debtors what we owed them" so that it would have been "unwise" to do more for one of the belligerents. Moreover, talks that were held at the time with the Department of State in Washington, which was anxious to preserve strict official neutrality, had merely resulted "in some utterances unfavorable to this country engaging in any large loan to belligerents." Fortunately, after the "helter-skelter" start of British and French purchases in the United States and a loan largely negotiated by Morgan, centralized purchasing had brought some order and stability. Due to Morgan's dominance there had been further tensions over the fact that one institution, that is, Morgan, "was making very great profits." In short, early disorganization had been followed by reluctant cooperation.

Last, but by no means least, there was the problem of the larger number of German Americans, among whom there was "a small minority of opinion favorable to the German cause," even if "speaking broadly, there is practically but one sentiment outside of those who by racial ties are naturally committed to Germany, and that sentiment is wholly with the Allies." Although the sinking of the *Arabic* by a German submarine that had meanwhile occurred had "not yet [been] digested," it could well be that pro-Allied sympathies became "crystallized into a positive alliance." But, as Vanderlip concluded, the country as a whole still "does not want war" and was "woefully unprepared for it."

The continuing general reluctance of the population also explains the lack of investments in foreign securities, which in turn was also related to the developing military situation on the Western Front and in Russia. There was also the fact that some corporations, such as Union

Pacific, were, under their charters, not allowed to hold foreign securities. Finally, it had to be considered that "in the boards of many institutions there may be one at least among the directors who is of German origin and strenuously objects to his institution giving financial aid to the enemies of the Fatherland." In the end, though, Vanderlip, in his letter to Poniatowski, felt compelled to return to his more general pessimism about "the consequences that may flow from this unprecedented struggle." Occasionally, it is true, there were references to the recovery of the United States from the destruction of the Civil War. But whatever the differences, Vanderlip expressed his faith in the ultimate redemption of the obligations that Britain and France had entered into, even if the burdens were great.

In the end, he asked his correspondent in Paris what he thought should be done. The Allies needed a minimum of $500 million between now and 1 January 1916. Should they meet that new obligation by shipping gold that the United States did not need? "Indeed, it would be a dangerous thing for us to have it." Gold would merely add to the strong reserves that banks held already, stimulating "sooner or later" further inflation. Hence other ways of repayment had to be found. A certain amount of British securities might still be placed in the United States, but the country had no appetite for taking more French or Russian government bonds, and confidence even in Britain's national efficiency had been shaken.

While all these dilemmas arose from the ever more astronomical costs of the war on the Allied side, the German-American relationship continued to deteriorate. As we have seen, Bethmann-Hollweg succeeded in pouring oil on the rough seas after the *Lusitania* and *Arabic* disasters. In 1916, there was another incident involving the *Sussex*. While Wilson was looking for ways of bringing about negotiations for an armistice and eventual "peace without victory," Washington also stepped up its military preparedness, perhaps also because, beyond all Anglophilia among the business community, there was disappointment not only with German but also with British policy making. As Vanderlip put it in August 1915, "the decadence of England's national virility, of which we have heard so much in the last few years and seen evidences of in her political and labor troubles" had "really come to the surface very prominently during the past year."[61] Of course "out of this war, if the Allies win, there may come a new national spirit, but England today is certainly facing the greatest crisis in her history and one which might easily take away some of her imperial prestige."

For a long time the populations in the Midwest in particular remained opposed to a direct American involvement in the war. However, by early 1917 this mood had begun to change, and not just because of the German resumption of unrestricted submarine warfare in February. At that time at the latest even the more pro-German businessmen had given up their neutralism in despair. In the case of Jacob Schiff of Kuhn, Loeb & Co., it was the outbreak of the Russian February Revolution that had pushed him to abandon his opposition, with his bank announcing that they were now "prepared to enter Allied financing if they are wanted."[62] Meanwhile the Anglophile Vanderlip felt that NCB was in good shape "to meet any strain that will come as a result of war, if we are to have war." This was so despite the fact that by then "we are loaning twice the French amount through Morgan to the English interests."[63] Of course, as a precaution Vanderlip had segregated "the collateral which is American securities with a very ample margin of foreign securities."[64]

5. The American Entry into the War and the Dilemmas of Peacemaking

The prospect that the United States would abandon their neutrality also shifted the burdens of war finance that had hitherto fallen on the private sector. By the end of March 1917, there arose the "possibility of a very large Government bond issue," if the country did "what it seems to me we ought to do—[i.e.,] give a great credit to the allies or certainly to France."[65] When, on 6 April, America found itself at war with Germany, it was clear that expenditures would rise even more steeply than people had ever imagined. Now Washington took the lead in initiating bond issues, seized German vessels anchored in American ports, and intervened much more directly in the domestic economy. Following European precedent, war boards were set up. Given that the country had no compulsory military service, mobilizing and preparing American men for combat on the Western Front proved difficult. Without a standing army, it took almost a year before American troops arrived in northern France. But they landed just in time to support the French and British in their effort to repulse the German offensive of March 1918.

This was the kaiser's last major push to achieve victory in the west only a few weeks after signing the Treaty of Brest-Litovsk, which, following the Bolshevik Revolution of November 1917, had secured an end to the war in the east.[66] By July, the American contingent had increased to close to two million, and this force made a major contribution to stopping the German offensive. With the tide now reversing and the German army collapsing, Wilhelm II was told by General Erich Ludendorff and his other military advisors that the war had been lost. It was time to negotiate an armistice with the Western Allies, which was finally signed on 11 November 1918. The United States had lost around 113,000 men. Some 220,000 had been wounded.

In light of America's great military-industrial potential, which merely had to be mobilized to tip the scales, Wilson sent a set of peace proposals to Congress on 8 January 1918, divided into Fourteen Points.[67] Some of these referred to territorial claims and demands for autonomy and self-determination, especially in East-Central Europe. But the most revolutionary clauses postulated an end to traditional secret diplomacy, a reduction of armaments, freedom of the seas, and a general association of nations "for the purpose of affording mutual guarantees of political independence and territorial integrity to great and small states alike."

If it was one of Wilson's peace aims to "make the world safe for democracy" and to usher in a new era of international relations, his program ran into trouble for the first time during the armistice negotiations with Germany. Anxious to avoid serious conflicts with Britain and France, he had already withdrawn the idea to secure the "freedom of the seas" that the British government was opposed to. The French then succeeded in upending the American negotiating position on reparations: the defeated countries and Germany in particular would now be expected to pay for the damage they had caused. By the time the peace conference opened in Paris in the spring of 1919, several cracks had appeared in the wartime alliance.[68] At a most fundamental level it had become clear that neither Britain nor France was genuinely interested in creating the kind of new diplomacy that Wilsonian idealism represented. At one end of the spectrum were the Bolsheviks, who were not represented at the conference table and who were promoting a radical revolutionary vision of a new world order based on Marxism-Leninism. At the other end stood Wilson's Western Allies who wanted to continue a diplomacy that was based on national interest and traditional power politics. The French position, strongly supported by the population, was also guided by its understandable desire to gain security against its neighbor to the east against whom they had fought two major wars in 1870 and 1914. British public opinion, already in a high state of agitation and bitterness over the huge losses in human lives and wealth and worried about the cohesion of its Empire, had been whipped up further by Lloyd George's jingoistic campaign during the national elections in the fall of 1918.[69]

If the "special relationship" between the British and Americans had been strengthened during the war, it was now beginning to fray, first at the Paris Peace Conference. In 1920–21 there were attempts at cooperation, which came under strain again at the time of the Genoa Conference in 1922, to be examined later in this chapter. Ultimately, Wilson's wartime Allies' resistance to his peace aims at Paris became so disconcerting to him that he dug in his heels. But the conference majority, led by Britain and France, ultimately got its way, and their victory became enshrined in a number of peace treaties signed by the vanquished in various Parisian suburbs. The most important among them, also in terms of the future development of international economic and political relations, was the treaty signed by Germany at Versailles in June 1919. It contained not only some quite painful territorial losses, a demilitarization of the Rhineland, a drastic reduction of the country's armed forces to one hundred thousand men, and reparations clauses that soon became the object of very sharp contention, but also the Covenant of the League of Nations, the first large international organization in history. Wilson had viewed this organization as a guarantor of the new diplomacy that he had been pushing for during and immediately after the war.

The Covenant was an incomplete work. Its clauses put to rest the Wilsonian principle of self-determination. In contradiction to this principle, East-Central Europe saw the emergence of states that comprised several nationalities and ethnic groups. The consideration of the peacemakers here was to create larger entities, such as Yugoslavia, Czechoslovakia, and Poland, that were strong enough to act as a cordon sanitaire against the Bolshevik "bacillus" to the east, while at the same time facilitating the containment of a militarily weakened but demographically and economically still strong Germany, now situated between France and a belt of Eastern European states with which Paris subsequently concluded separate alliance agreements. Meanwhile, the peoples in the European colonial empires, who, partly in response to Wilson's proclamations, had founded national unification movements of their own, were denied self-determination, and many of them had to wait until after World War II before achieving independence, often after bloody wars of liberation against European colonialism. Finally, the territories that had been under the rule of the now collapsed Ottoman Empire as well as Germany's former colonies were put under a Mandates system.[70] Its inhabitants were told that they would continue to be administered by foreign powers, mainly France and Britain, until they were deemed to be ready for independence. The nationalist ferment that this delay created in Asia and Africa finally exploded after World War II, leading to the creation of a welter of new nation-states.

However, this is not the place to discuss the problems of the Paris Peace Conference in more than broadest outline. The point is that when Wilson returned to the United States and these results, which bore the hallmark of the old international order, were put to the U.S. Senate for approval, its members were split into three factions: supporters of the president and his bid to obtain ratification, the "irreconcilables" who totally opposed the Versailles Treaty and the League of Nations, and the "reservationists" who were prepared for the United States to join the new international organization, but only if certain conditions were fulfilled and a number of amendments inserted. In order to swing the balance in favor of passage, the president began to tour the country to appeal directly to the people and thus to exert pressure on the senators. It was on this tour that he suffered a breakdown on 2 October 1919, followed by a stroke. On 19 March 1920 the Senate rejected America's accession to the League of Nations.[71]

No less disastrous for the future of Europe and European-American relations was that the peace with Germany was also not accepted, since the Covenant had, rather incongruously, been made part of the Versailles Treaty. It was only eighteen months later that the United States signed a separate peace with Germany (and also with Austria and Hungary, the two truncated remnants of the Austro-Hungarian Empire). By this time the popular mood in the United States had also turned more firmly against any further political and economic commitments to Europe. The "isolationist impulse" among parts of the American population proved stronger than the country's desire to reach out into the postwar world, as advocated by an assortment of East Coast industrial and commercial elites engaged in international trade.[72] In these circumstances the Europeans were largely left to sort out on their own the truly staggering socioeconomic and political legacies of World War I.

6. American Big Business and European Reconstruction

This is therefore the point at which to look more closely at the relationships that American big business developed with Britain and Germany after World War I. The best way to move into the larger question of American businessmen's perceptions and policies toward these two economies and toward Europe more generally is to begin with Frank Vanderlip. Time and again, he had raised his influential voice on the topics of the day in letters to friends, colleagues, and men involved in the Wilson administration. He had also firmly committed himself to the organization of the war effort. He was put in charge of the government's "war savings certificate program" and actively contributed to the war effort in many other ways.[73]

But in early 1919, he decided to leave the NCB at age fifty-five. At the time, there was a good deal of press speculation as to why he had taken this step. There were rumors that he had fallen out with James Stillman, who had expressed a desire to take over the NCB presidency.[74]

Retrospectively, Vanderlip wrote to W. S. Cassell in 1933 that, as the "relinquishing of the presidency was what I wished," he had signaled his intention to the board, provided that "my stock in the bank (I was the second largest stock-holder at the time) was taken at a price that was satisfactory to me." Although "some members of the Board rather vigorously objected," a settlement was eventually reached between the Rockefellers, Stillman, and Vanderlip that was satisfactory to the three parties. It seems therefore more likely that he was simply exhausted from the stresses and strains that his many jobs and activities had imposed upon him. He wanted to be free of daily chores in order to be able to read and travel and to use his great knowledge and experience to write articles and books that would influence American elite opinion.

He, who had always had wider intellectual interests, had become wealthy enough to live a more contemplative life. To be able to step back and to take a more long-term view of the future may also have been related to the fact that from the start of the war he had always seen the destructive effects of a conflict that had become ever more total, devouring millions of human lives and huge material resources all around the globe. He never doubted that the American economic and political system was strong and resilient enough to withstand the shock and secure victory against Germany and its allies.[75] When it was all over, he hoped for the inauguration of a successful reconstruction program, provided that it was launched without delay. At the same time, he found it impossible to join the optimists in the business community who expected a quick and almost automatic general recovery under the leadership of the greatly strengthened United States with its highly productive industries and powerful banks.

After his resignation from NCB, Vanderlip spent the spring of 1919 in Western Europe. His analyses of the situation there are to be found, in the first instance, in a number of letters that he wrote to friends and politicians after his return. Their tone is quite different from the optimism that many American companies exuded in the summer of 1919. Writing to W. B. Wilson, the U.S. secretary of labor, on 20 May 1919, he was quite firm that "a return to prewar conditions at an early stage" was "impossible."[76] He had found industry and agriculture in Europe "completely disorganized." Production costs would remain high "for some time to come which will affect world prices." He realized how important exports had become in peacetime for an industrial system that had been greatly expanded for military production and now, that the conflict was over and conversion to civilian production took place, had to find new markets. Accordingly and as early as November 1918, he submitted a plan to improve the efficiency and quality of American production to William Redfield, the secretary of commerce in the

Wilson administration.[77] It was to be "the basis of a movement which would be of great value to our industries and to our people" and "one of the incidental results would be a great stride in foreign trade." Recommending a certification system for American goods, he wrote, "We know, as we get into the scientific management business, how essential it is, in buying large quantities of material, to have some authoritative knowledge of what it is we are buying." While he encouraged the government to set an example, he also felt that "many large business organizations now [similarly] see the wisdom of having a real scientific knowledge of the quality and character of the things they buy."

The problem was that this efficiency drive to increase foreign trade was of limited use if the trading partners were distressingly weak. As he wrote on 7 July 1919 after his trip to Europe,[78] "Just now, with a fresh view of the suffering of Europe in my mind, I feel that the world is really in a very seriously troubled state." A "serious disorganization" was part of "the economic breakdown in Europe." Anglophile that he was, he had spent some part of his trip to Europe in Britain and now reported to Frank Trumbull, a British friend in Ashdown Forest, that he very much appreciated the "difficulties of the English situation" and the pressures of American competition that had vexed British industry long before 1914:[79] "We are sending ship-plates to England" and have "recently successfully bid on rails for the Glasgow tramways." In New England he was told that "they are now making cotton goods actually [at a] lower [price there] than they are at Lancaster," one of the traditional centers of the British textile industry. Worse, they were "opening up a large market in the Far East." In a letter to H. S. Pritchett in California of 16 July 1919, he confessed that he was glad to be relieved of his NCB job.[80] But not only the Russian but also the Western European situation had made him pessimistic: "The march of events in Europe seems to me to pretty well dovetail with the conclusion which I had in mind when I returned."

Pessimism was also more generally the thread running through a book that he wrote during his return sea journey on the basis of a diary that he had kept while traveling in Europe.[81] Published soon after, it garnered considerable public attention and led to invitations to give lectures about his experiences in Europe. It must be seen as a key document relating to banking and big business at this time. Vanderlip began with a description of economic conditions in northern France with its battlefields before he went on: "In picturing the devastating effect of the war on European industry, however, one must not confine the view to the Hindenburg line." Important industries were also destroyed in Poland. Some four hundred thousand had starved there in the fighting between the Russian and German armies. Now "that great territory, the size of Kansas, is barren and without means of sustaining life. The industry of Warsaw was systematically sacked, as was that of most cities on the eastern front." Romania, once a major exporter of grain, would, as its prime minister had told him, "be able to raise this year only a sufficient amount of food for her own population." Finally, "Serbia was utterly despoiled." He concluded, "If it were possible to show the exact percentage of the industrial life of Europe which has been sacrificed with shell, bomb, and incendiary torch, it would be seen that the destruction, vast as it is, bears no overwhelming relation to the whole."

Why, Vanderlip then asked, will it be so difficult to revive European industry? He suggested to leave aside the industries of the devastated regions in northern France and to take "an unharmed industrial plant in any place located in the interior of any one of several countries." He enumerated a few of these difficulties and then "let any American manufacturer try to imagine [that] his plant [was] faced with such a series of difficulties." He ventured to speculate that this manufacturer, too, would have found them insurmountable. To begin with, there was the breakdown of the system of domestic transportation, compounded by the problem of a lack of raw materials, most of which had to be imported. Next there was the question of finding customers who were able to pay for finished goods. In Scandinavia or Spain they would probably have the means to settle their debt, but not in many other nations, especially those in Eastern Europe. The latter were all scrambling to obtain credit. All in all, there was a great need for goods, "but the difficulties surrounding their production and marketing are so great that up to the present time there is a condition of idleness" that was unprecedented. And so Vanderlip had come home convinced that "there can be no secure peace until the way is found to supply . . . credits to all industrial centers."

After further analysis of the transportation problems, Vanderlip devoted a whole chapter to the British predicament. He reminded his readers, perhaps a bit too diplomatically, that "at no time prior to the war did she cease to make progress, although Germany and the United States in later years progressed on so much more rapid a scale that England's premier position was being endangered." He thought that the impression of the country "that is in the mind of the average American manufacturer who is looking forward to international competition" is that British industries had "greatly benefited by the war," as was true of the American ones. There was also the belief "that the war would result in a great revival in British industry." It was these notions upon which Vanderlip then poured a lot of cold water. Apart from poor housing conditions, average wages were lower "than the point at which physical efficiency of labor could be maintained." There had been little economic change from before 1914 at home. As far as international trade before the war was concerned, "the great customer of England was the continent of Europe." Indeed, that market had been "essential" for earning "the margin that she requires for her food imports from other countries."

However, Britain's European markets had experienced "an almost inconceivable disorganization." So, unless the economies of Continental Europe were brought back to life, Britain would not be able to regain those markets. Worse than that, "our own position in international industrial markets will be in large measure influenced by England's ability to continue successfully to compete in those markets." The general European disarray and paralysis had now resulted in "a rapidly growing army of unemployed which was increasing directly as the demobilization of the army proceeded." These workers had to be found jobs. Only then was there some hope that, if realized, would carry "the future of England's industry . . . beyond anything ever dreamed of."

In another chapter on the perilous state of France Vanderlip praised it for never having "stopped to count the price in courage and manhood that she must pay to defend herself from the Hun." Maybe it was this disdain for the Germans that he did not inspect and discuss the state of the German economy. Although its industry moved to the center of the stage again a few years later, conditions were as desperate as those of Britain. To give just a few indices, by the middle of 1918 the provision of foodstuffs, if measured against one hundred points in 1913, had reached twelve index points for meat, five for fish, thirteen for eggs, and seven for vegetables. In 1920 coal production compared with 1913 stood at two-thirds, iron at one-third, and steel at 50 percent. The consumer price index had quadrupled since 1914 and the cost of living in 1920 had risen more than eightfold.

It is against this background that Vanderlip unfolded a plan that he thought could still save the situation: truly massive American credit. In fact, "the role that American banks can play in the credit situation in Europe is of vast importance and, if they will hold firmly to the line of sound commercial banking it is a role which they can play with security and profit." However, this strategy, he continued, had to be accompanied by an American-style liberal capitalism that was based on "comfort and liberty," and not just for a small dominant minority, but for all. After all, America was, in his view, "the greatest of democracies, pledged to the sovereign rule of majorities," while the country "should beware of the power of minorities." Accordingly, what had struck him "as most significant" in the state of Britain was "the changed and liberalized attitude of employers." Vanderlip felt he had encountered this attitude among businessmen whom he had interviewed and whom he now quoted at length. The country, his interlocutors had reportedly said, would be efficient if it had a forty-eight-hour week and security against unemployment for its workforce as well as greater worker control. Here the "final step is to give labor a real interest in the profits in the business." This would be "the lowest price at which the capitalistic regime can buy itself off from the danger of revolution," that is, the threat of Bolshevism that was constantly on the mind of not only Vanderlip but also most other American businessmen in this period.

Even though the news that the banker brought back from his European trip was gloomy, he did not throw up his arms in despair. On the contrary, he not only was convinced that this was the great opportunity for American banking to help Europe to get back on its feet, but also asked the question, "Is New York to become the financial center of the world?" That, he added, was "a question which first arose in the minds of boasting ignorance [before the war]; but today it has become a question that is entitled to be asked in seriousness, examined with care, and answered in the light of new conditions." This led him to a discussion of the advantages that the London City still had over the Americans. So, even if Wall Street could not yet replace London, he was convinced that the former would most certainly become "the depository of a great part of the international bank balances coming from every quarter of the world," not least because the United States had now moved from its prewar status as a debtor nation to being a creditor country. Furthermore, "we are the greatest producers of food and raw materials and minerals in the world" so that "for years to come our commodity trade balance seems likely to run several hundred million a year in our favor."

7. The Idea of an International Loan for European Reconstruction and Its Failure

In Vanderlip's eyes, the United States therefore had a great opportunity to develop a plan for the reconstruction of Europe. Certainly, the country could not simply stand apart "from the rest of the international system." Consequently, he now proposed an "international loan to Europe." No time was to be lost, also in light of the ever-present Bolshevik threat: "Unless there is speedy action in the direction of restarting paralyzed industry, there may follow a quick march of events toward revolutionary outbreaks in any country where idleness is continued and is followed by hunger and want." Given the size of the international loan that would be required, it was in his view necessary to mobilize the entire financial sector. Waiting for government participation would take too long, as all legislation had to pass through U.S. Congress. Having discussed the question of loan security and other principles, Vanderlip made his appeal for the kind of huge loan that he was thinking of, "to be participated in by the United States of America, the Netherlands, the Scandinavian countries, Switzerland, Japan, those South American countries which are important exporters to Europe, and Great Britain, although the latter to perhaps a limited amount, if British interests so desired."

This "peace loan" was to be supervised by an International Loan Commission, headquartered "in the Peace Palace at The Hague." The commission "would determine from the facts regarding the industrial situation in each of the possible borrowing countries, the proportionate allocation of parts of the total loan to each borrowing nation." At a later date, the commission would also decide, "in conjunction with representatives from the borrowing nations, the definite amounts of machinery, raw material, rolling stock, etc., which should be furnished." The borrowers would "pledge a first lien upon its customs revenue to meet the interest and amortization service of that portion of the international loan allocated to that particular nation." This, so Vanderlip ended his book, would be the first step toward "furnishing the minimum necessary to restart industry in all European nations concurrently." To make certain that he would be heard in Washington, he wrote a memorandum [titled "1919 in Genoa, Report No. 4"] that he submitted to Colonel Edward House, Wilson's advisor at the Paris Peace Conference, proposing "that Europe must issue Receivers' certificates, that is to say that new loans should rank in front of all other indebtedness."[82] He repeated his idea of "a great international loan, the proceeds of which should be so administered as to best serve the reconstruction of industry" and then added, "The Conference of leading London financiers" later resolved "that they would be willing to join America substantially in making such a loan."

There can be little doubt that this was a very farsighted plan that might, in some ways, be compared with the Marshall Plan after 1945, when the United States, having learned the bitter lessons of interwar politics and economics and having won another world war that it did not want, promoted the reconstruction of Western Europe, again in the face of a widely perceived threat of Bolshevism. This story will be presented in chapter VI where the differences with the post-1918 situation will also have to be discussed.[83] This later development, too, will be analyzed in terms of the central theme of this book, first against the background of the current chapter, then for the period 1922–33 in chapter IV, ending with the Great Slump of 1929 and the rise of Nazi Germany, and finally for the years of World War II and the post-1945 decades.

It seems that Vanderlip was not alone with his plan. As early as April 1919, *WSJ* had carried an article announcing that "U.S. bankers prepare to finance Europe." By September the paper estimated that Europe needed some $5 billion as credits. Fearing a collapse of trade, John McHugh, the chair of the Commerce and Marine Division of the American Bankers Association, proposed in early 1920 to convert some $4 billion held by American investors in short-term bills of exchange into long-term investments to "open up again the flow of our [American] goods [to Europe] where they have ceased to flow." He also tried to give this program an institutional foundation with the help of an "Edge corporation organized as a debenture bank" whose debentures would attract savings from depositors "in banks outside the main centers (New York, Chicago, Cleveland, Detroit, and San Francisco)."

There are also the ideas of former Secretary of Commerce Redfield, now president of the American Manufacturers Export Association, who took an even more long-term view than McHugh. As he put it, the problem of American manufacturers did not lie "in our lack of competing power." Rather it was that, without branch banking of its own, all American "drafts went through banks owned by our competing countries." The challenge was therefore for American business to show "vision and courage to do a very simple thing . . . [i.e., to] put American money into American-owned and American-run and American-controlled industries around the globe."[84]

Such statements show the frustrations that many American bankers and manufacturers felt that so much of international business was not transacted through New York, Chicago, or California, but through foreign banks and the City in particular. This was to be changed. New York was to become the center of global finance, so that Britain, which had already been squeezed out of its prime place in manufacturing, would also be relegated to playing second fiddle in the world of finance. It was a strategy without which the subsequent treatment of Britain in the 1920s and beyond World War II and that country's resistance to it cannot be understood. Redfield's vision should also be seen against the backdrop of the passage of the 1918 Webb-Pomerene Act, which mitigated the strict antitrust rules of the Sherman Act. American firms were now permitted to cooperate in international trade without fear of being prosecuted by the Department of Justice.[85]

While Vanderlip's book had a positive reception at the time, the aim of the rest of this chapter is to hold his proposals against the realities that existed first during 1919 and then to look at developments that turned the dire situation that he had encountered during his trip into a general European socioeconomic collapse. This was followed by outbreaks of political violence and attempts in 1923 at emulating the example of

Benito Mussolini's Fascist seizure of power in the previous year, that is, to overthrow, especially in Germany, the constitutional order that had been built, very precariously, in 1918–19. Once again the United States, Britain, and Germany played a key role in these developments. It took the virtual collapse of the German economy and a major crisis in the French one to find a way out, this time successfully and with the active help of American bankers and industry.

8. The State of the American, British, and French Economies in the Early 1920s

A good starting point would seem to be to look at the state of the American economy at the end of the war. By becoming a major supplier of food and military hardware to Britain and France and, from April 1917, also to its own war effort, American industry experienced a great expansion of its capacities. One indicator of this was the additional factory space that had been created. In 1915 it had amounted to some 64 million square feet; by 1918 it was 181 million. Between 1914 and 1919 the number of employees in the car industry alone rose by 162 percent from approximately 127,000 to about 343,000. Electricity generation increased threefold and iron production doubled to 37.5 million tons by 1920, far outpacing Britain's at 8.2 million and Germany's at 6.4 million tons.

The U.S. merchant fleet now occupied second place behind Britain's, with a tonnage that had quadrupled since 1914 to 9.77 million. In 1918, the tonnage of merchant vessels built in American shipyards was twice the British one. Since freight rates had risen over sevenfold during the war, shipping companies kept placing large orders with the shipbuilding industry. These additional capacities were crucial to the ultimate winning of the war, but they were bound to pose a problem for the period after 1918. There was, it is true, some pent-up domestic demand due to the wartime emergency. But partly because the American involvement in World War I was relatively brief, living standards did not decline markedly and there had been no rationing as in Britain or food shortages and mass starvation as in Germany. Of course, in no way should it be forgotten that the American statistics reflected national averages and that poverty levels in the United States remained high among the lower classes and some ethnic groups, especially among African Americans in the still segregationist South and the slums of cities such as New York.[86] In this respect, the global figures of large-scale studies never tell the full story. But the literature on the more detailed picture of living conditions in various parts of the country is readily available.

As was to be expected, American industry first tried to satisfy domestic demand, which turned out to be a flash in the pan, and "postwar restocking" and export initiatives soon also ran into trouble. Domestic iron production slumped by 50 percent to 16.5 million tons by 1921, that of copper even by 80 percent; automobile output shrank by 50 percent. Soon both industrial workers and farmers were being hit hard by a slump, as wholesale prices kept rising from 100 index points in 1915 to 228 by 1920 before sinking back to 150 points in 1921. The early optimism about domestic demand now evaporated very quickly. On 15 January 1919, *Forbes* gave as total war damage the figure of $13.2 billion, which, the journal hoped, meant "heavy purchases of U.S. materials" by Europe.[87] The article was full of statistics about European needs and lists of what those countries would therefore want to buy from the United States. The huge losses in British shipping would, it was said, be replaced. The hopes and fears that these developments generated in American manufacturing circles must be seen together with the information on domestic and international conditions that circulated among the financial community.

Although it is difficult to know how much direct exchange there was between the bankers and the big manufacturing corporations about the situation, both were in touch with the politicians and bureaucrats in Washington and certainly both wanted something to be done long before oversupply at home put the economy into reverse gear. Creating an export outlet for surpluses required credits that would stimulate demand for American goods in Europe, much of whose own wealth had been destroyed by the war. What were the prospects of this? Judging from the available statistics, they looked good at first. In 1919, American exports reached $5.2 billion and generated a surplus of $4 billion. But, calculated in current dollars, this figure had dropped to $2.1 billion by 1921. In 1922, the surplus was a mere $700,000, reflecting a declining demand in Europe. It was exacerbated by insufficient credit that only the United States could furnish. Yet, its banks were merely prepared to give short-term loans and—a further complaint of industry—all too frequently to American agriculture, whose food exports to starving Europe were much in demand and certain to be paid for without long delays.

Thus in 1920, the United States exported grain to the value of $57.7 million, rising to $104.7 million in 1921; meat and meat product exports rose from $46.0 million in 1919 to $56.4 million a year later, before dropping to $49.0 million in 1921. The value of cotton exports quadrupled from 1919 to 1920 to $110.6 million and stayed at this level in 1921. But other industries that had expanded during the war were deeply worried about their future and were looking for export opportunities to Europe to complement declining domestic demand. How did things look in Europe?

Starting with Britain, the postwar boom there that lasted for a little over a year from the spring of 1919 was in effect due to an inflationary boost.[88] By March 1920 wholesale prices had increased by 200 percent in comparison to July 1914. Iron and steel production illustrates the severity of the subsequent slump particularly well, the more so since it was made worse by a decline in orders from manufacturing industry and a three-month strike by the miners in the spring of 1921. By July of that year all steelmaking had come to a standstill, so that by the end of the year steel production was 40 percent below its peak in 1917. Iron production was even lower at 25 percent of its 1913 peak. The downturn in coal production in comparison to 1913 was over 50 percent. Shipbuilding that, like the United States, witnessed an upswing after 1918 had dropped to some 38 percent from its peak in the fourth quarter of 1920.

The psychological impact of all this on the population was made worse by the British government's wartime promise to reintegrate returning soldiers into their former jobs. There was also the hope of job creation through investments and imports by its American ally. With the levels of poverty high, Whitehall focused on the expansion of welfare programs to provide not only for disabled veterans but also for war widows and orphans. To make things worse, the labor reintegration program was much less successful than expected. By June 1921, the British unemployment rate reached 23.1 percent so that some 2.1 million Britons and their families had to rely on welfare benefits.[89] The annual average for the year was 15.3 percent, to which must be added some one million in part-time work. Clearly, government and Parliament had to do something about these conditions. The 1920 National Insurance Act brought some 12 million Britons into this particular system of welfare. Another wartime promise to provide better housing at affordable rents had been created by the 1919 Housing Act. None of these measures were able to stem a rising tide of protests and demonstrations that reached a first peak on Armistice Day in 1922.

Badly battered by these developments, British businessmen, headed by the Federation of British Industries (FBI), responded with attempts to rationalize production, streamline management, and put pressure on the workforce to work longer and harder and to accept lower wages. While the government and the Labour Party were in basic agreement with FBI strategy, tensions arose over the level of dividends and over whether the reduction of high prices should come before wage reductions. In short, it was not in a condition to pay for American imports, and the plight of Britain was therefore another reason why the early postwar boom in the United States was running out of steam.

In France, economic problems arose not so much in the south of the country, where agriculture was still dominant, but in the industrial North.[90] If factories had not been leveled by the fighting, the Germans had flooded the mines and wrecked the iron works on their retreat in 1918. During the war female industrial labor had increased quite tangibly. Thus the Renault car factories employed a mere 4 percent of women in 1914. By 1918 the percentage was 31.6. However, in order to create jobs for returning soldiers, women were urged to devote themselves to their families and to have children. As a result the number of births did in fact rise from 313,000 in 1913 to 403,500 in 1919—a welcome increase in light of the high wartime losses of men and the traditional French fear of being demographically far behind Germany, their dangerous eastern neighbor. All these measures did not prevent massive protests. Lorraine's miners went on strike as early as 1919, followed by the metal workers, railroad workers, and white-collar employees in 1920, and on 1 May of that year the Confédération Générale du Travail (CGT) called for a general strike. As elsewhere in Europe, there was pressure on the government in Paris to look after the victims of the war. French casualties had been twice as high as Britain's (1.34 million as against 700,000). So, it was not only the disabled veterans who were clamoring for support, but also widows and orphans.

9. American Big Business and the Postwar Crisis in Germany

A few German key figures on the collapse of production, the undersupply of basic foodstuffs, and inflation in 1918–19 were given a moment ago. Economic deprivation was exacerbated by the chaos resulting from the November Revolution and the civil war that followed in 1919 between leftist radicals in the industrial centers of the country and the Free Corps units. The latter had been raised to stop attempts by German Bolsheviks, inspired by the Leninist revolution in Russia, to seize power.[91] As far as the reestablishment of economic relations with the United States was concerned, there was a good deal of perfectly understandable hatred of the Germans who were blamed for having unleashed the war and for causing the death of millions.

Playing on popular feelings, anti-German articles continued to appear in the American business press. Thus, on 3 June 1919 *WSJ* published a piece about the Versailles Treaty that warned,[92] "So long as the

well-known qualities of arrogance, impertinence, bad faith and hypocrisy go to make up the German mind, it is impossible to argue with the
German." Referring to the question of responsibility for the outbreak
of the war, the paper added, "Germany cannot say she did not know
that going to war meant risking all she had." But even if the Allies took
"all she has in public and private" property, "the damage inflicted by
Germany would not be made good."

Inevitably perhaps, there was also hostility toward German firms,
most expressly with regard to the chemical industry that reveals much
about pre-1914 German-American rivalries, discussed in chapter II.
On 28 December 1918, *Forbes* announced somewhat triumphantly,[93]
"Germany thought she had us eating out of her hands" in the field of
chemicals, and this may have been true before the war. But now "our
chemists have produced as good dyestuffs as Germany was ever able
to make, and moreover we have not only equaled the skills of the Huns
in producing pigments for the coloring of cotton, woolens, and silk fab-
rics, but we have in some instances excelled them." Consequently, the
"nation is now independent of German supplies of dyes and potash."
The article concluded, "For our entire chemical industry, the war has
undoubtedly been a blessing in disguise. We have long been possessed
of the materials and the technical brains for the work, but before the
war we lacked the plants and the incentives to bestir ourselves to bring
our production of chemicals up to its proper place in relation to the
world's output." If true, this was certainly a striking reversal of fortunes in the chemical industries. And yet, behind this so blatantly articulated animosity, cooperation quietly resumed in this branch of industry as in others.[94]

Many American companies—anxious to revive prewar markets in
Europe—took a pragmatic approach. Even before Washington relaxed
the restrictions of the Trading with the Enemy Act in the summer of
1919, American firms had made contact with their German counterparts. As early as October 1919 the Berlin government signed an agreement with Standard Oil—before 1914 an unwelcome trust with a tendency to dominate—to deliver oil and gasoline. American farmers tried
to sell their surplus production to starving Germans. In June 1920 the
HAPAG shipping firm made an agreement with the American Ship
and Commerce Company (which was part of the Harriman empire)
to cooperate. Two months later, North German Lloyd followed suit by
signing a contract with the U.S. Mail Steamship Company. While this
helped to restore disrupted transatlantic shipping links, the resumption
of contact between Walther Rathenau's AEG and General Electric, on
the one hand, and between Siemens and Westinghouse, on the other,
was no less significant. Other companies, most of which had invested

in and traded with Germany before 1914, also put out feelers, among them International Harvester, Otis, Singer, NCR, and the Guggenheim copper empire. The chemicals trusts also began to talk to each other with a view to reestablishing prewar cooperation and the sharing of patents that had been officially confiscated during the war.

All these efforts at exploiting the superior post-1918 international position of the United States were moderately successful in the very early postwar period. This was also a time when American banks were prepared to extend credit lines to agriculture and industry. They, too, harbored a good deal of optimism when they considered what had been destroyed by the war and—objectively correct—now ought to be replaced. But as Vanderlip had suggested in his book, much larger sums of money were required to finance these exports and European reconstruction. It was not just Vanderlip's reports on economic conditions in Europe but also their own observations that caused American big business to wonder whether they would ever get paid for their deliveries and whether the upheaval that the war had created in all spheres of life was so profound that Britain and Germany were not at all to be seen as the promising foreign market that the Americans were so eagerly looking for. Given these uncertainties in both the domestic and foreign markets, the recession finally hit the United States with full force in 1921.

10. American Big Business, Washington, and the Question of European Loans

Sensing the beginnings of this recession, America's financial institutions were reluctant to commit themselves without guarantees from the administration in Washington. They looked at the loans that had already been given during the war—before 1917 mainly by the private sector, and after the American entry into the war by the federal government. Even at that time there had been some question as to whether the British and the French would be able to repay those wartime loans and whether government loans had priority over private ones. After 1918 it was clearly even riskier to extend credit for postwar reconstruction, all the more so since the U.S. government refused to guarantee private loans and, given the political mood in the country, was even less inclined to commit any further official funds to Britain and France, let alone Germany. Due to the war, the gross domestic debt of the federal government had increased to $25.3 billion, over $10 billion of which had gone as loans to the Allies. Banks were prepared to grant short-term domestic loans and to some small extent also to Western Europe.

But what was needed was a long-term commitment to reconstruction from both the private and public sectors. Vanderlip's American-led international loan project required billions, not a few millions.

Before dealing with the further development of an already badly tangled situation, it is useful to return to Vanderlip's large correspondence with American business community. He was among the first whose mood had lapsed into pessimism. It is doubtful that he ever hoped that his grand European rescue plan with the Scandinavians and Swiss was more than a dream. If nothing else, achieving coordination with the banks in several countries was probably unrealistic in those years. If any one national economy could fulfill the role he had assigned in his plan, it was the American one. But only a few months after advancing his proposal, he wrote to the owner of the Robert Benson Company in London on 22 September 1919,[95] "There seems to have been nothing done in any adequate way in the direction of financing the needs of Europe." One reason for this was that Washington "has not been disposed to forward any comprehensive movement while awaiting the Ratification of the Peace Treaty, and the bankers have been so busy with important affairs flowing over their desks that they have not seemed to feel the necessity for coordinated action for mobilizing [the] credit that I believe is desirable." The United States, to be sure, might well experience a shock when the export drive of 1919 ran into trouble. Worse, Vanderlip could not see "how Europe can continue to pay for [American] exports on the scale that she has been paying unless new credit can be granted." Consequently he expected Europe to pass through an "extremely serious period" in "the next few months."

This meant, as he wrote to Ellery Sedgwick in Boston on 3 January 1920, that no loans to Europe would be forthcoming:[96] "In view of the great expansion of credit" that had already taken place, he doubted "whether we will be able to make loans" that Europe needed "if people are to be put back to work in time to save Europe from a financial breakdown." Certainly past European expenditures, large imports, and small exports had made a breakdown a serious possibility, and "what effect that would have on our own affairs seems to me but faintly comprehended."

Two months later, Vanderlip, writing to George Burnham in Philadelphia, put his finger on the main problem:[97] "The great difficulty in granting" credit to Europe "at the present time lies in the political instability of these governments." Not yet quite expecting an American recession, he continued that American manufacturers had large domestic markets and were hence reluctant to sell goods abroad when payment was so uncertain. This, Vanderlip admitted, opened up a "vicious circuit" that "in truth we have [already] been travelling." America's banks would not "give credit because there will be risk as long as there is industrial paralysis" in Europe. Conversely, "there will be industrial paralysis until credits can be obtained with which to pay for food and raw materials." Referring back to his book, he wrote, "The plan I proposed last May would have been large enough to have broken into that circuit." However, by March 1920 it had become "impossible to do anything on a large scale to make funds available between now and the next harvest." If the Europeans can tighten their belts till then, "some such plan might be helpful." But "our inertia will be in part to blame," should privations lead "to revolution in the meantime." Vanderlip could not have put the dilemmas of the moment more succinctly.

In a letter to Senator Maggiorino Ferraris, dated 19 March 1920, Vanderlip harkened back to what he had urged a year ago:[98] "Had we last May recognized the economic forces at work in Europe and mobilized credit in a comprehensive effort to start European industries, I think we could have accomplished a great deal." To be sure, some additional credit that had been given had resulted in an export surplus of $4 billion over imports. But he then enumerated once more the dangers of the situation: many European industries were still without food and raw materials, and bank credits had expanded "to a dangerous point of inflation." There were high taxes and, while the wealthy held back with their investments, not much capital was coming from small investors either. In short, American businessmen did not "dare . . . make fresh loans for fear that the governments are unstable" while the latter "cannot be stable when people are cold, idle, and hungry."

Vanderlip had reserved his worst fears for Central Europe, where revolutionary movements might lead "to the extension of the Bolshevik area." Indeed, only a week earlier he had written to Charles A. Stone, evidently with reference to the Right-radical anti-Republican Kapp Putsch in Berlin in March 1920, that, while the news of it was not "in the least surprising," it was nevertheless "the sort of thing that makes any serious consideration of immediate business enterprise of any kind, in Central Europe at least, out of the question."[99] Vanderlip's wavering between hope and pessimism continued into 1921. On 18 September, sitting in his room in the Grand Hotel in Florence, he described conditions between Europe and the United States to his colleague Dr. Norman Barnesby of the Bank of Commerce.[100] Those in America, he thought, were "so superior to those existing anywhere here that it makes one cheerful in comparison." Yet he was "by no means altogether pessimistic about European affairs." There may be "some financial smashes of governments, but Europe is [also] getting down to work." He believed that the region was "going to pull out of this awful mess." But a week later, he wrote to H. E. Benedict in New York: "I am extremely pessimistic about the financial conditions of several of the countries, particularly Austria and Germany, though industrial conditions" were looking up. This made him less pessimistic "overall" than he had been "two years ago." On 30 September 1921 he wrote in another letter to Benedict that the German mark was in the crisis that he had anticipated:[101] "I see nothing that can save it." In short, Vanderlip was at sea and so were his colleagues.

By the autumn of 1921 it had become increasingly clear to the big business community that the reconstruction of the European economies was foundering on a set of interrelated problems stemming from the terrible costs and sociopolitical legacies of World War I. The French were concerned not only about getting reparations payments from Germany but also about their military security against their eastern neighbor. Meanwhile, the German economy was going downhill even before an exact figure of Allied reparations demands had been agreed upon by all sides. The amount was expected to be sizeable also because the Americans were not prepared to cancel the wartime loans that they had given to Britain and France. As Stephen Schuker has shown, all attempts in Congress to reduce or even cancel those debts ran into strong opposition because the American taxpayer would have had to foot the bill.[102] This in turn made the American banking community increasingly unwilling to provide fresh credit on the scale that Vanderlip had outlined in his book. It might have been different if Washington had guaranteed long-term credits that were needed, but such guarantees were impossible to obtain as long as the popular mood was opposed to an official reengagement in Europe. Although the banks were in principle free to give credit, they were not prepared to take the full risk. Congress had to agree to be part of a deal, underwritten by American tax dollars, and that was impossible to achieve, at least as far as aid for Europe was concerned.

11. The Origins of the Washington System in the Far East

By 1921, American big business, facing a recession and looking for exports to sell its surplus production, was lobbying the administration to do something, and this time attention turned not to Europe but to the Far East and hence to transpacific relations that dated back to the pre-1914 period. Here it was to some extent a concern about the rise of Japan as an industrial power that had kept out of the war and was now also looking for markets in its immediate neighborhood on the Asian mainland. By focusing on Asia, there was also the realization that

the United States did not face in the Far East the same hopelessly in-
tractable problems as in Europe, with reparations, war loans, economic
exhaustion, unstable territorial border agreements, and high popular
emotions on all sides. Might it be easier in the Far East to put together
a set of agreements between the great powers that guaranteed territorial integrity, security, a reduction of armaments, and expanded trade
that a troubled American industry was desperately looking for in 1921
and that American public opinion was not reluctant (as with respect to
Europe) to support?

These were the calculations behind a diplomatic initiative, developed
by the U.S. administration, that led to a major international conference,
held in Washington from 12 November 1921 to 6 February 1922.[103] After
weeks of negotiations no fewer than three treaties were signed by the
invitees that became collectively known as the "Washington System."
Reminding the world that the United States was not just an Atlantic
power but also a Pacific one, it may be said to have represented the
postwar *Pax Americana* in Asia after the *Pax Americana* and the reconstruction plan that Vanderlip and others had in mind for Europe had
run into trouble and now had to wait until 1923–24. Without going
into the details of the negotiations in Washington during the winter of
1921–22, they ended in three international treaties:

1. A Four-Power Pact among the United States, Britain, France, and
   Japan that represented in a way an extension and enlargement of
   the British-Japanese accord of 1902, guaranteeing the territorial
   status quo in the Far East.

2. A Five-Power Pact among the United States, Britain, Japan, France,
   and Italy that limited the number of battleships deployed in the
   Pacific to ratios of 5 (United States) to 5 (Britain) to 3 (Japan) to
   1.75 (France) to 1.75 (Italy). The important point was that Japan
   accepted these ratios, although it was clear that they were also designed to contain Japanese naval power and as such created resentments that were to become virulent in the 1930s.

3. A Nine-Power agreement, signed on 6 February 1922, among the
   United States, Britain, France, Italy, China, the Netherlands, Belgium, Portugal, and Japan, securing equal commercial treatment
   for China, which also promised to establish a stable government.
   Put differently, this treaty introduced a principle that Wilson had
   been pushing for at the Paris Peace Conference, that is, the Open
   Door, that the other signatories—all of them, except for China, colonial powers—were otherwise anxious to maintain their possessions with their protectionist trade barriers.

Given that the myth and lure of the "unlimited China market" had been propagated before and that American industry was clamoring for unencumbered access to foreign markets, it was clear that big business welcomed not only the security arrangements but particularly also the opportunities for exports that the Washington System was expected to offer. But without this being loudly trumpeted, the Open Door in Asia was also directed against the Closed Door of preferential tariffs that the British, Dutch, Portuguese, Belgian, Italian, and French Empires had maintained and, indeed, promoted.

12. Britain's Rival Attempt to Spearhead a European Recovery Plan

It appears that these moves in the Far East and the American un-willingness or inability to forge a European Washington System in 1919–22, in turn stimulated the British government to try to take a lead in Europe where the Americans feared to tread. It will be remembered that Britain under Lloyd George's leadership had been among those powers at Paris that had opposed Wilson's ideas on self-determination, peace, and postwar prosperity. As Wilson had observed at the time "the British have appointed a lot of committees . . . to maintain Britain su-preme commercially all over the world." London and the other colonial powers hence thought it essential to preserve their empires with their protectionist tariffs. Thanks to the Paris Peace, they had even enlarged their possessions through the Mandates system under the League of Nations. This is where fresh cracks had appeared in the "special re-lationship" that the two Anglo-Saxon powers had forged during the war and that London was now hoping to perpetuate by inviting the United States to join a rescue operation of its own. But Washington re-mained suspicious of British motives, and after weeks of talks "consid-ered Lloyd George's grand scheme for European reconstruction [to be] premature at best."[104]

A further reason for growing tensions between the "Lion and the Eagle" (Carl Parrini) had been that Britain, seeing itself as one of the victors, was not prepared to play a secondary role in the international financial system behind the United States. The City seems to have been aware of the ambitions of Wall Street that Redfield had articulated in 1920. According to assistant secretary of state Norman Davies, the Brit-ish had been afraid ever since the Paris Peace Conference that they had lost their prewar position in finance.[105] Hence the quest to return to the gold standard that the country had so humiliatingly had to abandon in 1918. Although exhausted by the war, Britain continued to see both its financial and its manufacturing systems to be strong enough to put forward its own solutions to the postwar crisis. If the Americans could not bring themselves to help in the reconstruction of Europe, the Empire and Commonwealth would seize an initiative. For London such an effort included the reconstruction of Bolshevik Russia that Washington, more fiercely anticommunist than the more pragmatic Britons, was even less prepared to contemplate than the reconstruction of Germany or Western Europe.

Finally—and a factor never to be underestimated in politics—there was the personality of Prime Minister David Lloyd George, a man of great self-confidence, if not even arrogance, who believed that he could pull off a major success for his country that would reshape Europe. In the spring of 1919, he had tried to draw the Wilson administration into a joint venture by arguing that "in the financial sphere, the problem of restoring Europe is almost certainly too great for private enterprise alone."[106] Consequently, he saw "only two possible courses, [i.e.,] direct assistance and various forms of guaranteed finance."[107] He asked Wilson to guarantee American private bank loans to lift Europe out of its troubles. In a plan that John Maynard Keynes had drafted, these loans would be issued as long-term bonds linked to future German reparations payments. The U.S. president refused to be drawn into this bargain. As he wrote to Lloyd George, "it would not be possible for me to secure from the Congress of the United States authority to place a Federal guarantee upon bonds of European origin."[108] He added, "Our Treasury also holds the view (and in this again I concur) that to the very limit of what is practicable such credits as it may be wise to grant should be extended through the medium of the usual private channels rather than through the several governments."

It was a position that his Republican successor upheld in subsequent years. Worse, by the end of 1921, the attitude of the U.S. administration had hardened. What Lloyd George had presented as a mere economic conference had, in Secretary of State Hughes's view, "a wider political purpose." U.S. Secretary of Commerce Herbert Hoover even went so far as to suspect that the proposed Genoa Conference and the preconference at Cannes aimed at reasserting Britain's position "as the hub of a revived world economy and to lure Germany and Russia into the British orbit."[109] No American official—certainly not Hughes—would have been prepared to join such a plan. It was irritating enough to Washington that the United Kingdom continued to rely on its Empire as a preferential trading bloc.

With his appeal for a partnership rebuffed in the fall of 1921, Lloyd George went ahead without the Americans in his aim to reintegrate both Germany and Russia into a treaty structure of Western Europe that, with the City as the hub, would facilitate commercial cooperation and uplift the economies of the entire region. Once the door to greater trust and prosperity had been opened, Lloyd George hoped that the other thorny problems of the time, including the Franco-German conflict, could also be tackled. In this sense, the plan, just like the Washington System and the Consortium in the Far East, also contained a security element—the idea to reduce armaments in Europe not merely as a confidence-building measure, but also to contain the still enormous costs of the postwar military establishments and thereby to relieve national budgets when reductions of welfare expenditures were impossible for reasons of electoral politics.

In this complex web, Britain was thus not just interested in better relations with Russia that Lloyd George thought would benefit British industry and finance, he was probably also spurred by the fact that on 25 August 1921, Berlin and Washington—until then still in a state of war because of the American failure to ratify the Versailles Treaty—had signed a separate peace.[110] While, as has been mentioned, contacts between German and American firms and German-American trade had been resumed as early as 1919, the treaty certainly made future trade relations easier that, in light of the size and importance of the German industrial economy, everyone knew was crucial to any future American reconstruction effort in Europe. The treaty was strengthened in the fall 1923 by a trade agreement with a most-favored-nation clause—a topic to be examined in detail in the next chapter in connection with the reparations issue.

With two million Britons unemployed and also the Irish problem on his hands, Lloyd George found a partner for his plan in Aristide Briand, the French prime minister, who, unlike his much more nationalist successor Raymond Poincaré, also preferred conciliation to confrontation. A first sign that the British prime minister had overrated his ability to bring his plan to a successful conclusion emerged at a preliminary meeting at Cannes in January 1922 at which German and Russian participation as well as a Franco-British alliance were discussed.[111] Unhappy about the impact that the German presence might have on the reparations payments that Berlin had been told in October 1921 it would have to pay, deputies of the French Chamber rebelled and Briand was called back from Cannes to Paris where he was forced to resign on 12 January. Poincaré stepped into his shoes. Lloyd George was undeterred, and invitations went out to the governments of Europe, including the Germans and the Bolsheviks, to convene at Genoa in April 1922. With a major objective being to rebuild economic relations with Russia and to try to stabilize the European economic and political situation without American leadership, the Cannes meeting had agreed on a number of principles on which the negotiations with the Bolsheviks were to be based.

While the details of these principles need not be enumerated here, it is important that the Genoa initiative was based on a British commitment of the kind that Washington had declined to make to its own bankers: A few months earlier, the British Parliament under Lloyd George's leadership had passed the Exports Credits Act that gave official guarantees to British foreign trade. It was now hoped that at Genoa it would be possible to establish an International Corporation charged with stimulating trade with Russia that would similarly be underwritten by the other participating governments.[112] Washington, as reluctant as ever, merely sent observers.

Once the conference had started on the basis of the Cannes principles, another major setback to the negotiations with the Russia occurred: the Germans and Russians signed, right in the middle, a separate agreement at Rapallo that, apart from an expansion of trade, resumed diplomatic relations.[113] Although an accord between the two outsiders to the Paris Treaty System of 1919 had been on the cards since 1920–21,[114] it put a huge damper on the Genoa Conference's more optimistic beginnings. There was still the question of whether, if nothing else, a nonaggression pact might come out of weeks of formal and informal meetings, modeled after the earlier Pacific treaty that had laid down specific naval ratios. But eventually, facing a French refusal to shrink its land forces even after the reduction of the German army to one hundred thousand men in the Versailles Treaty, Lloyd George became disheartened that his vision of a British-led stabilization and reconstruct of Europe could be realized.

This is not to say that it should not have been tried. Yet it showed that Britain, whatever its global ambitions, just did not have the power and influence to pull it off. Its demise (and that of Lloyd George) had the unfortunate consequence that it reinforced the tensions with France over how to deal with the enormous problem of German reparations. This had become so hopelessly entangled that the knot needed to be cut by one mighty stroke that could be delivered only by the Americans with their superior financial power.

If this is the larger picture that we can glean retrospectively from the relevant sources and the secondary literature on the Genoa Conference and its context, it is fortunate that, apart from the delegation of American observers, we also have the notes and impressions of an experienced American businessman who went to Genoa in the spring 1922 and subsequently gathered his own information on the state of the various European national economies: Frank Vanderlip.

Having arrived in Genoa and keeping his ear to the ground, Vanderlip reported on 17 April that there existed two viewpoints at the end of the first week.[115] According to the first one, there was no hope of finding a "quick formula for the economic reconstruction of Europe."

The second view was that it was "a real achievement to bring together the highest representatives of thirty-four nations and . . . to hold them together in a fairly amiable state of mind." Overall, Vanderlip felt that there would be many more conferences "before Europe's economic reconstruction is accomplished." Still, he was also impressed by the "great many bankers and captains of industry" who had also come and who were fully aware of the "growing seriousness of the general European situation." Consequently, "the need for the Conference is beyond all question."

He added that on opening day Lloyd George had "put the greatest emphasis on the pressing need to reestablish economic relations with Russia."[116] The trouble was that that country was not at the "center of the European problem," and "its rehabilitation would in any case" take many years. Nor would the opening of the Russian market do more than "create a plan to sell goods on credit," and it would take a long time before there would be "a surplus of production" to enable Russia to participate in a mutual exchange for the general welfare of Europe. To Vanderlip, Germany's problems were the really "pressing [and] menacing" ones and among those reparations were at the top of the list: "With reparations demands unaltered, Germany faces inevitably financial collapse." This in turn would have political and social consequences of "vital importance" that were "likely to be contagious."

Furthermore there was France's financial situation, with an unbalanced budget and an extensive floating of obligations. The amount of "short-term treasury notes" stood at [$?]80 billion.[117] These debts, he observed, were sustained "by the hope that reparations expenditures would be recoverable from indemnities." But should Germany experience "a financial collapse, the French financial position will fall as a sickening weight on the French people." This is why French politicians had to retain "the financial confidence of their constituents" and "why they present[ed] a front as hard as steel against any discussions of reparations" at Genoa. Worse, this predicament was "what may drive France to extreme military measures, hoping to collect [from Germany] by force what she has been unable to collect by treaty." At the same time, there was the German situation whose greatest danger lay "in its contagious possibilities." If France's confidence were shaken, "it may incite France to measures of force" against Germany. Indeed, as Vanderlip feared himself, the possibility of a French occupation of the Ruhr region was already looming on the horizon. And so, the "storm center of the European situation" was on the Rhine and "not on the Volga."

In his Report "No. 2," Vanderlip agreed that "this conference was not the place for American participation," since it was "not economic," but political.[118] However, in his view this did not mean "that we should not participate in a future one." In this respect, "Wall Street could learn a lesson from Washington" which is "one of reserve, and of conserving ammunition for a time when its use will be much more effective than at present." This applied especially "in the matter of fresh European credits until the situation has further ripened." When the time for financial commitments by the United States had come, "financial statesmanship" would be deployed.

For yet another time, Vanderlip came back to the problem of broad reparations demands that "would financially ruin Germany" resulting "in social and political upheavals there which would create fresh dangers of the first importance to Europe."[119] But he had also been hearing views that "the blindness of the French view with regard to the ultimate significance of the French attitude to indemnities" was "believed to be paralleled by the blindness of the American view in demanding full satisfaction of the debts due by European countries." Turning to the British role in the Franco-German conflict, the American banker felt that London would use economic pressure to prevent a French invasion of the Ruhr area and that some other road had to be found to provide France with further funds to enable her to keep her financial equilibrium and the confidence of the French investor.[120]

One scheme that Vanderlip seems to have heard of relating to Genoa was a loan by banks in Britain and France to the tune of £108 million over three years; another one was to fix reparations at £100 million per year for forty-two years. The idea behind the loan was that "a breathing spell [was] being given to Germany before payments began at this rate."[121] What is so interesting about all these notes and the reason why they have been quoted here is that they contained all the various elements that were later cast into American-led reparations plans and implemented in 1924.[122] The tragedy was that this became possible only after the French had invaded the Ruhr in January 1923 and wrecked both the German economy and their own in precisely the way that Vanderlip had feared in the spring of 1922. This is why his notes from Genoa, some of which were published in the United States, are so invaluable for an understanding also of American policy that will be examined in the next chapter.

While all these ideas were being formulated at Genoa, "the political turmoil arising out of the German-Russian Treaty" began to upset the deliberations of the Financial Section of the conference.[123] Some people thought that a "real Entente" had been forged "between those two great countries" and "persons holding that belief picture the development of a vast Teutonic-Slavic coalition and see the division between eastern and western Europe moving from the Vistula to the Rhine."[124]

It would mean a crumbling of Poland and the absorption of Austria and Hungary by this coalition. For Vanderlip, it was also intriguing to learn that "American interests now working with German interests in the shipping business have extended their participation to a German-Russian shipping undertaking." Perhaps the worst consequence was that the Rapallo Treaty had "made all discussion of a breathing spell for Germany impossible for the moment."[125] There had been some chance of this before the Treaty. Now it was gone.

Though critical of German behavior, Vanderlip also heard plenty of criticism of the American banks from European bankers. However, he also thought that, if they were in the American position, they, too, would "for the time being withhold loans and discourage the transfer of funds to make investments" in Europe.[126] He continued, "They would reserve their financial strength and then use it freely when the opportunity offered [itself] to use it more effectively for Europe's [re]habilitation and more certainly for American prestige." When this "proper time" had come and "when the right action has been taken here [in Europe] and a united front presented, we should contribute most liberally from our redundant stock of gold." For the moment, though, Vanderlip doubted "the wisdom of involving the resources of the Federal Reserve Bank in the enterprise."

His conversations with "the most eminent Financiers of Germany who are in attendance here," seem to have confirmed him in his caution.[127] They had told him "that if Germany does not have relief, this will ensure the most serious economic consequences within [a time frame of between] 90 days and six months, and that is without reference to whether France should invade the Ruhr or not." The German bankers foresaw the "danger of a revolutionary development as a result of rising prices that will follow [the] continued depreciation of the Mark, and they regard such depreciation as inevitable unless relief is offered." The great disadvantage of the whole conference was, of course, that the agenda prohibited discussion of intergovernmental debts and reparations. Consequently Vanderlip's interlocutors felt that "they are permitted only to discuss external symptoms, but are prevented from dealing with the real disease."

On 21 April 1922, Vanderlip produced his sixth assessment with discussions of the "English Project for an International Corporation" to which the British delegation attached "great importance."[128] This corporation was to be set up "under English law" and to be run by "a British Chairman and Secretariat." The other countries were then to create National Corporations "under their domestic laws." Belgium, Holland, Norway, and Sweden, he learned, had indicated their support, while "France is hesitating, Germany is expected to cooperate and, it is hoped, America will" as well. The calculation behind this was apparently openly spoken about. It was based on the belief "that financial power will for the next ten years be the most potent influence in making European governments behave themselves." Consequently, the "scheme really takes on a strong political flavor as well as promising an important instrument for the economic development of backward eastern European countries—perhaps Russia in particular."

Overall, the corporation was to take on only "large matters" that, for reasons of their volatility, private enterprises would not touch.[129] Its proponents, Vanderlip continued, had "exceedingly clear ideas of its potential importance as a powerful instrument to influence the conduct of eastern European government[s]." They were deemed to be more potent than "military sanction." He also noted that the Russian reply to the schemes and demands that were put to them was "surprisingly moderate and promising"—no doubt helped by that fact that Lenin had meanwhile promulgated his New Economic Policy. After the rigidities of war communism during the civil war, he had created a freer market for domestic and foreign entrepreneurs.

Vanderlip then came back to the plight of the Germans.[130] They had argued that their situation was hopeless unless there was a moratorium on reparations payments in gold, and temporary help to buy food. They felt that Britain understood the emergency, "that America, except for very few, is profoundly ignorant, and that France's vision is obscured by a Chamber of Deputies that has learned nothing since the armistice." Ultimately, the Germans with whom the American banker had been talking had said "that the moral force of America is the only thing that can bring order out of chaos." The stress was thereby on "our moral force," and there was "distinctly" no suggestion that American dollars be invested "at the present time." They had added "that America could perform the greatest of world services if we could make it clear that we insisted upon Europe setting its political house in order before we give financial aid." Still, the Germans did not merely exhort and blame others at Genoa. They acknowledged "that they have injured their situation with the nations of western Europe by the German-Russian treaty incident." They regretted "the injury, but not the action."

After further notes about the complexities of Anglo-French relations and about American caution, Vanderlip summarized the discussions on a nonaggression pact with Russia as an antidote the British fears of Bolshevism.[131] Lloyd George had proclaimed that Genoa would be a failure without such a pact.[132] But the French kept opposing it, arguing that it should not apply to the enforcement of the Paris peace treaties. There was also the point that France wanted protection against future German aggression for which a British guarantee was needed. Beyond this, everything revolved in the end around money. For Russia a "great cash credit is sine qua non of any rapprochement with Western Europe."[133] But the Europeans were "utterly unprepared to pledge any such credit," and Vanderlip could therefore only turn to his colleagues back home telling them that "directly in front of American financiers is opening the opportunity profoundly to influence the European situation for good. The world needs at the moment statesmanship on the part of American bankers. If they will shape their course on lines of both sound finance and sound statesmanship, Americans make an important contribution to the salvation of Europe."[134]

Until the end of his stay in Genoa, Vanderlip continued to hammer home the points that he had been making in previous weeks: the crisis of the German economy, the threat of a French invasion of the Ruhr industrial region, the inability of France to see that "she cannot milk the cow and cut her throat at the same time," Russo-German cooperation and the menace of Bolshevism, and the American financial capacity to help but its political reluctance to make a move.[135] In the end, he thought that the conference had failed because Lloyd George had not prepared it sufficiently. And ultimately there was also "a defect of moral fiber of the British Premier: He undertook to deal with the situation in a spirit of compromise where compromise was impossible."[136] He had been too much of an "opportunist" who had no more than a "superficial" understanding of the facts and a feeble grip on principles. This was no doubt a harsh verdict on the British prime minister, but it tallies fairly well with the conclusion that Carole Fink reached at the end of her important monograph.

However, there was also the problem of the "selfish nationalism" of France that was shaped "by domestic political necessities" rather than by a "broadminded sincere desire to reconstruct Europe."[137] Vanderlip also had a few proposals for what might be done with Russia, but ended up by admitting that it was difficult to predict the future. Since Lloyd George's nonaggression pact had also been scuttled—"effectively torpedoed by Benes," the Czech president—he saw a 75 to 80 percent chance of fresh European hostilities breaking out during the current year. If one thinks of the Ruhr occupation that began in January 1923, he was not far off the mark. Nor was he in his analyses of the European situation and the suggestions he had made to get out of the hole into which the region had fallen as a result of a catastrophic world war. It is to the slow realization of many of these suggestions insofar as they involved the United States that we must turn in the next chapter. It will look at the (ephemeral) successes of American policies toward Europe and toward Germany and Britain in particular in the mid-1920s, up to the Great Depression. During the first phase, the German-American business relationship became "special" again in a positive sense in that big business made Weimar Germany its main base in Europe.

By contrast, U.S. relations with Britain were vexed by various political problems, also relating to London's trying to uphold its position as a great power with a large colonial empire. As to British-American business relations, many links continued from World War I and even from before 1914. But, as Genoa had shown, the country's commercial and industrial clout had further weakened after the war. On the Russian question, Washington's resistance had won the day against Lloyd George's design, while at the same time "the State and Commerce Departments combined had . . . opened the door to the possibility of commerce in Russia and the Near East on American terms."[138] Nor had the British prime minister succeeded in activating the promises that the more modern potential of German industry seemed to offer, also for a more general stabilization of Europe as a whole. Again it was only the Americans who had the capacity to do that.

Notes to Chapter III

1. Quoted in John Röhl, "Admiral von Müller and the Approach of War," *Historische Zeitschrift* 4 (1969): 670.

2. See, e.g., John Röhl, *Wilhelm II. Der Weg in den Abgrund, 1900–1941* (Munich, 2008), esp. chaps. 34 and 38–41, with detailed and up-to-date documentation.

3. See, above all, Konrad H. Jarausch, *The Enigmatic Chancellor* (New Haven, CT, 1973), esp. 148ff. on "The Illusion of Limited War." On the role of the Austro-Hungarian leadership, see Samuel R. Williamson, Jr., *Austria-Hungary and the Origins of the First World War* (New York, 1991), 164ff.

4. Gerhard Ritter, *The Schlieffen Plan* (New York, 1958); Annika Mombauer, *Helmuth von Moltke and the Origins of the First World War* (New York, 2001); Holger Afflerbach, *Falkenhayn* (Munich, 1994).

5. Wolfgang Michalka, "Kriegswirtschaft und Weltkrieg," in Helmut Böhme and Friedrich Kahlenberg, eds., *Deutschland und der Erste Weltkrieg* (Darmstadt, 1987), 173ff.

6. On London's moves in July and early August, see, e.g., Gustav Schmidt, "Contradictory Postures and Conflicting Objectives: The July Crisis," in Gregor Schöllgen, ed., *Escape into War? The Foreign Policy of Imperial Germany* (Oxford, 1990), 135–60. On Russia see now, Christopher Clark, *The Sleepwalkers: How Europe went to War in 1914* (London 2012).

7. Quoted in Fritz Fischer, *War of Illusions* (New York, 1975), 402.

8. Quoted in Niall Ferguson, *The Pity of War* (New York, 1999), 33.

9. On Herbert Spencer's differentiation between a "militant" type of society and an "industrial" one, and also on the wider debate about the future of capitalism within which Norman Angell's book was also written, see, e.g., Volker

Berghahn, *Militarism. The History of an International Debate, 1861–1979* (Leamington Spa, 1981), 11ff.

10. Ferguson, *Pity of War* (note 8), 33.

11. *WSJ*, 28 July 1914.

12. *WSJ*, 1 August 1914.

13. CUA, Vanderlip Papers, B-1-6, Vanderlip to his wife Narcissa, 30 July 1914.

14. *WSJ*, 1 August 1914.

15. Quoted in Ferguson, *Pity of War* (note 8), 192.

16. Quoted in ibid., 193.

17. Quoted in ibid.

18. Quoted in ibid., 192.

19. Ibid.

20. Alfred Vagts, *Deutschland und die Vereinigten Staaten in der Weltpolitik* (New York, 1935), 2:2017, also for the following.

21. Quoted in Richard F. Hamilton, "The Origins of the Catastrophe," in Hamilton and Holger H. Herwig, eds., *The Origins of World War I* (Cambridge, 2003), 488.

22. Ibid.

23. Quoted in Gerhard A. Ritter, "Der Kaiser und sein Reeder. Albert Ballin, die HAPAG und das Verhältnis von Wirtschaft und Politik im Kaiserreich und in den ersten Jahren der Weimarer Republik," *Zeitschrift für Unternehmensgeschichte* 2 (1997): 154; Lamar Cecil, *Albert Ballin* (Princeton, 1967), 341–42, in discussing the suicide issue, thinks it more likely that Ballin's death was an accident. Niall Ferguson disagreed, and so did Hella Kemper, "Auf hoher See," *ZEITGeschichte*, 4/10, 39.

24. Quoted in Ferguson, *Pity of War* (note 8), 193.

25. See Cecil, *Albert Ballin* (note 23), 205ff.

26. See the studies on the arms manufacturers such as David Hermann, *The Arming of Europe and the Making of the First World War* (Princeton, 1996); Clive Trebilcock, "The British Armaments Industry, 1890–1914. False Legend and True Utility," in Geoffrey Best and Andrew Wheatcroft, eds., *War, Economy and the Military Mind* (London, 1976), 89–107; Michael Epkenhans, *Die wilhelminische Flottenrüstung, 1908–1914* (Munich, 1991), 149ff.

27. CUA, Vanderlip Papers, B-1-6, Vanderlip to his wife Narcissa, 30 July 1914.

28. Ibid., Vanderlip to his wife Narcissa, 4 August 1914.

29. Ibid., Vanderlip to Lucy Evan Chew, 11 August 1914.

30. *WSJ*, 3 August 1914.

31. See the reports on sailings and cancelled sailings in *WSJ*, 5 August 1914. See also Cecil, *Albert Ballin* (note 23), 214ff., with a chapter titled "Phantom Fleet."

32. See the reports in *WSJ*, 3 August 1914; *WSJ*, 4 August 1914; *WSJ*, 5 August 1914; *WSJ*, 6 August 1914.

33. *WSJ*, 8 August 1914.

34. CUA, Vanderlip Papers, B-1-6, Vanderlip to his wife Narcissa, 11 August 1914.

35. *WSJ*, 1 August 1914.

36. CUA, Vanderlip Papers, B-1–6, Vanderlip to his wife Narcissa, 11 August 1914.

37. Ibid., Vanderlip to William Sloan, 21 August 1914. See also Hans W. Gatzke, *Germany and the United States. A "Special Relationship"?* (Cambridge, MA, 1980), 58ff.; Clara E. Schieber, *The Transformation of American Sentiment toward Germany, 1870–1914* (Boston, 1923), 263ff.; Alexander Sedlmaier, *Deutschlandbilder und Deutschlandpolitik* (Stuttgart, 2003), 45ff.

38. See *WSJ*, 3 August 1914.

39. See *WSJ*, 5 August 1914. See also John W. Coogan, *The End of Neutrality. The United States, Britain and Maritime Rights, 1899–1915* (Ithaca, NY, 1981); Edwin J. Clapp, *Economic Aspects of the War: Neutral Rights, Belligerent Claims, and American Commerce in the Years 1914–1915* (New Haven, CT, 1915); Patrick Kelly, *Tirpitz and the Imperial German Navy* (Bloomington, IN, 1911), 388ff.; Gerhard Ritter, *The Sword and the Sceptre* (London, 1973), 3:119ff.

40. See, e.g., Arthur S. Link, *Wilson. The Struggle for Neutrality* (Princeton, 1960); Henry F. May, *The End of American Innocence* (New York, 1979); Reinhard Doerries, *Imperial Challenge. Ambassador Count Bernstorff and German-American Relations, 1908–1917* (Chapel Hill, NC, 1989), 216ff.

41. See, e.g., *Los Angeles Times*, 11 July 1916; *NYT*, 22 July 1916; *NYT*, 8 November 1916. See also Christopher Kobrak, *Banking in Global Markets. Deutsche Bank and the United States, 1870 to the Present* (New York, 2008), 180ff.

42. See, e.g., George C. Herring, *From Colony to Superpower* (Oxford, 2008), 401ff.; Barbara Tuchman, *The Zimmermann Telegram* (New York, 1966).

43. On the organization of the British economy in World War I, see, e.g., Kathleen Burk, ed., *War and State. The Transformation of British Government, 1914–1919* (Boston, 1982); Arthur Marwick, *Britain in the Century of Total War* (Harmondsworth, 1970), 62ff.; Jay M. Winter, *The Great War and the British People* (London, 1985); Nicholas A. Lambert, *Planning Armageddon. British Economic Warfare in the First World War* (Cambridge, MA, 2012).

44. On German naval calculations, see, e.g., Ritter, *Sword and the Sceptre* (note 39), 318ff. The larger backdrop to this is the strategic defeat by the Royal Navy that the German battle fleet suffered at Jutland in June 1916 and the stalemate in northern France, where the indecisive Battle of the Somme began later that month. See, e.g., A. Templeton Patterson, *Jellicoe* (London, 1969), 99ff.

45. *WSJ*, 6 August 1914.

46. CUA, Vanderlip Papers, B-1–6, Vanderlip to Stillman, 18 September 1914.

47. Ibid., Vanderlip to Stillman, 9 October 1914.

48. Ibid., Vanderlip to W. S. Prince (Mayor of Duluth), 5 February 1915.

49. Ibid., Vanderlip to Stillman, 5 March 1915.

50. Ibid., Vanderlip to Stillman, 13 March 1915.

51. Ibid., Vanderlip to H. G. Selfridges (Selfridges & Co.), 6 April 1915.

52. Ibid., Vanderlip to Stillman, 7 May 1915.

53. Ibid., Vanderlip to Sir Felix Schuster, 1 June 1915.

54. Ibid., Vanderlip to Stillman, 11 June 1915.

55. Ibid., Vanderlip to Stillman, 25 June 1915.

56. CUA, Vanderlip Papers, B-1–7, Vanderlip to Stillman, 2 July 1915.

57. See, e.g., Gerald D. Feldman, *Army, Industry, and Labor in Germany, 1914–1918* (Princeton, 1966); Roger Chickering, ed., *Great War, Total War* (Cambridge, 2000).

58. CUA, Vanderlip Papers, B-1-7, Vanderlip to Stillman, 13 August 1915.

59. Ibid.

60. Ibid., Vanderlip to Poniatowski, 20 August 1915, also for the following. See also Katja Wüstenhagen, *Deutsch-Amerikaner im Ersten Weltkrieg* (Stuttgart, 2007). On Germanophobia, see Hans-Jürgen Schröder, *Deutschland und Amerika in der Epoche des Ersten Weltkrieges, 1900–1924* (Stuttgart, 1993), 25ff.

61. CUA, Vanderlip Papers, B-1-7, Vanderlip to Lyman J. Gage, 31 August 1915.

62. Ibid., Vanderlip to Stillman, 23 March 1917.

63. Ibid., Vanderlip to Stillman, 10 February 1917.

64. Ibid., Vanderlip to Stillman, 2 March 1917.

65. Ibid., Vanderlip to Stillman, 30 March 1917.

66. On developments between the Treaty of Brest-Litovsk and November 1918, see, e.g., Martin Kitchen, *The Silent Dictatorship* (London, 1975).

67. Klaus Schwabe, *Woodrow Wilson, Revolutionary Germany, and Peace-Making, 1918–1919* (Chapel Hill, NC, 1985), 58ff.

68. Margaret Macmillan, *Paris 1919. Six Months That Changed the World* (New York, 2002). See also Arno Mayer, *The Politics and Diplomacy of Peacemaking* (New York, 1967).

69. See, e.g., Bernd Dohrmann, *Die englische Europapolitik in der Wirtschafts-krise, 1921–1923* (Munich, 1980), 31.

70. See, e.g., Quincy Wright, *Mandates under the League of Nations* (New York, 1968); Michael D. Callahan, *Mandates and Empire. The League of Nations and Africa, 1914–1931* (Brighton, 1999); Roger W. Louis, *Great Britain and Germany's Lost Colonies* (Oxford, 1967).

71. See, e.g., Thomas A. Bailey, *Woodrow Wilson and the Lost Peace* (Chicago, 1944); Herring, *From Colony to Superpower* (note 42), 378ff.

72. Selig Adler, *The Isolationist Impulse* (New York, 1915).

73. See the documents in CUA, Vanderlip Papers, B-1-7 and B-1-8. Looking back on this period, he wrote in 1933 that, as president of NCB from 1909, he had been a director of over thirty-five corporations. As chairman of the War Savings program in 1918, he had "put together the organization which sold a billion dollars of 25c War Savings Stamps in the twelve months following the sale of the first stamps." CUA, Vanderlip Papers, B-1-10, Vanderlip to A. M. Urnes, American Institute of Banking, Minneapolis, 31 January 1933.

74. See, including the speculations about the reason for his resignation, in *WSJ*, 4 January 1919; *WSJ*, 6 January 1919; *WSJ*, 9 January 1919. His retrospective letter is in CUA, Vanderlip Papers, B-1-10, Vanderlip to W. S. Cassell, Baltimore, 1 December 1933.

75. In the early summer *WSJ* was full of reports on the postwar boom. See, e.g., *WSJ*, 28 June 1919; *WSJ*, 25 July 1919, that was expected to continue; specifically with reference to General Motors: *WSJ*, 24 June 1919; *WSJ*, 9 July 1919; to Ford: *WSJ*, 27 June 1919; *WSJ*, 24 July 1919; to Studebaker: *WSJ*, 30 July 1919. There was also much optimism about exports: *WSJ*, 26 July 1919. However,

there were also reports that the American steel industry was working at under capacity—not a good omen.

76. CUA, Vanderlip Papers, B-1-8, Vanderlip to W. B. Wilson, 20 May 1919.

77. Ibid., Vanderlip to William Redfield, 2 November 1918.

78. Ibid., Vanderlip to Joseph T. Talbot, 7 July 1919.

79. Ibid., Vanderlip to Frank Trumbull (Ashdown Forest), 7 July 1919.

80. Ibid., Vanderlip to Henry S. Pritchett (Santa Barbara), 16 July 1919.

81. Frank Vanderlip, *What Happened to Europe* (New York, 1919), passim. See also Frank Vanderlip and John H. Williams, *The Future of Our Foreign Trade. A Study of Our International Balance in 1919* (New York, 1919).

82. CUA, Vanderlip Papers, D-11, Report No. 4, 2.

83. One of the key lessons learned from the 1920s by the economic and political elites of the United States was that the government could not leave the initiative to the private sector. Washington had to commit itself to postwar reconstruction either by guaranteeing the loans to Europe or even leading through an official program that the Marshall Plan became. This made it easy for American finance and industry to follow. See chapter VI, pp. 299ff.

84. *WSJ*, 11 April 1919; *WSJ*, 18 September 1919. On the McHugh and Redfield initiatives and the larger ambitions of American business, see Carl P. Parrini, *Heir to Empire. United States Economic Diplomacy, 1916–1923* (Pittsburgh, 1969), 78ff.

85. See, e.g., Mira Wilkins, *The Maturing of Multi-national Enterprise: American Business Abroad from 1914 to 1970* (Cambridge, MA, 1974).

86. See, e.g., William H. Harris, *The Harder We Run. Black Workers since the Civil War* (New York, 1982); A. H. Spear, *Black Chicago* (Chicago, 1967).

87. *Forbes*, 15 January 1919.

88. Dohrmann, *Die englische Europapolitik* (note 69), 28, 37ff.

89. Marwick, *Britain* (note 43), 143ff.; Adam R. Seipp, *The Ordeal of Peace. Demobilization and Urban Experience in Britain and Germany, 1917–1921* (Farnham, 2009). On FBI policies, see Dohrmann, *Die englische Europapolitik* (note 69), 40ff.; Juliet Nicolson, *The Great Silence. Britain from the Shadow of the First World War to the Dawn of the Jazz Age* (London, 2009); Richard Overy, *Twilight Years. The Paradox of Britain between the Wars* (New York, 2009), with the title of the British edition: *Morbid Age. Britain between the Wars* (London, 2009).

90. See, e.g., Jean-Jacques Becker, *The Great War and the French People* (New York, 1986); Patrick Fridenson, *Histoire des usines Renault*, vol. 1 (Paris, 1972).

91. See, e.g., David Morgan, *The Socialist Left and the German Revolution* (Ithaca, NY, 1975); A. J. Ryder, *The German Revolution of 1918* (Cambridge, 1967). On the economic situation, see Carl-Ludwig Holtfrerich, *Die deutsche Inflation, 1914–1923* (Berlin, 1980).

92. *WSJ*, 3 June 1919.

93. *Forbes*, 28 December 1918. On the general mood, Alexander Sedlmaier, *Deutschlandbilder und Deutschlandpolitik* (note 37), 116ff.

94. For further details on the situation of the German chemical industry and the resumption of its cooperation with its prewar partners, see chapter IV, pp. 195ff.

95. CUA, Vanderlip Papers, B-1–8, Vanderlip to Robert Benson, 22 September 1919.

96. Ibid., Vanderlip to Ellery Sedgwick, 3 January 1920.

97. CUA, Vanderlip Papers, D-28, Vanderlip to George Burnham, Philadelphia, 1 March 1920.

98. CUA, Vanderlip Papers, B-1–8, Vanderlip to Maggiorino Ferraris, 19 March 1920.

99. Ibid., Vanderlip to Charles A. Stone, 13 March 1920.

100. Ibid., Vanderlip to Norman Barnesby, 18 September 1921.

101. Ibid., Vanderlip to H. E. Benedict (New York), 26 September 1921; ibid., 30 September 1921.

102. Stephen Schuker, "American Policy toward Debts and Construction at Genoa, 1922," in Carole Fink et al. eds., *Genoa, Rapallo, and European Reconstruction in 1922* (Cambridge, 1991), 98.

103. See, e.g., Thomas H. Buckley, *The United States and the Washington Conference, 1921–1922* (Knoxville, TN, 1970); W. E. Braisted, *The United States Navy in the Pacific, 1909–1922* (Austin, TX, 1971); Erik Goldstein and John Maurer, eds., *The Washington Conference, 1921–1922* (London, 1994), also for the following summary of the conference's results.

104. Thus Schuker, "American Policy" (note 102), 105. For the Wilson quote, see Edward M. Lamont, *The Ambassador from Wall Street. The Story of Thomas W. Lamont, J.P. Morgan's Chief Executive* (Lanham, MD, 1994), 103.

105. Quoted in Frank Costigliola, *Awkward Dominion. American Political, Economic, and Cultural Relations with Europe, 1919–1933* (Ithaca, NY, 1984), 34.

106. On Lloyd George see, e.g., Andrew Williams, "The Genoa Conference of 1922: Lloyd George and the Politics of Recognition," in Fink et al., *Genoa, Rapallo* (note 102), 29–47.

107. Quoted in Parrini, *Heir to Empire* (note 84), 66.

108. Ibid., 66–67.

109. Patrick Cohrs, *The Unfinished Peace after World War I. America, Britain and the Stabilisation of Europe, 1919–1932* (Cambridge, 2006), 87.

110. The American-German peace treaty was signed in August 1921 and came into force in October of that year. One of its consequences was that the Americans were obliged to return assets that had been taken over during the war.

111. On Cannes, see, e.g., Cohrs, *Unfinished Peace* (note 109), 72; Zara Steiner, *The Lights That Failed. European History, 1919–1933* (Oxford, 2005), 206ff.

112. Still the best study on the Genoa Conference and its preliminaries at Cannes: Carole Fink, *The Genoa Conference. European Diplomacy, 1921–1922* (Chapel Hill, NC, 1984).

113. See, e.g., Gerald Freund, *The Unholy Alliance, 1918–1926* (London, 1957); Walter Laqueur, *Russia and Germany* (London, 1965). See also Hartmut Pogge von Strandmann, "Rapallo—Strategy in Preventive Diplomacy. New Sources and New Interpretations," in Volker R. Berghahn and Martin Kitchen, eds., *Germany in the Age of Total War* (London, 1981), 123–46.

114. On the interests of German industry in trade with the Soviet Union, see Hartmut Pogge von Strandmann, "Grossindustrie und Rapallopolitik.

Deutsch-sowjetische Handelsbeziehungen in der Weimarer Republik," *Historische Zeitschrift* 222, no. 2 (1976): 265–341.

115. CUA, Vanderlip Papers, D-11, folder 1, Report "No. 1," 17 April 1922, 1–2. It is not always clear if these notes were produced by Vanderlip himself or by his assistant, i.e., if Vanderlip wrote or dictated them or whether they were secondhand notes. What is certain, though, is that the documents represent Vanderlip's words and thoughts.

116. Ibid., 2–3.

117. Ibid., 4ff.

118. Ibid., folder 2, Report "No. 2," n.d., 1–2.

119. Ibid., 3.

120. Ibid., 5.

121. Ibid.

122. See pp. 170ff.

123. CUA, Vanderlip Papers, D-11, folder 3, Report "No. 3," 18 April 1922.

124. Ibid., folder 5, "5th" Report, n.d., 1.

125. Ibid., 2–3.

126. Ibid., folder 3, Report "No. 3," 18 April 1922, 4–5.

127. Ibid., folder 5, "5th" Report, n.d., 4.

128. Ibid., folder 6, "Article No. 6," 21 April 1922, 1–2. It is not clear if, with one or two exceptions, these "reports" were in fact published. It seems that they were, at least to some extent, meant for publication.

129. Ibid., folder 6, "Article No. 6," 21 April 1922.

130. Ibid., folder 7, Report "No. 7," 22 April 1922, 2–3. This report was written for *New York World* and apparently published at the end of April.

131. Ibid., folder 8, "Article No. 8," 23 April 1922, 1 ff.; ibid., "Article 9," 25 April 1922, probably also written for *New York World*.

132. Ibid., folder 10, "Article No. 10," 27 April 1922, 1.

133. Ibid., 2.

134. Ibid., folder 11, "Article No. 11," 29 April 1922.

135. Ibid., folders 12–16.

136. Ibid., folder 17, "Article No. 17," 8 May 1922, 2.

137. Ibid., folder 18, "No. 18 Article," 10 May 1922, 2, apparently produced again for a syndicated issue of *New York World*.

138. Ibid., folder 21, "Article No. 21 for 'World' Syndicate, Genoa," 14 May 1922, 2.

IV

///

The North Atlantic Triangle

ECONOMIC RECONSTRUCTION
AND COLLAPSE, 1923–1933

1. Introduction

The years covered by this chapter began with a further deepening of the postwar crisis, culminating in the occupation of the Ruhr industrial region by French and Belgian troops. The Germans resorted to passive resistance to the occupiers' efforts to extract reparations by force, followed by the collapse of the German economy, with hyperinflation reaching astronomical figures in the autumn of 1923. Due to the radical German reaction, the French economy also suffered quite badly. The heavy industries of Lorraine were hit hard, and the franc had to be devalued. The years that followed the 1923 crisis ended with another and even more severe economic breakdown in the autumn of 1929, with consequences to be analyzed in chapter V.

The following pages deal with a distinct period of the years in between. This period saw an engagement of the United States in Europe that had not been possible in the immediate postwar years, generating a few years of relative stability and prosperity in which American manufacturing companies and banks played a major role. It was the phase in which the United States succeeded in deploying its superior industrial and financial power in an attempt to uplift the economies of Europe. During those five years it was not only American ideas and practices of rationalized mass production that came to Europe through massive FDI; rather Europe, again for the first time, got a taste of mass consumption, even if it was still quite limited in terms of affordable consumer durables. Instead material consumption was complemented and partially compensated by the offerings of modern mass entertainment, particularly film, some 70 percent of which were imports from the dream factories of Hollywood. However, before the role of American big business in the mid-twenties can be examined we have to pick up the thread from the previous chapter and discuss the ramifications of the 1922–23 wreckage.

2. German Reparations and the Harding Administration

The question of German reparations payments proved to be a very hard nut to crack, occupying and frustrating the efforts of politicians and businessmen alike who tried to find a way toward economic stabilization and political reconciliation. Scholars have scoured the archives and written countless articles and books in search of answers. There was the vigorous exchange of views between David Felix and Sally Marks in the 1970s that essentially continued the earlier debate between John Maynard Keynes and Etienne Mantoux.[1] They, as well as many others who later joined in the discussion, argued about whether Germany was economically capable of making the payments that had been imposed in May 1921, but refused to pay for political reasons; or whether the country had indeed been so weakened economically by war and civil war between 1914 and 1920 that, even with the best intentions, it could not have fulfilled Allied demands and was therefore constantly forced to delay or to ask for a moratorium.[2]

Meanwhile the administration in Washington continued studiously to avoid entanglements with crisis-ridden Europe, while London, in trying to achieve some forward movement via Lloyd George's reconstruction plan presented at the Genoa Conference, proved too weak to facilitate a solution of the reparations issue. France now became the key power. Aristide Briand might have been willing to contemplate bilateral Franco-German negotiations, but Raymond Poincaré, who replaced him in the winter of 1921–22, was a much more uncompromising protagonist of French national interest. He disliked Lloyd George's plan and pursued an "ever more wooden" policy.[3] When the Germans signed the Rapallo accord, he felt confirmed in his view that the Germans did not want to pay and should therefore be forced to. One reason for his government insisting on a strict fulfillment of reparations was, of course, that it was under enormous popular pressure to extract indemnities so that Paris could support the livelihoods of all those many French families who had suffered from the mass slaughter in the trenches. *Les Boches*, who were held responsible for the misery of war widows, orphans, and veterans, were to be made to pay. Massive investments were also required to rebuild the industries of northern France. Finally, there were the obligations that Paris had entered into when it took up loans from Britain and the United States to prosecute an increasingly costly war.

The British might have been prepared to enter into negotiations about the monies that France owed them. But they, too, just like France, had taken loans from America, and it was Washington that proved totally inflexible when the question, not of a cancellation of debts, but of their reduction and rescheduling was raised. Thus in August 1922 the British government had stated that it would not demand more from its debtors than what it had to pay to the Americans. But Washington again refused to make any concessions. There were, it is true, a number of people in the Wilson administration who had been thinking of forgiving the $10 billion that had been lent. There was also the *New York World*, for which Vanderlip had written his articles, that criticized the Harding administration's rigidity and indeed "obsession" with the debt question.[4] But Secretary of Commerce Herbert Hoover, who had Harding's ear, would hear nothing of it. And he had the support of such papers as the *Washington Post* that France and Britain were merely trying to place the burdens of the war on the backs of the American tax payer.[5] Aware of the financial power of the United States, he also wanted economic diplomacy to replace the tired power politics of Old Europe—a view shared by Secretary of State Charles Hughes.[6]

With Washington continuing to sit on its hands, the conflict between France and Germany escalated into a power-political and ultimately military struggle. But given the far-reaching disarmament of the latter by the Versailles Treaty, Berlin had no chance of mounting an effective military resistance against an invasion of the Ruhr when, after the failure of the Genoa Conference, rumors of such an invasion began to circulate. It was not merely that the French wanted to get hold of Ruhr coal, but also that they were toying with, or preparing for, the separation of the Rhineland from Germany and the creation of a buffer state.[7] There were various desperate attempts to avert an escalation that Poincaré correctly thought he could rebuff. When Germany again defaulted on a reparations payment due at the end of December 1922, France and Belgium marched into the Ruhr area. This move unleashed a passive resistance of the local population and of the miners in particular. It might be argued that there have been other conflicts in modern history where things had to hit rock bottom before the antagonists, having added up the great and futile costs of the clash, stopped in order to make a fresh start.[8]

As things went from bad to worse in the summer of 1923, the American government was stirred out of its wait-and-see posture. After their election victory, the Republicans had moved into the White House in early 1921 and Charles Hughes had taken charge of the State Department. He was a sophisticated man with wide-raging experience in the public and private sectors and with many excellent qualifications to fill the job. He had also surrounded himself with thoughtful advisors, one of whom was Norman Davis, a survivor from the Wilson administration. It was Davis who on 12 March 1921 had sent Hughes a personal letter with the following assessment:[9]

> Through the highly industrial developments of Europe prior to the war, Germany has become the axis, and the rehabilitation of Europe and its continued prosperity is most dependent on that of Germany. Unless Germany is at work and prosperous, France cannot be so, and the prosperity of the entire world depends upon the capacity of industrial Europe to produce and purchase. Into this enters the element of credit, and credit will not be forthcoming as long as there is no stability and confidence, and until the German reparation is settled constructively on the basis which will inspire confidence, the credits necessary for the reestablishment of normal conditions will not be forthcoming.

In some ways Davis's appeal was similar to a letter that advisor Jan C. Smuts had written to Lloyd George as early as 26 March 1919 from which it is also worth quoting at some length because it provides the even broader context in which the position of industrial Germany must be seen:[10] "I am seriously afraid that the peace to which we are working is an impossible peace, conceived on the wrong basis; that it will not be accepted by Germany, and, even if accepted, that it will prove utterly unstable, and only serve to promote the anarchy which is rapidly overtaking Europe." To Smuts two points were "quite clear and elementary: 1. We cannot destroy Germany without destroying Europe; 2. We cannot save Europe without the co-operation of Germany. . . . The fact is, the Germans are, and will continue to be, the *dominant factor* on the Continent of Europe, and no permanent peace is possible which is not based on that fact. The statesmen of the Vienna Congress were wiser in their generation; they looked upon France as necessary to Europe." His fear was "that the Paris [Peace] Conference may prove one of the historic failures of the world; that statesmen connected with it will return to their countries [as] broken, discredited men, and that the Bolshevists will reap where they have sown."

There is finally the statement of Ellis Dresel who had been a key member of the American delegation to the Paris Peace Conference and who, traveling in Germany in 1920, had, like Vanderlip before him, gained firsthand experience of the disastrous material and financial conditions of the country and thus worried about the increasingly unstable political system of Weimar. Being a member of the Republican Party, he became the chargé d'affaires in Berlin who officially signed, in August 1921, the separate German-American peace. As he wrote in January 1921, "I am dead against a 'forget and forgive' policy, but we are obviously soon coming to the point where we shall be distanced by England and other nations in our approach to Germany."[11] He added that "the surest guarantee against another war of revenge" would be to establish "close economic relations with Germany."

But just as Smuts's warning of 1919 went unheeded, Dresel's and Davis's advice was not taken onboard in 1921 either. Nor was that of Keynes who, in a paper and also a book, had argued against the imposition of punitive reparations on Germany that he believed were counterproductive.[12] In short, the leaders of the two Anglo-Saxon powers knew of the risks of leaving the reparations issue to the French and remaining inflexible on the question of Allied debts. And just as Lloyd George had tied his hands before the Paris Peace Conference in the 1918 election campaign with his anti-German sloganeering, the Harding administration remained passive for the reasons that Wilson had given to the British prime minister and that were mentioned in the previous chapter.[13] Harding and Hughes felt they could not offer any overt support or provide public guarantees for loans that American banks might have been prepared to float for European reconstruction. To offer such help without any guarantees seemed too risky to the banks.

No one seems to have been unhappier about this development than the American manufacturing industry. As has been seen, they had reconnected with their prewar commercial partners, including German companies. Facing a downturn in the domestic economy after the initial postwar boom, they were keen to export their products. They also apprehended that the Europeans needed credit to pay for goods imported from across the Atlantic. Some of them had begun to rely on their own financial resources, but they also appreciated that Germany, however important to any reconstruction effort, was a particularly unreliable partner, all the more so, when hyperinflation set in and the mark became the object of currency speculation.[14] Solid American corporations feared that the credit lines extended by them for their exports might never be honored.

In this volatile economic climate American business had welcomed the signing in August 1921 of a separate peace treaty with Germany after the Versailles Treaty had foundered in the U.S. Senate. This, it was felt, would place the United States on a par with the other former Allies. It was also beneficial to American interests, "especially regarding the legal status of sequestered German property."[15] Even greater was the interest of American industry in the conclusion of a commercial treaty that the administration had said would be facilitated by the peace accord. While the foundations for this treaty were being laid in 1922, Hughes was under increasing pressure to prepare an American response to the increasingly likely French occupation of the Ruhr. Thus Thomas Lamont, the chief executive of the powerful Morgan Bank, had, on 2 October 1922, criticized Americans for being timid and fearful of entanglements and called for sacrifices that would be light in comparison to those that Britain and France had made in the war. In light of such pressures, the plan came to be circulated in Washington, and on 29 December, the secretary of state made a speech at Yale University. He may have hoped that it would prevent an occupation, but also provide a road map to what Washington was prepared to do to help tackle the reparations question. He offered the constitution of a committee of experts to make an objective assessment of Germany's capacity to pay. He then added, "I do not wish to see a prostrate Germany. There can be no economic recuperations in Europe unless Germany recuperates. There will be no permanent peace unless economic satisfaction is enjoyed. There must be hope and industry must have promise of reward, if there is to be prosperity."[16]

A few weeks later, on 13 January 1923, the French invasion of the Ruhr "prostrated" Germany. Hughes response was, perhaps remarked more helplessly than cynically, that France and Germany apparently needed to experience a "bit of chaos" before they would come to their senses and be prepared to accept a committee of experts.[17] By the summer of 1923, with the German economy collapsing, there was the threat that the Weimar Republic might be overthrown by the nationalist Right and the officer corps.[18] In desperation, the civilian Berlin government not only accepted the Hughes Plan, but also offered guarantees of regular payments of annuities if a more permanent solution to the reparations problem could be negotiated with the Allies, leading not only to a stabilization of the economic situation but also to a withdrawal of France and Belgium from the Ruhr region.

3. American Big Business and the Crisis of 1923

The evolution of the political situation and the impact the economic collapse had on the daily lives and health of ordinary Germans has been examined in a number of studies. Klaus Schwabe has called it a "turning point in international relations."[19] Its details need not be summarized here, except to say that it was very hard, especially for blue-collar workers and their families, and for pensioners and other middle-class people who were relying on their savings and now found them wiped out by hyperinflation.[20] The news of all this slowly traveled also across the Atlantic. The response that it generated in American business circles is reflected in Vanderlip's correspondence of 1923. Thus he wrote to Albert von Bary in Berlin on 2 January that "there is really a very large sympathy here for the situation in which Germany now finds herself and a growing belief that the French attitude is not helpful to the restoration of Europe." But he also noted that at the same time "there is a feeling that a good many of the German industrialists have not been especially patriotic or high-minded." He concluded that "as a whole, we have very mixed opinions as to what our attitude ought to be, but it seems to me [that] there can be no room for two opinions about feeding a hungry child."[21]

A few months later Vanderlip wrote to another acquaintance that conditions in Germany since the "Ruhr Invasion are, of course, very much worse than they were a year ago. The enormous issue of German marks, the incredible increase of German debt and the natural growth of German hatred of France under the circumstances makes the outlook in Germany a bleak one for the present."[22] To him the reconstruction of Europe had become "a spiritual question and in some way there must be brought about a greater feeling of brotherhood and good will before there can be any sound foundation for reconstruction."

Writing to Professor Gustav Cassel in Sweden, he added on 27 April 1923 that "there is danger in the pressure on Germany resulting in disorder that will amount almost to revolution."[23] He thought that the French financial situation would also "become increasingly worse" and that Paris would eventually be forced into a devaluation of the franc. On the other hand, American "productive capacity was never greater, even during the height of the war." A "fair measure" of this was, in Vanderlip's view, that just under a million freight cars had been loaded. Last month was the greatest "peak ever reached." Yet, remembering the disorder of 1920–22, people were still afraid and made "little or no use of the potential good of the Federal Reserve System." The United States held about half the gold stock in the world. So, while he felt no optimism about the outlook for the countries of the European Continent, "our period of prosperity here is resting on firm ground, and it is likely to continue for some time." In a letter to Countess Treuberg in Heidelberg, written from California on 14 April, he noted with approval that there was a growing interest in events in Europe even on the West Coast and that there were "indications here of a reopening of the question of America joining the League of Nations."[24] Consequently, there was "a steadily growing sentiment in this country in favor of participation of the United States in European Councils." At the same time he urged Countess Treuberg "to make no mistake" that the "basis of this feeling was economic."

As such sentiments were spreading across the American continent, it is not surprising that the first step taken was to sign, on 19 October 1922, a commercial treaty with Germany. The administration had finally made a general decision to move from a conditional most-favored-nation trade policy toward an unconditional one.[25] Significantly, Germany was supposed to become the first partner in this new scheme. Another factor in the acceleration of the process was worries about the private contacts that, it was rumored, the Ruhr industrialists were trying to establish with their French counterparts in Lorraine.[26] Since Washington had insisted on the Open Door, whether in the 1922 Far Eastern treaties or in Europe, this idea looked like a protectionist arrangement to the detriment of American exports. With Poincaré's occupation failing, industrialists in Lorraine and the Ruhr were, like a growing number of politicians, beginning to look for more constructive relations between the two countries. Finally, with Germany in chaos and its currency in free fall, the British government, following the United States, also changed its posture. When Paris once again rejected a German offer to negotiate a reparations agreement, London also became completely disillusioned with Poincaré and was ready openly to confront him.[27]

One manifestation of this was a fresh initiative on British war debts to the United States. Even though the British government was still prepared to develop a joint Anglo-French approach, by the autumn it resumed its attempts to at least settle its own obligations. The result was an agreement between Treasury Secretary Andrew Mellon and Prime Minister Stanley Baldwin that fixed the debt to the United States at $4.3 billion plus $300 million in interest to be repaid over a period of sixty-two years. Believing that Britain had no choice but to sign, it left a good deal of bitterness toward Washington in America's closest wartime ally.[28] Putting all these initiatives together, it becomes clear that by the autumn of 1923 the United States had moved very close to implementing the Hughes Plan of the previous year. The Germans had already signaled their consent to a committee of experts and had furnished American politicians and businessmen with material that Senator William Borah and others in Washington incorporated in their increasingly anti-French speeches. There was also the impact of the book by H. G. Moulton and G. E. McGuire, published, with covert German assistance, by the Institute of Economics, titled *Germany's Capacity to Pay*, which illustrated just how dire the country's situation supposedly was.[29] It was now merely

for Poincaré to come, cap in hand, to the Americans and agree to setting up the committee of American experts that would pave the way
for an end to France's Ruhr occupation and the beginning of orderly
payments, adjusted to Germany's projected financial capacity.[30] On 14
January 1924, the experts began their deliberations, chaired by Owen D.
Young, chairman of GE and Radio City of America (RCA) as well as a
nonexecutive director of the Federal Reserve Bank of New York.[31]

4. Political Stabilization through the Locarno Pact

The research that traces the adoption of the Dawes Plan in the summer
of 1924 and its ratification by Germany that same autumn is rich and
comprehensive and therefore needs to be only footnoted here.[32] Instead
and before discussing the economic developments that followed in the
wake of the Dawes reparations settlement and the role of American
big business in this period, it seems helpful to look at the plan's impact on European politics. The general point to be made here is that
it facilitated a stabilization of domestic affairs as well as a diplomatic
rapprochement between nations that had been locked in bitter conflict
in the early 1920s, especially France and Germany. This rapprochement
was spearheaded by Aristide Briand and Gustav Stresemann.

Stresemann had meanwhile undergone a major ideological transformation.[33] In World War I he had been a National Liberal who supported
the territorial annexations of the Reich government. After 1918, when
he was deemed to be too right-wing and politically compromised to
be one of the leaders of the pro-Republican Deutsche Demokratische
Partei (DDP), he had formed the anti-Republican Deutsche Volkspartei
(DVP). But Stresemann, who had studied economics and had been an
executive of industrial associations in Saxony, began to move toward
the political center, as he witnessed how Germany kept falling into
the abyss. He was among those who, instead of further resistance to
France, wanted to revive the economy. He knew that a fresh start could
not be achieved without the help of American diplomacy and big business. After a brief spell as Reich chancellor in the fall 1923 at the height
of the crisis, he joined a reconstructionist cabinet as foreign minister in
November 1923—a position that he occupied until his death in October
1929. This long tenure enabled Stresemann to initiate and complete a
number of political projects that gave collateral support to the reconstruction of the German economy.

The most important among these was the negotiation and ratification
of the Locarno Treaty in December 1925.[34] With Briand having become

his counterpart in Paris and French and Belgian troops withdrawing from the Ruhr, negotiating a treaty that recognized the territorial status quo in the west was viewed as an indispensable contribution to the political but also to the economic stabilization in Western Europe. Locarno meant that Germany promised to stop challenging militarily the territorial acquisitions that France and Belgium had made under the Treaty of Versailles. In return, Germany was protected under a treaty that blocked another Ruhr occupation. Locarno also provided an opening for a withdrawal of the Inter-Allied Military Control Commission (IMCC) that had been monitoring German compliance with the disarmament clauses of the Versailles Treaty.

The good "Spirit of Locarno" also facilitated talks that Briand and Stresemann held at Thoiry to the west of Paris in September 1926, designed as a *"quid pro quo* transaction that once again followed the principle [of] 'economic concessions from Germany *versus* political concessions from France.'"[35] The political aim was to accelerate the French retreat from the Rhineland and to hand the Saar region back to Germany. The Belgians were to agree to a return of the Eupen-Malmedy area. The wider hope was that agreements on these issues would lead to a more general reduction of armaments that Washington had been pushing for even before 1924 as a confidence-building measure and a way of freeing scarce resources in Europe for industrial reconstruction, Allied debt services to the United States, as well as steady German reparations payments.

Arguably the most momentous consequence of Locarno was the French decision to abandon their forward strategy of 1922–23 that had been aimed at consolidating the country's hold over the western parts of Germany and even to promote the creation of a separate state in the Rhineland in the hope of weakening Germany over more of the long term economically as well as militarily. The strategy to secure a *Pax Gallica* by keeping its Eastern neighbor in the "chains of Versailles," as German nationalists called it, and to establish French hegemony in Europe in the face of Washington's unwillingness to create a *Pax Americana* was finally abandoned in 1925. There is no more telling evidence of France's new defensive strategy than the decision to build the Maginot Line of fortifications along the eastern border in Alsace-Lorraine.[36]

With Paris's worries about German industrial and demographic superiority continuing (as reflected in the metaphor of the "chains" that a restrengthened Germany might one day cast off), Briand was also tried to rope in the Americans by proposing a Franco-American security pact. But Washington was still determined to avoid all European *political* entanglements. What emerged was an international treaty

signed in 1928 also by Germany outlawing wars of aggression. It bore
the names of Briand and the then U.S. secretary of state Frank H. Kel-
logg. This treaty did not prevent the wars of aggression of the 1930s and
became significant only at the postwar trials of major war criminals in
Germany, Japan, and Italy, one of whose indictments was that they had
resorted to blatant military aggression.[37]

The "Spirit of Locarno" helped to clear the way for Germany to be
invited to join the League of Nations and to assume a seat on its council
in recognition of its status as a great power next to its former enemies.
The room for maneuver that Stresemann had been gaining diplomatically in 1925–26 also made it possible for him to formalize relations
with the Soviet Union. The treaty with the Bolsheviks of April 1926
opened the door not only to closer relations between the Red Army and
the Reichswehr, but also between Soviet state enterprises and ministries, on the one hand, and German industry, on the other.[38] Some very
illuminating work is now available on the links that firms, such as AEG,
Siemens, and Krupp, established with the Soviets and the problems
they encountered in doing business with a state-controlled economy.[39]
Their experiences must be seen within the context of the political risks
that private firms took when dealing with dictatorships—an aspect of
international business that will be discussed in greater detail in the next
chapter with regard to American industry and the Nazi regime. What is
significant here is that both Germany and Britain knew after the failure
of Lloyd George's consortium plans at Genoa in 1922 that they had no
choice but to rely on the United States, if they wanted to revive their
battered economies.

5. The American Business Community
and the Dawes Plan

Returning therefore to the Dawes Plan, that was first published in April
1924 and was to replace the 1921 London Reparations Schedule, it is
striking how far American manufacturing industry and banks were
prepared to commit resources to Western Europe, once the Dawes Plan
had been officially accepted by France and Germany.[40] There were, it
is true, some intriguing differences between the Wall Street bankers
and the big industrial corporations. While the bankers "believed they
were making a contribution to easing European entry into a general
community of interest," they were cautious about taking on the City
and merely argued "that ultimately the vast productive power of the
United States" would convert a British-controlled international banking system into an instrument largely serving the needs of United

States international commerce. This implied that the "immediate foreign market interests of the manufacturers should be subordinated to the long-run interests of the community," which in turn looked to the managers of industry "suspiciously similar to the immediate short-run interests of the bankers."[41]

With the economic depression of 1921 still haunting industry, the reason for this dissatisfaction among manufacturers emerges from the report of the Sixth National Foreign Trade Convention that concluded,[42] "Foreign trade is an absolute economic necessity. Without it our industries would wither and dwindle, and we should be unable to comply with the fundamental condition of prosperity—steady occupation for our workers in all lines. American productive capacity, both agricultural and industrial, is now so great that in order to maintain remunerative occupation we must have steady access to foreign markets for the sale of part of our products, and at the same time we must have constant and large supplies from foreign sources of numerous kinds of raw materials." Apart from reiterating the need of highly productive American industry to export, it was also a covert criticism of Britain with its imperial preference system and the difficulties that London was causing for American industry to gain better access to primary products such as rubber. It was a grievance that was not forgotten and that re-emerged in World War II, when the Americans insisted on the Open Door, while Britain tried to preserve its Empire and Commonwealth as a preferential tariff zone at the same time as the Hitler, Mussolini, and the Japanese were brutally erecting their autarkic empires in Europe, North Africa, and Asia.

In the end, with Wall Street keen on short-term profits and industry interested in long-term investments, the two sides arrived at something like a compromise, mediated by the Commerce and State Departments. But, as will be seen below, it was a precarious compromise in that it proved difficult to devise a foreign investment program that tangibly modernized European industry. Nor was it easy to find "a secure basis for the operation of the German economy and its ability to fulfill its reparations obligations" agreed under the Dawes Plan—the key to a hitherto elusive "economic peace" as a precondition to political stabilization.[43] For the moment, Dawes and his colleagues were therefore very happy to have created a framework that provided for an orderly payment of staggered and rising reparations, calculated in terms of the expected growth of the German economy once its recovery had begun with the aid of American bank loans and direct investments by the big manufacturing corporations. The expectation was also that Germany's economy would be strong enough to service those loans on top of reparations payments to the Allies.

Frank Vanderlip, writing to L. S. Rowe at the American Academy of Political and Social Sciences in Philadelphia on 16 January 1924, had still sounded a note of caution: "Europe hope[s] that America ultimately will become an important investor in European securities."[44] He then reminded his correspondent that "in the first six months of 1922 we did invest one hundred million dollars per month," adding that "an essential for sound investment is sound basic information." He felt that "we do not have that [even] about so simple a thing as what one might term the balance sheet of different European nations." He therefore insisted that the Europeans should be compelled to disclose in full and authoritatively "what they owe in detail," directly and indirectly. Vanderlip also wanted to know what their earning assets were and what direct and indirect incomes and expenditures they had.

However, just a month later WSJ reported,[45] "Full of optimism over the success of the Experts' Committee No. 1 in Berlin, Dawes, its chairman, has its sub-committee preparing final details of a plan for securing reparations from Germany and rehabilitating German finances." The Germans, Dawes elaborated, "gave us everything we asked for and treated us with the greatest cordiality in a spirit of cooperation." When the full Committee of Experts submitted its report in April 1924, the State Department, though not officially involved in these negotiations, "let it be known that the report . . . was 'highly pleasing' from an American point of view." The American diplomats continued, " 'We earnestly hope that this excellent piece of work will mean the solution of this serious problem of reparations.' " One "high department official" hastened to add that of course " 'we cannot express governmental approval of it.' " As before, the administration was prepared only to channel trade rather than to become directly involved.

Perhaps in partial response to this, first Wall Street reactions were more subdued. According to the WSJ article, bankers proclaimed that they had been able to peruse the report only "hastily." They also thought that the report was "rather complex and indefinite and, in a measure, disappointing because it fails to tell just those things about Germany and reparations that bankers have been most desirous of knowing." Furthermore they questioned if the report offered "a proper basis at this time for consideration of foreign loans." After all, the document still had to be "submitted first to the [Allied] Reparations Commission and then to the various governments, by which time many of the recommendations may be abandoned, while others may be changed." While J.P. Morgan, the most important player on Wall Street, had just raised a loan of $100 million to help Paris deal with the economic fallout from the Ruhr adventure, another banker who remained nameless conceded that at least this was "the first plan capable of practical operation . . .

and unless its application is blocked by political dissension among the Allies, it should furnish bases for both commercial and financial reconstruction in Europe, and for a steady expansion of business in the United States."

It was perhaps typical that the ever cautious J.P. Morgan also warned against overoptimism. As he wrote to E. C. Grenfell in July 1924,[46] "We must, however, be very sure not to let our desire to help the politicians to straighten out the tangled affairs of Europe lead us away from fundamentals." And these fundamentals were that it was the bankers' duty "that any issue which [the Morgan bank] sponsored rested on so strong a foundation that 'the small, private investors in the USA' would not be led astray." Yet, so great was the appetite for the Dawes loan bonds that, once offered, they were oversubscribed within fifteen minutes and subsequent American lending went through the roof.[47]

If ratification of the Dawes Plan by Germany and France was obviously considered crucial, Britain's role was also mentioned as very important. As *WSJ* wrote, providing a brief glimpse of attitudes in previous years, "the report is regarded here as a complete vindication of the French stand on reparations since the war, and a repudiation of the British viewpoint that the burden should be lightened if world commerce and stability in Germany is to be restored."[48] Such sentences that reflected the traditional American hard line toward Allied debts hint at the tensions between London and New York that will have to be discussed in more detail in a moment as part of a closer look at the state of the Anglo-American "special relationship" in the mid-1920s and the ambitions that Wall Street continued to pursue to dismantle the influence of the City.

Two weeks after these early responses, when more information on the Dawes Plan had become available, *WSJ* wrote that the committee's recommendations spoke of "only a modest loan of $200,000,000," with a "large participation from Americans." The possible total of international financing was pegged at "over $8,000,000,000, though it is probable that half that amount may be subscribed by German capitalists." Another $7 billion might be needed later. The paper also gave details on how any loans to Germany would be secured by mortgages on "German railways and industries, while the new railway company which is to take over the German lines is to sell preference shares and give ordinary shares to the government which itself will probably sell them in part or whole sooner or later."

Since the plan was not merely about these huge foreign loans to Germany but also about reparations payments that would increase annually, the Allies were said to be "at liberty to float loans on the basis of the German revenues under their control and up to a certain limit earmarked for Reparation purposes." The paper felt that "the external loan and the probable appeals on the basis of German railways and industries are worth considering." It added reassuringly that in the view of the committee "it has secured safety for the foreign investor, given a stable German currency." The experts were also "firmly convinced that Germany is a sound economic proposition from the start. All they stipulate is that the proceeds of the loan should be used to finance internal payments to the Allies in the form of reparations in kind or military outlays on German territory."

Given the prioritization of reparations over private loans, *WSJ* mentioned further elements by which investors were to be reassured that the risks were acceptable. Loans to specific German industries would be guaranteed by the Reich government and "in case of default recourse can be had to receipts from the controlled German revenues." And finally, "like the railway mortgage bonds," they would be "tax-free"—a covert way for the Washington administration to put some *public* money into European reconstruction without alarming the traditional opponents to any entanglements. The larger intentions of the Mellon tax reforms were—to quote Gilbert Ziebura—a typical ploy of the Republicans "designed to reduce taxes in such a way that the lion's share of the benefit accrued to high-income earners."[49]

However, giving up a source of internal revenue was the extent to which the U.S. government became involved in the Dawes enterprise. As before, all else depended on the expectation that the general situation would look sufficiently stable for the private sector to come to Europe *without* official guarantees. Both Germany and France were anxious to remove the 1923 wreck of reparations. There was also the agreement with the British over Allied debts to the United States that would soon be followed by negotiations between Washington and Paris to get the French debt problem out of the way as well. Taking all these developments together, it suddenly looked worthwhile for Americans making loans, buying bonds, and restarting FDI in Europe. True to the administration's position of nudging the private sector without direct commitment on Washington's part, the U.S. secretary of commerce did his best to whet American investors' appetites. After all, unless there was international trade, "not a single automobile would run, not a dynamo would turn, not a telephone, telegraph or radio would operate." Trading goods and raw materials was simply "the life blood of modern civilization."[50]

By May 1924 the first optimistic reports on the European and German economies appeared in the American financial press. It had always been assumed that German industry was not only the biggest in Europe, but also had the greatest potential for development. On 10 May 1924,

B. C. Forbes wrote in his magazine under the heading "Will Europe and Washington Give Business a Spring Tonic?"[51] that he was "very hopeful that the Dawes report will lead to a full agreement between Germany and the Allies." He continued that not only the Germans were serious: "France, too, gives every indication of being anxious to end the acute uncertainty," even if understandably France "insists upon clear-cut provisions for compelling Germany to live up to the agreement after it is signed."

On 21 June 1924, Julius Klein, the director of the U.S. Bureau of Foreign and Domestic Commerce, also put Germany at the center of the stabilization effort.[52] Referring to trade with Britain, he noted an increase from some $29 million to $41 million between April 1923 and April 1924 and believed that the "present depression in the coal trade" was "largely seasonal." British textiles were the other major producer with respect to which he noted an element of continued rivalry. Washington, confident of its strength on the international market, advocated the Open Door, whereas Britain tried to strengthen its Empire as a protectionist trading bloc. Accordingly, Klein commented on "the steady shift of the raw cotton imports from American sources to India and other producing areas in the Empire." No doubt to the irritation of American big business, he saw "further evidence of this determination to relieve itself of too great dependence upon uncertain American supply" by looking toward improving trade relations with Brazil.

From the vantage point of American big business Britain's shift, however irritating, related to textiles that were not part of the dynamic industries of the Second Industrial Revolution, such as electrical engineering, machines, and chemicals where Germany had much more to offer. Accordingly, the American Committee of the International Chamber of Commerce at its annual meeting in Cleveland had passed a resolution on 6 May welcoming the reparations plan and lending its support to its implementation.[53] Optimism was strong enough to ignore that factory orders from Germany were still volatile and "money and credit . . . scant."[54] German manufacturers, while "getting large orders for goods at home," were "all seek[ing] credit, but on short-time because they expect good returns from trade and better credit terms in the near future"—no doubt an irony in light of later problems when short-term loans were being used for long-term investment projects. For the moment, German industry's strategy made sense, considering that interest rates were "between 12 percent and 16 percent." Rates did indeed go down, but now German manufacturers began to look for long-term loans when they decided that the fulfillment of current orders had to be complemented by a modernization of their factories that required such loans and American FDI. According to *WSJ*, "several commercial loans are being negotiated" with the Americans. The trouble was that many of them continued to be short-term rather than long-term loans. In other words, the Germans signed up for a system that was less than sound. They did so in the hope that monies would continue to flow from across the Atlantic. This, as will be seen, turned out to be a very dangerous assumption in 1928–29.

For the moment, no one was prepared to contemplate another downturn, and so *WSJ* reported on 6 August 1924 that "American financial aid to Germany will not end with the floatation in this country of $100,000,000 of the $200,000,000 external obligation to be offered under the Dawes plan. At the conclusion of that financing, say bankers, large industrial financing undertakings unquestionably will come to the United States."[55] The paper continued that future requirements were already being considered: "Prominent New York Banking institutions with strong German connections are said to be quietly sounding out German industrialists' private needs," should the Dawes Plan go through. Dow, Jones & Co. had learned "that already important international bankers have made tentative proposals to German industrialists, which financing will probably materialize some time after the launching and disposition of the $200,000,000." Even bankers who were more skeptical for the moment thought "that with the acceptance of the Dawes plan, safe and lucrative financial operations, such as loans and credits, can be carried on with big German business interests."

In another article, of 30 August, *WSJ* focused on Julius C. Meyer, the managing director of the Hamburg-America Line after his return to New York on the United American liner *Resolute*:[56] The Dawes Plan, the journal quoted him, " 'will affect every phase of business in Germany, including shipping. [It] will revive business in Germany.' " People needed " 'money with which to carry on business.' " He therefore expected " 'all important industrial concerns of Germany to look to America for capital to carry out their work.' " No less important, " 'the German loan will tend to restore confidence throughout Europe.' "

Less than a week later, the U.S. ambassador to Berlin and a glass manufacturer from Corning, New York, Alanson B. Houghton, sailed into New York aboard the *George Washington*, "enthusiastic over the German Reichstag's prompt acceptance of the Dawes plan and confidence [recte: confident] that Germany will" implement its terms.[57] To make certain that the Reich government would ratify the plan despite considerable right-wing opposition, Houghton added that Hughes had paid a visit to Berlin "to acquaint the administration with his own views of probable developments at Berlin," following "the victory won by Chancellor [Wilhelm] Marx and Foreign Minister Stresemann on the Dawes report" over the nationalists. The secretary of state had apparently left Germany feeling satisfied that the Germans realized "that any other road would lead straight to chaos and irretrievable disaster for them, coupled with the loss of whatever remnant of the world's respect they had left."

Houghton went on that the $200 million loan "in which we are so heavily to participate is probably the best guaranteed loan in financial history," not least "because virtually the entire resources of the German nation are pledged as collateral." Of course, American capital had "an even wider interest in the adoption of the Dawes report and what will be its beneficent aftermath." Germany would become "a practically unlimited field of opportunity" for American investment. The country was "starved of capital requisite for her development in almost every conceivable direction," and interest rates offered would be "highly attractive to the foreign investor." Indeed, in many ways, Houghton waxed, "Germany resembles one of our great western states before eastern capital came into them and hewed, as it were, out of the primeval soil a vast industrial enterprise." He ended by hoping that British capital might join in this supposedly heroic effort of American capital's "pacific penetration of Germany." In light of what happened in the next couple of years, Werner Link correctly concluded that Weimar Germany became a "penetrated political system," and this also applied to Britain, with the relationship between the two and the United States now more distinctly asymmetrical than ever before.[58]

More restrained than Houghton but in typical State Department fashion, Hughes, too, continued to make encouraging noises, suitably complemented by apocalyptic ones, when, on 19 September 1924, knowing of the J.P. Morgan's traditional caution, he wrote to Dwight Morrow, a partner at the "House of Morgan," that the plan had opened "an avenue to economic recovery abroad."[59] Its failure would be a disaster because "we should have, in my judgment, not only chaotic conditions abroad, but [also] a feeling of deep despair." This in turn meant that American business "would not wholly [!] escape the reactions of such widespread economic distress."

When the plan was finally all signed and sealed, the New York business community organized a dinner at the Waldorf-Astoria in honor of Owen Young and the other members of the Dawes Committee.[60] On this occasion and in a spirit of gentlemanly generosity, the "Harding-Coolidge administration was given full credit for [the] creation and adoption of the Dawes plan." As Young then put it in his speech with considerable pride, "'The plan would not have been adopted without America.'" He mentioned that the "original suggestion of the experts committee came from our Secretary of State." The Commerce Department "'furnished the largest amount of helpful information.'" Young also praised the U.S. ambassadors in Berlin and London. Even the U.S. president had taken an interest " 'in the choice of an American citizen to sit on the reparation[s] commission for the purpose of administering the plan.' " The banks had given their support through the extension of credits to Germany, while Dawes was credited with having " 'sold' " the plan to Europe and the United States.

Young finally warned against overoptimism and an overextension of credit: " 'A steady, firm, conservative policy is better for Europe and for us because after all we must remember that the ravages of ten years of economic and social demoralization cannot be repaired overnight. The surest rehabilitation of Germany will be a slow and steady and healthful growth. There should be no encouragement for her to react from the great depression into an unhealthy boom.' " He also reminded his audience that the restoration of Germany must be seen as part of a larger reconstruction of Europe. He found warm words for the British and especially also for the French who had been very helpful during the London Conference at which the Allies agreed to the plan. He hoped that the disagreements that the whole effort had produced in Washington would now yield to a spirit of cooperation and support of the American people as a whole: " 'We may debate political participation in the affairs of the world, but we must participate in its business, and business, like science, knows no political boundaries and in its dictionary there is no such word as isolation.' " He ended with the hope " 'that business may be carried on internationally without sentiment, but with wisdom and courage' " and he prayed " 'that the spirit behind that business may be a worthy expression of the character of our people and worthy in the sight of God.' "

Apart from WSJ, Forbes joined the effort to generate broad support in the business community. Under the heading "German Revival Will Be Boon to America," it published an interview with John Hays Hammond after his five-month trip to Europe.[61] The magazine introduced him with the following comment: "In this interview he records his observations so clearly and concisely—with a notable lack of the mental fog that afflicts so many who have gone across to size up things—that they may be regarded as an important contribution of America's understanding of European conditions as they are today." Referring to his visit to Germany, he remarked, " 'The Germans whom I met, with hardly an exception, admitted that the Dawes plan would render a greater service to the economic regeneration of Europe and peace of the near future than any service America could have performed had she been a member of the League of Nations.' " But, he added, " 'the German Captains of Industry are hopeful that Germany will soon secure a position in the sun in her competition for foreign markets.' " After all, " 'the Germans are past masters in the peaceful penetration of foreign markets.'" Certainly, "'Germany, at the time of my visit late in September, was expectant and ready. Her industrial plants and equipment are in excellent condition. She expended large sums in expanding and equipping her industrial plants since the Armistice.'" Hammond felt that increased German competition had already been noted in the United States. But, given American superiority, it was not perceived as a serious threat. At the same time he raised questions with regard to Britain that sounded familiar. Because it had remained "'satisfied with profits as brokers,'" the country had "'allowed Germany in the past to secure'" competitive advantages. Consequently, Britain, "'unless she radically changes her policy, will suffer more than any other nation when Germany gets on her feet financially, industrially, and commercially.'"

6. American Big Business and the British Economy

An article by Julius Klein, the director of the U.S. Bureau of Foreign and Domestic Commerce, seemed to confirm this assessment.[62] There had been, he wrote, a marked decline in British exports to the United States and a rise in imports. He pointed to the continued weight of coal mining and textiles and that there had been a shift from a reliance on American cotton producers to those of the Empire and Commonwealth. If the importance of the textile industries in the British economy reflected an older difficulty of developing the new industries of the Second Industrial Revolution, the structural weaknesses of the country's industrial system emerged quite clearly also from the decline in coal production. The 1926 General Strike was followed by renewed labor troubles in the industry. Coal exports saw a disastrous drop by 60 percent.

Although the output of the electrical engineering, machine tool, and chemical industries had risen from 6.5 percent of total industrial production to 12.5 percent, this rise proved insufficient to overcome traditional weaknesses, to reduce the weight of the financial sector, and markedly to increase employment. To take the chemical industry, it, like coal and textiles, continued to focus "for the most part on older and simpler operations in inorganic chemistry" instead of developing dyestuffs and drugs. As a result it was by 1924 becoming "uncomfortably apparent" that chemicals were "in serious danger of being hopelessly outclassed, in scale and scope," by the Germans and Americans.[63] The picture was arguably even worse with respect the steel industry: "Not only were British furnaces small, but as the figures of stagnating labour productivity" indicated "they were also ill-provided with modern ancillary equipment." This left steel in "a condition of chronic depression and wild uncertainty about its true state and prospects."[64] Meanwhile, as will be seen in a moment, the German steel industry underwent a massive rationalization program, modeled on the big American trusts, though with ambivalent results. Finally, British mechanical engineering had also little to show for. Even if the overall state concealed "a considerable variety of experience, both between and within trades," there were many inefficiencies that the higher productivity of some of the more modern sectors could not equalize.[65]

This being the state of Britain's industries, old and new, a further growth in exports to parts of the world other than the sterling bloc with its preferential tariffs could hardly be expected. Indeed, between 1921 and 1930 exports stagnated overall. One reason was that textiles and coal as staple products "were relatively uncompetitive in world markets because of high unit costs of production arising from the technical inefficiency of the industries concerned and also because of lack of competitiveness on non-price counts."[66] Nor was the picture prettier at the level of prices. The brief explosion of wages immediately after the end of the war had increased the price differentials between the United States and Britain from 8 percent to 23 percent, and probably even more with respect to Germany.[67] Then hit the 1921 slump. Wages fell and unemployment rose sharply so that in February 1923 the percentage of unemployed trade union members was almost 15 percent. By August 1924 it had declined to 7.2 percent only to rise again to 8.6 percent a month later. With 1.5 million still out of work in 1924, the year saw a series of strikes, including buses and trains. By the summer of 1925 the share of unemployed union members reached 12.3 percent.

Not surprisingly, the demonstrations that Britain had seen in the early 1920s, for example, on Armistice Day 1922, escalated, leading to further protests, especially by the well-organized miners, and finally to a fully fledged general strike in the spring 1926.[68] This strike officially lasted for twelve days, but when it was called off on 12 May, bitterness was still so great that it went on spontaneously for another day. The miners continued their industrial action for another six months, until they also gave up having gained virtually nothing. Subsequently, the government not only tried to prevent a repetition of the damage that the general strike had caused to the economy and among foreign investors by passing the restrictive Trade Disputes Act, but, on a more positive note, attempted to stimulate the economy. Still, neither the Labour Cabinet under Ramsay Macdonald nor the Conservatives under Stanley Baldwin were able to bring about a more lasting turnaround.

To be sure, it was not just the anger and frustration of the working population, its proclivity to go on strike and disrupt production that accounted for the stagnation. If in his interview with *Forbes* Hammond had identified the smug lack of dynamism of "British capital" as a serious drawback to an economic revival,[69] Keynes was even harsher when, in November 1926, he raised the question of the "suitability and adaptability of our Business Men to the modern age of mingled progress and retrogression."[70] The explanation he gave was that too many of the current generation of businessmen had gained their executive positions through their fathers and grandfathers rather than by rising on their "own legs."

In fairness, though, another factor must be added that the British-American historian Jay Winter has called the "Lost Generation" syndrome. As he shows, all too many of those who had volunteered to fight in 1914 and were wiped out in the trenches had been the young university students especially at Oxford and Cambridge. They were now sorely missing, as they were to be the next generation to move into positions of responsibility in the economy and politics. Neither Germany, with its universal service army in which the losses were highest among the working class, nor the United States, which had entered the war late and took until the spring of 1918 to send larger contingents to the Western Front, faced the generational problem of older and less adaptable managers in the way Britain did.[71] Nevertheless, the verdict of the British historian Corelli Barnett will have to stand the "the war rendered British businessmen more self-satisfied rather than less, because, [by] forgetting that foreign machines had alone made the colossal output of munitions possible, they took victory as being proof that British industry was superior to German."[72] While the problem of managerial inertia and conservatism had existed before 1914, the war had indeed brought little change. Nor did it help the recovery of the British economy that the spending power of the average consumer also barely increased.

In these circumstances the arguments that Patrick Cohrs, Michael Hogan, and Kathleen Burk have advanced in their books with regard to Anglo-American relations look plausible on the surface. Burk was struck by the amity and cooperation between the two nations, as reflected in the public and private archives that she found. To her, relations between the two banking systems were "symbiotic."[73] In Cohrs's view the mid-1920s saw a close relationship between Britain and America and even the conclusion of a *"Pax Anglo-Americana"* that he interpreted as a transitional phase from the *Pax Britannica* of the nineteenth century to the *Pax Americana* of the post-1945 period.[74] He also purported to show that "the reorientation of American policy under Hughes and the new mode of Anglo-American co-operation fostered by MacDonald paved the way for what was indeed the first 'real' peace settlement after 1918:

the London reparations settlement of 1924."[75] Hogan wrote (as is also reflected in the title of his study) "that instead of the wide great-power community envisioned by Colonel House in 1916, an informal Anglo-American economic entente had emerged by mid-decade."[76] However, like Cohrs, he then goes on to mention a number of factors that do not quite fit this interpretation.

One of these that has already been mentioned both in the context of the Paris Peace Conference and the meeting at Genoa was the British determination to keep the Empire and Commonwealth together as a trading bloc. Thus British FDI underwent a marked shift, with some 50 percent now going to the Commonwealth. In the view of B. C. Forbes, "Britain is adhering more earnestly than ever before to 'trading within the Empire.'"[77] This policy, he continued, "is stimulated by her natural desire to cut down the industrial lead attained by the United States during and since the World War." It was of course a policy that had irritated the U.S. administration from Wilson to Coolidge as well as the American business community who, confident in their newly won economic strength, pushed for the Open Door, whether in the Far East or in other parts of the world. Parrini, it is true, claimed that "the British imperial preference system did not in most cases forbid American investment." But he then added, "It gave to competing British investors a significant advantage."[78]

Beyond manufacturing industry, there was also the tension between the City and Wall Street. The American banking industry had resented for a long time that so much lucrative international commissioning business had been flowing through London—before 1900 still the undisputed financial center of the world with large "invisible earnings." This was to be changed after World War I, when New York's bankers were quite unabashed about their ambition to replace their British competitors. Paul Warburg was particularly blunt about this when he wrote to Owen D. Young on 21 March 1924,[79] "The opportunity that the present emergency in Europe offers is unique, and I don't believe it will ever be again within as easy a grasp of the United States as it is today. It is the question of whether the Dollar shall permanently retain a dominant position or whether we are willing to surrender financial mastery to the Pound Sterling for good and all!" He added, "England realizes that, and that is why the Bank of England is willing to go to a considerable length in granting facilities." And indeed, "Britain's political and financial elites never lost sight of their underlying aim: to re-establish the *status quo ante bellum* as far as possible, with The City still seeking to regain pre-eminence from Wall Street."[80] In light of these realities, it is a bit is difficult to discern a symbiosis or anything like a continuation of the wartime "special relationship" between the two World War I allies

in the 1920s. If B.J.C. McKercher is correct, Britain's politicians and diplomats harbored a "deep and latent mistrust" of the Americans.[81] Nor
in light of Warburg's remark to Young, had suspicious City bankers
changed their mind about Wall Street's hegemonic ambitions.

It did not help the British position that some policies relating to the
erosion of Britain's financial hegemony were self-inflicted. The British Conservatives and their allies in the City had always regretted that
the country, badly battered by the total war effort, had been forced to
abandon the gold standard in 1918. An early return to this standard
and to the convertibility of sterling had therefore constantly been at the
back of the Conservatives' minds. When the issue reappeared in 1924
in connection with the expected general stabilization of the economies
of Europe following the implementation of the Dawes Plan, Benjamin
Strong, the governor of the New York Federal Reserve Bank, encouraged, for not entirely altruistic reasons, his colleague Montague Norman of the Bank of England to pursue the reintroduction of the gold
standard. As the former put it to Norman on 3 June 1924, returning to
the gold standard as soon as possible would be "for the ultimate benefit" of British trade and "facilitate paying her debt to us."[82]

However, from the start there had been serious questioning of
whether any advantages would in fact accrue to the British economy
from a return to gold. Keynes, for example, was convinced and said so
very loudly that it would reinforce the country's dependence on the
United States. In an article in *Forbes* of 15 January 1927, Merryle Stanley
Rukeyser also referred to "the critics of the British Treasury [who] asserted that a return to gold would entail a recognition of the economic
supremacy of the United States."[83] These critics were no doubt correct,
and it seems that this is why Norman was being nudged by Strong.
And behind him stood the American banking community whose members had repeatedly articulated their ambition to replace the City as the
financial center of the world.

Yet there was not merely the transatlantic rivalry between New York
and London. On closer inspection, the return to the gold standard was
also a major issue of contestation between the City, on the one hand,
and British manufacturing industry, on the other. Again the question
was whose interests the Conservatives in Parliament and the Cabinets
of the mid-twenties put first. The war was not even over when the idea
began to circulate that the best way to revive a civilian economy was to
have a sound currency by returning to the gold standard.[84] Norman and
his supporters in the City were convinced that this was the only path
to a stable international system of payments and a renewed flourishing
of world trade. If the Bank of England introduced a moderate increase
of its rate and thereby also gently fueled inflation, sterling's position

would be strengthened. British industry, by contrast, feared that dearer money and rising inflation would negatively affect its competitiveness, increase wage pressures, and reduce its capacity to hire more workers.

The back and forth between the two sectors continued until 1925 after Winston Churchill had become chancellor of the Exchequer and found himself between three stools. He shared the suspicions of Lord Beaverbrook and the right-wing press that Wall Street was trying to steal the City's clothes and undermine the Empire and Common-wealth as a preferential tariff zone centered on sterling.[85] Nevertheless, the pressure of Norman and the bankers on him was strong enough for him to opt for a return of the gold standard in April 1925 at the risk of higher unemployment and the other negative consequences for British industry that its spokesmen had warned about. Prime Minister Baldwin argued that the standard was a "safeguard against [the] sub-version of [the] existing order."[86] The move pleased the City. As had been warned, the strength of the pound handicapped British industry and especially the branches of the Second Industrial Revolution to com-pete with the Americans and Germans. The Federation of British In-dustries (FBI) and also Sir Alfred Mond, the chemical industrialist, pro-tested but to no avail. As one paper put it, industry had been "crucified on a cross of gold" or, to invoke the title of Barry Eichengreen's study, had been put in "Golden Fetters."[87] But it was not the first nor the last time that Britain's productive economy was disadvantaged for the sake of the banks and their much vaunted "invisible earnings."[88] In light of this outcome of the power struggle between manufacturing industry and the City, with Wall Street always hovering in the background, it is not too farfetched also to see a connection between this decision and the industrial unrest that reached its first culmination point in 1926. But even after the end of the General Strike, the British economy shuffled from crisis to crisis until the Depression produced further hardship from 1929 onward.

Churchill later reproached himself for having allowed himself to be pushed into his decision by Norman and his advisers, calling it the "biggest blunder of [my] life."[89] But the damage had been done and the decision could not be reversed until the country went off the gold standard again in September 1931. The point to be borne in mind is what it meant for the dynamics of the North Atlantic Triangle that is at the center of this book. While the Baldwin Cabinet and the City had their eyes firmly fixed on the United States as a rival in pursuit of its antiprotectionist strategy and opposition to the Empire, Germany's ma-neuvers to regain its former position in the international markets also appeared in London's visor. The suspicion was that with the Americans favoring industrial Germany, they would make her "an even greater

commercial rival than she had been before the war."[90] The City also
worried about "the establishment of German-American commercial
links that by-passed London and reduced its entrepot role." As Walter
Leaf, the chairman of the Westminster Bank, put it in June 1925, there
was the possibility that a "depreciated pound would be squeezed out
of world finance between the two great gold currencies, the dollar and
the mark."[91]

British anxieties of 1925 must also be seen against the background of
a proposal that the Anglophile Hjalmar Horace Schacht, the president
of the Reichsbank, had put to his colleague Norman as early as January
1924.[92] He offered the creation in Germany of a sterling-based "gold
discount bank" that would oblige the new bank as well as the Reichsbank "to deal solely with and through the Bank of England in Great
Britain," provided that Norman participated in the funding of this
institute to the tune of five million pounds sterling. Arguing that this
step could provide German industry with much-needed credits, subsequent negotiations yielded, in addition to the undertaking from the
Bank of England, a promise from a consortium of British private banks
of another five million. Although Owen Young as Dawes's deputy in
the Committee of Experts was more annoyed with Poincaré's procras-
tination on the Ruhr and Rhineland questions than with Norman and
Schacht, it was no secret that the proposal was an attempt by Schacht
who feared the Reichsbank's dependence on Wall Street to create a joint
Anglo-German front. It was a futile move and the "Americanization" of
the British financial system and the Weimar economy continued.

Given these developments, the disputes over the supply of rubber
that arose between the American Rubber Association and British grow-
ers may seem unimportant.[93] But they, too, are indicative of the fact
that the *Pax Anglo-Americana*, if it ever existed in this period, was not
as harmonious as some scholars have postulated. As has been mentioned above, ultimately the World War I Allies envisioned two different economic world orders. The British elites thought in terms of the
Imperial preferential tariff zones which the City dominated, backed by
gold and a strong sterling. Free Trade now meant open markets within
the Empire and Commonwealth for British industry, with other trading
nations having to overcome the tariff walls around it. Wall Street and
the big manufacturing corporations aimed at a global economy with
open markets and open access to raw materials that was run by American money. It was these realities of Anglo-American relations in the
postwar period that led Hogan to conclude that the erstwhile "informal
understanding had broken down" by the middle of 1925.[94] Even if affinities continued to exist between the British and American business
communities that dated back to the war years, after the ratification of

the Dawes Plan American banks and manufacturing industries were increasingly looking toward Germany for their investments and exports.

The statistical material on the relatively poor performance of British industry, the number of strikes and unemployed therefore should be viewed together with less tangible sociocultural research on the country's economic and political predicament. There is, to begin with, the fragmentation of manufacturing with its many family firms "rubbing shoulders with bankers and financiers at board meetings," whose members saw the world "essentially in terms of their particular sector of industry."[95] World War I had not strengthened the organization of British industry. The FBI remained weak if compared with the powerful German industrial lobbies. As Eyre Crowe at the Foreign Office observed rather disdainfully in April 1916, the Association of British Chambers of Commerce, with its fifty thousand members in the 1920s, was "really nothing more than a very incompetent debating society."[96] In these circumstances, it was difficult to establish a cooperative relationship with the unions and to gain an effective voice in the City and among its supporters in the Conservative Party in Parliament, many of whose members were educated in the same public schools and Oxbridge colleges.

Understandably, there was resentment "at the American dismissal of Britain as inefficient, unstable and hovering on the brink of revolution."[97] But the trouble was that this view was shared by Norman who believed that "if British manufacturers were unable to hold their place in foreign markets, it was chiefly because they were un-enterprising and too 'individualistic' to rationalize their operations."[98] It was a view shared not only in the City but also by Arthur Balfour, later lord president of the council, when chairing the Committee on Industry and Trade. He noted in his final Committee Report, published in 1928, that "American trade has increased to a considerable extent" in many markets and seemed to have done so "at the expense of British trade."[99] He therefore urged the British business community to become more efficient through "large-scale production, elimination of waste, standardisation, and simplification of practice," in short through " 'rationalisation.' "

It is telling of the reservations that British businessmen and members of the House of Lords harbored about this concept that Balfour, as the chair of an industry and trade committee that had been asked to investigate Britain's industrial problems, put the term in quotation marks. At the same time, they were "envious of the Americans' peaceful labour relations and boundless optimism about business prospects."[100] The Rothermere press tried to drive this point home when insisting that "America has shown" how rationalization and mass production can be achieved "without 'sweating' the worker."[101] These attitudes may explain why in the power struggle between the City and manufacturing industry over the return to the gold standard the former and its allies in the Baldwin Cabinet and the Bank of England opted for what they thought was the stronger of the two main pillars of the industrial Britain. It was a preference that not even the resurgence of British manufacturing in World War II succeeded in changing in the long-term after 1945.

7. American Investments in Weimar Germany and Their Risks

Compared to the British reaction to the larger issue of the American economic pressure upon Europe in the 1920s, the Germans were indeed more responsive when it came to modernizing their factories with American help, now that the 1922 trade agreement was fully operative and loans were flowing into the country. Werner Link, in totting up American long-term and short-term loans between 1924 and 1930, arrived at a total of 137 to the tune of $1.3 billion with annual amounts reaching close to $250 million in 1926 and 1928. Short-term American loans amounted to some $94 million. Carl-Ludwig Holtfrerich, in his very meticulous account of American capital exports, has put together a set of data in which he compared the years 1919–23 with 1924–29.[102] These figures have to be held against a total of $9 billion that had been invested worldwide up to February 1930, with world trade between 1925 and 1929 rising by 21 percent.

Apart from the bankers and investors, American firms also returned to Germany to revive pre-1914 and early postwar commercial links or to forge new ones. American FDI went into agencies and production facilities. According to Commerce Department figures, 1,150 American firms sold their products in Germany through permanent representations, and some 79 reopened or built factories. The branches were much the same as before 1914, that is, electrical engineering, chemicals, automobiles, steel and iron products, shoes and leather, and so were the companies. The total value of capital they invested amounted to close to $139 million, with the car industry, to be discussed in detail at the beginning of the next chapter, taking up the largest chunk. As Karl Heinrich Pohl put it in his study of the Weimar economy and foreign policy, "the question of reparations had been transformed from a weapon of French foreign policy into an international business—with preference given to the U.S. . . . A far-reaching identity of interests had been established between the two countries."[103] He added that the more German indebtedness grew, "the greater would be the interest of

American capital in the well-being of the German debtors also in the future." America's dynamic optimism spread into virtually all branches of industry.

However, with the benefit of hindsight, it would be very misleading to say that all was well with the expansion and modernization of German industry, even if the indigenous business culture was different from that of Britain and tended to draw positive American comments rather than criticism. Just as in Britain, the problems arose from the structural and attitudinal conditions with which the German economic system, marked by a number of peculiarities, continued to wrestle. There was first of all the issue of the channeling of American loans. Its dimensions and broader implications have become clearer after William McNeil and other historians began to evaluate the files of Parker Gilbert, the Wall Street banker and official Reparations Agent in Germany.[104] He was supposed to supervise the implementation of the Dawes Plan.

As Young had stressed in his speech at the Waldorf-Astoria dinner in the middle of December 1924 when the ratification of the settlement was being celebrated, there were no solutions that would work overnight.[105] The Committee of Experts had also always known that they would not be able to produce more than a transitional arrangement for the payment of reparations. Although the Dawes Plan worked for the time being, sooner or later it would have to be revised for both Germany and the recipients of payments to have something more durable in hand. Moreover, the Committee of Experts almost expected that the Germans would be the first to push for a revision, as the payments gradually increased from year to year. This revision was in fact initiated in 1928 and resulted in the Young Plan that was finally adopted in August 1929. Essentially, it amounted to a rescheduling of the debt and provided for a more extended payment period of some fifty years.

Apart from the Reich government, Gilbert himself began to raise the issue of an eventual revision soon after assuming his duties as Reparations Agent in Berlin. But his activities inevitably also involved him in a close monitoring of the German economy. He was particularly anxious that American loans went into the modernization of industry. It did not take him long to discover, though, that many bonds offered to investors on the American market were not from private companies to be used to make production more efficient. Instead they originated from German cities that wanted to strengthen their infrastructure. Of course, as long as American loans were used to improve roads, ports, or public utilities, they could be deemed modernizing investments. But many city fathers who tried to attract American money were also politicians who thought of the next election and were keen to remain popular with their voters.[106] Gilbert therefore observed with dismay how, say, city of Cologne bonds were used by its mayor, Konrad Adenauer, to build recreational facilities or the impressive "Green Belt" (*Grüngürtel*), a park that hugs the inner city of Cologne to this day. There was no effective way to stop the flow of money into such issues, not least because they looked safer to an investor sitting in the American Midwest than those floated by manufacturing firms whose economic soundness it was difficult to gauge from afar.

Another area of potential trouble was that the gains from the revival of the German economy were quite unevenly distributed. By 1925–26, urban centers such as Berlin, Hamburg, Frankfurt, Stuttgart, or Munich experienced a good deal of prosperity. It was enjoyed primarily by those commercial and educated middle classes who had not lost their savings in the hyperinflation of 1923 and whose well-paid jobs left them with quite a lot of spending power in their budgets. While agriculture was ailing after the war and people continued to move to the urban centers in search of better jobs, the white-collar and white-blouse professions expanded. These were the socioeconomic groups that could pay for consumer goods and leisure activities that in turn stimulated the supply of cultural offerings. They ranged from "high" culture, such as concerts of classical music, opera, theater, and art exhibitions, to "popular" culture and entertainment, such as dance halls, fairs, or movies. Most films were directly imported from Hollywood, but there were also adaptations to other American imports. Moreover, there arose an intriguing competitive tension between the American market-based approach films made to entertain and the more experimental and "darker" German movies that, though they benefitted from a protectionist *Filmkontingenzgesetz*, were no money-spinners. In 1925, Coca-Cola built a bottling plant in Essen and marketed its fizzy drink in competition to German *Brause* and beer. Overall, the mid-1920s was an enormously creative period for cultural experiments at all levels in theater, music, visual arts, architecture, and dance.[107]

While living standards rose for some groups, others were left behind, not only in agriculture but also among blue-collar workers. Since unemployment remained high, rising from a relative low of 682,000 (3.4 percent) during the first boom year of 1925 to 2 million in 1926 (10 percent), then hovering around 1.3 million (6.1 percent) in 1927 and 1928 before rising to 1.9 million (8.5 percent) in 1929, several million family members barely participated in the new prosperity. This also applied to those whose hours were cut.[108] Those who kept a full-time job were seeing both their wages but also their leisure time reduced. The eight-hour workday—one of the few genuine economic achievements for industrial workers in the 1918 Revolution, but a thorn for the employers—had been scrapped again during the crisis of 1923. Trade union membership had been high during the early 1920s at between 8 and 9 million in 1922–23. It dropped to 5.3 million in 1924 and stayed at around 4.7 million between 1925 and 1928, rising again to 5.5 million in 1929 and 1930. In short, just as Zara Steiner has concluded for Britain that the "golden twenties" were not so golden, the German economic historian F.-W. Henning came to similar conclusions with respect to the Weimar Republic.[109] Nor did agriculture fare better.[110] So, before we extol the achievements of "Weimar culture" too much, there was a dark side to the glitter and successes of the 1920s: continued working-class deprivation and distress.

Partly in an effort to avoid further losses of members, the union leaderships became interested in American industry where workers were rumored to have high wages, a car, and a house. In her *Visions of Modernity* Mary Nolan has examined how it was that German industrialists traveled to the Unites States, as they had done before 1914, to visit modern factories in Michigan, Ohio, or Pennsylvania.[111] They were joined by trade unionists interested in American labor relations and in how far American work practices, factory organization, and management might be transferable to Germany. They often came back feeling that their country still had a long way to go to achieve blue-collar lifestyles that they had seen in Detroit or Pittsburgh. Although few, if any, of these trade unionists ever went to see the poverty in the American South, in the sticks of northern Maine, or in the slums of Chicago, Harlem, and Los Angeles, they sensed that the lives of their American colleagues also had a marked downside that included little social security and protection against employer arbitrariness. It was only the New Deal that changed these conditions of insecurity in the 1930s.

This meant that those trade unionists who had taken a closer look came back to Europe feeling that their system of social security but also the labor practices in the new industries were in fact more progressive than America's. But they also knew that back home conditions could be quite varied, too, depending on whether the employer was the head of a small family firm with traditionally more rigidly paternalistic traditions, a large steel firm or coal mine run by a management with strong antiunion sentiments and practices, or a company like Bosch or AEG whose executives inclined toward cooperation and compromise with their workforce rather than responding to a strike with a lockout and by calling the police.[112]

The state of labor relations back home was to no small degree also driven by larger discourses about "Americanization," the "rationalization" of production, and standardization that had resumed among unions and employers after 1923. One of these revolved around the treatment of work forces and a metamorphosis that pre-1914 Taylorism had undergone. As will be remembered, Taylor's approach to work organization had been harsh. He saw industrial workers as unskilled humans who merely had to be taught repetitive tasks in return for higher wages and bonuses. It was, as Charles Maier has demonstrated, an engineering view of modern industrial labor.[113] But by the early 1920s, if not before, the discovery of the "human soul" by psychology and psychiatry had spilled over into the industrial world. After 1918, many managers were no longer just supervisors who issued rulings from the top. They had become more sensitive to the immaterial aspects of labor and had come to see the "factory as a society," involved in a common productive enterprise. By the 1920s, Scientific Management had "extended the original approaches of Taylorism into all areas of labour productivity, technological efficiency, and even corporate organization," but in a less disciplinarian guise. If the tempo of production was stepped up, the fast pace—true to the arch-capitalist slogan that "time is money"—also became the hallmark of people's lives outside the workplace.[114]

In Germany, the interest in ideas about how to organize and run a modern corporation became suffused with concepts of more centralized planning and economic forecasting not just within a multilevel firm but also between industry and government. Against the background of the experience of the war, American business had pushed hard for a full restoration of a liberal-capitalist economy that kept the state out and relied exclusively on the forces of the market to generate growth and prosperity. In Britain and Germany, where the organization for total war had unfolded between 1915 and 1918 and had therefore also struck deeper roots, it was not just socialists and communists who talked about the permanent involvement of the state in the economy. While the workers and their leaders who adhered to Marxism in its various guises hoped to transform the capitalist economy into a socialist one, some more moderate trade unionists were not merely prepared to collaborate with reform-minded employers of the "Siemens camp" on collective bargaining rights and containment of conflict through the institutionalization of conflict but also on the larger definitions relating to the changing relationship between "capital and labor" as well as between industry and the government. Discussions on the rationalization and standardization of work to increase productivity constituted an integral part of these debates, some of which became intertwined with discourses on managers as technocratically minded "engineers of the soul."[115]

Finally, these developments must be related to Ford's ideas that were not merely about rationalized production and assembly line work at an attractive rate of $5 per day. They were also about how to motivate workers by appealing to their desire to own and consume. His recipe was to pass a larger portion of the gains achieved through rationalization on to the workers as consumers and to lower prices in the expectation that, with more money in their pockets, they would spend it not merely to cover their daily needs in food and housing, but also to buy consumer durables. It is this side of Fordism that employers and unionists also witnessed on their visits to the United States or assembled from the newspaper articles, company brochures, and books that were being published in large numbers in Germany as the economy recovered in the mid-1920s with the help of American loans and FDI.

However, the picture becomes more complex when the responses of different industrial branches and their lobbies are considered. The electrical engineering industry had, not surprisingly, a strong interest in the designing, production, and marketing of consumer durables, such as vacuum cleaners, electric tea kettles, fridges, radios, telephones, or washing machines that were also pleasing to the eye and practical. AEG, Siemens, and Bosch were at the forefront of these movements. A growing number of department stores were keen to display and sell such products in their glittering "palaces of consumption," with the more modest chain stores not far behind. Together with the automobile industry these branches were the leaders of the Fordist revolution that was also reflected in the ever faster pace of both factory production and life outside the workplace.[116] To be sure, there was ample criticism of other aspects of Americanism, such as the alleged tendency toward uniformity. Frank Lippert has even argued that the ubiquitous German cartelization movement, first discussed in chapter III and to be examined again in chapters V and VI, must be seen as an "attempt to mitigate the negative consequences of rationalization at the firm level by higher-level planning and to transfer them, inter alia, through price increases, to the demand side."[117]

It should be clear by now that the response of the Germans—be they workers, trade union leaders, editors of factory newsletters, or cultural critics and academic economists—was quite polyphone and that this was no less true of the men who were in charge of corporations and their lobbies. The power and influence of the latter was particularly strong in Germany and was concentrated in the peak associations whose presidents and officers often spoke for an entire branch. However, there has been a scholarly debate about their actual power and unity. While rejecting the Marxist-Leninist-Stalinist notion of a single bloc of a "monopoly-capitalist" ruling class that not only determined economic policy making, but was also responsible for bringing Hitler to power, a larger number of historians have asserted that there existed a split between a liberal-capitalist and a conservative-nationalist camp. The former was embodied in the policies of export-orientated and socially reformist-minded companies such as Siemens, Bosch, and chemicals companies that gained the upper hand in the mid-1920s also in the peak association, the powerful Reichsverband der Industrie (RDI). But, as Bernd Weisbrod has shown, this did not mean that the conservative bosses of coal and steel, especially in the Ruhr region, had been successfully sidelined. Rather they retained a "veto" position that was strong enough to put a brake on reformist initiatives.[118]

The very bitter *Ruhreisenstreit* of 1928 that badly undermined worker-management relations is a good case in point. On this occasion, the managers of iron, coal and steel, especially in the Ruhr region, reacted very harshly to their labor dispute with the metal workers' union and unceremoniously locked their work forces out. The problems that came to the surface in such disputes concerning the positions of employers on domestic and foreign issues were glaring enough for Peter Hayes to disagree with the two-camp hypothesis and to insist that industry was even more fractured than earlier scholarship had assumed.[119] Sensibly enough, he wanted to get away from "an ahistorical schematization that elides differences in the national and international contexts at different periods" and "blinds us to important changes." He added, "We [also] need to recognize the distorting effect of the extraordinary phenomenon of the Ruhr." It was "more compact, more coordinated by a common 'culture' and entrepreneurial 'mentality' and by sociological as well as economic ties than most other aggregations of commercial energy." But, though "for a time absolutely pivotal to most of German industrial production, the Ruhr was neither imitable nor imitated by other industrial constellations, either regional or sectoral." This meant that "we must stop chasing the chimera of an industrial two-party system."

Even if Hayes's interpretation of "industrial factionalism" is accepted, he, too, stresses the power of the Ruhr heavy industries. Their weight grew markedly with the onset of the Depression when the consensus-building efforts between the unions and the "Siemens camp" began to fray and class conflict resumed in the face of mass unemployment and escalating austerity programs by the government of Reich Chancellor Heinrich Brüning. As Paul Reusch, of Gutehoffnungs-hütte steel trust and then president of the Ruhr iron and steel association (aka *Langnamverein* because of its long title), put it in June 1928,[120] "It will have to be examined if, due to the development of conditions, entrepreneurs will be forced to leave the defensive position adopted since the end of the war."

Accordingly, Weisbrod came to the conclusion that it was "erroneous to suppose that the protagonists of heavy industry were [ever] ready to depart on that 'experiment in modernity' which has been described as the 'societal corporatist solution,' if it implied recognition of organized labour as an equal in their domain."[121] By 1930, the Ruhr was no longer merely using its veto powers but actively tried to shape industrial and economic policy making as successive Reich governments became increasingly paralyzed. When Hitler came to power in January 1933, they began to collaborate with an antidemocratic regime that immediately persecuted and then banned the unions and the Social Democratic Party and destroyed the Weimar Republic. Hitler also lost no time to promise industry large public expenditure programs. Since they involved government orders for a rearmament of the Reichswehr, they amounted to a "military Keynesianism" that gave a big boost to heavy industry.[122] There were, it is true, also major power struggles within the RDI with its more diverse central committee membership and leadership. In other words, the bridges that had been built to the unions in the 1920s were not burned completely and talks continued to find ways of jointly tackling the economic and political crisis of the early 1930s. Ultimately, the conservative coal and steel bosses of the Ruhr region won the day and decided in 1933 to support the policies of the Nazi government.

The foregoing discussion of attitudes toward rationalization, mass production, mass marketing, and mass consumption that had its parallels in Britain is very relevant to this chapter's themes of American big business attitudes toward loans, FDI, and the economic reconstruction of Europe in light of what visitors and also readers of the *WSJ* learned and, no less important, what they missed. They were informed about the broad impact that American money had on the German economy, and, at least between 1924 and 1928, they felt assured that the recovery would enable the country not only to pay its reparations agreed under the Dawes Plan but also honor its loan and interest payment obligations. American corporations that made new investments were similarly optimistic that these would pay off. What they also welcomed was that the German firms that belonged to the "Siemens camp" were not merely interested in American ideas and practices of production, management, and marketing, but also in reconnecting with prewar partners. While Anglo-American and German-American relations in the automobile industry will be discussed in detail in the next chapter for the 1920s as well as 1930s, the cooperations that AEG, Siemens, or Bosch developed provide good cases of how Fordism was studied, taken up, critically tested, and integrated into those practices and traditions of a company's culture that seemed to mesh well with Fordist concepts.

But many visitors from the United States missed almost completely what was going on in the field of labor relations and the tensions between divergent branches of industry. At least one of the visitors left with the quite erroneous impression that there was no unemployment to speak of. After the 1923 crisis, the Ruhr industries rarely commanded the interest of American bankers and corporate leaders. And yet, coal and steel were not only groups influencing the domestic balance of economic power, but also the processes of rationalization and "Americanization." Put in a nutshell, the Ruhr steel industry with its vertical links to mining (*Verbundwirtschaft*) rationalized its production, but with anti-American objectives in mind. They took U.S. Steel as their model by bringing about a massive merger of major corporations that would give the new entity a virtual monopoly position in its branch.

8. The Problem of International Cartels, Trusts, and Cooperations

As early as 1905, August Thyssen, one of the promoters of concentration, had argued that "the age of syndicates is really over; we must now move towards trusts."[123] Since Germany did not have a Sherman Act that gave the Justice Department, in the name of preserving competition, the powers to break up firms that had acquired a dominant position in the marketplace, there was no threat to the construction of a German United Steel, the Vereinigte Stahlwerke AG (VSt), in 1926. This time it was Fritz Thyssen, who, in writing to Albert Vögler in July 1927, looked back on the creation of VSt as follows:[124] "Our model is the splendid example of America [where] the wealth in natural resources [and] a large market have promoted the development of mass production. On the basis of this favorable foundation American scientists have done outstanding things." By contrast, Germany "first had to create artificially through our actions the foundations of concentrated mass production." Alfred Reckendrees has investigated this founding process in considerable detail and seen it as part of the "Americanization" of German heavy industry.[125] It is worth comparing this merger movement with what has been said about the British steel industry and also to look across to the German chemical industry and its development of the I.G. Farben conglomerate. Clearly, by the mid-1920s the "special relationship" with Britain was no more than a shadow of what it had been during World War I. By then a "special relationship" had been restored between American big business and their German counterparts both as partners in FDI and joint ventures and as competitors.

Trying to buttress their position in the international economy against the American corporations, but not having the advantage of a very large internal market, it is not surprising that VSt began to see its neighbors, especially French heavy industry in Lorraine, as potential partners in an international cartel. After all, VSt boss Vögler had insisted as early as December 1925 that "mass production is inseparably linked to mass sales."[126] It therefore did not take long for the International Raw Steel Community (IRG), as it came to be called, to be designed as a European bloc.[127] This was patently anathema to the Open Door policies that Washington had established in Asia and in opposition to the British Empire as a closed trading area. Consequently, the United States was also intent on introducing the Open Door in Continental Europe. But there was an escape from the impression of American politicians and businessmen that the Europeans were "ganging up" against them that probably prevented a more direct confrontation.[128] Under the Webb-Pomerene Act of 1918, it was possible for the American companies "to join together for exports without fear of anti-trust prosecution" and thus also to participate in international collaborations.[129]

Perhaps to clarify a complex situation, *Forbes* published a long article by Arthur S. Grey in September 1928 under the title "Germany—the World's Business Partner." In it the former U.S. trade commissioner in Berlin between 1921 and 1924 first analyzed the party-political situation in Berlin. He then gave a description of the organization of that country's industry with clarifications of what were "vertical trusts," "horizontal trusts," "cartels," and "communities of interest."[130] Also going back to the information that had circulated in the United States about German cartels and monopolies, American big business had at least some understanding of the structures of German capitalism.

Given VSt's size and clout, it is not surprising that IRG came to be dominated by the Ruhr trusts. The trouble was that it was soon racked by disagreements between the Germans and the other members, the more so when it turned out that the profits from cooperations were below those of returns from a firm's own ventures.[131] Reckendrees has added that there was also the problem that in many respects German heavy industry, like its British counterpart, remained steeped in mentalities that dated back to the pre-1914 period so that—as will be seen in chapter VI—a genuine reorientation did not occur until after 1945 when the Americans insisted on a fresh start and the abolition of the cartel structures in all of Europe via Germany. And so IRG collapsed in May 1929. It was only in 1933 that a successor, the International Raw Steel Export Community, was set up.

Given that the conditions of American hegemony were not yet those of the post-1945 period, cooperation with European competitors was preferable to exporting American corporations whenever such arrangements seemed "more profitable than uncompromising competition that depressed prices."[132] The founding of the American Steel Export Association was designed to counter the trend toward intra-European cartelization but also to prepare a transatlantic understanding about production and distribution at the global level. Accordingly, the American Steel Export Association signed an agreement with IRG in 1928 to coordinate deliveries of steel pipes to the oil industry around the world. At the same time, U.S. Steel assured Ernst Poensgen of VSt and the IRG vice president that the American steelmakers would desist from lobbying the U.S. government to reintroduce the tariffs that had been lifted in 1927. But such cooperations that also occurred in the fields of rail and copper manufacturing were, inevitably perhaps, badly undermined by the Great Depression.

Beyond these often precarious arrangements, American-style steel production offered monopolists such as VSt yet another bonus: it was under no or little pressure to pass its rationalization gains on to the consumers. Moreover, putting up large steel mills with cutting edge technology, it was also able to reduce its work force, unloading the unemployed onto the Reich budget. The fact that the Ruhr was opposed to unions and the SPD was therefore not merely a reflection of nineteenth-century patriarchal mentalities, but also of bitterness on the part of labor to the threat of redundancy and the technocratic mindset of many Ruhr managers. The above-mentioned *Ruhreisenstreit* of 1928 was thus in part also a confrontation that had its origins in the peculiarities of the rationalization movement in this particular industry. Vögler's mass production was not complemented by mass demand. It soon became clear that overcapacities had been created that the consumer goods industries of the 1920s were still too weak to relieve, and this weakness was exacerbated when the Slump produced a collapse of consumer demand. In other words, steel rationalization produced a downward spiral until Hitler came along with his massive "military Keynesianism"[133] of placing public orders that once again uplifted heavy industry and created jobs in the Ruhr.

The above-mentioned article in *Forbes* on horizontal German cartels also pointed to "communities of interest" (*Interessengemeinschaften*) as "a peculiarly German formula" that "in the German sense, is a rather generic" and hard-to-define term.[134] An example would be that "two firms, making a similar line of products, may find that one is better equipped for manufacturing the heavier units, while the other finds itself better adapted to making the finer units or parts." This community of interest "formula" was adopted by a number of major chemical corporations at about the same time as VSt was created. The I.G. Farben, as it came to be known, included the Farbwerke Hoechst, the Bayer Farbenfabriken, AGFA, the Badische Anilin- und Soda-Fabrik (BASF), Leopold Casella, Kalle & Co., and the Riedel de Häen Chemische Fabrik.[135] Among the companies that remained independent were Schering A.G., Rudolph Koepp chemische Fabrik, C.F. Boehringer & Sons, and Chemische Fabrik von Heyden.[136] On the British side, concentration continued primarily through Imperial Chemical Industries (ICI), Lever Brothers, and Burroughs Wellcome.

But all these efforts to concentrate German and British industry must be seen, just as in steel, against the power and influence of the large American chemical firms such as Du Pont de Nemours, Monsanto, Dow Chemicals, Union Carbide, Minnesota Mining and Manufacturing, and Procter & Gamble. Again the self-confident Americans furthered international competition, but were also prepared to enter into agreements. In 1927, I.G. Farben signed a treaty with Standard Oil of New Jersey. The American IG Chemical Corporation was a joint venture among Standard Oil of New Jersey, Ford, and I.G. Farben.[137]

Meanwhile Du Pont developed its cooperations through its subsidiary, Du Pont Rayon Co. In Germany, the Köln-Rottweil Company became one of its partners that was in turn a subsidiary of the ubiquitous I.G. Farben. But relations were difficult, largely, it seems, because "Du Pont wanted German technology, yet it did not want to be in any way junior to the Germans." It was ready to cooperate, but "only on its own terms," and it is was "fiercely competitive."[138] In December 1929, Du Pont jointly with Kokswerke und Chemische Fabriken A.G. took over "the Oskar Mosebach A.G., with the newly founded Duco Lackfabrik A.G., in which Du Pont has about a 50 per cent interest."[139] In the field of pharmaceuticals, there is the story of Merck & Co., which, after the sale of its American properties to George Merck, cooperated as separate entities—a relationship that apparently worked well and was continued when George W. Merck took over from his father in 1925.[140]

The Americans made similar agreements with a number of French companies. In Britain they took a 49 percent stake in Nobel Chemical Finishes Ltd., with "the controlling interest being held by Imperial Chemical Industries Ltd." Nobel Britain in turn signed an agreement with Germany's Nobel Dynamit A.G. But as first mentioned in chapter II, overall the British had made the strategic mistake of "concentrating for decades on inorganic chemicals and natural dyes for supplying the large home demand of textile, steel, glass, and soap industries for different acids, intermediates, and other raw materials." Here Brunner, Mond & Co. and United Alkali were "among the world's largest" in soda production. Crossfield and Lever Brothers had specialized in soap. While they may still have had competitive advantages in these fields, they failed to move decisively into organic chemistry. Lacking the know-how, British chemicals continued to depend on imports and thus were part of the continuing decline of the country's industries.[141]

There is no space here to examine the new transatlantic links in optics, film, gramophone, and other new industries. The expansion of Hollywood into Britain and Germany has been analyzed in a number of studies that show how movies became an industry that lured millions of people into the cinemas every week and how some 70 percent of the films shown were Hollywood products. The economic but also the cultural impact that the screening of the products of the Californian dream factory had on its British and German viewers can hardly be overestimated.[142] Movies were therefore part of the "Americanization" process that had intrigued men like William Stead before 1914 and that scholars, intellectuals, journalists, and the educated and commercial bourgeoisie debated extensively during the interwar period.

This discussion of the restoration of prewar German-American business connections would be incomplete without a look at the electrical engineering industry. Powerful even before 1914, GE's financial and technological clout had greatly increased during the war. Led by Owen D. Young, International GE's (IGE) ambitions knew few bounds. In a speech to his executives on 26 July 1922, he tried to inspire them with the words: "You have all the world as your field, undeveloped."[143] Advertising was to be used to create "new demands," and, in pursuing its goals, the corporation was not reluctant to work closely with Washington as early as the fall of 1920. By this time IGE president Gerald Swope and other managers had refreshed their prewar links with AEG and Walther Rathenau to discuss the dividing up of foreign markets and patent sharing. As far as Britain was concerned, there was the nuisance of "London's command of the world cable network,"[144] so that the secrecy of American diplomatic and commercial information was never secure. To counter this situation, the Americans turned to radio communication, leading to the rise of the Radio Corporation of America (RCA), whose "expansion fit with GE's sophisticated plan for global expansion."[145] Rather than establishing its own production facilities in Europe, GE, by the late 1920s, began to take a closer interest in AEG. In August 1929 "it was confirmed that 14 million marks of common AEG stock" were to be issued to International GE. This enabled the trust to put no fewer than "five directors on the AEG governing board." Young became a member of the supervisory council. Also, "a closer working agreement was signed between the two companies, providing the German company [with] U.S. technology and patents."[146] Talks also took place between AEG and IGE about Osram, the light bulb manufacturer.

By 1930 IGE had invested $111.6 million, up from $24 million in 1927. By that time, the corporation had "participated in a significant reorganization of the English electrical manufacturing industry."[147] In early 1928 it acquired a share majority of Metropolitan Vickers Electrical Company from its parent Vickers Ltd. While the penetration of the British market continued, IGE apparently used some $11 million to buy Siemens debentures in the hope of gaining an influential position in that company. It was negotiated with the help of Dillon, Read & Co. through which many American loans and investments were being channeled during this period.[148] This time, however, the strategy of gaining a major influence in German electrical engineering failed, even if it was still deemed "a historical economic event of the first order and an important step toward a future world electric trust."[149] As *Vossische Zeitung*, the influential Berlin daily, put it,[150] "The American electrical industry has conquered the world, and only a few of the remaining opposing bastions have been able to withstand the onslaught." The reasons for this strong interest, especially in AEG and Siemens, emerge from the rise in turnover that the electrical engineering industry achieved from 1928 to 1930. In the case of the big Siemens empire it increased from 735 million marks in 1928 to 820 million in 1929, before it was halved to 410 million in 1932 under the impact of the Great Slump. AEG's performance was not quite as impressive, reaching 510 million marks in 1928, including majority participations, and 580 million in 1929. By 1932, turnover had fallen back to 220 million.

For the year ended 30 September 1925, the journal listed gross earnings for GE (Germany) of $8,523,306, a considerable increase over the $5,451,891 of the previous year. Net income after taxes and depreciation for 1925 was $1,900,759, as compared to $1,719,142 for 1924.[151] It seems therefore that both foreign and indigenous electrical engineering was doing quite well in mid-twenties Germany.

Finally, there is a report by Thomas J. Watson, the president of International Business Machines Corporation (IBM), who returned from "an extended business trip" to Europe in the autumn of 1924.[152] He found that there was "more confidence and more hopefulness" all over Europe and that conditions were improving. He thought that in Germany "factories, highways and railroad equipment" were in good shape and was impressed "by the prospect of Germany making a good showing as soon as the Dawes-Young agreement" had been implemented. IBM's German factory that "commenced operations about a month ago . . . is turning out excellent work." At Stuttgart, IBM was "making scales and parts of Hollerith Tabulating machines" and was now "preparing to turn out time recording equipment." Overall, he was expecting "a substantial growth in the company's business abroad," while back home IBM's sales for September 1924 "were the largest of any month in the company's history, surpassing August which was also a record month." It seems that Watson did not visit Britain, but if the above-mentioned assessment for mechanical engineering there is any guide, the picture certainly looked rosier for Germany.

And yet this prosperity remained precarious, just as politics achieved no more than a semblance of stability. Moreover, in light of the concentration and cartelization efforts in steel and chemicals, American corporations always also worried that the Europeans might erect higher tariff barriers, since neither the "Siemens camp" nor the chemical industry were completely averse to moderate protection.[153]

9. The Instabilities of Weimar Politics and American Business Optimism

While the foregoing analysis of the economic aspects of the American-European relationship is indispensable to an understanding of big business's engagement with Britain and Germany, it should never be forgotten that the Weimar Republic also had to grapple with the political fallout from the postwar crisis and the hyperinflation of 1923. The Reich Constitution had introduced a proportional system of representation, rather than a majority vote as in Britain and the United States. This gave even very small parties a chance to gain a few seats in the Reichstag. In view of the fragmentation of Weimar politics, this meant that all Reich cabinets had to be cobbled together from a coalition of parties. This in turn led to unstable governments that were repeatedly toppled when one coalition partner decided to withdraw its ministers. On occasion it was also necessary to form minority cabinets that had to rely on the ad hoc support of parties outside the government. Invariably they demanded concessions relating to their specific agendas and interests.[154]

From his lair in Berlin, Gilbert soon worried not only about reparations payments and about the flow of American investments, but also observed employment statistics, labor relations and the volatility of parliamentary government. He was alarmed when Paul von Hindenburg was elected Reich president in 1925. This was the old field marshal of World War I who, together with Erich Ludendorff, had become the virtual dictator of the wartime monarchy and who, though he knew that Germany had been militarily defeated, refused to refute the poisonous legend of the stab in the back, that is, that the country had allegedly been brought down in 1918 by socialists, communists, Jews, and other "traitors." There was indeed something odd about this election of a man who in his heart of hearts was still a monarchist.

He was surrounded by advisors who in 1926 and again in the early 1930s were talking about how to transform a parliamentary-democratic republic into an authoritarian presidential regime of unelected "experts."[155] Small wonder that, next to Gilbert, Wall Street became rather alarmed first by the nomination of Hindenburg and then by his actual election.[156] To calm the atmosphere, the German ambassador Adolf Georg Otto "Ago" von Maltzan decided to invite a group of Wall Street bankers for a breakfast meeting.[157] Those who accepted, among them apparently some who were pro-French, gave Maltzan a cool reception at first. But when the Q&A session that followed his introduction ended, he received a round of applause. Paul Warburg subsequently told the ambassador that the mood had changed again.

While Gilbert must have been pleased with the diplomatic stabilization of the mid-1920s and especially the passage of the Locarno Pact and other international arrangements, he also had to bear in mind the interests of those American institutions and individuals who were committing their resources to German reconstruction without official guarantees from Washington. These investors and companies were attracted because Germany, as has been seen earlier in this chapter, was advertised as the European country with the greatest potential for growth and lucrative returns. Unlike British industry, its enterprises were assumed to be modern. Its system of education and training, comparatively speaking, was still deemed as excellent as it had been before 1914, and its service sectors as dynamic. In 1925–26 *WSJ* repeatedly treated its readers to articles that reassured them that all was well, especially in contrast to Britain whose industries were run by Oxbridge classics graduates with little understanding of a modern factory whose operations were said to be frequently disrupted by strikes of an allegedly "communist" labor movement.

The main concern with regard to Germany was whether the American monies were channeled into "productive" ventures. Gilbert monitored this closely and urged the State Department to warn the banks to make certain that nonindustrial investments were sound. In line with this consideration, Reichsbank president Schacht "wanted to curtail borrowing by German states and municipalities," arguing that "foreign borrowing by local governments would not stimulate the kind of productive economic growth that would make payback of the mounting indebtedness possible."[158]

In the middle of August 1925, A. L. Humphrey, the president of Westinghouse Air Brake Co. and Union Switch and Signal Co., talked to *WSJ* after returning from a two-month tour of Britain, France, Belgium, Italy, and Germany. In Britain, the company had concluded an agreement with its former subsidiary, Metropolitan-Vickers, that ran until

1929 and could then be renewed on a yearly basis. In Germany West-inghouse had signed a contract with Siemens-Schuckert in October 1924, valid for ten years—presumably a sign of greater confidence in the Germans. It gave Central Europe to Siemens as its exclusive terri-tory, with Siemens promising not to compete in North America.[159] It is against this background of cooperation and optimism that Humphrey noted an " 'abrupt recovery' " with respect to Germany that he felt was " 'due primarily to the stabilizing of currencies, balancing of budgets and proved workability of the Dawes plan.' "[160] Railroad moderniza-tion, Humphrey believed, was "imitating American working methods, particularly as regards the substitution of machinery for man power" in Britain, Germany, and the countries of the Continent. Although orders for new equipment had of late been slow, Humphrey was "encouraged by the outlook for new business." He thought it was merely a matter of time "before all railroad equipment manufacturers will be running at capacity."

The journal also had good news for all businessmen on the occasion of the first anniversary of the Dawes Plan. Economists, it reported, had "generally conceded" that the program had been a success, even if "this first year can by no means be regarded as a test."[161] German gold mark payments had been duly received. More than that, in a review of the past year's operation, the New York Trust Co. had found that " 'besides making possible a stabilization of German currency and restoring order into German industry' " the receipt of " '1,000,000,000 marks is by no means all that has been accomplished' " since September 1924. After listing a number of delays and snafus, the journal mentioned "the con-trol of German revenue" as one of the plan's achievements.

In December 1925 Gilbert confirmed the earlier optimistic assess-ments during a visit to New York.[162] He was quoted as saying that the Dawes Plan was " 'functioning smoothly.' " Germany now had a stable currency and a balanced budget. There was in fact " 'a consider-able surplus even in the face of mounting expenditures.' " He added that " 'from the viewpoint of German reconstruction, the plan marked a turning point in the recovery from disorder and disorganization of the inflation.' " German industry, it was true, was still in need of capital and there were various " 'problems of reorganization.' " But they were inevitable and " 'necessary phases of the recovery itself.' "

Six months later, on 9 August 1926, *WSJ* wrote that "private enter-prises are now borrowing much more than German governments and municipalities." Indeed, in 1925 the German federal states and cities had borrowed to the tune of 422 million marks, with another 391 mil-lion having gone to public works. Meanwhile private enterprises had received 693 million. During the first six months of 1926, the total for states and cities was 141 million marks, with 263 million for public works. Corporate loans were 488 million for the same period. The paper concluded, "Reckoning average interest on the 3,800,000,000 marks [in] loans at 8 per cent, Germany would have 324,000,000 marks to pay. This does not seem an excessive burden when compared with German national income which is now put at around 60,000,000,000 marks."

On 26 October 1926, Henry M. Robertson, president of the First National Bank of Los Angeles and a former member of the Dawes Commission, while not doubting Germany's "'ability to pay'" reparations, pointed to apprehensions expressed by German nationalist politicians who "'desire to make the matter a popular issue.'"[163] On the other hand, "'the present attitude of Germany's business community does not afford any ground for doubt concerning the country's'" ability to fulfill its obligations. The opposition, Robertson added, was "'part of a campaign carried on by the Nationalists against the foreign policy of the Social Democrats and other middle groups.'"

Reporting from Washington on 19 January 1927, *WSJ* referred to the gradually increasing reparations payments that were lying ahead for Germany.[164] There had been criticisms "aimed at the growing volume of German securities sold in the American market." These critics asserted that "sufficient attention had not been given to the fact that reparations are a first charge on German resources," that is, "that foreign loans are junior to reparations." There was also the "argument that during the standard years of reparations payments transfer problems might complicate the payment of charges on foreign loans because of the greatly increased use of exchange for reparations commitments." But "experts inquiring into the situation two years hence" had reached the conclusion "that barring a serious economic crisis Germany should be able to carry the burden of maximum reparations commitments and carry annual payments on loans floated in the United States with ease." The strength of the German budget was "the test of that country's ability to meet its obligations." The article continued by listing the increased reparations payments, whereas "German loans floated in this country since the beginning of 1924 at about 600,000,000, including the 120,000,000 gold loan of 1921" with an average estimated yield of 7 percent and an amortization of 4 percent would mean an "annual charge of German loans obtained in the United States" of "only $60,000,000." Given also the reduction of military expenditure, "the relatively small amounts due to American investors as interest payments should present no difficulty."

In September 1927, J. S. Bache, a heavyweight on Wall Street, came back from a trip to the European Continent feeling that conditions were "'very favorable, particularly in Italy and Germany.'"[165] He claimed, quite inaccurately for a year when the rate was at 6.2 percent, that "'there is no unemployment at present'" and "'industry everywhere shows signs of progress.'" Referring to the Dawes Plan, the banker said that "'it will be a mighty task for Germany to meet the heavy gold payments due in the next few years'" and it would be "'a difficult question to answer'" where the gold would come from in light of the fact that Gilbert "'is not going to permit the gold that is sustaining the mark to leave Germany and since all the gold is right here in America.'" On 20 August, the *Journal of Commerce* was quoted as saying that reparations were marginal since the main issue was Germany's position as a trading nation.[166]

Leon Fraser, the general counsel for the Dawes Plan, who sailed into New York on the same day as Bache, immediately disclaimed "any cause for alarm over the future" of the plan.[167] Germany, he explained, was "'enjoying greater prosperity today than at any [time] since the war and her industries in particular appear to be prospering on a sound foundation.'" Germany's payments since the start of the Dawes Plan had been "'$1,000,000 a day,'" rising to $1,150,000 per day from "'next week.'" This would not raise any problems right now, but the largest payments would fall due in two years' time and this would put the plan "'to its severest test.'" Still, he saw no need to revise the reparations payments that the country had met until now "'without difficulty.'" Of course, there continued to be "'extravagance in government expenditures.'" Fraser ended with the remark that "'sentiment throughout Germany toward America is very cordial, although there is a general desire for some early action on alien property legislation in Washington.'"

In the middle of December, John Moody of "Moody's Investors Service" chipped in after returning from "an exhaustive study [tour] of financial and business conditions" including interviews with "a large number of Germany's important bankers and business leaders."[168] Germany, he explained was of course "'depleted of capital'" and therefore had to import large amounts "'before she can hope to build her production to the point where her annual export balances will fully offset her foreign debt and reparations payments.'" Some "'alarmists,'" Moody continued, were pointing "'to the fact that thus far she has not succeeded in building up any export balances whatever and on the strength of this fact are predicting that there will be a transfer crisis next year.'" However, the rating specialist assured investors, "'there is nothing in this,'" also because Gilbert had means at his disposal to prevent any difficulties. Moreover, Germany had good intentions and "'anyone who has looked carefully into the matter will realize how important the German regards the building up and maintenance of Germany's credit with the outside world.'" Understandably, "'the Germans wish to see reparations terms modified as soon as possible, but her responsible leaders all realize that the building of confidence and credit is infinitely more important to her than any reparations revision at this time.'" In conclusion, Moody took "'a distinctly constructive view of Germany as a field for investment of American capital for genuinely constructive purposes and with the exercise of proper discrimination.'"

A few days later, another key figure, Ferdinand Eberstadt of Dillon Read & Co., spoke about his experiences.[169] He averred that the country had now borrowed a large amount of money from the United States and was seeking to place additional loans. So far these funds had "'been devoted to productive purposes and further loans appear to be necessary and desirable so long as the proceeds are used for purposes which enable the borrower to earn a margin above the requirements for service of the loan.'" As to reparations having priority over private investments, he felt that there was "'no good reason'" for maintaining this principle. If nothing else there was "'general recognition of the moral obligation due to those who have made loans through which the German economy has been rehabilitated, and thus additional power afforded to the German government to provide reparations payments.'" Having touched upon these neuralgic points of the American engagement in Germany, in the end Eberstadt circumnavigated them by proclaiming the Dawes Plan to have been a success, also because it had enabled Germany's "'participation in the movement toward combination and rationalism in European industry'"—an aspect of the larger picture that has been discussed at some length above.

One final article from *WSJ* of January 1928 shall be mentioned here because it quoted no lesser figure than Paul M. Warburg as agreeing with Gilbert "that the time has arrived to limit Germany's obligations," that is, to revise the Dawes Plan after all.[170] The sober comments and reassurances of the readers of *WSJ* that appeared throughout 1927 are likely to have left investors and firms that were thinking of entering the German market in some confusion.

10. Parker Gilbert's Pessimism and American Business Gullibility

It was obvious that the information these investors were receiving was imperfect and in part even misleading. But they did not have access to the reports that Gilbert kept sending to his superiors in the United States. It has already been mentioned that the Reparations Agent in Berlin had been quite concerned about economic and political developments in

Germany, about where American investments were going, and whether the Germans would be able to make rising reparations payments and service those sizeable loans. Overall, he hoped to postpone the revision of the Dawes Plan that the German government was urging him to initiate without delay. The fear was that the German economy was being overburdened by both these foreign obligations and the promise to maintain a social welfare system for those who were still heavily dependent upon this safety net.

In the 1970s the German economic historian Knut Borchardt argued with respect to the economic policies of Reich Chancellor Heinrich Brüning in the early 1930s that his government was faced with a serious overburdening of the economy that dated back to the late 1920s. He therefore had no choice but to adopt a brutal austerity regime.[171] Looking at the relevant statistics and the policies of Brüning's predecessors who were grappling with a similar though still less serious overburdening of the economy with both foreign and domestic financial obligations, the American "alarmists" were not as wrong as their more optimistic respondents in *WSJ* suggested. There was a crisis in the making.

The sword that was hanging over the servicing of German reparations and loans, precarious as it was from the start, seems to have been on the mind of Arthur J. Grey, who had been the American trade commissioner in Berlin between 1921 and 1924. Writing on 1 September 1928, he started his analysis by reiterating that "Germany has held the center of the political and economic arena for the last two decades with a persistency yet to be equaled by any nation. She has awakened among the nations of the world a cycle of reactions ranging from admiration and respect to fear and hatred; then turning back to admiration."[172] But now a point had been reached where the "immediate problem" was that the "Reparations Committee is required by the Dawes plan to transfer the marks into respective currencies of the creditor nations without disturbing international exchange." Grey felt that the way forward was not panicky retreat into protectionism. Although clearly uneasy about the tension between German reparations obligations and the servicing of American loans, he returned to extolling the Open Door that would solve the international economy's woes under American leadership.

On 7 November 1927, Gilbert finally went public with his own serious qualms about Germany's capacity to meet her obligations in a memorandum to the Reich government whose full text he gave to *WSJ* for publication.[173] In it he criticized the "increasing fiscal outlays" as posing an "economic menace" that "seriously jeopardized [the] Dawes Plan." One of his points was the apparent overburdening of the Reich budget with unemployment relief and other social welfare costs. He charged that "the German public authorities are developing and executing constantly enlarging programs of expenditures and of borrowing with but little regard for the financial consequences of their actions." These expenditures undermined public finances: "If present tendencies are allowed to continue unchecked, the consequence is almost certain to be serious economic reaction and depression and a severe shock to German credit at home and abroad." Gilbert's suggested remedies consisted "primarily in reversing the present tendencies toward over-spending and over-borrowing and applying instead a regime of strict economy and of ordered public finance." The Reich government, he added, had the powers to do this and "if they will act promptly and effectively," they could still "prevent a crisis."

Gilbert then retraced the legislative steps that the country had taken to inflate public budgets and the speeches Reich ministers had made to justify their policies. He also quoted the figures involved and mentioned that the Reich government had, from 1 April 1927, taken on "practically the entire responsibility for advancing, when necessary, the supplementary funds for the purposes of unemployment relief beyond those furnished by employers and employe[e]s, though up to that time the States and communes had been obliged to furnish five-ninth of these supplements." Gilbert did not think this to be a "'provident arrangement for the Reich.'" In fact the federal states and communes were now "'drawing larger payments from the Reich than ever before, and will get the principal benefits from any income, corporation and turnover taxes in excess of the amount to fulfill the guarantee already given.'" There was also more and more confusion about who had responsibility for taxation and public expenditure. Worse, despite increased transfers to the federal states and communes, the latter were now pressing the Reich for more "'to meet their constantly increasing expenditures'" while the Reich had also put forward new proposals that would add further burdens to the states and communes. And on top of it all there were the proposed increases of public service salaries that were being mooted at 10 percent.

What emerges from this report is how far the German government by now had the Americans over a barrel. The loans were becoming a bottomless pit. As reparations payments rose, more American money was needed to make certain that foreign debts were being covered in a Reich budget that was increasingly under pressure to fulfill rising domestic claims all the way down to the communal level. But it should be added that the Reich government did not resort to these measures out of spite for the Allies and out of opposition to reparations, even though the nationalist parties exploited this issue with relish in their fundamental hatred of the Reich government and the Weimar Republic as a political system. Unemployment was indeed rising and politicians, having to cope with a democratic voting system and a welter of small parties, among which was one that merely tried to represent those "damaged by hyperinflation" (*Inflationsgeschädigte*), were anxious to maintain or increase their popularity.

The cabinets that had been formed between 1924 and 1928 had been made up of bourgeois coalitions that excluded the Social Democrats. The latter, being internationalist and in favor of reconciliation, had been welcome to vote for Stresemann's foreign policy initiatives when the right-wing middle-class parties in the Reichstag were rejecting them. But when it came to issues that were close to the SPD's blue-collar members, such as working hours or social security benefits, the bourgeois coalition governments had ignored them. The conservatives in industry, especially in the Ruhr, regularly also blocked demands put forward by the Social Democrat trade unions. This changed when after the May 1928 Reichstag elections the Social Democrats gained over twenty seats and, as the largest party, were asked to form the government. The new Hermann Müller cabinet still supported Stresemann's pro-Western policies. But it also began to try to correct some of the defeats that the SPD had suffered on the domestic and economic front while they had been kept out of power by the middle-class coalitions between 1924 and 1928.[174]

It is not clear how far the visitors to Germany whose reports have been quoted above understood these complexities of Germany's domestic and foreign situation and especially the Reich's fiscal policies until the more knowledgeable Gilbert set them out in his report, subsequently published in *WSJ*. The paper's readers would no doubt have begun to wonder how secure their investments still were. Indeed, it seems that behind the scenes the banking community was quite shaken, and it may well be that the above-mentioned reassuring words that prominent men found in interviews and articles in the American press were not based merely on their own continued optimism and gullibility, but were rooted in their inside knowledge, also designed to calm investors' nerves. Now that Gilbert had himself issued a warning people began to appreciate fully that reparations payments had priority over private investments.

No less alarming, American private funds were not necessarily going into "productive" industrial modernization, but into communal swimming pools and green belts. It was a confusing picture with contradictory information coming from a faraway country. Seeing this with the benefit of hindsight seems to have led Joan Wilson to conclude that "the discrepancies that did exist between business thought and action in foreign policy between 1920 and 1933 revealed the confused and often inadequate attempts on the part of businessmen to cope with altered postwar conditions that they did not fully understand, without abnegating their traditional prewar values." Ziebura similarly felt that, while Gilbert and Hoover were increasingly nervous, they were uncertain about what to do.[175]

Nor did Vanderlip develop a better grasp of the situation when he visited Europe in February 1928. Writing to Edwin Harden in New York from Paris on 24 February 1928, he believed that "affairs are undoubtedly improving."[176] Having made some positive comments on the French situation, he referred to Elmar Roberts of AP, whom he had known for thirty years and who had told him over lunch that he felt "confident that there is nothing to cause apprehension in the general outlook in Europe" and "that practically all countries are improving economically." While there were "still many financial problems and the recovery is not likely to be rapid," he saw no grounds to be worried.

When, still in Paris a week later, Vanderlip dined with Judge Woodward, the general counsel of GE, he found him "pretty thoroughly familiar with business conditions throughout Europe" and gave him "a fairly cheerful outlook."[177] It was no more than "quite an optimistic" view of the future, but Woodward thought that "conditions are improving and he sees nothing that is likely to cause serious difficulty." In particular, the judge "was more optimistic about the German financial situation than I would have supposed." He believed "that it is possible for Germany to continue payments under the Dawes Plan unless the Germans decide that it is better not to." He also confirmed "what has been my opinion for a good while, [meaning] that German industrial practices are not sufficiently advanced to make serious competition with the United States." A few years back, Woodward had still assumed that Germany's comeback would create "the very sharpest competition with our producers." But he had now concluded that was "not in the books; that we are more efficient in our manufacturing methods and distribution and have little to fear."

Another of Vanderlip's letters from Paris is dated 27 March 1928 and addressed to H. E. Benedict.[178] Talking over lunch to "P.R." [?], who had just completed a trip around Europe, the latter had reinforced Vanderlip's "earlier impressions that the situation is generally showing much improvement." He believed that if Europe "gets by the next few months without any financial difficulties developing, the Continent is in for a period of 'Victorian prosperity.'" Apparently speaking of the boom in the United States, Vanderlip's interlocutor "professed to feel that the market had gone quite wild and that sooner or later there would be a crash." One reason for this assessment was "that last year's earning would show a decline of twelve and one half percent and that so far this year" earnings were much the same as in 1927. It is difficult to understand this optimism when Gilbert had signaled serious problems several months earlier, except that it seems best to see it against the background of the boom back home in the United States.

11. America's Domestic Boom and the "Wild" Years of 1925–1929

In assessing the economic situation in the United States, Vanderlip's message had been distinctly uplifting, when he wrote to a Japanese colleague on 18 January 1927,[179] "We have enjoyed, during the last few years, an era of great prosperity. The present year promises a somewhat reduced industrial volume as compared with 1926, but the outlook is for a year of high activity. Funds are plentiful and there seems [to be] a pretty clear tendency toward lower rates." The situation of American banks looked to Vanderlip "particularly strong and favorable to continued plentifulness of credit and aid to industry." Fifteen months later, Vanderlip still had not changed his mind and, in another letter to Benedict, thought that "few people have yet dreamed the dream that will match the reality of America's future."[180] He was not forecasting "what the ticker tape will read in a month or a year, but rather in a generation or epoch." His point was "that the wildest Los Angeles boomer is a pessimist." Benedict would "live long enough to see an accumulation of wealth which would stagger a John Law to dream."

Vanderlip's reference to the period of plenty that the United States experienced in those years until it was followed by collapse in 1929 can be traced in the national statistics for those years. There are also many studies of the "roaring twenties." But the book that still describes this era and its culture best in no more than a little over two hundred pages continues to be John K. Galbraith's *The Great Crash 1929*.[181] To begin with, there are his illuminating statistics. Thus, the Federal Reserve index of American industrial production that had declined to 67 points in 1921 and had still been precarious in 1923 had nearly doubled to 110 in July 1928 and added another 16 points during the following twelve months. In June 1925 production of cars and trucks reached 396,000, the largest figure for any June so far. But the news on these industrial figures and on increasing business volumes was not the only information investors relied on. There was also the real estate boom, especially in Florida, with its attractive opportunities for wealthy buyers and retirees from the North to spend the winter in a mild and sunny climate. Accordingly, in 1925 some $1.6 trillion was cleared, as land and house prices went through the roof.

Meanwhile an even bigger bubble was inflating in the stock market. In December 1924, the *New York Times*, which listed the average share prices of the twenty-five most important industrial corporations, had reached 134 points, and 181 points a year later.[182] To be sure, there were ups and downs in the market that should have reminded investors that they were putting their money into companies that involved risk. But the trend continued upward and credit, as Vanderlip had written, was plentiful. There was also the possibility of putting your money into an investment firm, such as the Goldman Sachs Trading Corporation, which maintained diversified portfolios of their own and attracted investors with the allegedly diminished risk that their diversification offered. The crucial point was, though, that many Americans took their money out of their savings accounts with local banks in the highly decentralized American banking system and consulted with their local bank manager, who advised them to put it into this or that allegedly flourishing manufacturing corporation, real estate company, or even an enterprise in Europe whose published balance sheet looked good.

If foreign investments in manufacturing industry seemed too risky, speculators would turn to municipal bonds, which were assumed to be safer than the private sector. The lure was invariably that the returns would be higher than the interest on an ordinary savings account. Many Americans who were dreaming in this period of boundless optimism of becoming rich were even encouraged by their local banker to take out a loan. This money would then be put into the stock market not merely to obtain high dividends, but also with a view to selling the shares at some higher point, to repay the bank loan and to pocket the rest.

It is not difficult to see what this speculative risk taking would sooner or later lead to. First, share prices were pushed up to levels that bore no relation to the current value of a company or its future potential. Galbraith shows this very impressively by reference to those companies that were leaders in modern production methods and innovation. To give a few examples, in 1928 Du Pont chemicals went up from 310 to 525 points, Wright Aeronautics from 69 to 289, and the RCA from 85 to 525 points.[183] Things became even crazier in 1929, when established corporations such as U.S. Steel, Westinghouse, and General Electric became the target of speculation, in some cases also doubling their stock market quotations. By 1928 some 18 million out of 120 million Americans owned stocks and hence had joined the stampede. The fallout was much larger once the reversal came.

Although the performance of American industry after the 1921 slump was impressive and living standards were rising, structural imbalances continued to exist. They were partly the result of the system of taxation. With the Republicans in power, Andrew Mellon at the helm of the Treasury Department devised tax laws that blatantly favored the wealthy strata, resulting in overaccumulation.[184] The disposable incomes of the top 1 percent of the population increased from 13.1 percent to 19.1 percent. Meanwhile wages, whose rise was so vital for the mass production of civilian consumer goods to fuel consumption, did not keep up with the gains in productivity. No less than 22 percent of America's families had to make do with less than $1,000 per year, while another 44 percent had $1,500 to spend. The picture was even bleaker in agriculture, where the income level of some seven million farming families was below that of urban dwellers. Many of them had very high debts, and some 90 percent of the nation was excluded from the blessings of the "roaring twenties."[185] Nevertheless, an estimated eighteen million stockholders participated in the deceptive bonanza.

For the moment, these problems were largely ignored. The press was full of hype about the economic boom. What was brushed aside was, for example, the indebtedness of the lower strata, who should have been more cautious with their budgets. But it was now increasing dramatically. In the early 1920s, individual indebtedness stood at $1.4 billion. It had risen to $29 billion by 1929. Even more alarming, in the climate of mid-1920s optimism, middle-class people who had some savings were encouraged to take out a loan to join the stock market speculation. Many more also took great risks of a different kind. This supposedly being the American age of modern mass production of goods for the average consumer, they took out loans to pay for a car or other consumer durables, often acquired on a hire-purchase basis, which made this kind of family expenditure alluring but also very vulnerable to an economic downturn.

In looking at these statistics, Galbraith and other scholars have been interested not only in the quantities, but also in the qualitative impact of this boom. As he put it so aptly,[186] "The striking thing about the stock market speculation of 1929 was not the massiveness of the participation. Rather it was the way it became central to the culture." Accordingly, to quote Joan Wilson once more,[187] "Business leaders felt little necessity, at least until 1929, to temper their public statements on foreign policy to any significant degree." There are remarkable cultural continuities extending forward to the 1990s and the bubble that finally burst in 2008, but also back to the pre-1914 period. Thus the British *Banker's Magazine* wrote as early as 1906, perceptively but probably not without a slight dose of envy at the success of the industrial power across the Atlantic, that "the Americans of today are a nation of champion earners, champion spenders, and champion speculators."[188] The article added that this was leading to wild fluctuations in the financial system as well as to "violent extremes of wealth and poverty."

There was one early warning sign in February 1929, when the Federal Reserve Bank became very nervous about the "easy money" that fueled speculation. There were calls demanding a curbing of speculative investments and inside the Federal Reserve system discussions began about an increase in the bank rate. The rumors about this promptly led to a decline in the stock market. But, fearful of a panic, it seems that the administration quickly blocked the plan. The markets calmed down again, and the *NYT* index showed further gains. To offer a few more figures from the index at the height of the stock market bonanza in the summer of 1929: In June the index gained 52 points and added another 25 points in July and 33 points in August. From 31 May to 31 August the increase was thus from 339 to 449. A number of industrial shares proved once more particularly popular:[189] "During the three summer months Westinghouse went from 151 to 286." General Electric "was up from 268 to 391 and Steel from 165 to 258." Investment trusts also attracted ample funds and in some cases doubled their paper value. The first break came in September when industrial production began to decline. On Wednesday, 23 October, the *NYT* index dropped from 415 to 384, and, while still showing some volatility, continued its steep descent into the Depression over the next few days.[190] In 1929, the peak value of all stocks was $87 billion. By November of that year it had shrunken to $56 billion. When the bottom was reached in 1933 the total value hovered around $18 billion.

12. The Great Slump
and Its Consequences
in International Politics

These figures should provide sufficient evidence for what happened on Black Friday and thereafter. The panic that began in October 1929 forced innumerable investors, who had overreached themselves financially, into bankruptcy.[191] But their bankers were also hard hit when, sitting on ever larger numbers of bad loans, their savers, made nervous by rumors, started a run on their accounts. The early birds still succeeded in withdrawing their money. The rest found the counters closed. With more and more banks in liquidation, credit also dried up for local businesses. Production declined and unemployment rose. In 1929 the annual index of industrial production reached its height (in comparison to 1913 = 100 points) in the United States at 180.8 in Germany 117.3 and in Britain, still trailing behind, 100.3. Two years later it had shrunken to 121.6 (United States), 85.1 (Germany), and 82.4 (Britain). In short, the financial crisis become a massive crisis of the economy at large.

A similar chain reaction set in with regard to foreign loans. Many of them were short-term, but had been used by firms and municipalities, especially in Germany, for long-term development projects in the expectation that fresh loans would be available once an earlier one had to be repaid. With American money now drying up, borrowers had to profess that they could no longer repay the loans that were being called in. Many investors were therefore also driven into bankruptcy because their certificates had become worthless paper. In 1935, there were still some six hundred thousand Americans with sufficient staying power to avoid bankruptcy holding defaulted bonds. Beyond the American market, there was also the fallout in the domestic markets of Britain and Germany, the largest debtor nation. As the crisis escalated it was not just the private sector that unleashed mass unemployment. The public sector, faced with declining tax revenues and higher social security expenditures, also began to declare redundancies. In short, it was austerity everywhere.

Turning more specifically to the reactions of the big American corporations and Wall Street, it would be wrong to assume that they experienced the crisis as a continuous steep decline and therefore also lost their nerve. More than once between 1929 and 1932 it looked as if the depression was bottoming out. In the autumn of 1930, Ford saw fresh opportunities for increased production in Britain and Germany.[192] At the same time, IBM reported that its 1930 profits had been the highest on record, while Bosch Germany and Bosch America reinforced their cooperation.[193] Nor did GM beat a retreat, predicting in November 1929 that its investment in Opel Cars would lead to the production of fifty thousand cars per annum and, as shown above, proceeded with its full acquisition of the Rüsselsheim plant.[194] The following two years would reveal that such plans were all too optimistic with respect to Britain and even more so to Germany until Hitler came to power.

Meanwhile American bankers watched the unfolding of the British crisis with ambivalence. The growing weakness of the pound did not provide significant boost to British industrial exports. When, after repeated sterling crises and the undiminished opposition of British industry to the gold standard, this weakness forced London in the autumn of 1931 to abandon this panacea of the City and the Bank of England, American gold reserves grew and the dollar became the lead currency. The drawback was that these developments moved Britain in the direction of higher Imperial and Commonwealth tariffs, finally agreed at Ottawa in November 1932.[195] They undermined Wall Street's capability of challenging the City and the Empire and the latter saw an opportunity to shift the balance again in Britain's favor. Economic nationalism and protectionism were now spreading fast, including in the

United States when Congress passed the Smooth-Hawley tariffs in June 1930. With no end to the international crisis in sight, there were efforts to increase cooperation between the Bank of England, with an increasingly pessimistic Norman at its head, and the Federal Reserve. At one point George Harrison, the governor of the New York Federal Reserve Bank, apparently even tried to persuade Wall Street to provide a large loan to the United Kingdom.[196]

However, as in previous years, the German situation caused the American banking community more serious headaches. In the Reichstag elections in September 1930 the Nazis had increased their votes from 810,000 (1928) to 6.3 million and the number of seats from 12 to 107, resulting in further heavy withdrawals of money from Germany. In November 1930, when German unemployment stood at close to 4 million, Schacht had warned in a speech in Chicago that German reparations payments that had just been rescheduled by the Young Plan might be in doubt if higher tariffs hampered Germany's capacity to earn through exports.[197] He also raised the other thorny question of American private loans, all of which, he boldly asserted, were safe. It did not take long for this to prove a false claim. A month later, H. C. Maclean of the International Chamber of Commerce expressed his confidence that Germany would weather this crisis.[198] Instead the crisis escalated so that the Reich government began to push for a moratorium on reparations that U.S. president Hoover in the end had no choice but to announce.[199] With the moratorium expiring, the final stage in the reparations nightmare was reached at Lausanne in the autumn of 1932 with the cessation of reparations.[200] Inevitably, this raised the question as to whether Allied war debt payments to the United States should also be suspended.

After Lausanne the next question was whether Germany would be able to meet its repayment obligations of private debts. Once more, some Wall Street bankers exuded optimism at the end of 1931. Thomas Lamont of J.P. Morgan Chase then began to put the problem into the larger context of the need to preserve peace and stability.[201] A month later, he discussed the situation of short-term credits and long-terms bonds, concluding that the good faith of the Germans was not in doubt. Otto Kahn of Kuhn Loeb &Co. sounded a similarly optimistic note a few days later.[202] Finally, in December 1932 James Speyer, another banker with strong connections to Germany, came back from a trip stressing the importance of the country's obligations to American bond-holders.[203] But long before that time, more articles had begun to appear on the rising strength of the Nazi movement, ventilating the possibility that Hitler might come to power.[204] A few weeks later, he was indeed nominated Reich chancellor by Hindenburg, opening up an entirely new chapter of Anglo-German-American relations. According to Ziebura, the special partnership of the Weimar Republic with the United States came to an end and the two countries soon became bitter enemies.[205]

If the mid-1920s saw an attempt at the "economization" of politics, in the 1930s Europe's national economies, and the German one in particular, were being repoliticized, with the Americans, fearing another power-political conflict, maneuvering to effect a "re-economization" of international relations.[206] Even more important is another factor. It seems that the reconstruction effort of the mid-1920s failed not only because American money came to Europe too late and only after the failure of the audacious plans of 1920–21 to float a major loan had further exacerbated the postwar crisis. This means that the years 1924–29 were too short to let American loans and FDI do what they were intended to achieve. But there was also another weakness: to be effective, American support should have been accompanied by a recasting of the organization of German industry and banking. As we have seen, Germany but also the rest of Western Europe had structures of cartelization and protectionism that were dysfunctional in an Open Door liberal-capitalist and multilateral transatlantic trading system. This was one of the great lessons that were learned from the mid-1920s: material reconstruction had to be accompanied by a *recasting* of the European protectionist ways of organizing industry and that of Germany in particular. The next two chapters therefore will have to include an analysis of the ways in which this was done by the United States and its big business community during the 1940s.

Notes to Chapter IV

1. John M. Keynes, *The Economic Consequences of the Peace* (New York, 1920); Etienne Mantoux, *The Carthaginian Peace. The Economic Consequences of Mr. Keynes* (New York, 1946); Sally Marks, "Reparations Reconsidered. A Reminder," *Central European History* 2 (1969): 356–65; Marks, "Reparations Reconsidered. A Rejoinder," *Central European History* 5 (1972): 358–61; David Felix, "Reparations Reconsidered with a Vengeance," *Central European History* 4 (1971): 171–79.

2. Zara Steiner, *Lights That Failed. European International History, 1919–1933* (Oxford, 2005), 198, 206ff.; Theodore Balderston, *Economics and Politics in the Weimar Republic* (Cambridge, 2002), 18–19, with additional references to the positions of Mark Trachtenberg, Gerald Feldman, and Barry Eichengreen.

3. Balderston, *Economics and Politics* (note 2) 16, 21.

4. Quoted in Stephen Schuker, "American Policies toward Debts and Reconstruction at Genoa, 1922," in Carole Fink et al., eds., *Genoa, Rapallo, and European Reconstruction in 1922* (New York, 1991), 112. Ibid., 97, on advocates of cancellation.

5. Ibid., 112.

6. Patrick Cohrs, *The Unfinished Peace after World War I* (Cambridge, 2006), 82–83.

7. On Rhenish separatism, see below (note 18).

8. For the best study on the Ruhr occupation, see Conan Fischer, *The Ruhr Crisis, 1923–1924* (Oxford, 2003).

9. Quoted in Werner Link, *Die amerikanische Stabilisierungspolitik* (Düsseldorf, 1970), 56.

10. J. C. Smuts to Lloyd George, 26 March 1919, in W. K. Hancock and J. Van Der Poel, eds., *Selections from the Smuts Papers* (Cambridge, 1966), 9:82–87.

11. Quoted in Alexander Sedlmaier, *Deutschlandbilder und Deutschlandpolitik* (Stuttgart, 2003), 354.

12. Keynes, *Economic Consequences* (note 1).

13. See above, pp. 139ff.

14. Steiner, *Lights That Failed* (note 2), 190n, with American losses; Michael Wala, *Weimar und Amerika* (Stuttgart, 2001), 110.

15. Elisabeth Glaser-Schmidt, "German and American Concepts to Restore a Liberal World Trading System after World War I," in Hans-Jürgen Schröder, ed., *Confrontation and Cooperation. Germany and the United States in the Era of World War I, 1900–1924* (Providence, RI, 1993), 355.

16. Link, *Die amerikanische* (note 9), 174, and ibid., 191, for Hughes's speech at Yale University. Link, "Ruhrbesetzung und die wirtschaftspolitischen Interessen der USA," *Vierteljahrshefte für Zeitgeschichte* 4 (1969): 372–82.

17. Link, *Die amerikanische* (note 9), 183.

18. On Mussolini and his march on Rome in 1922 as a model for the Hitler-Ludendorff putsch and a detailed account of the latter, see Hanns Hubert Hofmann, *Hitlerputsch* (Munich, 1967); on Rhenish separatist putschism, see Fischer, *Ruhr Crisis* (note 8), 243ff.

19. Klaus Schwabe, *Ruhrkrise 1923: Wendepunkt der internationalen Beziehungen nach dem 1. Weltkrieg* (Paderborn, 1984). See also Link, *Die amerikanische* (note 16), 378.

20. Gerald D. Feldman, *The Great Disorder. Politics, Economics, and Society in the German Inflation, 1914–1923* (New York, 1993); Carl-Ludwig Holtfrerich, *Die deutsche Inflation, 1914–1923* (Berlin, 1980).

21. CUA, Vanderlip Papers, B-1–9, Vanderlip to Albert von Bary, 2 January 1923. See also Robert Gottwald, *Deutsch-amerikanische Beziehungen in der Ära Stresemann* (Berlin, 1965), 21 The German industrialist who is usually mentioned in this context is Hugo Stinnes. See Peter Wulf, *Hugo Stinnes. Wirtschaft und Politik, 1918–1924* (Stuttgart, 1979); Gerald D. Feldman, *Hugo Stinnes* (Munich, 1998); Conan Fischer, "Scoundrels without a Fatherland? Heavy Industry and Transnationalism in Post-First World War Germany," *Contemporary European History* 4 (2005): 441–64.

22. CUA, Vanderlip Papers, B-1–9, Vanderlip to Balhanyi, 26 April 1923.

23. Ibid., Vanderlip to Professor Gustav Cassel, Djursholm, Sweden, 27 April 1923.

24. Ibid., Vanderlip to Countess Treuberg, Heidelberg, 14 April 1923.

25. See, e.g., Hans-Jürgen Schröder, *Deutschland und die Vereinigten Staaten, 1933–1939* (Wiesbaden, 1970), 50; Michael Wala, *Weimar und Amerika* (note 14), 107.

26. Cohrs, *Unfinished Peace* (note 6), 111; Link, *Die amerikanische* (note 16), 380; Eberhard von Vietsch, *Arnold Rechberg und das Problem der politischen Westorientierung nach dem 1. Weltkrieg* (Boppard, 1958); Fischer, *Ruhr Crisis* (note 8), 249ff.

27. See Bernd Dohrmann, *Die englische Europapolitik in der Wirtschaftskrise, 1921–1923* (Munich, 1980), 139ff., 149ff.

28. Clemens Wurm, "Interalliierte Schulden, Reparationen—Sicherheit and Abrüstung. Die Kriegsschuldfrage in den britisch-französischen Beziehungen, 1924–1929," in Gustav Schmidt, ed., *Konstellationen internationaler Politik, 1924–1929* (Bochum, 1983), 89–121; Michael J. Hogan, *Informal Entente. The Private Structure of Cooperation in Anglo-American Economic Diplomacy, 1918–1928* (London, 1977). A Franco-American debt agreement was finally completed in 1926. See Karl-Erich Born, *International Banking in the Nineteenth and Twentieth Centuries* (Leamington Spa, 1983), 205.

29. See, e.g., Gottwald, *Deutsch-amerikanische Beziehungen* (note 21), 59, 62; Wurm, "Interalliierte Schulden" (note 28), 89–121.

30. First signals from Poincaré in early August. See Link, *Die amerikanische* (note 9), 207. One of these signals seems to have been France's long delayed ratification of the naval ratios negotiated at the 1922 Washington Conference. See ibid., 175.

31. But there was no change in Hughes's detached attitude, as he had put it again in a telegram to the U.S. embassy in London on 15 August 1923. Quoted in Link, *Die amerikanische* (note 9), 184.

32. See Born, *International Banking* (note 28), 209; Emily Rosenberg, *Financial Missionaries to the World. The Politics and Culture of Dollar Diplomacy, 1900–1930* (Cambridge, MA, 1999), 166–67; Gilbert Ziebura, *World Economy and World Politics* (Oxford, 1990), 83.

33. See, e.g., Jonathan Wright, *Gustav Stresemann. Weimar's Greatest Statesman* (Oxford, 2002); Karl Heinrich Pohl, *Weimars Wirtschaft und die Aussenpolitik der Republik, 1924–1926* (Düsseldorf, 1979), 7ff. See, e.g., Gottwald, *Deutsch-amerikanische Beziehungen* (note 21), 29, 59ff.; Gregor Johnson, ed., *Locarno Revisited* (London, 2004); Cohrs, *Unfinished Peace* (note 6), 201ff., 325, 383ff. The latter (p. 222) sees in Locarno a quest by Britain to establish a concert of Europe. This effort must therefore also be viewed in the context of attempts to assert British power and influence against the United States.

34. Jon Jacobson, *Locarno Diplomacy*, (Princeton 1971).

35. Cohrs, *Unfinished Peace* (note 6), 385.

36. See, e.g., Conan Fischer, *Europe between Democracy and Dictatorship, 1900–1945* (Chichester, 2011), 171–72. Gustav Schmidt, "Die Position und Rolle Deutschlands in regionalen und internationalen Strukturen von der Jahrhundertwende bis zur Weltwirtschaftskrise," in Jürgen Kocka et al., eds., *Von der Arbeiterbewegung zum modernen Sozialstaat* (Munich, 1994), 643, argues that, together with the stabilization of the French currency, the Maginot Line was also designed to provide more room to maneuver for French foreign policy. See also

the comprehensive study by Stephen Schuker, *The End of French Predominance in Europe* (Chapel Hill, NC, 1976).

37. On this pact, see, e.g., Gottwald, *Deutsch-amerikanische Beziehungen* (note 21), 77; Cohrs, *Unfinished Peace* (note 6), 222, 448ff.; George C. Herring, *From Colony to Superpower* (Oxford, 2008), 447ff.

38. See, e.g., Francis L. Carsten, *Reichswehr und Politik, 1918–1933* (Cologne, 1964), 141ff., 253ff.

39. Martin Lutz, *Siemens im Sowjetgeschäft* (Stuttgart, 2011). See also Robert Mark Spaulding, *Osthandel and Ostpolitik* (Providence, RI, 1997).

40. See, e.g., Herring, *From Colony to Superpower* (note 37), 456ff.

41. Carl P. Parrini, *Heir to Empire. United States Economic Diplomacy, 1916–1923* (Pittsburgh, 1969), 265–66.

42. Link, *Die amerikanische* (note 9), 264.

43. Parrini, *Heir to Empire* (note 41), 267; Link, *Die amerikanische* (note 16), 362.

44. CUA, Vanderlip Papers, Vanderlip to L. S. Rowe, 16 January 1924.

45. *WSJ*, 16 February 1924, also for the following.

46. Quoted in Kathleen Burk, "The House of Morgan in Financial Diplomacy, 1920–1930," in B.J.C. McKercher, ed., *Anglo-American Relations in the 1920s. The Struggle for Supremacy* (Basingstoke, 1991), 141.

47. Steiner, *Lights That Failed* (note 2), 249.

48. *WSJ*, 10 April 1924.

49. Ziebura, *World Economy* (note 32), 45–46. See also Cohrs, *Unfinished Peace* (note 6), 301.

50. Quoted in Herring, *From Colony to Superpower* (note 37), 445.

51. *Forbes*, 10 May 1924, 145, 166.

52. *Forbes*, 21 June 1924, 389, 391.

53. Link, *Die amerikanische* (note 9), 267–68.

54. *WSJ*, 5 May 1924.

55. *WSJ*, 6 August 1924.

56. *WSJ*, 30 August 1924.

57. *WSJ*, 3 September 1924.

58. Link, *Die amerikanische* (note 9), 589.

59. Ibid., 318–19.

60. *WSJ*, 12 December 1924.

61. *Forbes*, 15 November 1924, 223–24.

62. See above, note 52.

63. W. J. Reader, "The Chemical Industry," in Neil K. Buxton and Derek H. Aldcroft, eds., *British Industry between the Wars* (London, 1979), 166.

64. K. Warren, "Iron and Steel," in Buxton and Aldcroft, *British Industry* (note 63), 113, 115.

65. T. R. Gourvish, "Mechanical Engineering," in Buxton and Aldcroft, *British Industry* (note 63), 147.

66. Derek H. Aldcroft, *The British Economy 1: The Years of Turmoil* (Brighton, 1968), 1:13. According to Simon Molton and Ronald Michie, "The City of London as an International Commercial and Financial Center since 1900," *Enterprise and Society* 3 (September 2012): 538–81, purchasing and shipping were also

poorly prepared for "a new world when imperial power was no longer dominant, when local governments might well be hostile and when competition in
the world markets was the norm" (ibid., 549).

67. Aldcroft, *British Economy* (note 66), 13.

68. Arthur Marwick, *Britain in the Century of Total War* (Harmondsworth,
1968), 163ff.; Ziebura, *World Economy* (note 32), 107ff.; Stephen N. Broadberry,
The British Economy between the Wars (Oxford, 1986).

69. *Forbes*, 15 November 1924, 223–24.

70. Quoted in Marwick, *Britain* (note 68), 145.

71. Jay M. Winter, "Britain's 'Lost Generation' of the First World War," *Population Studies* 31 (1977): 449–66.

72. Quoted in Aldcroft, *British Economy* (note 66), 7.

73. Burk, "House of Morgan" (note 46), 126–27.

74. Cohrs, *Unfinished Peace* (note 6), 15, 185–86.

75. Ibid., 9.

76. Hogan, *Informal Entente* (note 28), 218.

77. *Forbes*, 1 October 1927.

78. Parrini, *Heir to Empire* (note 41), 246.

79. Link, *Die amerikanische* (note 9), 234.

80. Cohrs, *Unfinished Peace* (note 6), 189.

81. B.J.C. McKercher, "'The Deep and Latent Mistrust.' The British Official
Mind and the United States," in McKercher, ed., *Anglo-American Relations in the
1920s. The Struggle for Supremacy* (Basingstoke, 1987), 208–38. See also Harold
James, *The Role of Banks in the Interwar Economy* (Paris, 1991).

82. Quoted in Link, *Die amerikanische* (note 9), 239. See also H. S. Kenan, *Federal Reserve Bank* (Los Angeles, 1966).

83. *Forbes*, 15 January 1927.

84. Robert W. D. Boyce, *British Capitalism at the Crossroads, 1919–1932* (Cambridge, 1987), 31ff., also for the following.

85. Ibid., 71ff.

86. Ibid., 95.

87. Ibid., 172; Barry Eichengreen, *Golden Fetters. The Gold Standard and the
Great Depression, 1919–1939* (Oxford, 1992). This important book complements
Boyce's excellent study. Although this section relies primarily on the latter,
Eichengreen also highlights Churchill's presumption concerning the benefits of
the gold standard that the latter regretted later on.

88. Marwick, *Britain* (note 68), 146; Steiner, *Lights That Failed* (note 2), 186.
Churchill's budget speech in which he announced the return to the gold stan-
dard is reprinted in Shepard B. Clough et al., eds., *Economic History of Europe:
Twentieth Century* (New York, 1968), 148–52.

89. Boyce, *British Capitalism* (note 84), 139.

90. Ibid., 60, also for the following quote.

91. Ibid.

92. Link, *Die amerikanische* (note 9), 225. See also Harold James, *The Reichsbank and Public Finance, 1924–1933* (Frankfurt, 1985).

93. Burk, "House of Morgan" (note 46), 127.

94. Hogan, *Informal Entente* (note 28), 197. See also the excellent compara-tive study on the rubber and tire industries by Paul Erker, *Vom nationalen zum globalen Wettbewerb. Die deutsche und die amerikanische Reifenindustrie im 19. und 20. Jahrhundert* (Paderborn, 2005).

95. Boyce, *British Capitalism* (note 84), 10.

96. Ibid., 9.

97. Ibid., 112.

98. Ibid., 176.

99. Frank Costigliola, *Awkward Dominion. American Political, Economic, and Cultural Relations with Europe, 1919–1933* (Ithaca, NY, 1984), 143. See also the report as reprinted in Clough et al., *Economic History* (note 88), 164–71.

100. Boyce, *British Capitalism* (note 84), 102.

101. Ibid., 88.

102. See Werner Link, "Zum Problem der Kontinuität der amerikanischen Wirtschaftspolitik im Zwanzigsten Jahrhundert," *Amerikastudien* 20, no. 1 (1975), 128. And Karl-Ludwig Holtfrerich, "Amerikanischer Kapitalexport und Wie-deraufbau der deutschen Wirtschaft, 1919–23 im Vergleich zu 1924–29," *Viertel-jahrsschrift für Sozial- und Wirtschaftsgeschichte* 4 (1977): 497–529.

103. Pohl, *Weimars Wirtschaft* (note 33), 14.

104. William C. McNeil, *American Money and the Weimar Republic. Economics and Politics on the Eve of the Great Depression* (New York, 1986).

105. *WSJ*, 12 December 1924.

106. McNeil, *American Money* (note 104), 240.

107. See Eric D. Weitz, *Weimar Germany. Promise and Tragedy* (Princeton, 2007), 207ff.; Walter Laqueur, *Weimar. A Cultural History* (New York, 1975); Peter Gay, *Weimar Culture* (New York, 1968). On consumption see Victoria de Grazia, *Irresistible Empire* (Cambridge, MA, 2005); Karl Dittl, *Zweite Industrialisierung und Konsum* (Paderborn, 2011); Claudius Torp, *Konsum und Politik in der Wei-marer Republik* (Göttingen, 2011).

108. Pohl, *Weimars Wirtschaft* (note 33), 155–56.

109. Henning quoted in Ziebura, *World Economy* (note 32), 89. See also Torp, *Konsum und Politik* (note 107); Moritz J. Bonn, *Prosperity* (Berlin, 1931); Irene Witte, *Amerikanische Verkaufsorganisation* (Munich, 1926); Bruno Birnbaum, *Or-ganisation der Rationalisierung: Amerika und Deutschland* (Berlin, 1927).

110. Robert G. Moeller, *German Peasants and Agrarian Politics, 1914–1924* (Chapel Hill, NC, 1976).

111. Mary Nolan, *Visions of Modernity. American Business and the Moderniza-tion of Germany* (New York, 1994), 17ff.; Alexander Michel, *Von der Fabrikzeitung zum Führungsmittel. Werkzeitungen industrieller Grossunternehmen von 1890 bis 1945* (Stuttgart, 1997); Carl Köttgen, *Das wirtschaftliche Amerika* (Berlin, 1925).

112. On labor relations in Weimar Germany, see, e.g., John A. Moses, *Trade Unionism in Germany from Bismarck to Hitler*, vol. 2 (London, 1982); Heinrich August Winkler, *Der Schein der Normalität. Arbeiter und Arbeiterbewegung in der Weimarer Republik, 1924 bis 1930* (Berlin, 1985).

113. Charles Maier, "From Taylorism to Technocracy: European Ideologies and the Vision of Industrial Productivity in the 1920s," *Journal of Contemporary*

History 2 (1970): 27–61; Maier, "The Factory as Society. Ideologies of Industrial Management in the Twentieth Century," in Roger Bullen et al., eds., *Ideas into Politics* (London, 1982), 147–63.

114. Peter Borscheid, "Die Tempomacher," *Zeitschrift für Unternehmensgeschichte* 2 (1996): 125–38; Wolfgang Kaschuba, *Die Überwindung der Distanz. Zeit und Raum in der europäischen Moderne* (Frankfurt, 2004); Theodor Lüddecke, *Das amerikanische Wirtschaftstempo als Bedrohung Europas* (Leipzig, 1925).

115. Bernd Weisbrod, *Schwerindustrie in der Weimarer Republik* (Wuppertal, 1978); Philipp Gassert, *Amerika im Dritten Reich* (Stuttgart, 1997).

116. For a full study of Henry Ford and his life and work, see, e.g., Robert Lacey, *Ford. The Man and the Machine* (London, 1987). See also chapter V, pp. 261ff.

117. Frank Lippert, "Rationalisierungsstrategien in der deutschen Flaschenindustrie. Technische und betriebswirtschaftliche Entwicklungen in der ersten Hälfte des 20. Jahrhunderts," *Zeitschrift für Unternehmensgeschichte* 2 (1995): 98–109.

118. Bernd Weisbrod, "Economic Power and Political Stability Reconsidered: Heavy Industry in Weimar Germany," *Social History* 2 (1979): 232. See also Hans Mommsen et al., eds., *Industrielles System und politische Entwicklung in der Weimarer Republik* (Düsseldorf, 1974); David Abraham, *The Collapse of the Weimar Republic* (New York, 1986); Pohl, *Weimars Wirtschaft* (note 33), 14.

119. Peter Hayes, "Industrial Factionalism in Modern German History," *Central European History* 2 (1991): 122–31.

120. Paul Reusch quoted in H. H. Hartwich, *Arbeitsmarkt, Verbände und Staat* (Berlin, 1967), 333.

121. Bernd Weisbrod, *Schwerindustrie* (note 115), 262.

122. On German big business and the collapse of the Weimar Republic, see Henry A. Turner, *German Big Business and the Rise of Hitler* (New York, 1985); Reinhard Neebe, *Grossindustrie, Staat und NSDAP, 1930–1933* (Göttingen, 1981); Neebe, "Industrieverbände und das Ende der Weimarer Republik," in Kurt Düwell and Wolfgang Köllmann, eds., *Von der Reichsgründung bis zur Weimarer Republik* (Wuppertal, 1984), 381–97; Udo Wengst, "Unternehmerverbände und Gewerkschaften in Deutschland im Jahre 1930," *Vierteljahrshefte für Zeitgeschichte* 1 (1977): 99–119. On Hitler's "military Keynesianism," see Wolfgang Sauer, "Die Mobilmachung der Gewalt," in Karl Dietrich Bracher, Wolfgang Sauer, and Gerhard Schulz, eds., *Die nationalsozialistische Machtergreifung*, pt. 3 (Opladen, 1962), 787ff. Sauer does not use the term explicitly, but it is implied and he lists Keynes in the index with reference to these pages.

123. Gerald D. Feldman and Heidrun Homburg, *Industrie und Inflation* (Hamburg, 1977), 38.

124. Alfred Reckendrees, "Die Vereinigte Stahlwerke A.G. 1926–1933 und das 'glänzende Beispiel Amerika,'" *Zeitschrift für Unternehmensgeschichte* 2 (1996): 159.

125. Ibid. See also Alfred Reckendrees, *Das "Stahltrust"-Projekt. Die Gründung der Vereinigten Stahlwerke A.G. und ihre Unternehmensentwicklung, 1926–1933/34* (Munich, 2000).

126. Dieter Spethmann, "Begegnung mit einer jüngeren Ansicht über die Vereinigte Stahlwerke A.G.," *Zeitschrift für Unternehmensgeschichte* 2 (2001): 239.

127. Pohl, *Weimars Wirtschaft* (note 33), 233ff.

128. Link, "Zum Problem" (note 102), 130.

129. Mira Wilkins, "German Chemical Firms in the United States from the Late 19th Century to Post-World War II," in John E. Lesch, ed., *The German Chemical Industry in the 20th Century* (Dordrecht, 2000), 302.

130. *Forbes*, 15 September 1928.

131. Reckendrees, *Das "Stahltrust"-Projekt* (note 125), 589. See also the text of the International Steel Agreement, with the national quotas that were agreed in Clough et al., *Economic History* (note 88), 172–75.

132. Link, *Die amerikanische* (note 9), 367.

133. Sauer, "Die Mobilmachung" (note 122), 787ff.

134. See above, note 130.

135. On I. G. Farben, see Peter Hayes, *Industry and Ideology. I.G. Farben in the Nazi Era* (New York, 1987). See also Hayes, "I.G. Farben Revisited: Industry and Ideology Ten Years later," in Lesch, *German Chemical Industry* (note 129), 7–14; Elisabeth Glaser-Schmidt, "Foreign Trade Strategies of I.G. Farben after World War I," *Business and Economic History* 1 (1994): 201–11.

136. On Schering, see Christopher Kobrak, *National Cultures and International Competition. The Experience of Schering AG, 1851–1950* (Cambridge, 2002).

137. Frank A. Southart, *American Industry in Europe* (Boston, 1931).

138. Wilkins, "German Chemical Firms" (note 129), 303. See also Pilar Barrera, "The Evolution of Corporate Technological Capabilities: Du Pont and IG Farben in Comparative Perspective," *Zeitschrift für Unternehmensgeschichte* 1 (1994): 31–45.

139. Antony C. Sutton, *Wall Street and the Rise of Hitler* (Seal Beach, CA, 1976).

140. Wilkins, "German Chemical Firms" (note 129), 305.

141. Reader, "Chemical Industry" (note 63). See also W. J. Reader, *Imperial Chemical Industries*, 2 vols. (Oxford, 1970ff.). See also Ulrich Marsch, "Transforming Strategy and Structure: The German Chemical Industry and its Role as an Exemplar for Other Industries in Germany and Britain," in Lesch, *German Chemical Industry* (note 129), 217–41, with Germany as the model. See also above, p. 198.

142. Ursula M. Saeckel, *Der US-Film in der Weimarer Republik—ein Medium der "Amerikanisierung"?* (Paderborn, 2011); Sarah Street, *British National Cinema* (New York, 1997); Wala, *Weimar und Amerika* (note 14), 119ff., with a graph of film screenings in Britain, France, and Germany, 1926–1931. See also David Ellwood, *The Shock of America* (Oxford, 2012), 106ff., 133ff.

143. On Young, see, e.g., Josephine Young, *Owen D. Young and American Enterprise* (Boston, 1982).

144. Costigliola, *Awkward Dominion* (note 99), 152.

145. Ibid., 153.

146. Sutton, *Wall Street* (note 129), 52.

147. Southart, *American Industry* (note 137), 21.

148. See Robert Sobel, *The Life and Times of Dillon Read* (New York, 1991, esp. 92ff.

149. Sutton, *Wall Street* (note 129), 53.

150. Ibid., 52.

151. On Siemens and AEG, see Heidrun Homburg, *Rationalisierung und In-dustriearbeit* (Berlin, 1991), 350. On GE (Germany), see *WSJ*, 27 May 1926.

152. Ibid., 4 October 1924.

153. Pohl, *Weimars Wirtschaft* (note 33), 47–48.

154. Michael Stürmer, *Koalition und Opposition in der Weimarer Republik, 1924–1928* (Düsseldorf, 1967).

155. On Hindenburg and his presidency, see Andreas Dorpalen, *Hindenburg and the Weimar Republic* (Princeton, 1964); Wolfram Pyta, *Hindenburg* (Munich, 2007).

156. *WSJ*, 15 May 1925; *WSJ*, 26 May 1925; Gottwald, *Deutsch-amerikanische Beziehungen* (note 21), 37.

157. Gottwald, *Deutsch-amerikanische Beziehungen* (note 21), 38ff.

158. Rosenberg, *Financial Missionaries* (note 32), 172.

159. Southart, *American Industry* (note 137), 32ff.

160. *WSJ*, 15 August 1925.

161. *WSJ*, 22 September 1925.

162. *WSJ*, 22 December 1925.

163. *WSJ*, 23 October 1926.

164. *WSJ*, 19 January 1927.

165. *WSJ*, 1 September 1927.

166. Gottwald, *Deutsch-amerikanische Beziehungen* (note 21), 104.

167. *WSJ*, 1 September 1927.

168. *Forbes*, 15 December 1927.

169. *Forbes*, 23 December 1927.

170. *Forbes*, 18 January 1928.

171. Jürgen Baron von Kruedener, ed., *Economic Crisis and Political Collapse. The Weimar Republic, 1924–1933* (New York, 1990); Balderston, *Economics and Politics* (note 2), 88ff.

172. *Forbes*, 1 September 1928.

173. *WSJ*, 7 November 1928. See also Albrecht Ritschl, *Deutschlands Krise und Konjunktur, 1924–1934* (Berlin, 2002).

174. Michael Stürmer, *Koalition und Opposition* (note 154).

175. Ziebura, *World Economy* (note 32), 51. See also Wala, *Weimar und Amerika* (note 14), 114, on Hoover's position.

176. CUA, Vanderlip Papers, B-1-9, Vanderlip to Edwin Harden, 24 February 1928.

177. Ibid., Vanderlip to H. E. Benedict, 2 March 1928.

178. Ibid., Vanderlip to H. E. Benedict, 27 March 1928.

179. Ibid., Vanderlip to Sakio Imamura, Kobe, 18 January 1927.

180. Ibid., Vanderlip to H. E. Benedict, 14 April 1928.

181. John K. Galbraith, *The Great Crash 1929* (Harmondsworth, 1961). See also Edward M. Lamont, *The Ambassador from Wall Street* (Lanham, MD, 1994), 249ff.

182. Galbraith, *Great Crash* (note 181), 36.

183. Ibid., 45.

184. Ziebura, *World Economy* (note 32) 45–46.

185. Gustav Schmidt, *Geschichte der USA* (Darmstadt, 2004), 80.

186. Galbraith, *Great Crash* (note 181), 103.

187. Joan H. Wilson, *American Business and Foreign Policy, 1920–1932* (Lexington, KY, 1971), xiv.

188. *Banker's Magazine* 82 (July–December 1906): 24.

189. Galbraith, *Great Crash* (note 181), 91.

190. Ibid., 91ff.; Lamont, *Ambassador* (note 181), 272ff.

191. Balderston, *Economics and Politics* (note 2), 82ff.

192. *WSJ*, 3 November 1930; *WSJ*, 19 November 1930.

193. *WSJ*, 31 November 1931; *WSJ*, 4 November 1930.

194. *WSJ*, 2 November 1929. See also *WSJ*, 22 December 1930.

195. *WSJ*, 19 November 1932.

196. See Boyce, *British Capitalism* (note 84), 321.

197. *WSJ*, 15 November 1930.

198. *WSJ*, 15 December 1930.

199. Balderston, *Economics and Politics* (note 2), 25.

200. Link, *Die amerikanische* (note 9), 489ff., 525ff.

201. *WSJ*, 18 November 1931; *WSJ*, 19 December 1931; *WSJ*, 19 November 1932.

202. *WSJ*, 22 December 1931.

203. *WSJ*, 25 December 1932.

204. *Atlanta Constitution*, 20 December 1931, with a heading that reflected the deceptiveness of Hitler about his actual long-term aims and that many foreigners, including businessmen, took a long time to recognize: "Hitler Modifies Drastic Views as He Draws Closer to Power."

205. Ziebura, *World Economy* (note 32), 27.

206. Gustav Schmidt, "Der gescheiterte Frieden. Die Ursachen des Zusammenbruchs des Versailler Systems," in Hartmut Elsenhans et al., eds., *Frankreich—Europa—Weltpolitik* (Opladen, 1989), 174–96.

V

//

Nazi Germany, Appeasement, and Anglo-American Big Business, 1933–1941

1. Introduction

In terms of the overall argument of this book, this chapter, covering the years up to the official American entry into World War II on the side of Britain and the Soviet Union against Germany, Italy, and Japan, presents a most dramatic moment in world history. It was during the years 1933–41 that strategies were developed by those six countries and then turned into actual policies that determined the shape of the relations of American big business with Britain and Germany during the subsequent wartime and postwar periods. And this decade was also decisive for the organization of both the world economy and world politics for the following fifty years until the collapse of the Soviet Bloc in 1989–90.

This larger context explains the structuring of this chapter. It begins with an analysis of the visions of the future world and the strategies and policies that Adolf Hitler as the driving force in this picture had designed for Germany and began to implement as soon as he came to power in 1933. These strategies will be related, albeit briefly, to those of the two other dictatorial and expansionist powers, Italy and Japan. From 1936–37 onward these three countries came together in a coalition that aimed at world domination and that between 1939 and 1941 slowly drew the British Empire, the Soviet Union, and the United States into a total war. It was after five years of war with enormous sacrifices that the Axis powers were finally defeated in 1945.

This means that following an examination of Hitler's quest for territorial expansion and his rapid rearmament program, the second subsection will look at relations in the German-British-American triangle before the behavior of American big business in this force field will be treated. Here the focus will be on a number of major American corporations and their maneuvers that represent a spectrum of responses to the increased political risk they faced in the international system. These responses were due not only to the world economic crisis but also to the extraordinary dynamic of the Nazi dictatorship that neither the Western countries nor Stalin knew how to handle.

Faced with this dictatorship, many American companies that had come back to Germany after World War I and had invested in the Weimar economy cut their losses as the political and economic climate in the Third Reich became more and more inclement. But there were a number of firms that present intriguing case studies of the behavior of larger enterprises when forced to operate within an increasingly controlling political and economic regime that is heading unswervingly toward a major war of conquest. Some of these companies, such as Woolworth and Coca-Cola, belonged to the civilian mass consumption sector and raise questions about the basic character of the Nazi dictatorship. Others, such as General Motors, Ford, and IBM, while also involved in supplying civilian markets, were as manufacturers increasingly drawn into Hitler's industrial preparations for war.

All these case studies will also facilitate an examination, in chapter VI, of the socioeconomic models and structures of the United States, Germany, and Britain that American big business, learning from the interwar experience, hoped to implant into the economies of Europe after a victorious war, this time with the support of Washington. It was the German and American concepts of international relations that, together with Japanese ideas of the Greater East Asia Co-prosperity Sphere and Mussolini's ambitions in North Africa, clashed between 1941 and 1945. After 1945, when Stalin's alliance with the West fell apart, yet another global clash occurred between the American and Soviet models of how to organize a modern industrial society. Although the United States and the Soviet Union came close to World War III on more than one occasion, they succeeded in avoiding another descent into the abyss of total war, in no small degree thanks to the fact that their policies, unlike Hitler's, remained sufficiently rational and ultimately desirous of détente rather than a further escalation into an all-out military conflict.

2. Hitler's Ideology of Conquest and
Ultimate War Aims

It seems best to begin the study of international relations between 1933 and 1941 with a consideration of three basic points:

1. The appearance on the scene of the Hitler dictatorship infused the unfolding of events in the 1930s with an unprecedented and extremely radical dynamic, accelerated further by the decisions of the Italian and Japanese governments, that is, the three powers that were responsible for the outbreak of World War II and the forging of the Anglo-American-Soviet counteralliance in 1941.

2. It would be misleading to view the Hitler dictatorship as being driven exclusively by one individual, when it came to German domestic affairs. Here, as Hans Mommsen and others have shown, the regime practiced a bureaucratic Social Darwinism, with ministerial and party officials engaging in cutthroat power struggles.[1] In terms of the theme of this book, it left American companies that had come to Germany before 1933 in a huge quandary about whether to get out or to play along—the theme of the second half of this chapter. However, in the design and decision-making processes in the field of Nazi foreign policy and the push toward war, Hitler was unquestionably the key figure. By 1937–39 he had the final say in questions of war and peace. It was he who unleashed the war in 1939, invaded the Soviet Union in June 1941, and declared war on the United States in December of that year.

3. There were a number of points in Hitler's *Weltanschauung* on which he had a dogmatic fixation. But this did not mean that within this basic ideological framework there existed no space for tactical maneuvering and cool Machiavellian calculation as long as it did not lead him away from his strategic objectives. If Hitler's crucial role in Nazi foreign policy making is by now widely accepted in the community of scholars, what were the axioms of his view of history in general, of the more specific world situation of the 1920s and 1930s, and, third, of the New Order that he was determined to build?

Apart from the many speeches and statements that he made in public or in his entourage from the mid-1920s onward, his book *Mein Kampf*, first published in 1925, and the manuscript of his "Second Book" (which he wrote in the later 1920s but never published) contain all the basic components of an ideology that, though contradictory, implausible, and irrational, if its many thought fragments are considered separately, nevertheless had an inner logic to it, provided one accepts the premises and takes them en bloc.[2] These premises were that Social Darwinist power politics, a biological racism, and the missionary will of a strong leader were the perennial forces of world history. Human-made socioeconomic and cultural factors, while not irrelevant, were definitely secondary. Applying these concepts to the German predica-ment after World War I, the first political task was therefore to find a solution to the "food question," which had become so acute during the Allied blockade in 1916–18, and to deal with the problem of Germany's population and its allegedly inadequate "living space." Alternatives, such as population control or urban-industrial concentration, were briefly discussed by Hitler but rejected on racist grounds. The acqui-sition of "living space" was seen by him as the only escape from the threat of biological extinction. Violent struggle and self-assertion alone would lead to the ultimate triumph of the "Germanic race."

For the Germans, Hitler continued, this "living space" was in the first instance to be found to the east on the Eurasian continent, at a later stage to be complemented by colonies in other parts of the globe. Given that these eastern regions were inhabited by Slavic and other non-German "races," territorial conquest and displacement by military force was seen by Hitler as the only viable means to secure this space for the Germans. Conquest in the east also meant that the indigenous populations would be ruthlessly decimated to make room for German settlers. Those who survived the onslaught would, after their defeat and, most importantly, that of the Soviet Union, live as helots under direct German rule, laboring for the dominant Germans. This was to be a *formal* empire, not an informal one that German businessmen had been envisioning before and after 1914.

It was the task of Germany's existing industrial infrastructure to pro-vide the modern military equipment for the acquisition of this "living space" by the country's armed forces. After victory they and Himmler's police units would guard the townships and farmsteads. Once this Nazi New Order had been established, industry was to shift its main focus from military production toward the provision of mass-produced civil-ian goods for a racist mass consumption society for which the United States furnished the *productionist* model, though Hitler disdained America's sociopolitical and cultural organization. Politically, the Nazi New Order would be autocratically organized, built on mass acclama-tion by a majority of the *Volksgenossen*. They would be soaked in Nazi propaganda. Their material dreams and needs would be satisfied and paid for through the exploitation of the occupied countries.[3] Whoever resisted the New Order or was deemed not to belong to the "Germanic race" would be killed or worked and starved to death.

However nightmarish this vision of the future was, its implementation was not bereft of at least some coolly calculated elements. Hitler was not so irrational as not to formulate some lessons that Germany had to learn from its earlier history in order to be successful at the imperial mission that lay ahead. His writings contain an assessment of the pre-1918 power constellation and a criticism of the "mistakes" he believed his Wilhelmine predecessors had made when they launched their *Weltpolitik*. Dividing the world into sea powers and continental states, Hitler chided the kaiser and his advisors for having been over-ambitious and for initiating an exorbitant naval rearmament program before the country's living space position on the European Continent had been secured with the help of Germany's land forces by defeating France and Russia.[4] As a result of this miscalculation the *Kaiserreich* had found itself at war with both its Continental enemies as well as the British Empire in 1914 and with the United States from 1917. These enemies had brought the monarchy to its knees—a disastrous defeat that Hitler said had been accelerated by the "treason" of Germany's Social Democrats and Jews, who were said to have stabbed the army in the back. Just as many other right-wing Germans, Hitler never accepted this defeat and was therefore firmly wedded to undoing the peace settlement of 1919.

In "learning" from the kaiser's mistakes, he concluded that the second attempt to establish the country as a world power would have to be taken in two steps. The first one would involve the conquest of "living space" on the Eurasian Continent while keeping the "sea powers" neutral by reassuring them that their position was not being challenged. Only after the territories in the east had been secured by military force, did Hitler envisage, as a second step, a confrontation with Britain and ultimately with the United States in a struggle for world domination. Since this vision also implied a struggle between societies that were democratically organized and geared toward civilianism and peaceful commercial exchange, on the one hand, and states constituted along militaristic lines, it was clear that the attempt to build a Nazi New Order was not just about economic and political structures, but rather about fundamental principles of how to run a modern society. In short, World War II was in this sense a gigantic struggle between the racist Nazi New Order and a constitutional Anglo-American one. The Soviet system represented a third alternative that, in conjunction with the Anglo-American effort in the Atlantic, in the Pacific against Japan, and in North Africa against Fascist Italy, defeated Hitler in the east.

This very compressed analysis has, it is hoped, laid bare sufficiently clearly the contours of the Nazi New Order, as reflected in Hitler's writings (and also his speeches) to highlight two basic points essential to an understanding of international developments after 1933. First, when Hitler seized power he quickly gained dictatorial control of a country that was large and economically as well as militarily strong enough to enable him to tackle the historic mission that he had assigned to himself and to those Germans who were prepared to follow him into the realization of his racist utopia. However, in line with the "lessons" he had learned from the past, he proceeded at first only with implementing the continental stage of his "program," while reassuring the "sea powers" and Britain in particular that he was not a Wilhelminian.[5] He showed this initial restraint in his foreign policy also because he calculated, again quite coolly, that he needed several years to consolidate his dictatorship at home and to expand his land forces before he could begin to conquer "living space" in the east. Let me pursue Hitler's actual foreign policies after 1933 in more detail before turning to the reactions to them by Germany's political and economic elites, on the one hand, and by Britain and America, on the other.

3. Hitler's Foreign Policy in the 1930s

At the beginning of his regime, Hitler adopted two domestic policies that were very visible to both ordinary Germans and to foreign governments.[6] In the spring of 1933, he destroyed the trade union movement and the political parties of the Left. He also purged the civil service and higher education by dismissing those who had been identified as politically unreliable because of their service under the Weimar Republic or because they were Jewish or both. It was a time when Germany's prisons filled up with brutalized victims. This policy was billed as a restoration of law and order after years of alleged corruption during the Weimar Republic and the ravages of the Great Depression. It was also the phase of the first carefully organized anti-Semitic outrages with the boycott and maltreatment of Jewish shop owners and others in April 1933. By the summer of 1933 the other parties that had still garnered seats in the Reichstag elections of March 1933 had all been dissolved.

On 30 June 1934, Hitler turned against his critics within the Nazi movement in a further step to gain unchallenged control of both the government and the by then very large Nazi movement.[7] On that night, Ernst Röhm and the Storm Troopers (SA) leadership, who had been talking about a "Second Revolution" against Hitler's conservative partners in the Cabinet as well as in the Reichswehr officer corps, were unceremoniously murdered. The SA was politically emasculated. Heinrich Himmler, the leader of the SS (Schutzstaffel), originally created as Hitler's body guard contingent, was expanded and by 1936 had been put in charge of both the party's intelligence service and the entire state police apparatus. Finally, in order to buttress his popularity not only with "law and order" measures and rigged plebiscites but also through "constructive" initiatives, he announced a work creation program funded by public investments in road and autobahn construction and other infrastructural improvements.

These initiatives lent themselves well to the efforts of Joseph Goebbels, the propaganda minister, even though they did not create more than a few hundred thousand jobs. The more important reduction of mass unemployment occurred in the industrial sector of the economy after Hitler had announced an expansion of the armed forces to an approving assembly of the top officer corps on February 1933. Although, as Adam Tooze has shown, the blueprints for the highway building program were prepared before 1933, the impetus behind the Nazi program was different from that of the civilian Weimar Republic:[8] Hitler's autobahns were built with military-strategic considerations and the projected overthrow of the territorial status quo in Europe in mind.

The plans for an expansion of the Reichswehr were also based on an anti-Versailles territorial revisionism among the nationalist officer corps. His speech to the Reichswehr's top brass about his rearmament program was not hot air. In line with his own long-term plans, it was put into practice, with the additional advantage that the ordering of military equipment began to fill the depleted order books of industry. Before 1933, its captains, whether in charge of the steel works and coal mines of the Ruhr region or of the chemical, machine manufacturing, and electrical engineering corporations, had had many reservations about the Nazis. But now there was the prospect of renewed production. The specific attitudes and policies this triggered both among domestic industries and among American firms operating in Germany will be examined later in this chapter.

With Germany having few natural resources of its own, the rearmament boom that began straightaway in the spring of 1933 required the importation of large amounts of raw materials. It was first thought that these could be paid for from the foreign exchange earnings of increased exports. However, with production for the domestic market, and for the armed forces in particular, being given priority, the country's exports soon proved too small to generate the foreign exchange to pay for much-needed raw materials. By 1934, a crisis point had been reached that was so serious that Hjalmar Schacht, the president of the Reichsbank and a key economic planner, devised the so-called New Plan. It was made up of three components:[9] First, it imposed quantitative limits on imports in accordance with an "economic urgency scale." Second, it abandoned the multilateral trade policies of the Weimar period as enshrined in the German-American commercial treaty of 1922 with its most-favored-nation clause and introduced bilateral trade agreements. Finally, to promote German exports but to save foreign exchange, it moved to a system of barter, export subsidies, and preferential allocations of raw materials to companies that brought in export orders. Mineral-rich countries such as Brazil and Sweden were henceforth courted to subscribe to Nazi bilateralism. At the same time the nations of Southeastern Europe were nudged and increasingly cajoled to barter their agricultural produce and oil for whatever manufactured goods were left in German industry (now primarily engaged in armaments production) to be sent to them.

Due to the rapid expansion of the Wehrmacht, the New Plan of 1934 proved to be no more than a band-aid. It became clear that a much stricter system of resource allocation had to be introduced that gave absolute priority to industries charged with fulfilling the targets set by Hitler to ready the armed forces for a war of territorial conquest in the east. Tight controls were also needed after the introduction of universal conscription in March 1935. This was another program that the generals had covertly prepared during the Weimar years and that, to their delight, Hitler now implemented. The need to issue uniforms and other equipment put a further strain on the provision of raw materials, including cotton that had hitherto been imported for civilian purposes in relatively small quantities from the United States against payment in hard dollars. And so a successor to the New Plan was drawn up to overcome the latest and ever more dangerous bottlenecks. It came in the shape of the Four-Year Plan of 1936 that put the preparation for an early war of expansion into the hands of Hermann Göring.[10] Even more important, the document that detailed the next coordinated phase of war preparation had a secret appendix in which Hitler ordered that the Wehrmacht be ready for war in four years' time and that industry be put into high gear to secure military readiness.

It is in this context that a speech by Hitler becomes significant in showing that he was beginning to look beyond a conquest of the Eurasian continent and the building of a closed self-sufficient empire whose food and raw material needs could be satisfied from within this bloc and that could be largely detached from the rest of the world economy. Mindful of his idea of expansion in two stages and still hoping for a deal with Britain, he had sent Joachim von Ribbentrop, his trusted foreign policy advisor, to London as German ambassador in October 1936 in hopes that he would be able to negotiate an alliance.[11] Following the signing of the Anglo-German naval agreement of 18 June 1935, which was supposed to reassure Britain that he was not a reincarnation of the kaiser, Hitler believed that London could be lured into a formal agreement on the basis that he would not touch British Imperial interests in return for being given a "free hand" with his plans of conquest in the east.

By November 1937, it had become clear that an alliance with Britain could be had only on terms that were unacceptable to Hitler, that is, that there would be no revision of the territorial status quo in Europe and an eastward expansion that used force instead of negotiation and compromise. Worse, a few weeks earlier U.S. president Franklin D. Roosevelt had made a speech warning that Germany, but also Japan and Italy, had to reckon with American opposition to their expansionist ambitions in Europe, North Africa, and Asia.[12] It was in response to this changing power constellation that Hitler made a speech before the leadership of the Wehrmacht and key Nazi figures on 7 November. According to the notes by one of his adjutants, Col. Friedrich Hossbach, Hitler now envisioned a compression of his earlier "time-table."[13] In light of Britain's refusal to cut a deal on his terms and of the growing hostility of the American administration, he now expected a war with the "sea powers" by 1943–45. This meant that the Continental phase of his expansionism had to be completed by that date, with a shift from the army toward naval and air force rearmament to begin without delay in 1938. In line with this reassessment of the evolving strategic situation, Germany's preparations for aggression on the Continent now proceeded apace. Austria was incorporated in March 1938. The Czech Sudetenland came next in October of that year, followed by the destruction of the whole of the Czechoslovak Republic in March 1939.

Still looking east, the invasion and swift defeat of Poland began on 1 September 1939.[14] Hitler, as the decisive instigator of this military operation, had been assuming that Britain and France would again stay away. He believed that with the government of Neville Chamberlain still in power, France in continuous domestic turmoil, and both London and Paris stunned by his pact with Stalin of 22 August 1939, the two major Western powers would not respond militarily. He was wrong, but since neither Britain nor France took offensive actions on the Western Front, Hitler continued to hope that it was possible to negotiate a truce, enabling him to concentrate on completing the acquisition of "living space" in the east, to be gained by throwing the Nazi-Soviet pact to the winds and defeating Stalin in another lightning war. This would have given Germany the territorial base to be exploited for food, raw materials, and forced labor. It also was large enough to face, together with Japan and Italy, the "sea powers" in a global struggle for world domination. A war of looting in the east would also enable him to recoup the enormous investments that had been made in the Wehrmacht and to pay for the huge public debts that had accumulated in

the 1930s. By exploiting the national economies of the occupied countries the regime aimed to rebalance its budget and to provide civilian
consumer goods, including—as will be seen—the Volkswagen that he
had held out to the German population before 1939. It was a path that
Hitler *had* to take in light of the fact that the German economy had for
several years been geared to war and had become completely unhinged
in order to fulfill the rearmament objectives of the Four-Year Plan and
its secret appendix.

Why Hitler failed to complete the Continental phase of his "program" and continued to find himself in a dreaded two-front war, escalating into a world war with the American entry in 1940–41, is to be
examined in a moment. The immediate task is to discuss British and
American reactions to Germany's preparations for war up to 1939–
40. Here it has to be remembered first of all that following the Nazi
seizure of power in January 1933 Hitler stopped speaking about his
long-term territorial ambitions and posed as a law-and-order politician who would maintain peace with Germany's neighbors. There
were, of course, alternative voices in the German government and the
Nazi Party, some of which will be discussed in connection with Anglo-
German and German-American diplomatic moves in this period. Still,
the key point remains that Hitler, even in the face of an embryonic and
ineffectual resistance movement, was firmly in driver's seat. It was he
who insisted on the invasion of Poland in September 1939, which objectively represented a point of no return in his all-or-nothing strategy
of conquest.

4. The Underestimation of Hitler and British Appeasement

The first group to fall for the ruse of Hitler as an "ordinary" politician were the conservative elites inside Germany and their supporters
among the bourgeoisie.[15] These elites had engineered Hitler's nomination as Reich chancellor. They knew from their pre-1933 contacts and experiences with him that he and his cronies were totally untrustworthy.
Moreover, the Nazis were very radical men who had resorted to lies
and crimes to get their way. And yet the conservatives thought that,
once he was given government responsibility, Hitler would moderate
his radicalism. If he didn't, the advisors of the old field marshal and
Reich president Paul von Hindenburg and the non-Nazi members of
the Reich cabinet thought they could contain the Reich chancellor and
his minority group of ministers. Should this containment not work, the
conservative-nationalist "watchdogs" would engineer the dismissal of

the Nazis from the cabinet under the powers that Hindenburg held via Article 48 of the Weimar Constitution.

It took just a few weeks and months for these conservative elites to discover that they had hopelessly underestimated the dynamism and cunning of Hitler and his associates. By the summer 1933, Germany had become a one-party dictatorship. After the political emasculation of the SA in the Night of the Long Knives in June 1934 the country had grown into an ever more terroristic police state charged by Hitler with preparing the first stage in the execution of the Nazis' "historic" mission, the creation of a racist Germanic New Order in the east. The generals were initially enthusiastic about Hitler's rearmament program. But by 1938–39 they and also the business elites were getting cold feet about the headlong rush toward war.[16] Some of them felt that the Wehrmacht was insufficiently prepared for such a war; others had more fundamental moral doubts that led a few of them to contemplate the violent removal of Hitler. Yet, in the end, they, too, went along with Hitler's decision to attack Poland.

If Germany's elites believed in 1933 that Hitler was an "ordinary" politician who could be tamed and hence underestimated the radicalism of his politics, it is not surprising that foreigners who had much less inside information fell into the same trap. In an attempt to make the interactions between Nazi Germany and Britain and America more transparent, British government reactions and policies will be discussed first. A subsequent section will then deal with American strategizing about what to do with Hitler in the 1930s and why it proved so difficult for London and Washington, even under the new circumstances of the 1930s, to overcome their post-1918 disagreements. A final section will then discuss the increasingly closer cooperation between the two powers from 1939 to 1941. It is only after this analysis that the ground will have been cleared to delve into how American big business operated within this complex and confusing force field.

There is a huge volume of literature on British diplomacy and foreign trade policy in the 1930s and the meaning of British-style Appeasement.[17] After many scholars had been very critical of Appeasement, the pendulum later swung more not toward a position, to be sure, of sympathy and apology, but toward a more sophisticated analysis and understanding of the constraints that the British government was working under, as it reacted to a seemingly irrational Nazi regime with its gigantic rearmament program and manifest preparation of war. There was a very healthy distrust in London of the German dictatorship. But there were also illusions based on the assumption that Hitler was an "ordinary statesman" with whom sensible deals could be struck that preserved the paramount principles of peace and international trade.

Because of the geographic proximity of Germany, British government attitudes were particularly concerned with the issue of peace and security. This explains why London was more interested in political negotiations rather than trade that Washington put upfront in its dealings with Nazi Germany. It was also clear that, given the world depression, neither Prime Minister Stanley Baldwin nor Neville Chamberlain, his successor from 1937, had much economic weight to throw into the scales. The aim was therefore to achieve a *comprehensive* settlement of all issues on the understanding that Germany would not resort to violent territorial conquest. Britain was in principle prepared to let Hitler move into East-Central Europe provided the gains came after peaceful negotiations, did not radically surpass the country's pre-1914 borders, and would lead to a reversal of the dangerous rearmament program. Under these conditions London thought Germany's political and economic reintegration into the European community of nations and the traditional commercial exchange among them could be achieved.

However, Britain's responses to Hitler's rise were not merely influenced by the international constellation. Baldwin and Chamberlain also had to reckon with the country's publics that, remembering the ravages of World War I, were in a broad sense quite strongly pacifist. Larger sections were moreover in favor of continued social reform. These conditions of a democratic society based on universal suffrage pushed Baldwin and Chamberlain in the direction of trying to strike a deal with Hitler on the above-mentioned terms.[18] There were also fiscal constraints that blocked higher military expenditure above the stepped-up efforts that had already been set in motion from 1935 onward, especially in the area of aircraft production, as news about Germany's rearmament and suspicions about Hitler's larger ambitions mounted.

It is against this background that the agreement has to be seen that Chamberlain struck with Hitler in Munich in September 1938.[19] The prime minister genuinely thought (though, as it turned out, quite erroneously) that the "peaceful," negotiated absorption of the Czech Sudetenland into Germany had not only prevented a major war, but also had satiated Hitler's territorial appetite. Of course, six months later Hitler, still in dogmatic pursuit of "living space" in the east, had occupied the whole of Czechoslovakia and had given orders to prepare the conquest of Poland in the autumn of 1939. After this, both the British government and the public were ready to stop Hitler's expansionism and to enter into a war against Nazi Germany. On 31 March 1939 London issued a guarantee in favor of Polish independence. There is no space here to do more than sketch this larger development. Just as inside the Nazi regime, there were also major debates and disputes in the British government and public about variations and alternatives to

Chamberlain's course of negotiating with Hitler. But given the existing balance of power, the voices of the Anti-Appeasers and of the Commonwealth counted for even less than the criticism coming from within the British government. As long as Hitler single-mindedly pursued his aggressive policies, the Anti-Appeasers were ultimately no wiser than the Appeasers.

5. American Foreign Policy in the 1930s

If there were thus many factors of domestic politics and economy as well as of foreign policy at work in London in developing its approach to the Nazi menace, the American administration forged an anti-Nazi strategy that has been labeled by some as "economic appeasement."[20] However, just as in the British case, there have also been misunderstandings about the meaning of this label. Again it is not possible here to examine the many different proposals that were put forward by key figures in the State Department, politicians and journalists, or top civil servants in other Washington ministries. At the risk of simplifying another complex story of Western reactions to Nazi dynamism and aggressiveness, the changing positions of three men shall be examined: Roosevelt, his secretary of state Cordell Hull, and his treasury secretary Henry Morgenthau.

Hull was brought into the Roosevelt administration not only because as a former senator from Tennessee he had many connections with politicians on Capitol Hill, but also because he represented the idea of multilateral trade in its most undiluted form.[21] He accepted the top diplomatic job determined that the U.S. government would abandon its own protectionist reaction to the Great Depression and lead the way toward the re-creation of an Open Door world trading system. This was a position not only that Hull deeply believed in, but also that had practical advantages when it came to reacting to Nazi Germany's descent into bilateralism, barter, exchange controls, and quest for self-sufficiency. Multilateralism could be used as both a stick and a carrot in Hull's attempt to get Germany to stop on its dangerous path.

The underlying concept was not so much to seek, like Chamberlain, a comprehensive settlement that would stabilize the political situation in Europe; rather Hull and some of his advisors, often against the opposition of others in the Roosevelt administration, were prepared to threaten the imposition of economic sanctions in the hope of putting the skids under the Nazi regime's rearmament policies. If, on the other hand, these reckless policies were rescinded and the economy reoriented toward the production of civilian goods so that it could be included in Hull's vision of a revived international trade, Germany could become part of a larger State Department effort to create this multilateral global trading system. Unlike Chamberlain, who did not think that a weakened Britain had much economic leverage and was therefore focused more on a territorial-political agreement with Hitler, the State Department felt muscular enough to believe that its economic approach might do the trick. Hull was encouraged in this belief because of the many rumors about disagreements in Berlin between "moderates" and "radicals," with the former advocating the abandonment of the massive rearmament program that by the late 1930s was unhinging everything. Accordingly and to the dismay of the Nazi "moderates," he refused to renew the MFN Trade Treaty that had expired in 1934. The mounting tensions are also reflected in American exports to Germany that in 1927 and 1928 had amounted to no less than 1.9 billion marks per annum, but between 1935 and 1938 vacillated around 250 million per annum. Except for 1937, American imports from Germany were below 200 million marks per annum during the same period, another dramatic reduction from the 1.7 billion in 1927 and 1928.[22]

The promulgation of the Four-Year Plan indicated that the "moderates," if they ever existed as a more powerful faction, were losing the internal battle. But this merely encouraged some strategists around Hull to insist on an even stronger reliance on the "stick" of trade sanctions to force Germany into bankruptcy and thus a change of course. One of the fields where this policy was particularly noticeable was in Washington's attempts to disrupt the bilateralism that Germany, in search of raw materials, pursued in Latin America. To be sure, the appearance of a competitor in that part of the world was also to be fought as a matter of principle, being a violation of the time-honored Monroe Doctrine. But when German efforts in Brazil, for example, blatantly undermined American multilateralism in the Hemisphere and on top of it strengthened anti-American authoritarian regimes, the State Department moved toward a more anti-German policy.[23]

Theoretically this anti-Germanism could have encouraged close cooperation with British attempts to stop Hitler from resorting to war. But London remained suspicious of American objectives, believing—not without reason—that Hull's multilateralism and Open Door rhetoric was also, albeit more indirectly, aimed at the Empire and Commonwealth and the City, with Wall Street waiting in the wings. Under the impact of the Depression, the Empire had been transformed into an economic bloc with even stronger preferential tariffs favoring British finance and industry. By 1938, it looked as if these Anglo-American tensions were being overcome in the face of the growing threat posed by Germany, Japan, and Italy through a trade agreement as a step toward closer cooperation.[24] But first it took quite long and difficult negotiations to sign this agreement that was also meant to be a warning to Germany's barter politics; worse, even after its conclusion, suspicions continued over the role of Canada as a member of the Commonwealth, on the one hand, and as America's neighbor and trading partner, on the other. There is the telling remark by Sir Ronald Lindsay, the British ambassador to Washington, who vented his frustration by calling the Americans "dreadful people to deal with." They "cannot make firm promises and so they jolly you along with fair prospects and when we are committed, they let you down. Taking a short view, it is hard to remember a bargain with them that has really been satisfactory to us in itself." Part of the problem was, of course, that American diplomats constantly had to look over their shoulders and take isolationist opinion into account. This had been a problem in the early 1920s, and it continued to be one not only in the 1930s but also in the early war years.

Chamberlain may have hoped that closer trade cooperation would lead the Americans to modify their official policy of "noninvolvement" in the *political* problems of Europe that the British prime minister was wrestling with both before and after Munich. But even though some of Hull's advisors were pushing for a firmer political commitment that they hoped would act as an even stronger deterrent to Hitler than the economic stick, it was Roosevelt, the other key figure in Washington in the Anglo-American-German triangle, who blocked such a commitment.

There can be no question that the U.S. president was anything but a friend of the Nazi dictatorship. Although he had quite positive childhood memories of his visits to Germany, the brutal policies of repression and anti-Semitism that were reported in the American press outraged him. As Hitler continued his rearmament and forged ahead with his Four-Year Plan, Roosevelt decided that it was time to express his opposition more explicitly. He was also worried by the aggressiveness of Japan and Italy in China and North Africa. This is the background to the president's Quarantine Speech of October 1937 in which he outlined a policy of containment of the fascist and militarist menace. The fact that this statement probably contributed to Hitler's decision to make his "Hossbach Speech" a few weeks later reflects the deterioration in German-American relations. Clearly, Hitler had now come to realize that he had to hurry up with his conquests in the east, as the two "sea powers" began openly to oppose him. So, if Britain was not prepared to go along with his plans in the east, he would pursue them without and ultimately even against the Western powers. Logically, this meant that he had to prepare for a war in the west in the 1940s by expanding the navy and the air force. This shift in the Nazi rearmament program promptly occurred from 1938 onward.[25]

However, even if Chamberlain had been hoping that rising German-American tensions would result in closer cooperation, Roosevelt, apart from his speech making, continued his policy of noninvolvement that dismayed his secretary of state. In 1933 Hull had been surprised when the president announced that domestic reconstruction and stabilization through protectionism rather than multilateral trade was his first priority. Given the economic state of the country, he probably had no other choice. And also in subsequent years, Roosevelt had time and again been guided by the country's internal problems and by electoral politics when his reelection was at stake in 1936 and 1940. He worried about the continued isolationist stance of larger sections of the American population, especially in the Midwest and their representatives in Congress. There was also the concern over how to sustain the recovery when in 1937 the economy dipped into a recession.

By this time, if not before, another member of Roosevelt's Cabinet, Henry Morgenthau, had emerged as an influential voice in the debates on the strategy the United States should pursue to counter the growing threat to peace and stability emanating from Germany, Italy, and Japan.[26] Hull continued to use the softer levers of economic pressure without escalating them to a point that would make negotiations with the two fascist powers and with Tokyo impossible. Morgenthau, by contrast, nudged by a number of loyal advisors and also by the persistent demands Bernard Baruch, the influential banker, had become increasingly convinced that America had to confront aggressors. He also wanted to support those European powers that were prepared to resist them and to lay the industrial and military foundations inside the country, should participation in a major war become inevitable, as he believed sooner or later it would. In this combative mood, he tried to counter not only Hull's more cautious line of "economic appeasement" but also the War Department that, in his view, was moving far too slowly in beefing up the country's defenses.

Morgenthau's advocacy of more determined (re)action can be followed at two interrelated levels:[27] First are his efforts to release the administration from the constraints that the isolationists in Congress had imposed through the Neutrality Act of 1933 and its revised version of 1937. The second level concerned his attempts to persuade American big business to obtain and fulfill expeditiously orders from the U.S. government, Britain, and France for military equipment and to expand its production capacities. His aim was for Washington to be able to respond to a growing demand for arms from Europe as well as from the American armed forces that, he was convinced, was bound to come. In a way, this was an American lesson learned from World War I when it took the country a full year to mobilize after the declaration of war in April 1917.

The Neutrality Act, after further revisions in 1939, improved the administration's position toward allies when the earlier strict weapons embargo against belligerents was at last modified. Arms could now be sold by American manufacturers, provided the buyer paid in cash and carried the goods on its own ships, and provided also that no American credits were given to finance these purchases. With fascist expansionism in Central Europe and in Africa as well as Japanese imperialism in Asia continuing, deliveries of all goods to the aggressors could be stopped, while aid to France and Britain was stepped up. After the fall of France in June 1940, Britain's "cash-and-carry" capacities became hopelessly overstretched, and a desperate Winston Churchill, who had replaced Chamberlain as prime minister, appealed to Roosevelt for American *loans* to enable Britain, now the last bastion in Europe against the Wehrmacht, to order vital military equipment.[28] Again it was Morgenthau who was at the forefront of crafting the Lend-Lease Agreement which, after many delays due to objections and demands for amendments from Congress and the State and War Departments, was finally ratified in March 1941. All the while, the Treasury Secretary was also involved in the organization of aid to China and Dutch Southeast Asia against Japanese expansionism. He argued with Hull over the State Department's traditionally more nuanced approach, as the diplomats were anxious not to provoke Tokyo into a declaration of war against the United States, if vital American exports of oil, oil products, and manganese were stopped.

6. American Big Business and the Roosevelt Administration

The confusing politics prior to the promulgation of the 1939 Neutrality Act and the no less complex debates surrounding Lend-Lease have been sketched here because they are important to an understanding of the role of American big business relating to attempts to develop a consensus about the vital questions of peace and stability at home and abroad and also to when the time had come to give up hoping that Hitler, Mussolini, and the Japanese leaders were reasonable men with whom war-avoiding deals could be struck.

There was first of all the initial split in the business community over how to assess Roosevelt's New Deal. Here it was above all the American Chamber of Commerce (ACC) with its many owners of small and medium-sized firms from all over the country, but also some big corporations that vigorously resisted the president's efforts to overcome the Depression. After a brief honeymoon in the spring of 1933 and even a willingness of accept Roosevelt's job creation programs, relations quickly went downhill. The National Recovery Act, with its provisions that guaranteed workers' rights, was totally unacceptable to most employers. When the president signed the Securities Exchange Act of 1934 into law, it was not just the banks that were up in arms over this attempt to regulate the financial markets. Nor did the business community see the benefits of the Glass-Steagall Act, which put a firewall between investment banks and ordinary commercial and savings institutions. The hoariest stories circulated about the United States sliding down the road toward socialism and regimentation by Washington.

Although there were periods of greater realism when the leadership tried to move the ACC toward the center, some of the opposition lasted beyond Roosevelt's two election victories into World War II. Still, the number of his often archconservative foes among the business community began to dwindle after the 1934 congressional elections had shown that the voters were in favor of reforms and then reelected Roosevelt two years later. It was Henry Harriman, the ACC's moderate president, who now, if not before, began to seek a rapprochement with the government.

The National Association of Manufacturers, which had similarly found it difficult to reconcile itself to the election of a Democratic administration, also became more flexible. And then there were a number of prominent businessmen who had never abandoned the positive stance that they had taken up toward Roosevelt in 1933. They had accepted an invitation to a meeting that Secretary of Commerce Daniel Roper had called to form a Business Advisory and Planning Council, later to be renamed Business Advisory Council (BAC), in an effort to harmonize government-business relations. Among the attendees were, apart from Harriman, such major figures as Gerard Swope (General Electric, GE) Walter Teagle (Standard Oil), Alexander Legge (International Harvester), and Alfred Sloan (GM). After the BAC's founding in June 1933, Myron Taylor (U.S. Steel), Walter Gifford (AT&T), and Robert Wood (Sears, Roebuck & Co.) also joined.

BAC's relationship with Roosevelt experienced a few ups and downs, but it did support the administration in its quest to introduce social security. It also came to accept that some comprehensive planning and coordination was necessary in a complex industrial economy and that some deficit spending might act as a welcome stimulus to employment and to overcome the Depression. Other prominent figures who were to play an important role in World War II were Beardsley Ruml (Laura Spelman Rockefeller Foundation, later Macy's), Paul Hoffman (Studebaker), Charles Wilson (GE), and Henry Luce (Time-Life). Overall, Roosevelt succeeded in assembling a political coalition that was made up partly of workers and southern Democrats but partly also of capital-intensive industries and banks that were internationally orientated.[29]

As Germany, Italy, and Japan were careening down the tracks toward another world war that would sooner or later also drag in the United States, the foundations were laid for a Hullian vision of a *Pax Americana*. Within this broader framework, many American corporations that had invested in Germany developed a peculiar schizophrenia. While continuing their business in Germany and supplying, directly or indirectly, Hitler's nascent war machine (as will be seen in a moment by reference to a number of American companies), key leaders abandoned their earlier reservations about the Roosevelt administration and began to see the benefits not only of its strategy of stimulating the domestic economy, but also of confronting Germany, Italy, and Japan without making the United States a belligerent. They appreciated that this strategy would kill several birds with one stone. It was designed (1) to meet whatever greater demand for civilian goods there was after 1938, (2) to be able to respond to British and French needs for military equipment, and (3) to replenish the gaps that had arisen in the arsenals of the War Department as well as to stockpile reserves.

There had been, it is true, indications in 1936 that private domestic investment and industrial production were picking up. But 1937 had seen an unexpected decline that accelerated in 1938. Thus in April 1938, the steel mills—a key indicator—were operating at a mere 32 percent of their capacity. Car sales in March of that year were 47 percent below what they had been a year earlier, and in January some 7.8 million Americans were registered as unemployed and if those who were no longer registered are added, the figure was closer to 10.8 million. In these circumstances, Roosevelt decided to try to stimulate the economy. If parts of industry responded positively to this effort, there was an additional bonus for the U.S. president: for the upcoming 1940 elections it was important that the unemployment figures that were still so distressingly high would come down.

7. Stimulating American Industrial Production

As Roosevelt was looking for ways of lifting the American economy out of another depression,, he had an influential ally in his cabinet who, unlike the more cautious Hull, had already tried to nudge him toward taking a harder line against Hitler, Mussolini, and the Japanese leadership: Henry Morgenthau. Accordingly, he began to support Roosevelt in his plan to focus, as a first step, on an expansion of aircraft production. As Morgenthau recorded in his diary in November 1938 soon after Roosevelt's Quarantine Speech, the president was apparently "leaning more and more towards giving private manufacturers the first chance."[30] He guessed that this idea had in part been conceived because Roosevelt had "become convinced that in England particularly the Government has been unable to manufacture planes in their own plants." This was, of course, a reference to the earlier British decision to concentrate its preparations for a possible war on the air force.

But the domestic economic situation in Britain had prevented Chamberlain from spending more on the military. If only—so the calculation— the United States could add to its five-thousand-plane air force a capacity expansion to ten thousand per annum, the selling or lending of a larger number to Britain and France became a viable proposition. There was also the calculation that, if these plans had been known to Hitler and Mussolini, it might have deterred them from their aggressive policies that, thanks to the Munich Agreement of September 1938, had barely avoided a descent into war. While, with Hitler already thinking of tearing up Chamberlain's "peace for our time" agreement, deterrence was no more than a pious hope, the proposed expansion did surpass the air power that Germany and Italy had been building. Supporting Roosevelt's antifascism, Morgenthau was also convinced that this stimulus to the American defense industry would lead to extra shifts and the hiring of more workers.

It is against this backdrop that the hitherto reluctant War Department was prepared to order, for example, Boeing's four-engine bomber. No less important, the French, also short of military aircraft, were prepared to advance the cash needed for Boeing and other corporations to expand their factories. To be sure, all this had to be done gingerly in light of isolationist feeling in the country and in Congress. It was therefore very awkward when one of Douglas's testing planes crashed and it was found that a Frenchman had been onboard. The opposition promptly cried foul and accused the administration of violating the Neutrality Act. Consequently, however urgently France and Britain pleaded to let them buy more planes, Congress had not even approved the additional funds needed for increased military production. At this point it was significant that a man as influential in American industry as Edward R. Stettinius, Jr., the president of U.S. Steel and an advocate of closer government-industry cooperation, remarked that French orders and cash could have an "almost revolutionary" effect on the aircraft industry and would lay "the groundwork for the great expansion" to come, while Roosevelt, with the 1940 elections in mind, talked of renewed prosperity at home.[31]

Six months later, Roosevelt abandoned holding back on approving British and French requests for munitions deliveries because of isolationist opposition in Congress. As war in Europe looked to him increasingly likely by the summer of 1939, he chose Stettinius to chair a newly constituted War Resources Board, on which Walter Gifford (American Telephone & Telegraph Company, AT&T) and William Knudsen (GM) also agreed to serve. Once the Neutrality Act had been revised, British and French orders for American military equipment were pouring in. With Hitler's attack on Poland in September 1939 and the British and French declaration of war on Germany a few days later, Roosevelt was more firmly convinced than ever that, while keeping out of the military conflict, production must be expanded to thirty thousand aircraft per annum and that this expansion could be achieved with the help of Allied purchasing.

The trouble was that American industry was still woefully underprepared for this boost. Some companies, whose leaders continued to be critical of Roosevelt and his New Deal in particular, were reluctant to respond positively to these initiatives. Earlier suspicions that the administration wanted to increase state controls were fanned by antitrust investigations that the Justice Department had begun under Thurman Arnold and that will be analyzed in greater detail in chapter VI. There were also firms that, with civilian consumption slowly picking up, had quite full order books to supply the large domestic market. For example, the output of American and Canadian automobile plants was estimated in September 1939 to be over twenty-five thousand vehicles per week. At the same time it seems that those who were willing to follow the administration in its quest to boost industrial production found it difficult to recruit and train the additional workers. For too long their recruitment and training of workers had been neglected. Skilled workers had been unceremoniously dismissed instead of keeping them on part-time in the expectation that the economy would improve. Morgenthau also discovered that there were a mere three corporations that were ready to manufacture engines of one thousand horsepower and that their monthly output capacity was at most two thousand. There was also the case of the GM-owned Allison Motors, which could not immediately switch to engine production that met War Department specifications, and when Edsel Ford, Henry's son, was approached, he saw similar problems. On top of it he had to persuade his stubbornly antiwar father to abandon his opposition to military production. At the same time, Pratt & Whitney was working around the clock in three shifts.

A further important step not only to increase production but also to create the bureaucratic structures for an economy that slowly became geared to aiding Britain and France and preparing for war occurred under the impression of the Nazi onslaught on France and the evacuation of the British Expeditionary Force from the beaches at Dunkirk. On 28 June 1940 Roosevelt created the National Defense Advisory Commission, which led to the rise of Knudsen, the GM president. He became the director of the Office of War Production Management, which included coordination of the crucial machine tool industry.

With Britain having become the sole opponent after Hitler's conquests in Western and Northern Europe by the summer of 1940, Winston Churchill presented a long wish list of desperately needed weapons for the continuation of the war.[32] On it was a request for a loan of American destroyers for convoy protection. But Roosevelt was in the middle of his reelection campaign in a political climate where isolationist feeling was still strong. So, he felt constrained to offer no more than fifteen old warships. In return, Britain would lease a number of bases to the Americans in Newfoundland and the British West Indies. He replied that, however much he would like to make a deal, Britain had to wait for more until after the November elections.

By this time the crisis in the Atlantic had become even more acute, as some fifty German submarines were torpedoing British ships at a calamitous rate and the country did not have enough destroyers to provide convoy protection. Under the "cash-and-carry" policy, ships on the transatlantic route could not be American-owned, even if some of them had already been registered under a different flag to circumvent this rule. With Roosevelt's election victory secured, preparations began to replace "cash-and-carry" with the Lend-Lease Agreement that was finally passed by Congress in March 1941. Meanwhile and after some delays, the destroyer-for-bases agreement had also been put in place, and Roosevelt also approved that repairs on the HMS Malaga could be made in a U.S. shipyard. Perhaps the most significant move to supply Britain with food and weapons and to stimulate the American economy had come in the autumn of 1939 when the British delegation in Washington ordered sixty tramp steamers. By November the total price of $96 million had been agreed, with some $9 million earmarked for the building of new shipyards. By January Washington had added its own accelerated shipbuilding program that until 1945 produced some 72,100 naval and 4,900 merchant ships.

Henry J. Kaiser, a dynamic entrepreneur who had come to value the benefits of the New Deal connections between government and industry when he established the Six Companies consortium that built the Hoover Dam, was among the first to seize these business opportunities.[33] Although he was an outsider to the shipbuilding industry, he from 1940 onward built pretty much from scratch and partly with public funds no fewer than five huge shipyards in Richmond (California) as well as farther north in Portland and Vancouver. This is where the "Liberty" class freighters were built that soon proved to be vital first for shipping supplies across the Atlantic and after the American entry into the war in December 1941 also American troops to be stationed in Britain. By this time the American security zone, that is, the limit of the American neutrality patrols, which since the beginning of the war had stretched from Halifax, via Bermuda to just north of Antigua and then into the mid-Atlantic west of Dakar, had been expanded to the seas west of the Portuguese Azores and ultimately the waters east of Iceland. This step now gave antisubmarine protection by U.S. Navy destroyers up to this mid-Atlantic line and was still deemed to be within the rules of the Neutrality Act. After Pearl Harbor the patriotic popular mobilization for the war against Japan and Germany gave all these measures, whether under Lend-Lease or other agreements, a further boost to a massive production program, now funded by both private investments and government bonds.

A number of other smaller steps were undertaken during the winter 1940 and 41 and spring 1941: Despite continuing opposition from the isolationists in Congress and from the America First Committee, with Charles Lindbergh still asserting that peace with Hitler could be achieved, the manufacturing and legal infrastructure for supplying Britain was being built. It also helped that the U.S. Army and Navy now wanted to place orders themselves, for which some $880 million had been allocated. With the Lend-Lease Bill before Congress, the constraints of the 1939 Neutrality Act were being relaxed further. In the autumn of 1940, Nazi bombing of London and other British cities and the Battle of Britain had given rise to fears of an imminent Nazi invasion of the United Kingdom. It was another reason for Churchill, banking on the increasingly close "special relationship" that he had forged with Roosevelt, to appeal to the U.S. president, whereupon the latter had promised Lend-Lease, that is, the end of ruinous "cash-and-carry."[34]

Although Roosevelt had won the elections and was now prepared to push Democrats and Republicans harder, he still tried to avoid upsetting his critics too much.[35] Accordingly, Knudsen, the industrialist in charge of expanding production, decided that only one-third of the $880 million would be immediately available to the armed forces. Nevertheless, the larger point to emerge from all this is that American industry did not "spend itself" out of the depression; nor did Roosevelt solve the unemployment problem until the United States finally entered the war. In fact, there was an earlier phase when, partly thanks to pressure from Morgenthau, the financial and organizational foundations for the mobilization of industry were put in place and production was increased, securing not only the supply of Britain. No less important, from the summer of 1941 onward, that is, well before Hitler's declaration of war on America in December of that year, the Soviet Union, which had been attacked by Germany in June, was included in American deliveries. As a result of these developments, it may be said that the Nazis had objectively lost the war in the autumn of 1941, both because the Wehrmacht had become logistically overstretched in the wide expanses of Russia and the Ukraine and because American supplies, next to the heroic effort of the ordinary Red Army soldier, helped prevent the collapse of the Soviet Union.[36]

In trying to draw a balance sheet on these developments from the perspective of American big business, it is not surprising that it was not easy for it to find a common approach not only to Roosevelt's New Deal but also to the administration's foreign and armaments policy. Even those entrepreneurs who were favorably disposed toward the administration's domestic policies and agreed to serve on its preparatory committees and boards were not in favor of expanding the war in Europe to a world war by the United States joining the anti-Axis coalition as an actual belligerent. They all feared the destructiveness of a global world war. This is why sections of the business community continued to speak up for pursuing a policy of noninvolvement, with some openly favoring an appeasement of the dictators. It may be that even those who took a harder line thought of July 1914 and believed that, perhaps, big business had not intervened forcefully enough then to preserve peace. This may explain why some of them—as can be seen from hindsight—all too naively thought that by talking to Hitler, Mussolini, or the Japanese they could still stop a catastrophe, even after the fighting was in full swing in Europe and the Far East. It is to the peace missions that took place in 1939–40 that we shall have to turn after discussing the policies and practices of a number of key corporations in the 1930s.

8. American Views of the
Hitler Dictatorship

With the Nazi seizure of power, American corporations that had established a base in Germany during the Weimar years were, like the diplomats, trying hard to come to grips with the basic character of the new regime.[37] Just as among Germany's conservative elites, there was little appreciation of the radicalism of Hitler and his entourage. To many American businessmen the regime looked at first like a continuation of the presidential regime of President Hindenburg. They noted that conservative nationalists and a Reichswehr general looked firmly entrenched in key cabinet posts. The argument that Hitler had been successfully boxed in seemed as plausible to foreign observers as it was to non-Nazi right-wing Germans. This perception was reinforced by Hitler's early assurances, given, for example, in interviews with correspondents of the American Hearst press, that he was a man of peace in international affairs.

Reports in the *WSJ* and the *NYT* during the early days reflect this initial credulity.[38] Thus, on 31 January *WSJ* headlined its account of the events in Berlin at the very end of January 1933 with the words "Hitler Granted Chancellorship. Hindenburg Puts Conservatives in New Chancellor's Cabinet, Checking Extremists." The *NYT* announced on the same day "Hitler Made Chancellor of Germany, But Coalition Cabinet Limits Power." A more detailed news item in the same paper said reassuringly that "Hitler Puts Aside Aim to Be Dictator" and, referring to economics minister Alfred Hugenberg and Reichswehr minister Lieutenant General Werner von Blomberg, added that "Contrasts Mark Hitler's Cabinet." A day later, *WSJ*, unsurprisingly concerned about the reception of Hitler by the stock market, wrote that "Berlin Views Hitler Calmly. Rise in Stocks Reflects Confidence He Will Not Disrupt Nation's Affairs." On 4 February, Vice Chancellor Franz von Papen, a conservative Catholic, denied that the cabinet was moving toward a restoration of the monarchy and declared that the "Hitler Government Will Make No Marked Changes in Foreign Policy." This seemed to confirm a *WSJ* item of 31 January that "Hitler News Fails to Stir Wall Street." The paper continued that "financial markets on the whole took the news calmly." German bonds "listed on the New York Stock Exchange reacted from a fraction to" a little under six percentage points, "but there was no great selling pressure."

In Britain the press took a more cautious line, with the London *Times* commenting that "the President has taken a great risk" and that the further development of Germany's "great political adventure" would be closely watched.[39] This applied in particular to German policies in the field of armaments. The *NYT* editorial of 31 January was similarly more cautious, arguing that "Germany has entered upon a perilous political adventure" and that the world would see if Hitler could be "tamed."[40] This may have been in part a response to a report by Associated Press of 30 January. It referred to "a proclamation that the present Cabinet is not truly representative of Hitlerism" and that the Nazi leader, after praising Hindenburg, was determined to "carry on the fight within the government as tenaciously as we fought outside."

Four days later Hitler began to use stronger language. Before a group of handpicked journalists he asked that the "press of the world" should not pass a "premature judgment" on him and his government. According to United Press, he complained that he had been presented as someone who delivered "bloodthirsty firebrand speeches."[41] But in fact "all the world has been surprised by my moderation." He denied having made inflammatory speeches. His speeches "even 10 or 15 years ago testify to that." At the same time he was "a tenacious person" with "strong nerves." But the manifesto he had issued to the Germans should not be taken as an "election campaign speech." If he had "wanted to do that, I could have said that unemployment would cease on March 15 and that agriculture would be back on its feet by May 1." He had refused to make such promises because he was "more honest than my political opponents." With an eye to the international community and referring to his frontline service in World War I, he then said, "No one who, like myself, knows war as we do—what immense squandering of effort and consumption of strength it involves." No one wanted "peace and tranquility more than Germany does and I do." However, "like all other nations we insist on equality and our adequate place in the world, just as any American would insist for his own country." All he wanted is to be given was a chance to implement a four-year program of domestic change. He was asking for a mere four years "after which the nation can pass judgment and even crucify me." The report then listed the main points Hitler had made in a radio address, among which were the "curbing of Communism," the "conquering of unemployment" within four years, and "arms equality, preferably through reductions by heavily armed nations."

To stress his determination to "fight against Communism," the *WSJ* printed a United Press item that the police had "raided Communist headquarters throughout Prussia in their search for documents to prove that the Communist party activities are illegal."[42] The report also mentioned that, if Hitler were unable to gain a majority in the next Reichstag elections either alone or in conjunction with Hugenberg's Nationalist Conservative Party, "he may obtain the majority by outlawing the Communists and abolishing their 100 Reichstag seats." In light of what happened at the end of February after the Reichstag building had gone up in flames (whether started by a young communist Dutchman or by the Nazis themselves), this was no doubt a prescient analysis of one of the measures by which Hitler proceeded to turn Germany into a one-party dictatorship within the next six months.[43]

American businessmen across the Atlantic gathered this and other information about events in Nazi Germany primarily through the national and regional dailies as well as weeklies and monthlies, such as *Business Week, Barron's, Forbes,* or *Fortune.* In 1994, Frank Biess undertook a careful analysis of these magazines and found overall that they reflected the difficulties that the United States had with understanding what was actually going on the Germany.[44] In April and again in June

1933 *Business Week* focused on the conservatives in the Hitler cabinet and on the "moderate" economics minister Hjalmar Schacht. Starting from the alleged "complete absence of planned economy ideas" in the Nazi program, the April issue assigned to Schacht the "dominant role" in the formulation of "governmental and financial economic policy."[45] On 27 March *Barron's* went so far as to compare the new Germany to the Hohenzollern monarchy. There were, it is true, some radical outbursts, but the expectation was still that the Third Reich would, like the Second Reich, take the shape of an autocratic regime that respected private property and would not interfere with business.[46] It was another gross underestimation of the Nazis.

Accordingly, the anti-Semitic outrages were interpreted by *Business Week* as a "strange interlude" before things would settle down again. Later both magazines but also *Fortune* turned to comparisons between Italian Fascism and National Socialism and pointed to the productionism and greater efficiency that John Diggins has analyzed in his 1972 study.[47] Discussing Hitler's recovery program in its 26 April issue, *Business Week* called Nazi economic policies "Germany's New Deal." Meanwhile on 1 April *Forbes* had raised the question of whether "many industries need[ed] dictators."[48] Although these and similar publications were widely read in the business community, it is of course difficult to know how far they influenced opinions. There was no lack of information, as they also had access to news and analyses in the publications of trade associations and research institutes. A few of them also benefitted from occasional briefings and informal conversations they had with ministerial officials in Washington or with German businessmen. But it is only with the benefit of hindsight that it becomes clear how widespread misperceptions were of the regime's basic character and how much wishful thinking also played a role.

Even the information that American consuls provided was often less than reliable, as they now dealt with a regime that imposed ever stricter censorship and spread ever noisier propaganda, and that also became ever more secretive and deceptive about its actual plans, especially in the field of foreign and armaments policy.[49] The more the regime tightened its grip on the political system, the more suspect published German sources and official statistics became. The massive rearmament program that began straightaway in 1933 was especially difficult to gauge. Official figures on industrial production, on exports, imports, and employment, on deficit-spending, or on inflation were more and more cynically rigged.

In these circumstances, the business press and business community with a direct interest in German developments came to focus on larger questions in an effort to gauge what made an economy tick that was

becoming increasingly centralized and dictatorial.[50] American businessmen with Jewish connections understandably reacted extremely
negatively to the Nazis unfolding anti-Semitic policies. For some these
policies alone were sufficient to break off all connections and to demand official protests by the State Department. Another and arguably
larger business group was more concerned to comprehend the evolving political economy of Germany. They were struck by some of the
modern features of both German and Italian fascism and its seemingly
technocratic decisionism. After all and notwithstanding the agrarian
utopianism of some Nazi leaders, flow production and rationalized
factory organization appeared to be spreading.[51] In light of the propaganda campaigns that extolled Hitler's public works program, comparisons were made with Roosevelt's initiatives to put Americans back
to work and to refloat the economy.

Those businessmen who were hostile to the president's proto-
Keynesianism warned that this policy would twist the structures and
principles of American capitalism in a fascist or, worse, a Bolshevik direction.[52] Others saw greater government intervention and regulation
as a way out of the Depression and a salvation of capitalism and democracy. They pointed to the differences between Roosevelt and Hitler.
Over time, early comparisons between the New Deal and fascist economic policies receded into the background.[53] National Socialism came
to be studied as a unique phenomenon that was headed toward wars of
conquest. By 1936, the National Industrial Conference Board, a research
and information outfit of American business, explicitly drew attention
to the links between the Nazi regime's restrictive trade policies and its
political dogmas of antiliberalism, anti-Semitism, antisocialism, and
territorial expansionism. The business press also began to comment on
the impression that Nazi economics made on the German population
and commented on the empty promises that were being made to the
ordinary consumers. The latter had gotten their jobs back. But with rising inflation resulting from the concentration on the production of military hardware and an ever more noticeable scarcity of durable civilian
goods as well as the spreading of economic and political controls, *Business Week*, for example, now wrote sarcastically about the bread that
German workers were given "without butter," as Hitler was "spending
[the] last pfennigs for guns."[54]

Meanwhile large sections of the American public and their representatives in Congress persisted in their isolationism, restraining the
Roosevelt administration from communicating with the business community on international affairs. Worried about Hitler's foreign and economic policies, the State Department began to counsel American firms
operating in Germany to get out. But even after Roosevelt's Quarantine

Speech of October 1937, his actual policy of noninvolvement left those still manufacturing and trading in Germany confused. The ambiguity of official American foreign policy and the differences of opinion about Germany within Washington produced a parallel ambiguity and uncertainty among American corporations with investments in Central Europe. Gabriel Kolko rightly called attention to this gap, but he was uncertain how far the business press can be used to fathom business attitudes and decision making.[55]

9. Hitler and German Industry

The approach taken here has been to analyze both the press and specific corporate practices in an attempt to avoid a generalized conclusion that American firms in Germany in the 1930s were all fascist collaborators. Even those who were initially more favorably disposed toward Hitler or misjudged his radicalism had (with a few exceptions, such as Henry Ford) by 1936 begun to reevaluate the situation. By then many of them had heard of the regime's brutalities at home and its preparations for foreign war.[56] Those who had decided to not cut their losses experienced in their daily operations that they lived under an increasingly state-controlled economy that limited their freedom of action to make decisions on the basis of what they had learned to be in the best interest of their particular enterprise and its bottom line. And having witnessed Nazi repression, Roosevelt's New Deal and the politics of the Democratic administration began to look more and more benign.

Economic historians of the Third Reich have argued among themselves how to assess the behavior of German companies during the 1930s. This debate is quite helpful to understanding the behavior of American firms that continued to manufacture and trade. These were on the whole companies that, rather than merely having agencies, had invested millions of dollars in factories and a sales infrastructure. Their political risk was, to be sure, not as great as that of indigenous corporations, such as Bosch, I.G. Farben, or VSt. Still, they, too, faced a problem.

Some early postwar Anglo-American scholarship reflects the black Allied picture of German managers as war criminals. Other scholars viewed them as victims of a totalitarian dictatorship who had no choice but to collaborate.[57] Resistance would have led to their firms' expropriation by the regime and would have been self-destructive. In the 1960s and 1970s the pendulum swung back again when, in the wake of neo-Marxist analyses of contemporary industrial societies, fascism was seen as an outgrowth of "monopoly capitalism." The criticism that this perspective encountered in turn during the 1980s is exemplified by Peter Hayes's book on I.G. Farben. Insofar as his work contained any a priori judgments, it was his conviction "that the organizing framework for good and evil in the modern age is not capitalism or socialism, but industrialization and its corollaries of bureaucratism and professionalism."[58]

With the rise of more complex interpretations of how the Third Reich supposedly ticked, views on German business began to change again. Christoph Buchheim and a group of business historians around him at Mannheim University argued that big business, rather than operating under an all-pervasive totalitarian dictatorship, had more room for maneuver, and that any collaboration was much more voluntary than extracted.[59] As this debate unfolded, Hayes raised his voice against what he thought was an approach "that presents economics in virtual isolation from politics . . . and the fluctuating relationship between business and the state as largely static." Ultimately, it was "Nazi economic policies [that] structured opportunities and thus corporate executives' choices. Did businessmen retain free will? Of course they did. Was their autonomy intact? I think not."

If it is thus a matter of both agency and structure, two further differentiations have to be introduced that relate to the findings of Henry Turner concerning the financing of Nazism *before* 1933.[60] Here the accepted view now seems to be that it was smaller and more local companies that, together with the sacrifices of ordinary party members, funded the Nazi movement and its propaganda campaigns. With more studies on family enterprises and middle-sized firms coming out, it has become clearer that collaboration was less widespread among the big corporations.[61] To be sure, Turner's findings did not let big business off the hook, considering their increasing opposition to the Weimar Republic, especially among the archconservative managers of the Ruhr enterprises; it was this opposition that helped to undermine the parliamentary system and promoted a sharp polarization that no democratic political system can survive for any length of time. After Hitler had come to power, it also made a difference whether one produced and retailed civilian goods or stuff that Hitler viewed as essential to his rapid rearmament program and to his ultimate aim of waging an expansionist war for "living space." Not surprisingly, the Ruhr heavy industries were therefore more prone to make their peace with the regime than the members of the former "Siemens camp," even though they, too, were ultimately drawn into the rearmament effort.

Finally, there is also a generational factor to be considered. By 1936 an older generation of executives and owners of big enterprises had become increasingly unhappy about the regime and the direction in which its economic policies were moving, even if they were not under pressure, like their Jewish colleagues, to leave the management. They decided to bow out, to be replaced by a younger generation who were keen to make their mark. These—as Lutz Count Schwerin von Krosigk later put it—were the men "whose dynamism degenerated into brutality and who could not be impressed by anything."[62] Yet even they were split into two camps: those who wanted to take Germany out of the world economy altogether and those who approved of the acquisition of a large empire in Europe but also wanted to keep their companies engaged internationally.

10. Doing Business in Nazi Germany

If this was the political-economic milieu in which American corporations were submerged in Nazi Germany in the 1930s, while also observing the opaque foreign policy of the Roosevelt administration, it is not surprising that they should join their German counterparts in calculating the "political risk"—a topic that Christopher Kobrak and Per Hansen have recently taken up again in their anthology.[63] They stressed that political risk "is really political uncertainty" and that contemporary actors obviously did not know in 1933 that the world would be engulfed in a world war less than a decade later. Since the situation did not look all that gloomy at the start of the Third Reich and there were plenty of views that things, even if they did not get better, would at least not get worse, many American companies decided to soldier on.

Among the producers and retailers of civilian products, Woolworth's presents a good case in point. The company—so famous for its offerings of cheap mass-produced textiles, household goods, and others things of daily use—had come to Britain and Germany before 1914 and after the disruptions caused by World War I had consolidated its German subsidiary during the optimistic Weimar years. By 1927 seven stores had opened their doors, a large distribution center had been built very strategically at Sonneberg in Thuringia, and the company was thriving.[64] In 1933 the radical anti-Semites in the Nazi movement erroneously suspected the company of being a Jewish enterprise and blocked the entrances to its stores during the boycotts in the spring of that year. When the company protested, the regime relented. The decision now read like this:[65] "Although it is forbidden to open any new one-priced stores in Germany until April 1934," permission was given "by the Prussian ministry to F.W. Woolworth Co. GmbH, an affiliate of the American Woolworth, to complete installation of four new stores." These stores brought the total in Germany to a respectable eighty-two, with sales around 50 million marks per annum. Officially this was "largely" in response to the company's complaint that the chain would have suffered "heavy losses in case the decree was too strictly carried out."

This special permission must be seen in the context of another important peculiarity of the Nazi regime. While the production of military goods had priority, this was also a dictatorship that tried to secure its popularity and hence its stability not merely by propaganda, but also by appeasing ordinary Germans through the provision of material goods and promises of an even higher living standard once "living space" had been won. But consumer durables remained in short supply, even when after the end of unemployment people again had more money in their pockets. The steel, chemical and electrical engineering, and machine tool industries were busy working primarily for the Wehrmacht. Nevertheless, the regime was anxious to put at least day-to-day necessities into the shops and to avoid shortages that would lead to popular grumbling.[66]

This is where besides Woolworth's and other mass retailers the entertainment industry came in. If Hollywood movies had dominated the silver screen in the Weimar Republic, they continued to be shown in German theaters. This was part of a calculated cultural policy that Joseph Goebbels, himself a film buff, had developed. He wanted the mass of the German population to enjoy movies also as a means of distracting them from their daily grind and from the abolition of all vestiges of an open society. Accordingly, Nazi propaganda was put across to the ordinary cinemagoers not in the main feature film.[67] Here the audiences were treated to soothing soap operas with an apolitical happy ending. Hollywood movies were perfect for this and hence were imported in large numbers as before 1933. The newsreels that were screened before the main program served as the moment of Nazi propaganda, skillfully put together by Goebbels's propagandists. There were a number of popular German film stars, but their Hollywood counterparts were no less well known to German moviegoers.

While Nazi racist attitudes and censorship soon banned American jazz that had had many aficionados before 1933, the soft swooning tunes of swing music continued to be played in the dance halls, clubs, and bars of the big cities, often by indigenous bands.[68] Benny Goodman's swing was forbidden, which did not mean that his music and also traditional New Orleans jazz or even more frequently a "Germanized" swing was not played privately. During the war swing was also in demand among the troops, and on at least one occasion a party functionary who wanted to stop a concert was booed off the stage.

The regime also promoted healthy living and offered vacation travel organized by the "Strength Through Joy" association, while other parts of the German Labor Front encouraged sports and other activities.[69] In the same vein, the Coca-Cola Company was also allowed and even encouraged to market its fizzy drink after 1933. As Mark Pendergast put it in his study,[70] "While the soft drink came to symbolize American freedom" back in the United States, "the same Coca-Cola logo rested comfortably next to the swastika." As sales almost doubled in the 1930s, a further seven bottling plants were added to the six that had existed since the mid-1920s, including the first one in Essen in the heart of the working-class Ruhr region. By 1939 there were no fewer than fifty Coca-Cola bottling plants, selling millions of bottles. Germans spent over 100 million marks to refresh themselves. Customers of all social groups and ages were enticed to buy the uplifting drink on large bill boards and other media, depicting "Germanized" happy people, indulging in this enjoyable beverage—"ice cold."[71] The 1936 Olympic Games in Berlin and the Schaffendes Volk Exhibition at Düsseldorf in 1937 gave the company opportunities for huge marketing campaigns that German competitors like "Afri-Cola" found difficult to match. As Walter Oppenhoff, one of its managers, remarked, "political issues played no appreciable role" for the company.

The development of an inexpensive *Volksempfänger* radio, again promoted by Goebbels, must also be viewed in the context of the provision of inexpensive consumer goods and mass entertainment. Amateur photography provides another telling example. Film rolls and cheap cameras were very popular and widely available, as photos were taken for the family album at birthdays and weddings, on vacation travel, and at local festivals. Agfa Photo, a subsidiary of I.G. Farben chemicals, had a strong position in this particular market, but the American Kodak trust was also allowed to operate. During World War II the Wehrmacht propaganda units became a major consumer, taking dramatic pictures of advancing German troops. They were incorporated into Goebbels's newsreels, displaying the alleged invincibility of the German army, navy, and air force. But in the early stages of the war enough film was still available for amateur photography, and photos were eagerly exchanged between soldiers at the front and their families back home. This is how in the 1990s the Wehrmacht Photo Exhibition came about that displayed depictions of executions and other atrocities that ordinary soldiers and officers had taken in the Nazi-occupied territories. Thus a consumer good that the regime had used to distract and to garner support was turned into one that documented its boundless criminality.[72]

Finally, there is the most ambitious plan to create an Aryan society of materially satisfied *Volksgenossen*: the Volkswagen.[73] The story of this automobile will be examined in a moment in the context of GM's position in the Third Reich. The point to be made here is that this project is a good example of delayed gratification in the regime's effort to develop an ethnically "pure" mass consumption society. The Volkswagen was to be an "automobile for all," but only after a victorious war in the east and after more autobahns had been built next to wide-track super-fast trains, some of which would service the Ukraine all the way to the Crimea.[74] Volkswagen owners would travel along these highways for a vacation on the Black Sea coasts—to be sure, also after the "Jewish problem" had been "solved" and while the Slavic populations in those regions, kept in appalling living conditions, were being exploited as slave laborers for the Greater German Reich.

In anticipation of this future, Germans could sign up for a savings plan that, once they had accumulated enough points, would enable them to take delivery of a Volkswagen. This is why Hitler insisted that this car should cost around 1,000 marks. After lengthy negotiations, the well-financed "Strength through Joy" organization stepped in to build a large factory complex northeast of Brunswick in Fallersleben/ Wolfsburg. Since the Nazis did not win the war, the savings were lost, except for a token that account holders were given by the Volkswagen Works after 1945. During that war, Ferdinand Porsche's air-cooled, rear-mounted, boxer-engine "ugly duckling" (whose basic concept was in fact developed before 1933 by Joseph Ganz, an engineer and motor journalist, who was forced to leave because of his Jewish background) was transformed into the *Kübelwagen*, the Wehrmacht's equivalent of the American Jeep.[75]

11. The U.S. Auto Industry and Mass Motorization

For Hitler and his entourage, mass motorization was a serious post-war project whose foundations were laid before 1939. Accordingly, they looked toward the American motor industry, which produced 4.8 million passenger cars in 1928, compared with Britain's 212,000 and Germany's 90,000. In a broader perspective Hitler's interest has to be seen as part of the rationalization movement that began in the United States with Taylorism and Scientific Management and then swept into Europe after World War I.[76] Whether to adopt American factory organization and management methods came to be debated in countless books and articles in the contemporary media in Britain, Germany, and France in the 1920s. The scholarly evaluation of this literature has preoccupied historians and social scientists to this day. In comparative perspective, this issue is of interest to the larger themes of this book because British industry was slow to introduce continuous production and assembly lines. In this case, though, the Germans were not much further ahead so that a committee set up in 1925 for the promotion of what came to be called *Fliessarbeit* found no more than some two dozen practical examples.[77] In the end it was Opel Cars that led the way in Germany, even if at a length of two kilometers it reached only a fraction of Ford's and GM's lines in Michigan.

The same widespread interest also applied to the other side of this coin, that is, the Fordist idea of mass production enabling companies to pass a larger portion of the gains of rationalization on to the consumer. Prices could be lowered and more people would be able to afford even more expensive consumer durables without bigger wage packets. The related topic of consumption therefore also has generated a considerable amount of more recent scholarship, as interest in the qualitative and cultural aspects of modern industrial societies increased.

Returning to Hitler's attitudes on these subjects, he was disdainful of America as a "racially" mixed, democratic society in which a minority of Jewish capitalists allegedly pulled the strings, misleading society into greed and decadence. At the same time, he had a good deal of respect for American technology and greatly admired Henry Ford as an innovator, charismatic genius, and anti-Semite.[78] Although Ford had publicly distanced himself from his earlier anti-Semitic publications in the late 1920s, he still felt many affinities with National Socialism. Hitler's affection was so great that he awarded Ford a special medal for foreigners, the Grand Cross of the German Eagle, in recognition of his achievements. Conversely, Ford remained so proud of this honor that, unlike IBM's Thomas Watson, Sr., he refused to return it at the beginning of World War II when the United States and Germany had become deadly enemies. It paid off in that Hitler continued to hold a protective hand over Ford's industrial properties in Germany.

The story of Ford's rise in the United States before 1914 and of his setbacks in the late 1920s when he procrastinated for too long to scrap his old best seller, the Model T, that had by then fallen technologically behind its competitors, and to develop the new Model A, has been told many times. The circumspection with which Henry Ford originally went into the British and German markets is a good example of the step-by-step method (discussed in chapters II and IV) with which American firms ventured into Europe. He began with the creation of a dealership network, and by 1925 some eighty-five dealers were under contract with him. The next step came in January 1926 when he built an assembly plant in Berlin-Plötzensee. As *WSJ* reported, this plant was scheduled to start production on 15 April on two acres of floor space and with a waterfront of 1,000 feet in the Westhafen quarter that, through an elaborate system of canals, was connected to the seaports of

Hamburg and Bremerhaven in northwestern Germany.[79] The plan was to build some seven hundred cars per month. The retooling during the changeover to the Model A led to a temporary shutdown of this plant. The break was used at the same time to reorganize Ford's European operations. As far as Britain was concerned, Detroit pursued a similar strategy to good effect. As Hugh Jenkins, the managing director of Ford Motors Co., reported in early 1927, the outlook for Britain was good with sales of Fords as well as tractors increasing. And in the middle of November 1928, the parent company announced that it had invested the princely sum of $35 million in the British company "to acquire all [of] Ford's European subsidiaries."[80] The plant to be built at Dagenham in the east of London was to have a capacity of two hundred thousand cars per annum.

Another peculiarity of Ford Germany was that I.G. Farben, the chemical trust, took a 35 percent stake, with 60 percent being held by the British arm and the remaining 5 percent by a number of suppliers and dealers.[81] The development of new models became a joint venture between Detroit and Dagenham, though the names of individual models were adapted to the country in which they were marketed. Thus the small car that had been developed, partly in response to GM's Opel Laubfrosch, was offered in Germany as the Köln, to which other regional names were later added, such as the Rheinland, the Eifel, and the Taunus, which came out of the main factory outside Cologne, completed in 1929–30. Sabine Saphörster has written a most interesting article on the decision to locate this plant outside Cologne rather than in Neuss, south of Düsseldorf. It is a story of modern local government lobbying to attract a major manufacturer to a city, in this case Cologne, where Konrad Adenauer was the mayor.[82]

However much Henry Ford was admired for his achievements, once the Nazis had come to power it was not his factories in Cologne or Brandenburg that were chosen to develop Hitler's pet project, the Volkswagen. While Ford did well under the new regime, it was GM that at first made the running. One reason for this was that Ford's great competitor had in the late 1920s and under the leadership of Alfred Sloan shifted to a multimodel policy that gave buyers a wider choice in terms of makes, color schemes, and power trains.[83] It all evolved when these concepts had first been exported to Britain, where GM took a major stake in an existing company, Vauxhall Cars—a strategy different from Ford's practice of building its own factories abroad. The original acquisition target had been the more established Austin Ltd., after the Americans had begun to penetrate the British car-making industry with their machine tools. Morris Motors had first bought "a large number of American specialized machines" for their engine plant in Coventry, just as "British industry [had more] generally imported large quantities of American stamping and pressing machinery and lathes."

In the expansionist investment climate of the mid-1920s, it was but a small step to start car production in Britain and also to move into the promising market of Germany. But GM's strategy was different from Ford's in that it took a major stake in or ultimately purchased a European carmaker. Thus, in August 1925 Austin Motors, which Herbert Austin had successfully reorganized after a financial crisis in 1922–23 and turned into "the most modern automobile company in England," was to be "amalgamated" with GM at a cost of £1.5 million, reduced to "£1,000,000 or less than $5,000,000, as the balance will be later used by the Austin Company to acquire the assets of the present General Motors Ltd. in England."[84] In the end, the deal, much to GM's regret, was not, as Sloan put it, "consummated." A few months later, on 16 November 1925, GM's negotiations with the much smaller Vauxhall Motors Ltd. at Luton were completed with the proviso that the management would remain the same and that there would also be no change in the firm's operations. If Vauxhall was acquired with an eye to export opportunities to the British Empire in mind, Germany was deemed to be a good location for exports to neighboring countries on the European Continent.

Over the next few years, GM's FDI policies were still crystallizing, with Germany being the next target. Here Rüsselsheim near Frankfurt became the main location, when GM first decided to take a stake and later to purchase Opel Cars, the first producer in Germany of the small Laubfrosch. Since Opel subsequently advanced to the largest carmaker in Germany, the price of some $33 million looked like a good bargain that GM forked out in 1931. But by that time the board in Detroit found itself in the middle of the Great Depression that hit Germany particularly hard. In 1933 it was also faced with the new Nazi government, led by a man who began to build a ruthless dictatorship at home and a militarized, centrally controlled economy. With little appreciation of Hitler's more far-reaching foreign ambitions and keen to be asked to develop an inexpensive automobile that the regime was hoping to offer to loyal *Volksgenossen*, Opel presented the Kadett, priced at 1,400 marks.

In the meantime and after hearing about Hitler's ambitions to motorize the Germans, Ferdinand Porsche, an energetic engineer from Austria, began to work on a design of a Volkswagen with a 1,000-cubic-centimeter air-cooled rear-mounted boxer engine. For complex reasons that also had something to do with Hitler's nationalism and determination to gain greater control of the economy, the Volkswagen plan was not placed with GM at Rüsselsheim. Instead the regime decided to build from scratch a huge state-owned complex in

Lower Saxony. In the autumn of 1936 Porsche traveled to Detroit to study American mass production methods before, after many delays and conflicts with the Nazi bureaucracy and the national car manufacturers association, his vision of an inexpensive car reached the point where the first exemplars could be built.[85]

Although GM had been excluded, by the late 1930s it had become Germany's largest car manufacturer of small and midsized automobiles and trucks, outpacing its rival, the Ford Works, and seeing better business prospects abroad than back home. It tried its hand at marketing a larger model, the Admiral, but otherwise left the production of very expensive models with eight or even twelve cylinder engines that Hitler loved to ride in at rallies or annual party celebrations to Daimler and other indigenous firms.[86] However, while doing well as a capitalist enterprise, over time Opel's political situation became more difficult. To begin with, there was the larger problem that elements in the Nazi movement and its leadership had been harboring anti-American resentments even before 1933. With the consolidation of the regime, these elements were growing increasingly hostile to the presence of competing foreign enterprises inside Germany. There were also those ideologues who wanted to enlarge the country's "living space" in order to create a self-sufficient territorial bloc that was to be taken out of the world economy altogether. This Closed Space Economy (*Grossraumwirtschaft*) was pretty much the exact opposite of the above-mentioned Open Door that Secretary of State Cordell Hull envisioned and that GM embodied.

As the Nazi dictatorship stepped up its preparations for an expansionist war, the GM leadership in Detroit came under increasing pressure to produce Opel cars not merely for the private and commercial vehicles market, but also to accept orders from the Wehrmacht.[87] The military was particularly interested in GM's light truck, the Opel Blitz. Meanwhile, back in the United States, Roosevelt became increasingly convinced that the country would one day find itself in a war against Germany, and the question was inevitably whether American corporations in Germany should be persuaded to refuse "working for the [future] enemy," even at the risk of Nazi reprisals and under the ultimate threat of being expropriated without compensation.[88]

There was yet another dilemma that the GM leadership in Detroit had to grapple with. On the one hand, Germany was fast becoming a tightly organized dictatorship in which Hitler was the key decision maker in military and foreign affairs. On the other hand, and as has been mentioned above, he was quite disinterested in the day-to-day handling of domestic politics. Wedded ideologically to the principles of Social Darwinism, Hitler's inattention led to the rise of all sorts of "Little Führer" at the lower levels of the party and state bureaucracy who battled their rivals next door. The struggle for survival that Hitler wanted to direct toward the outside world thus also turned upon the regime itself, resulting in a highly volatile system, placing all managers of capitalist enterprises, who had to keep their shareholders happy, in a very difficult predicament. Opel Cars is a good case in point of what many other American firms went through by the late 1930s, if not before. Located in the state of Hesse, Jakob Sprenger, the *Gauleiter*, developed a growing appetite for the Rüsselsheim complex. This appetite manifested itself initially in Sprenger's attempts to oust inconvenient Opel managers, especially those who were Americans, and to replace them with men loyal to him. Insisting on their right to make decisions for the good of the company and not for the whims of Nazi functionaries who had no knowledge of how to run a modern factory, Opel Cars began to increase the number of loyal German managers who nevertheless had amicable relations with, and the confidence of, Sprenger.

With the Nazi regime tightening its grip on the country as a whole, Sprenger's meddling also got worse, whereupon Detroit tried to find allies within the Nazi bureaucratic hierarchy. The hope was that they would act as a counterweight to Sprenger and protect the company. These allies were subsequently found in Berlin where heavies like Hermann Göring and the generals in charge of Wehrmacht procurement were alerted to Opel's problems. Once the chief of the Four-Year Plan and the military had been wheeled out, Sprenger beat the retreat. But the drawback of this search for protectors was, of course, that Opel Cars came under even greater pressure than before to yield to the Wehrmacht. Its generals knew that the moment of Hitler's war of expansion was fast approaching and insisted ever more urgently that the orders that its officers kept placing be fulfilled as soon as possible.

Meanwhile, as has been analyzed above, the attitude of the Roosevelt administration toward the Nazis was becoming more and more hostile and confrontationist, even if both in the country and in Congress the mood was still quite firmly opposed to an American entry into a war in Europe or in the Pacific.[89] As a publicly quoted joint stock company, GM, just like Roosevelt, had to take account of this larger political milieu. No less vexing, there were voices that accused the corporation of supporting, via Opel Cars, the war preparations of the Nazi regime. This criticism did not come merely from the American-Jewish community and its organizations, but also from other groups and politicians in Congress, especially after the anti-Semitic pogroms in Germany in November 1938. The leadership at the GM headquarters responded to the Nazi pressures on Opel Cars and the deteriorating German-American relationship with further maneuverings. Car sales had been going up in the American market, as the civilian economy saw some improvement after the 1937 recession. Yet, this was not the only reason why the management board was anxious not to jeopardize these gains merely because of the clouds of war appearing on the horizon. Opel Cars was also doing well, thanks in part to a stream of orders for light trucks from the Wehrmacht. A war between Germany and the United States would lead not only to a loss of income (even when German currency regulations prevented a repatriation of profits), but also to expropriation under Nazi decrees on enemy property.

In this atmosphere Knudsen came to the conclusion that the corporation had to talk to key figures in the Third Reich, such as Göring, not only to sideline Sprenger, but also to ward off attempts by BMW (Bayerische Motoren-Werke), whose leadership advocated the expropriation of the Rüsselsheim factories under the pretext that the industry had to be concentrated.[90] With the expansion of the *Luftwaffe*, aircraft engines were more urgently needed than passenger cars, and a German-owned Opel, run by BMW or Göring's ministry, could be ordered to give priority to airplane engine production. Finding themselves between a rock and a hard place, GM managers were, not surprisingly, most interested in helping to prevent German-American tensions escalating into war, while Knudsen simultaneously agreed to be recruited into Roosevelt's and Morgenthau's efforts to boost production in the United States, in particular of military planes that Britain had also made the focus of its underfunded rearmament program since 1935.

12. British and American Business and the Preservation of Peace

The question that several industrialists therefore asked themselves was what could be done concretely to prevent the spread of war or, once the war in Europe had in fact started in 1939, how an armistice might be arranged. Just as Norman Angell had argued before 1914 that a major war would be disastrous for all sides because of its incalculably high human and material costs, Americans and also the British held similar convictions in the late 1930s. It is in this context that attempts at peace preservation have to be seen. They originated in Britain in the summer of 1938 when the Federation of British Industries (FBI) drew the attention of the Department of Overseas Trade and the Board of Trade to a fall in British exports due to price-cutting practices by competitors.[91] In an effort to deal with this problem with respect to one of these, that is, Germany, that had been aggressively buttressing its trade positions in Central Europe and Latin America, the FBI had already put out feelers to the *Reichsgruppe Industrie*. The Board of Trade replied that the conclusion of new cartel agreements with European competitors might offer a way forward. Flanked by the Anglo-German diplomatic agreement that had been reached at Munich over the Sudeten question in September 1938, the talks could claim a first success on 28 January 1939 when, following British calls for a Coal Cartel, an Anglo-German Coal Agreement was signed.

Both sides now hoped that the foundations for a broader industrial accord had been laid. Encouraged by Chamberlain who, after Munich, was hoping for a more comprehensive settlement of all issues, the FBI and the *Reichsgruppe* concluded the so-called Düsseldorf Agreement in March 1939. The twelve-point final statement referred to the need for both countries to have "a substantial and profitable export" trade with fair returns that would promote prosperity.[92] It would be desirable to reach agreements that "eliminate destructive competition," but that "prices must be fixed at such a level as not to diminish the buying power of the customers." With this in mind, concrete steps should be taken "to increase world consumption of the products in which German and British industry are interested." Agreements on prices were merely one step, though "a most important one, towards a more ordered system of world trade." Individual branches should therefore make more specific agreements for which some contacts had already been established. In a clear reference to the United States, the two associations added that agreements between Britain and Germany "may be nullified by competition from the industry of some other country that refuses to become a party to the agreement." In this case "it may be necessary for the organization to obtain the help of their governments" that they would then be prepared to seek.

Not surprisingly, the news of such Anglo-German accords did little to relieve the tensions and suspicions between Washington and London that had arisen during the negotiations for the Anglo-American Trade treaty and that had continued at the time of the Munich Agreement. In July 1939 there followed the brief attempt by the commodity broker E. W. Tennant to see if Ribbentrop might agree to stop "further outbursts by Germany in Europe."[93] But with Hitler already thinking of the invasion of Poland, this initiative went nowhere. There may have been more promise in a meeting with Göring that, mediated by the managing director of the Swedish Elektrolux Corporation, Birger Dahlerus, a group of top-level British industrialists and insurance executives had in early August 1939.[94] But Göring was stringing his interlocutors along in line with the Nazi government's plan: instead of preventing a war, he, following Hitler's overall strategy, merely wanted to make certain that Britain (and France) stayed out of the campaign against Poland, to which the finishing touches were being made at this time. With

Chamberlain still in power, Hitler—in pursuit of the first stage of his expansionist "program," that is, the conquest of "living space" in the east—was anxious to avoid a two-front war against France and Britain in the west. To secure this was apparently also the mission of Göring's assistant Hellmuth Wohlthat, while members of the British government tried to win him over by pointing to the benefits of a "common foreign trade policy for the two great European powers." It was a futile exercise. On 1 September, the Wehrmacht attacked Poland.

Still keen to avoid a war in the west, Hitler tried to conclude a truce with Britain and France. But the differences between the two sides were now even greater than they had been before the outbreak of hostilities: he wanted the Western Allies to recognize his conquest of Poland in return for a promise not to touch British and French imperial interests overseas; London and Paris insisted on a retreat from Poland and a guarantee that Germany would abrogate the use of force in its forays into Eastern Europe.

With British and German industry now also locked in a military conflict, American businessmen appeared on the scene. The first in line was James D. Mooney, the man on the GM board in charge of Overseas Operations.[95] In this position he had a deep interest in the wellbeing of Opel Cars under the Nazis. During the discussions on the Volkswagen project, he had had a personal interview with Hitler in May 1934 and had also been dragged into the subsequent endless quarrels with Gauleiter Sprenger and others. After the beginning of the war in Europe he had paid another visit to Rüsselsheim in October 1939 to participate in negotiations, urged upon Opel by the Wehrmacht. The generals were now pressing the Americans to produce engines and other components for the Junkers Airplane Works that was assembling the Ju 88 fighter-bomber.

While GM was very reluctant to make such a deal, Mooney received a call from Opel's general counsel in Berlin who told him about hints that the Reich government was interested in talking to an unofficial American emissary. Apparently Hitler wanted to find out whether the administration in Washington might be prepared to act as a mediator in efforts to end the war—an inquiry that tallies with what we now know about the Reich governments attempts to engineer, after the defeat of Poland, a peace in the west. Mooney was no doubt a suitable target for these efforts. While not a Nazi sympathizer, he nevertheless felt that Germany had been given a raw deal after World War I. He had remained silent when Hitler began to conquer in Eastern Europe and apparently continued to believe that even after the destruction of Poland an arrangement could be forged with Germany, provided that Britain and France offered concessions. He was also convinced that the root cause of international tensions was economic and that Soviet communism posed a major threat.

After further news from a number of other intermediaries, Mooney went to Berlin on 18 October 1939 to have dinner with Wohlthat who in turn had already made an appointment for him with Göring on the following day. Mooney believed to have been given a unique chance to end the war. His next stop was therefore Paris, where he reported on his conversations in Berlin to William C. Bullitt, the American ambassador to France. But instead of gaining an ally, Mooney soon found that, his polished frankness notwithstanding, Bullitt was in fact warning his colleagues in the State Department who agreed that the Nazis were taking a naïve GM manager for a ride.

This did not deter Mooney from traveling to London to contact Sir Robert Vansittard, the undersecretary at the Foreign Office. He believed in Mooney's integrity and in turn reported the news about Göring to Foreign Secretary Lord Edward Halifax. The reply that the GM man memorized to take back to Berlin was not particularly encouraging. And yet Mooney was so firmly convinced of his mission that he began to see himself as a catalyst to get Germans and Britons to explore peace negotiations. When Mooney arrived in Berlin, Wohlthat who had promised to arrange another meeting with Göring was not in town. Mooney now went to Rome and after waiting for three weeks for news from Berlin finally met Wohlthat in Madrid. In this meeting the latter had nothing positive to say about Mooney's report on his London contacts. At this point the American returned to the United States. Knowing Roosevelt in person, he managed to get an appointment with the president, who merely talked sternly about how Germany must abolish its economic restrictions and return to multilateral trade. Mooney refused to give up even after this rebuff. It is possible that the Sumner Welles Mission raised his spirits again.

From all that is known, there is no direct connection between Mooney's reports to Roosevelt and the president's and Hull's decision to send Welles, the deputy secretary in the State Department, on a roundtrip to Europe in March 1940. However, it seems that the mission was in part triggered by the fears circulating in the American business community more generally that the United States might enter the war. William Langer and Everett Gleason argued in their 1952 book, *The Challenge to Isolation*, that Welles's trip to Europe showed "more clearly than any of its antecedents the illusion prevalent in this country in the final weeks of the phony war," though it had the merit "to shatter this illusion in high Washington circles."[96] Stanley Hilton by contrast took the view that the mission was "a shrewd realistic maneuver by the White House designed to bolster the position of the Allies by weakening the Rome-Berlin Axis and delaying the expected spring clash in order to give England and France additional time to secure war materiel in the United States." Hence, Hilton continued, there was a "continuity of policy and objectives between the repeal of the arms embargo and the Welles Mission."[97] If Hilton is correct, it may be that Roosevelt had something more in mind, that is, to reassure the American business community that, while everything was being done to avoid a direct involvement of the United States in the war in Europe, the need to supply Britain with military hardware in its struggle against Hitler provided an opportunity to shift the American economy into higher gear.

There is an odd sequel to Mooney's failed mission that shows him again as a man who found it very difficult to take no for an answer. On his next trip to Europe he learned of Welles's mission and desperately tried to get a meeting with the deputy secretary of state. He failed when Welles was on a visit to Rome; he then tried to reach him in Berlin. Again the several messages he left requesting an appointment were ignored. Finally, he literally gate-crashed a reception, organized by the American Embassy after Welles's meeting with Hitler. But the embassy staff kept Mooney away from the guest of honor so that in the end there was no more than a very brief exchange of a few pleasantries.

Still undeterred and mentioning his conversation with Roosevelt to his German contacts in Berlin, he succeeded in getting an appointment with Hitler. He used the opportunity to repeat his hopes that peace could be restored and cited Roosevelt's remarks during his interview that the president was looking for a liberalization of international trade. In his response, Hitler went into a long spiel about his purely defensive aims in Europe and demanded that the Allies give up their plan to destroy Germany. The only reason why he had occupied Czechoslovakia and Poland was to end Western domination in Eastern Europe and the persecution of the German minority in Poland.

What Hitler was therefore promoting was a solution that he and his political advisors were pursuing in the spring of 1940 and that Franz Halder, the chief of the Army General Staff, recorded in his diary on 21 May 1940 as follows:[98] "We seek contact with Britain on the basis of a division of the world." As late as 19 June Ribbentrop confirmed this position in a conversation with Count Galeazzo Ciano, his Italian counterpart:[99] "The 'Führer' does not desire the destruction of the British empire. He asks that England renounce some of her possessions and recognize the fait accompli [on the European Continent]. On these conditions Hitler would be prepared to come to an agreement." This meant that Mooney was still chasing a chimera.

However, instead of abandoning his quest to be a peacemaker, the GM manager typed a very long report summarizing all his impressions and through an intermediary succeeded in cabling it to the White House. Hoping for a positive response from Roosevelt, he waited for further instructions, not knowing that Welles had meanwhile made his own report on his talk with Hitler. It held out no prospect of peace.[100] When Mooney finally heard from the president about these latest developments, he was told that there was no interest in his role as a mediator. After offering his services in yet another letter, he finally published his conviction that the United States could use its great power to force the two sides to the negotiating table. When Roosevelt saw an advance copy of this article that appeared in the *Saturday Evening Post* he was, not surprisingly, decidedly unhappy about it and made one last attempt to persuade the GM man to give up.[101] But this conversation had to be cancelled because of more urgent commitments that Roosevelt had on his calendar for that day. Nor did the publication of the article on 3 August 1940 give Mooney much joy. He was accused of being in the Lindbergh camp and of being a Nazi sympathizer. In July 1940 he had already informed one of his German contacts that his efforts had come to naught, though he stuck to his guns that an arrangement was still possible.

Even at this late stage this optimistic view was shared by Henry Ford, another American businessman who offered himself as a mediator in 1939–40. He did so for reasons of economic self-interest, but also because he was anxious to keep international peace. He had had few qualms about selling his cars and commercial vehicles not only to the Wehrmacht but also to Himmler's police and SS. It has been estimated that one-third of army trucks were delivered by Ford Germany. The company, responding to Nazi pressures, advertised its cars as "German made" because their local content was said to have risen to 75 percent. There is a 1938 photo of Henry Ford receiving the Grand Cross of the German Eagle, but he was surprised when he was strongly criticized back home for accepting this medal. On the occasion of Hitler's birthday in April 1939, Henry Ford sent 35,000 marks as a special gift. When pressured by the Reich government, he appointed a purely German management board and on the occasion of Hitler's next birthday the magazine of his German subsidiaries published an ode to the "Führer," with Hitler's portrait on the front cover.[102]

As war loomed ever larger, it became more and more difficult to discern what drove Ford before the American entry into World War II. His attitude to the Third Reich was no doubt influenced by a strong dose of self-interest. But there were also the sympathies that he continued to feel for Hitler's dictatorship. As to his anti-Semitism of the early 1920s, he had, rather opportunistically, dissociated himself from it in 1927, when his company had run into difficulties and he did not want to antagonize the American-Jewish community as potential customers. In private, though, he evidently continued to harbor his prejudice. In the late 1930s he railed at the "Jew bankers" and their support of France and Britain. He approved of Frank Buchanan's Moral Rearmament movement and the "America Firsters" and, like Mooney, thought that peace was still possible.[103]

13. IBM in Germany

The third major American entrepreneur who similarly veered between self-interest and criticism of Roosevelt's policies and, up to the American entry into the war, advocated preserving the peace at any cost was Thomas Watson, Sr., the president of IBM.[104] While his post-1941 policies will be examined in the next chapter together with those of Ford and GM, he too provides a good example of what it meant to accept the political risk of staying in Nazi Germany. Watson had started his business career before 1914 with NCR until he left this firm to become, at the end of 1924, the chief executive officer of IBM a few months after leaving the Computing-Tabulating-Recording Co. (CTR). The latter had been the brainchild of Herman Hollerith, an ingenious inventor of tabulating machines on which CTR and then IBM held many patents.

These machines became an ever greater success, as private enterprises and government bureaucracies all over the world looked for an alternative to the increasingly voluminous but inefficient collection of statistics. IBM provided the ever more sophisticated mechanical tools to rationalize and systematize the keeping of a vast array of records. By the 1930s, the U.S. government had become IBM's largest customer. Germany had also bought Watson's machines, and the arrival of the Nazi regime threw him, IBM's consummate salesman of his company's labor-saving products, into the dilemma that all foreign companies faced after 1933: should he stop selling his machines or continue to market and service them, as he had done during the Weimar years? Watson's dilemma was exacerbated by the type of product he was selling. It was not cars and trucks like Ford's and GM's nor merchandise like Woolworth's, or refreshing drinks, like Coca-Cola's.

Like the heads of other corporations, he was easy prey if he thought at the beginning of the Third Reich that Hitler's radicalism would subside.[105] But even before American car manufacturers began to realize that they were supplying Hitler's preparations for war, Watson's tabulating and recording machines were being used by the police state that Himmler had perfected by 1936, when he became Reichsführer SS and chief of the German Police.[106] Germany had long required its citizens to be officially registered, and these inventories came handy when the Nazis began to identify their political enemies and minorities, such as Jews, homosexuals, and other "undesirable elements." These persecutions began straightaway in 1933 until they reached massive proportions by the late 1930s and during World War II. The continued operations of IBM in the Third Reich led to even more serious accusations against Watson's empire than were being leveled against the car manufacturers and other corporations during and after the war. Scholars have therefore argued that just as the moral compass of many indigenous businessmen who produced the tools for Hitler's wars and the murder of millions of people had failed them, Watson's had similarly broken down.

There is something of a tragic dimension to Watson's activities in Germany. He was not, like Henry Ford, an entrepreneur with fascist sympathies. Like Mooney, he believed that world peace could be secured through commercial contacts among nations. Toward this end, he worked hard, when elected president of the International Chamber of Commerce, against rising fears and hatreds. He supported Roosevelt and believed that a defeat of American democracy would lead to revolution. He sided with Hull in the search for reciprocal trade and the avoidance of war, believing that a major conflict would be catastrophic and that the "essence of civilization" was the "spirit of conciliation." He thought that Hitler could be turned away from his aggressive policies and, knowing that the Nazi leader appreciated the great value of Hollerith's inventions, tried to meet with him. Realizing that he was being duped and rejecting Nazi anti-Semitism, he, unlike Henry Ford, decided to return the German Eagle medal that he, too, had been awarded by Hitler. The "Führer" was furious.

In light of Watson's contributions to the American war effort after 1941, it is difficult to gauge the fairness of Edwin Black's verdict who wrote that "IBM NY always understood—from the outset in 1933— that it was courting and doing business with the upper echelon of the Nazi Party. The company leveraged its Nazi Party connections to continuously enhance its business relationship with Hitler's Reich, in Germany, and throughout Nazi-dominated Europe."[107] Even more damning, "IBM subsidiaries trained Nazi officers and their surrogates throughout Europe, set up branch offices and local dealerships throughout Nazi Europe staffed by a revolving door of IBM employees, and scoured paper mills to produce as many as 1.5 billion punch cards a year in Germany alone. Moreover, the fragile machines were serviced on site about once per month, even when that site was in or near a concentration camp." Finally, "When U.S. law made . . . direct contact illegal, IBM's Swiss office became the nexus, providing the New York office continuous information and credible deniability." So, perhaps Watson represents the case of an American investor who should have gotten out when it became clear beyond reasonable doubt what IBM's technology was being used for in the late 1930s and early 1940s.

As has already been discussed with reference to Du Pont, American corporations that had come to Germany without establishing production facilities or having a large sales force, but had relied on cooperations with I.G. Farben on the basis of patent and licensing agreements, also found it difficult to detach themselves from Germany while the American entry into the war was still in the balance and contacts with their partners were not illegal under U.S. law. And even after Pearl Harbor and Hitler's declaration of war on the United States in December 1941, contacts and transactions did not stop completely. The next chapter will therefore have to take a closer look at the behavior and activities of American big business between 1941 and 1945, before their role in the postwar reconstruction in both Britain and the western zones of occupation (which became the Federal Republic of Germany in 1949) is considered.

Notes to Chapter V

1. Hans Mommsen, *Beamtentum im Dritten Reich* (Stuttgart, 1966); Reinhard Bollmus, *Das Amt Rosenberg und seine Feinde* (Stuttgart, 1970). For a summary of the debate on the character of Nazi Germany, see Ian Kershaw, *The Nazi Revolution. Problems and Perspectives* (New York, 1989), esp. chap. 4.

2. Adolf Hitler, *Mein Kampf* (Munich, 1941); Gerhard L. Weinberg, ed., *Hitler's Second Book* (New York, 2004). See also Avraham Barkai, *Nazi Economics. Ideology, Theory, and Policy* (Oxford, 1990); James V. Compton, *The Swastika and the Eagle* (Boston, 1967); Rainer F. Schmidt, *Die Aussenpolitik des Dritten Reichs, 1933–1939* (Stuttgart, 2002), 103ff. The discussion of Hitler's ultimate aims has also raised the question of whether his regime not only wanted to revolutionize the international system and create a racist New Order, but also had initiated this revolution while in power. For a helpful recent summary of the debate and research that this question has generated, see Hartmut Berghoff, "Did Hitler Create a New Society? Continuity and Change in German Social History Before and After 1933," in Panikos Panayi, ed., *Weimar and Nazi Germany* (London, 2001), 74–104.

3. See, e.g., Philipp Gassert, *Amerika im Dritten Reich* (Stuttgart, 1997), 87ff.; Götz Aly, *Hitler's Beneficiaries. Plunder, Race War, and the Nazi Welfare State* (New York, 2007); Robert Hertzstein, *When Nazi Dreams Come True* (London, 1982); Werner Rohr and Brigitte Berlekamp, "Neuordnung Europas," in *Vorträge vor der Berliner Gesellschaft für Faschismus und Weltkriegsforschung* (Berlin, 1996); Lothar Gruchmann, *Nationalsozialistische Grossraumordnung* (Stuttgart, 1961). This focus on Hitler at the head of the Nazi regime is not meant to ignore the significance of the popular support that he succeeded in mobilizing. But in this

context the highly manipulative character of this regime should not be forgotten—a theme that will be examined below, pp. 258ff.

4. This had by then become a more widespread criticism of Wilhelmine *Weltpolitik*. As early as 1915, Admiral Alfred von Tirpitz heard of this critique when he recorded that "numerous circles in the Army and other right-wing forces" were arguing that "we should have conducted power politics, but as a continental policy. First the enemies on the Continent to be defeated for which everything to be invested in the Army. . . . World and naval policy has been 'premature.' We have overreached ourselves with the Navy." In May 1919 General Wilhelm Groener opined, "We have unconsciously aimed at world domination . . . before we had firmed up our continental position." Quoted in Volker R. Berghahn, *Der Tirpitz-Plan* (Düsseldorf, 1971), 600–601.

5. Klaus Hildebrand, *The Foreign Policy of the Third Reich* (London, 1973), 51ff. Later Hildebrand preferred to use the term "program" in quotation marks to stress that it was nothing absolutely fixed in terms of its execution. For a brief critique of the concept and the debate around it, see Schmidt, *Die Aussenpolitik* (note 2), 125–26.

6. See, e.g., Karl Dietrich Bracher, *The German Dictatorship* (New York, 1970); Peter D. Stachura, ed., *The Nazi Machtergreifung* (London, 1983).

7. See, e.g., Ian Kershaw, *Hitler, Vol. I, 1889–1936—Hubris* (New York, 1999), 510ff.

8. Adam Tooze, *Wages of Destruction* (New York, 2006), 37ff. See also Richard Overy, *War and Economy in the Third Reich* (Oxford, 1994), esp. 68ff., 93ff., 177ff.; Wilhelm Deist, *The Wehrmacht and German Rearmament* (London, 1981); Jonas Schermer, *Die Logik der Industriepolitik im Dritten Reich. Investitionen in der Autarkie- und Rüstungsindustrie und ihre staatliche Förderung* (Stuttgart, 2008).

9. See, e.g., Tooze, *Wages of Destruction* (note 8), 79ff.

10. See, e.g., Richard Overy, *Goering. The "Iron Man"* (Boston, 1984), 48ff.; Dieter Petzina, *Autarkiepolitik im Dritten Reich* (Stuttgart, 1968); Tooze, *Wages of Destruction* (note 8), 203ff.

11. Hildebrand, *Foreign Policy* (note 5), 38ff. Hitler sent him off with the words, "Ribbentrop, bring me back the British alliance!"

12. See, e.g., Arnold A. Offner, *American Appeasement* (New York, 1976), 188ff. Text reprinted in Detlev Junker, *Kampf um die Weltmacht* (Düsseldorf, 1988), 79ff.

13. Reprinted in *Documents on German Foreign Policy, Series D, Vol. 1* (Washington, DC), 29ff. For context, see Tooze, *Wages of Destruction* (note 8), 244ff.

14. Among the numerous studies on the immediate origins of World War II, see, e.g., Christopher Thorne, *The Approach of War, 1938–1939* (London, 1967), and most recently: Richard Overy, *Countdown to War* (New York, 2010).

15. See, e.g., Hermann Beck, *Fateful Alliance. German Conservatives and the Nazis in 1933* (New York, 2008); Martin Broszat et al., eds., *Die deutschen Eliten und der Weg in den Zweiten Weltkrieg* (Munich, 1989).

16. On the incipient conservative and military resistance to Hitler at the time of the Munich Crisis and later, see, e.g., Harold C. Deutsch, *Hitler and His Generals. The Hidden Crisis, January-June 1938* (Minneapolis, 1973).

17. Among the numerous studies, see, e.g., W. R. Rock, *Appeasement on Trial. British Foreign Policy and Its Critics, 1938–1939* (New York, 1966); Wolfgang J. Mommsen and Lothar Kettenacker, eds., *The Fascist Challenge and the Policy of Appeasement* (Boston, 1983); Maurice Cowling, *The Impact of Hitler. British Politics and British Policy, 1933–1940* (Cambridge, 1975); Arthur H. Furnia, *The Diplomacy of Appeasement* (Washington, DC, 1960); Martin Gilbert, *The Roots of Appeasement* (London, 1967); Callum MacDonald, *The U.S., Britain and Appeasement, 1936–1939* (London, 1980); Keith Middlemas, *The Politics of Illusion* (London, 1972); Neville Thompson, *The Anti-Appeasers* (Oxford, 1971). Karl Rohe, ed., *Die Westmächte und das Dritte Reich, 1933–1939* (Paderborn, 1982), contains a number of particularly thoughtful essays by the editor as well as by Gustav Schmidt, Berndt-Jürgen Wendt, Callum MacDonald, Klaus Schwabe, Gilbert Ziebura, and Roland Höhne.

18. See Gustav Schmidt, *The Politics and Economics of Appeasement* (Leamington Spa, 1986)—a study that is still important both conceptually and in terms of its focus on the interaction among military, domestic, and foreign policies. Schmidt developed the notion that armaments constituted the hinge between British domestic and foreign policy. See also Berndt-Jürgen Wendt, *Economic Appeasement. Handel und Finanz in der britischen Deutschlandpolitik, 1933–1939* (Düsseldorf, 1971). Stephen Broadberry and Peter Howlett, "The United Kingdom: 'Victory at all costs,' " in Mark Harrison, ed., *The Economics of World War II* (Cambridge, 1998), 47; Scott Newton, *The Political Economy of Anglo-German Appeasement* (Oxford, 1996). On the gloomy views of the City before Munich, see David Kynaston, *The City of London, Vol. 3: The Illusion of Gold, 1914–1945* (London, 2000), 444–45.

19. On the Munich Agreement and its aftermath see, e.g., the studies in notes 17 and 18 above; Keith Robbins, *Munich 1938* (London, 1968); Kynaston, *City of London* (note 18), 446ff.; Dwight E. Lee, ed., *Munich. Blunder, Plot, or Tragic Necessity?* (Lexington, MA, 1970), with a range of contributions to the early debate.

20. See, e.g., Offner, *American Appeasement* (note 12); Hans-Jürgen Schröder, *Deutschland und die Vereinigten Staaten, 1933–1939* (Wiesbaden, 1970), esp. 69ff.; Schröder, "American Appeasement Revisited," *Journal of American History* 64, no. 2 (1977): 371–93. P. J. Hearnden, *Roosevelt Confronts Hitler* (DeKalb, IL, 1987). Overall, it still holds true that American foreign policy toward Germany remained cautious and vague, but, for reasons discussed below, became more distinctly anti-Nazi by 1936–37.

21. On Hull, see, e.g., Cordell Hull, *The Memoirs of Cordell Hull*, 2 vols. (New York, 1948); Detlef Junker, *Der unteilbare Weltmarkt* (Stuttgart, 1975). See also the role of key advisors: George S. Messersmith, *Diplomat of Democracy* (Chapel Hill, NC, 1987); Nancy Hooker, ed., *The Moffat Papers, Cambridge, MA, 1919–1943* (Cambridge, MA, 1956).

22. For the export-import figures, see Gerhard Kümmel, *Transnational Economic Cooperation and the Nation State* (New York, 2001), 1:21. For the debates inside the Nazi regime, see, e.g., Rohe, *Die Westmächte* (note 17).

23. On the German penetration of Latin America, see, e.g., Hans-Jürgen Schröder, "Die Vereinigten Staaten und die nationalsozialistische Handelspoli-

tik gegenüber Lateinamerika, 1937/38," *Jahrbuch für die Geschichte Lateinamerikas* 7 (1970): 309–67, with several statistical appendices; Jana Wüstenhagen, "German Pharmaceutical Companies in South America: The Case of Schering A.G. in Argentine," in Christopher Kobrak and Per H. Hansen, eds., *European Business, Dictatorship, and Political Risk, 1920–1945* (New York, 2004), 81–102; Alton Frye, *Nazi Germany and the American Hemisphere, 1933–1941* (New Haven, CT, 1967).

24. Concerning the many difficulties that vexed Anglo-American relations even in the face of the rising fascist and Japanese threats, see, e.g., David Reynolds, *The Creation of the Anglo-American Alliance, 1937–1941: A Study in Competitive Cooperation* (London, 1981), who stresses the ambiguities and speaks of "a relationship of competitive cooperation." Ibid., 294. On the difficulties of finalizing the Anglo-American Trade Agreement see, e.g., Gerhard Kümmel, *Transnational Economic Cooperation and the Nation State* (New York, 2001), 83ff. On relations before and after the Munich Crisis, see Barbara Rearden Farnham, *Roosevelt and the Munich Crisis* (Princeton, 1997). The Lindsay quote can be found in Anne Orde, *The Eclipse of Great Britain. The United States and British Imperial Decline, 1895–1956* (New York, 1996), 104, and ibid., 106 with a few more pretty scathing quotes. See also Daniel Bennett Smith, *Toward Internationalism. New Deal Foreign Economic Policy, 1933–1939* (New York, 1900), 197ff.; Patricia Clavin, *The Failure Foreign Economic Diplomacy: Britain, Germany, France and the United States, 1931–1936* (London, 1996); B.J.C. McKercher, *Transition of Power. Britain's Loss of Global Pre-eminence to the United States, 1930–1945* (Cambridge, 1999), 126ff.; Walter LaFeber, *The American Age* (New York, 1989), 371–72. Erhard Forndran, *Die Vereinigten Staaten von Amerika und Europa* (Baden-Baden, 1991), 66ff., relating specifically to the "special relationship." Ritchie Ovendale, *Anglo-American Relations in the Twentieth Century* (Basingstoke, 1998), 27, believes that "a 'special relationship' did exist between Britain and the United States" even before the outbreak of World War II, "reflected in the full and frank exchange of information between the two governments." The situation seems to have been more complex and after the outbreak of war no less so.

25. See, e.g., Jost Dülffer, *Weimar, Hitler und die Marine. Reichspolitik und Flottenbau, 1920–1939* (Düsseldorf, 1973); Herbert Sirois, *Zwischen Illusion und Krieg. Deutschland und die USA, 1933–1941* (Paderborn, 2000), 105ff.; Newton, *Political Economy* (note 18), pp. 133ff.

26. On Morgenthau's early years in Washington: Bernd Greiner, *Die Morgenthau-Legende. Zur Geschichte eines umstrittenen Plans* (Hamburg, 1995), 31ff.

27. On the evolution of the neutrality question, see William E. Leuchtenburg, *Franklin Roosevelt and the New Deal, 1932–1940* (New York, 1963), 275ff.; Selig Adler, *The Isolationist Impulse* (New York, 1961), 201ff.; Detlef Junker, *Kampf* (note 12), 66ff., with the strict terms of the Third Neutrality Act of 1 May 1937; Robert A. Pastor, *Congress and Politics in US Foreign Economic Policy, 1929–1976* (Berkeley, 1980); Wayne S. Cole, *Roosevelt and the Isolationists, 1932–1945* (Lincoln, NE, 1983).

28. Churchill's letter that, after several drafts, was sent on 7 December 1940 in Warren Kimball, ed., *Churchill & Roosevelt. The Complete Correspondence, Vol. 1: Alliance Emerging* (Princeton, 1984), 102–9; Mark Harrison, "Resource

Mobilization for World War II: the U.S.A., U.K., U.S.S.R., and Germany, 1938–1945," *Economic History Review* 41, no. 2 (May 1988): 171–92.

29. See, e.g., Ira Katznelson, *Fear Itself* (New York, 2013).

30. Quoted in John M. Blum, *Morgenthau. Years of Urgency, 1938–1941* (Boston, 1965), 2:47.

31. Quoted in ibid., 78. See also ibid., 118, with Roosevelt's remark that "these foreign orders mean prosperity in this country and we can't elect a Democratic Party unless we get prosperity and these foreign orders are of the greatest importance."

32. See, e.g., David Edgerton, *Britain's War Machine. Weapons, Resources and Experts in the Second World War* (London, 2011), 47ff. See also, Junker, *Kampf* (note 12), 70ff., reprinting the results of Gallup polls, 1937–41, showing the shifts in the mood of the American public. Ibid., 107ff., also a calendar that Grand Admiral Erich Raeder, the commander in chief of the navy, produced for Hitler on 9 July 1941, which shows the small steps that Roosevelt took to aid Britain and to constrain German naval operations in the Atlantic. See also Kevin Smith, *Conflict over Convoys. Anglo-American Logistics Diplomacy in the Second World War* (Cambridge, 1996).

33. On Henry Kaiser and the shipbuilding industry, see Edgerton, *Britain's War Machine* (note 32), pp.81–82, with figures for both North American and British shipyards. It now also paid off that Roosevelt's public investment and job creation programs had built several dams that could now provide the electricity needed for the expansion of production. Tim Schanetzky (Jena University) is writing a comprehensive history of Kaiser and his empire.

34. On the origins of Lend-Lease, see Warren Kimball, *The Most Unsordid Act. Lend-Lease 1939–1941* (Baltimore, 1969). See also Corelli Barnett, *The Audit of War* (New York, 1984); Barnett, *The Collapse of British Power* (London, 1972); Edgerton, *Britain's War Machine* (note 32), who argues that Churchill exaggerated the depletion of British resources, partly because he did not mention the contributions made by the Empire and Commonwealth. It seems that Roosevelt suspected this. Nevertheless, he asked Churchill to send him a heartrending letter about the British predicament that he could use in a speech he was planning and also to put pressure on Congress. See above, note 28.

35. See, e.g., Cole, *Roosevelt and the Isolationists* (note 27), 456ff.

36. Although Hitler has been widely and rightly blamed as the one primarily responsible for the decision to invade the Soviet Union, the generals, although they later denied it, also bear their share for the impending disaster. Being used to warfare in confined territories and punch-drunk after their swift victories in Western and Northern Europe, they totally underestimated the logistical problems raised by a war in which the Wehrmacht had to be supplied across thousands of miles. See Barry Leach, *German Strategy against Russia, 1939–1941* (Oxford, 1973).

37. See, e.g., Hildebrand, *Foreign Policy* (note 5), 24ff.; Herbert Sirois, *Zwischen Illusion* (note 25), 38ff.

38. *WSJ* and *NYT*, with several articles on 31 January 1933 and subsequent days.

39. *The Times* as quoted in *NYT*, 31 January 1933. See also Brigitte Granzow, *Mirror of Nazism. British Opinion and the Emergence of Hitler* (London, 1964). On the United States, see Michaela Hoenicke Moore, *Know Your Enemy. The American Debate on Nazism, 1933–1945* (New York, 2010), 41ff., with reports filed by prominent American journalists. Kynaston, *City of London* (note 18), 430ff.

40. Quoted in *NYT*, 31 January 1933.

41. Quoted in *WSJ*, 3 February 1933.

42. Ibid.

43. On the Reichstag fire and its consequences, see, e.g., Richard J. Evans, *The Coming of the Third Reich* (New York, 2004), 328ff.

44. The following evaluation of business magazines was undertaken as part of a more comprehensive analysis by Frank Biess, "Echoes of a (Not So) Distant Thunder: American Business and National Socialism, 1933–1941" (paper, Brown University, 1994). I would like to thank him for allowing me to quote from this material.

45. *Business Week*, 12 April 1933.

46. *Barron's*, 27 March 1933.

47. See John P. Diggins, *Mussolini and Fascism. The View from America* (Princeton, 1972).

48. *Forbes*, 1 April 1933.

49. On the reporting by American diplomats in Germany and their cautious assessments, see Bernard V. Burke, *Ambassador Frederic Sackett and the Collapse of the Weimar Republic, 1930–1933* (Cambridge, 1994); Maynard Moser, *Jacob Gould Schurman. Scholar, Political Activist and Ambassador of Goodwill* (New York, 1982). It was only when William Dodd became ambassador to Berlin that reporting became much more critical. Robert Daller, *Democrat and Diplomat. The Life of William E. Dodd* (New York, 1968). Dodd wrote about the persecution of German Jews in great detail and on American and British firms involved in the rearmament business.

50. See, e.g., Michael Zampalas, *Adolf Hitler and the Third Reich in American Magazines* (Bowling Green, OH, 1989). This is a comprehensive evaluation of popular magazines, such as *Saturday Evening Post*, but also of political weeklies such as *Time*, *Newsweek*, *New Republic*, and *Nation*. The focus is on political developments in Nazi Germany. A good deal of space is devoted to anti-Semitic policies and these sources' more general anti-Nazism. Yet, Zampalas comes to the conclusion that "American magazines failed to galvanize the American people to oppose Nazism" (218) and that Roosevelt remained "more the captive" of insular opinion "than its transformer" (219).

51. On the agrarian wing of the Nazi Party, see, e.g., Gustavo Corni, *Hitler and the Peasants. Agrarian Policy of the Third Reich, 1930–1939* (New York, 1990).

52. On a somewhat risky comparison between Roosevelt's and Hitler's efforts to refloat their respective economies see Wolfgang Schivelbusch, *Three New Deals. Reflections on Roosevelt's America, Mussolini's Italy, and Hitler's Germany, 1933–1939* (New York, 2006).

53. See, e.g., Robert M. Collins, *The Business Response to Keynes, 1929–1964* (New York, 1981), 23ff., who discusses the "negativistic opposition to the New

Deal" as well as "patterns of positive business response[s]." See also the particularly vigorous opposition by Pierre Du Pont in Graham Taylor and Patricia Sudnik, *Du Pont and International Chemical Industry* (Boston, 1984), 146; Colin Gordon, *New Deals. Business, Labor, and Politics in America, 1920–1935* (Cambridge, 1994), 280ff., with an emphasis on the competitive and fragmented character of the economic policies of the United States. William J. Barber, *Design within Disorder. Franklin D. Roosevelt, the Economists, and the Shaping of American Economic Policy, 1933–1945* (Cambridge, 1996), 1, argues that Roosevelt was not firmly wedded to a particular economic doctrine.

54. *Business Week,* 7 December 1935.

55. Gabriel Kolko, "American Business and Germany, 1930–1941," *Western Political Quarterly* 15, no. 4 (1963): 713–28.

56. See Roland N. Stromberg, "American Big Business and the Approach of War, 1935–1941," *Journal of Economic History* 13, no. 1 (Winter 1953): 58–78.

57. On early postwar American views, see below, pp. 307ff. On German industry's positions toward its Nazi past, see Jonathan Wiesen, *West German Industry and the Challenge of the Nazi Past, 1945–1955* (Chapel Hill, NC, 2001).

58. Peter Hayes, *Industry and Ideology. I.G. Farben in the Nazi Era* (Cambridge, 1987), xix.

59. See Christoph Buchheim, ed., *German Industry in the Nazi Period* (Stuttgart, 2008); Buchheim, "Unternehmen in Deutschland und NS-Regime, 1933–1945. Versuch einer Synthese," *Historische Zeitschrift* 282 (2006): 351–90. On the subsequent debate, see Peter Hayes, "Corporate Freedom of Action in Nazi Germany," *Bulletin of the German Historical Institute* 45 (2009): 29–42; Christoph Buchheim and Jonas Scherner, "Corporate Freedom of Action in Nazi Germany: A Response to Peter Hayes," *Bulletin of the German Historical Institute* 45 (2009): 43–50, esp. 50; Peter Hayes, "Rejoinder," *Bulletin of the German Historical Institute* 45 (2009): 51.

60. See Henry A. Turner, *German Big Business and the Rise of Hitler* (New York, 1985). See also Arthur Schweitzer, *Big Business in the Third Reich* (Bloomington, IN, 1964); Willi A. Boelcke, *Die deutsche Wirtschaft, 1930–1945* (Düsseldorf, 1983); Reinhard Neebe, *Grossindustrie, Staat und NSDAP, 1930–1933* (Göttingen, 1981); Michael Grubler, *Die Spitzenverbände der Wirtschaft und das erste Kabinett Brüning* (Düsseldorf, 1982); Louis P. Lochner, *Tycoons and Tyrant. German Industry from Hitler to Adenauer* (Chicago, 1954).

61. On membership funding of the Nazi Party, see Turner, *German Big Business* (note 60); on the Kiehn family enterprise that closely collaborated with the regime, see Hartmut Berghoff and Cornelia Rauh-Kühne, *Fritz K. Ein deutsches Leben im zwanzigsten Jahrhundert* (Stuttgart, 2000).

62. Lutz Schwerin von Krosigk, *Die grosse Zeit des Feuers* (Tübingen, 1957/59), 3:560.

63. Kobrak and Hansen, *European Business* (note 23), 3, x.

64. See *WSJ,* 27 November 1929. On the history of F. W. Woolworth, see Jean Madden, *F.W. Woolworth and the Fine and Dime* (Jefferson, NC, 2003); John K. Winkler, *Five and Ten: The Fabulous Life of F.W. Woolworth* (New York, 1940). See also Andrew Godley, "American Multinationals in British Retailing, 1850–1962:

Performance and Identity," in Hubert Bonnin and Ferry de Goey, eds., *American Firms in Europe, 1880–1980. Strategy, Identity, Perception and Performance* (Geneva, 2009), 299–319.

65. *WSJ*, 7 May 1933.

66. See Timothy Mason, *Arbeiterklasse und Volksgemeinschaft* (Opladen, 1975). Richard Overy, *War and Economy* (note 8), 177ff., has rightly played down the importance of the "butter" question, arguing that Hitler's first priority was the manufacture of "guns" for his war. Nevertheless and although Himmler's police had by 1936 destroyed most of the covert opposition and hence had a firm grip on "grumbling," material appeasement of the population remained, apart from Goebbels's propaganda efforts, an important issue. See also Hartmut Berghoff, "Enticement and Deprivation: The Regulation of Consumption in Pre-War Nazi Germany," in Martin Daunton and Matthew Hilton, eds., *The Politics of Consumption. Material Culture and Citizenship in Europe and America* (Oxford, 2001); Berghoff, "Methoden der Verbrauchslenkung im Nationalsozialismus," in Dieter Gosewinkel, ed., *Wirtschaftskontrolle und Recht in der nationalsozialistischen Diktatur* (Frankfurt, 2005), 281–316; Jonathan Wiesen, *Creating the Nazi Marketplace. Commerce and Consumption in the Third Reich* (Cambridge, 2011), 60ff. Very illuminating, also with reference to the discussion of the American shoe industry and Europe in chapter II: Anne Sudrow, *Der Schuh im Nationalsozialismus. Eine Produktgeschichte im deutsch-britischen-amerikanischen Vergleich* (Göttingen, 2010). On the British experience, see Matthew Hilton, *Consumerism in 20th-Century Britain* (Cambridge, 2003).

67. On film and film propaganda, see Hilmar Hoffmann, *The Triumph of Propaganda. Film and National Socialism, 1933–1945* (Providence, RI, 1996); Philipp Gassert, *Amerika im Dritten Reich* (Stuttgart, 1997), 164ff.

68. On jazz, see Michael Kater, *Different Drummers* (New York, 2003). See also Andrew Wright Hurley, *Return of Jazz* (New York, 2009).

69. See, e.g., Shelley Baranowski, *Strength through Joy. Consumerism and Mass Tourism in the Third Reich* (Cambridge, 2007); Wiesen, *Creating the Nazi Marketplace* (note 66); Anson Rabinbach, "The Aesthetics of Production in the Third Reich," *Journal of Contemporary History* 11 (1976): 43–74.

70. Mark Pendergast, *For God, Country and Coca-Cola. A History of the Coca-Cola Company* (New York, 1993), 213; Hanne Freiburghaus, *Die Coca-Cola-Story* (Zürich, 1986); Helmut Fritz, *Das Evangelium der Erfrischung, Coca-Colas Weltmission* (Reinbek, 1985); Ulf Biedermann, *Ein amerikanischer Traum: Coca-Cola: die unglaubliche Geschichte eines 100-jährigen Erfolges* (Hamburg, 1985); Siegfried Pater, *Zuckerwasser. Vom Coca-Cola Imperium* (Bonn, 2003); Peter Aldenrath, *The Coca-Cola-Story* (Nuremberg, 1999); Peter Zec, ed., *Der Mythos aus der Flasche: Coca-Cola Culture im 20. Jahrhundert* (Essen, 1994). See also James L. Hunt, *Relationship Banker. Eugene W. Stetson, Wall Street, and American Business, 1916–1959* (Macon, GA, 2009), 95ff., on Stetson's relationship with Coca-Cola.

71. Jeff Schutts, "'Die erfrischende Pause.' Marketing Coca-Cola in Hitler's Germany," in Pamela Swett et al., eds., *Selling Modernity: Advertising in Twentieth-Century Germany* (Durham, NC, 2007), 151–81.

72. See Hartmut Berghoff and Bert Kolbow, "Konsumgüter im Rüstungsboom. Wachstumsstrategien der IG-Farben-Sparte Agfa," *Zeitschrift für Unternehmensgeschichte* 55, no. 2 (2010): 129–60. America's Kodak also participated in this photographic boom, on which Bert Kolbow is writing a study.

73. On the history of the Volkswagen, see Bernhard Rieger, *The People's Car. A Global History of the Volkswagen Beetle* (Cambridge, MA, 2013). See also Hans Mommsen and Manfred Grieger, *Das Volkswagenwerk und seine Arbeiter im Dritten Reich* (Düsseldorf, 1996); Wolfgang König, "Adolf Hitler vs. Henry Ford: The Volkswagen, the Role of America as a Model and the Failure of Nazi Consumer Society," *German Studies Review* 27, no. 2 (2004): 249–68; Paul Kluke, "Hitler und das Volkswagenprojekt," *Vierteljahrshefte für Zeitgeschichte* 8, no. 4 (October 1960): 341–83.

74. For references to this utopia, see Gerhard L. Weinberg, ed., *Hitler's Table Talk, 1941–1944* (New York, 2008). See also Jochen Thies, *Architekt der Weltherrschaft* (Düsseldorf, 1976).

75. See Paul Schilperoord, *The Extraordinary Life of Joseph Ganz: The Jewish Engineer Behind Hitler's Volkswagen* (Cambridge, MA, 2012).

76. For U.S. car production, see Anita Kugler, "Arbeitsorganisation und Produktionstechnologie der Adam Opel Werke" (Paper IIVG/pre-1985-202, Wissenschaftszentrum Berlin, 1985), 110. For British and German car production figures, see Kümmel, *Transnational Economic Cooperation* (note 22), 95. On the rise of mass production, see Mary Nolan, *Visions of Modernity* (New York, 1994); Michael Stahlmann, *Die erste Revolution in der Automobilindustrie. Management und Arbeitspolitik von 1900–1940* (Frankfurt, 1993); Harukito Shiomi and Kazuo Wade, eds., *Fordism Transformed. The Development of Production Methods in the Automobile Industry* (Oxford, 1995); Thomas P. Hughes, *American Genesis* (New York, 1989); Steven Tolliday and Jonathan Zeitlin, "Between Fordism and Flexibility," *Archiv für Sozialgeschichte* 28 (1988): 153–71; David A. Hounshell, *From the American System to Mass Production, 1800–1936* (Baltimore, 1984); Volker Wuttke, *Wie entstand die industrielle Massenproduktion?* (Berlin, 1996); Gunther Mai, "Politische Krise und Rationalisierungsdiskurs in den zwanziger Jahren," *Technikgeschichte* 62, no. 4 (1995): 317–32; Heidrun Edelmann, *Vom Luxusgut zum Gebrauchsgegenstand. Geschichte der Verbreitung von Personenkraftwagen in Deutschland* (Frankfurt, 1989); Fritz Blaich, "Motorization in Germany between the Wars," in Ted Barker, ed., *The Economic and Social Effects of the Spread of Motor Vehicles* (London, 1987), 148–64.

77. On the slow development of mass production in Britain, see Sue Bowden, "Diverse Paths to Mass Consumption: The Development of the 'Mass Market' for Motor Cars in the UK in the Interwar Period" (paper, 1992). For Germany, Jürgen Bönig, *Die Einführung der Fliessarbeit in Deutschland bis 1933*, 2 vols. (Münster, 1993); Michael Stahlmann, "Management, Modernisierungs- und Arbeitspolitik bei der Daimler-Benz AG und ihrer Vorläuferunternehmen von der Jahrhundertwende bis zum Zweiten Weltkrieg," *Zeitschrift für Unternehmensgeschichte* 37, no. 3 (1992): 147–80; Tilla Siegel and Thomas von Freyberg, *Industrielle Rationalisierung unter dem Nationalsozialismus* (Frankfurt, 1990); Heidrun Homburg, *Rationalisierung und Industriearbeit. Das Beispiel des Siemens-Konzerns in Berlin, 1900–1939* (Berlin, 1991); Reiner Flik, *Von Ford Lernen? Automobilbau*

und Motorisierung in Deutschland bis 1933 (Cologne, 2001); Theodore Balderston, *Economics and Politics in the Weimar Republic* (Cambridge, 2002), 74–75, noting that "even in Siemens in the later 1920s only a few hundred workers worked fully machine-paced assembly lines (mainly assembling vacuum cleaners!), although a few thousand more were working on self-paced assembly lines."

78. See, e.g., Wiesen, *Creating the Nazi Marketplace* (note 66); Swett et al., *Selling Modernity* (note 71). On Henry Ford, his car, and his universe, see, e.g., Robert Lacey, *Ford. The Men and the Machine* (London, 1986); Allan Nevins and Frank E. Hill, *Ford: Expansion and Challenge, 1915–1933* (New York, 1957); Nevins and Hill, *Ford: Decline and Rebirth, 1933–1962* (New York, 1962); Roy Batchelor, *Henry Ford. Mass Production, Modernism and Design* (Manchester, 1995); Douglas Brinkley, *Wheels of the World. Henry Ford, His Company, and a Century of Progress* (New York, 2003); Hubert Bonnin et al., eds., *Ford, 1903–2003: The European History* (Paris, 2003); Anne Jardin, *The First Henry Ford. A Study in Personality and Business Leadership* (Cambridge, 2003); James J. Flink, *The Car Culture* (Cambridge, MA, 1975), 49ff.; Klaus J. Hennig, "Das Auto an sich," *Die Zeit*, 25 September 2008, 106; Lee Iacocca, "Henry Ford," *Time*, 7 December 1998; Greg Grandin, *Fordlandia. The Rise and Fall of Henry Ford's Forgotten Jungle City* (New York, 2009); Ken Silverstein, "Ford and the Führer. New Documents Reveal Close Ties Between Dearborn and the Nazis," *Nation*, 20 January 2000, 11–16; Mira Wilkins and Frank Ernest Hill, *American Business Abroad: Ford in Six Continents* (Detroit, 1964). Also illuminating: Henry Ford, *Today and Tomorrow* (Garden City, NJ, 1926); Henry Ford, *Mass Production, Modernism and Design* (Manchester, 1995). On Ford's anti-Semitism and support of the anti-Semitic *Dearborn Independent*, see Max Wallace, *The American Axis. Henry Ford, Charles Lindbergh, and the Rise of the Third Reich* (New York, 2003), 123ff. This anti-Semitism was probably related to his contempt of bankers. See Henry Ford, *My Life and Work* (New York, 1922), 10. Ibid. also his Dickensian views of those unable or unwilling to work: instead of receiving the full value of community services, they should have the freedom to starve.

79. *WSJ*, 19 April 1926.

80. Ibid. See also Wallace, *American Axis* (note 78), 226.

81. *WSJ*, 3 February 1927; *WSJ*, 14 November 1928.

82. Sabine Saphörster, "Die Ansiedlung der Ford-Motor-Company 1929/30 in Köln," *Rheinische Vierteljahrsblätter* 53 (1989): 178–210.

83. See James Forman-Peck, "The American Challenge of the Twenties: Multinationals and the European Motor Industry," *Journal of Economic History* 42, no. 4 (December 1982): 865–81. See also Ed Gray, *Chrome Colossus. General Motors and Its Times* (New York, 1980), 218ff.

84. *WSJ*, 28 August 1925; *WSJ*, 5 September 1925; *WSJ*, 21 November 1925; John McDonald and Catherine Stevens, eds., *Alfred P. Sloan, Jr., My Years with General Motors* (New York, 1972). For a detailed analysis of the strategies of American carmakers in Britain and Germany, see Forman-Peck, "American Challenge" (note 83). On the British motor industry, see also M. Miller and R. A. Church, "Motor Manufacturing," in N. K. Buxton and D. H. Aldcroft, eds., *British Industry between the Wars* (London, 1979), 179–215. On Germany, see, e.g., Gerhard Kümmel, *Transnational Economic Cooperation* (note 24), 93ff.; on Opel:

Michael Stahlmann, *Die erste Revolution* (note 76), 60ff.; Henry A. Turner, *General Motors and the Nazis* (New Haven, CT, 2005); Reinhold Bilstein et al., *Working for the Enemy* (New York, 2000).

85. On Porsche, see Reinhard Osterroth, *Ferdinand Porsche. Der Pionier und seine Welt* (Reinbek, 2003); Karl Ludvigsen, *Ferdinand Porsche* (Cambridge, MA, 2009). But see also note 75 on Joseph Ganz.

86. See James D. Mooney's report after an extended visit to GM plants in Europe in *WSJ*, 1 February 1933. On the position of Daimler-Benz, see Neil Gregor, *Daimler-Benz in the Third Reich* (New Haven, CT, 1998); Hans Pohl et al., eds., *Die Daimler-Benz AG in den Jahren 1933 bis 1945* (Stuttgart, 1986); Elfriede Grunow-Osswald, *Die Internationalisierung eines Konzerns: Daimler-Benz, 1890–1997* (Königswinter, 2006); Caroline Schulenberg, *Renault und Daimler-Benz in der Zwischenkriegszeit, 1919–1938* (Stuttgart, 2008); Bernard P. Bellon, *Mercedes in Peace and War, German Automobile Workers, 1903–1945* (New York, 1990).

87. For a detailed history of GM-Opel's experience with the Nazi regime, see the excellent study by Turner, *General Motors* (note 84), passim, also for the following. See also Kümmel, *Transnational Economic Cooperation* (note 24), 100ff.; Eckart Bartels, *Opel at War* (West Chester, PA, 1991); Günter Neliba, *Die Opelwerke im Konzern von General Motors (1929–1948) in Rüsselsheim und Brandenburg* (Frankfurt, 2000); Jürgen Lewandowski, *Opel* (Bielefeld, 2000).

88. See Bilstein et al., *Working for the Enemy* (note 84).

89. See above, pp. 239ff.

90. On Knudsen, see p. 247 and Joseph Maiolo, *Cry Havoc. How the Arms Race Drove the World into War, 1931–1941* (New York, 2010), 378.

91. See Scott Newton, *Profits of Peace. The Political Economy of Anglo-German Appeasement* (Oxford, 1996), 99–100. See also Jonathan Kirshner, *Appeasing Bankers. Financial Caution and the Road to War* (Princeton, 2007).

92. The full text of the Düsseldorf Agreement is reprinted in K. L. Mayall, *International Cartels. Economic and Political Aspects* (Rutland, 1951). See also Bernd Martin, "Friedens-Planungen der multinationalen Grossindustrie (1932–1940) als politische Krisenstrategie," *Geschichte und Gesellschaft* 2 (1976): 66–88, esp. 74ff.

93. See Kynaston, *City of London* (note 18), 457ff.

94. On the Wohlthat discussions, see Newton, *Profits of Peace* (note 91), 124ff., 145.

95. On Mooney's missions, see Turner, *General Motors* (note 84), chap. 7. On Mooney's position within GM, see Kümmel, *Transnational Economic Cooperation* (note 24), 108ff.

96. William L. Langer and S. Everett Gleason, *The Challenge to Isolation* (New York, [1952] 1964), 361ff., with quotation on 375.

97. Stanley E. Hilton, "The Welles Mission to Europe. February-March 1940: Illusion or Realism?," *Journal of American History* 58, no. 1 (June 1971): 93–120, with quotation on 94. See also Cole, *Roosevelt and the Isolationists* (note 27), 332ff.

98. Quoted in V. R. Berghahn, *Modern Germany* (New York, 1987), 157.

99. Quoted in ibid., 158.

100. See Turner, *General Motors* (note 84), 188. It may be that an article by top I.G. Farben executive Georg von Schnitzler has to be seen in this context, which

appeared in *Atlantic Monthly* in 1940 (pp. 817–21), titled "Germany and World Trade after the War." It ended, "Thus, on the secure foundation of these natural premises, Central Europe and the Southeast of Europe are developing an exemplary economic cooperation which the practical American business man, who in economic matters has always followed a sound practical policy, will be able to appreciate fully. Germany, who everywhere strives for the development of the highest economic efficiency, believes that she is thus contributing a vital share to a new, organically linked, and intrinsically sound exchange of goods in the world, which we hope for in the future for the benefit of all concerned." What these words also indicated was that I.G. Farben was not totally wedded to Hitler's concept of a world of autarkic blocs, but hoped to resume participation in the world economy after the war.

101. Turner, *General Motors* (note 84), chap. 7. See also Kümmel, *Transnational Economic Cooperation* (note 24), 120ff.

102. See Wallace, *American Axis* (note 78), 218a, with title page photo.

103. Ibid., 146ff.

104. See Thomas G. Belden and Marwa R. Belden, *The Lengthening Shadow. The Life of Thomas Watson* (Boston, 1962), 33ff. See also Robert Sobel, *IBM* (New York, 1981).

105. Another example of this is Norton Co. of Worchester, Massachusetts, a medium-sized manufacturer of bonded abrasives. The company had been in Germany since 1909 and, operating as Deutsche Norton Gesellschaft, "was variously supportive of, indifferent to, or in opposition to the Reich's policies." See Charles Cheape, "Not Politicians but Sound Businessmen: Norton Company and the Third Reich," *Business History Review* 62, no. 3 (Autumn 1988): 444–67.

106. See, e.g., Helmut Krausnick, *Anatomy of the SS State* (New York, 1968); Richard Breitman, *Architect of Genocide* (Hanover, NH, 1992).

107. Edwin Black, *IBM and the Holocaust* (New York, 2001), 9–10.

V I

//

British and German Business and Politics under the *Pax Americana*, 1941–1957

1. Hitler's Quest for Victory in the East

Before examining the third round in the German-American-British business relationship from 1941 to 1957, it is important to stress how right Roosevelt, Morgenthau, and other key members of the U.S. administration were in suspecting that Hitler was everything but an "ordinary politician" with whom deals could be struck. Together with Italy and Japan, he had begun to launch the first stage of his violent conquest of "living space," at first against Poland in September 1939 and from 22 June 1941 against the Soviet Union. After consolidating his European victories, including those he had won in 1940 in Western and Northern Europe, and after the confidently expected swift defeat of Stalin, he, in line with his speech of November 1937, would have been in a good position to contemplate the second stage of his "program," that is, a campaign against the Anglo-Saxon world for global domination that, in conjunction with the other two Axis powers, he also hoped to win.

He came very close to victory in the Soviet Union. However, by November it became clear that he had failed to occupy Moscow—in his twisted worldview the citadel of the "Jewish-Bolshevik" arch enemy. After fierce Red Army resistance and a very harsh winter costing the Germans some 900,000 casualties, Hitler bypassed Moscow and moved southeast in the following spring into the Ukraine and the Caucasus. He was stopped at Stalingrad in the winter of 1942–43 and thenceforth gradually pushed back farther and farther to the west. With the American entry into the war in December 1941, it was all but certain that Hitler would lose the war, though it is noteworthy that this defeat came primarily in the east in 1942–43 and not in June 1944 with the Anglo-American invasion of Normandy.

For understandable reasons historians are not particularly fond of counterfactuals. But in light of developments on the Soviet front it is quite helpful to ask what would have happened if Hitler's expectation of victory in 1941 had come true. The usefulness of this counterfactual is reinforced by the point that, in anticipation of success outside Moscow, he had begun to put the next phase in place. Operation plans against Afghanistan and for the occupation of the Azores were being drawn up at this time.[1] While the Japanese were advancing in Southeast Asia, India, the "crown jewel" of the British Empire, was the prize to be taken after the occupation of Afghanistan. Assuming possession of the Indian Ocean, a Nazi Colonial Ministry, officially established in 1940, started to train administrators for service in Africa. Meanwhile Mussolini, already in possession of Libya, had set his sights on British Egypt and the Suez Canal.

Hitler also formulated ideas about how he wanted to organize his empire internally. Nazi occupation policies in Poland in 1939 and now in the Soviet Union in 1941 were harbingers of what was to come. In his Table Talks, recorded by a stenographer when he and his cronies sat together in the evening at his headquarters, he talked about how he expected to treat the conquered territories.[2] His plans to resettle Germans in the east and to exploit the Slavic populations as slave laborers were, however horrific, concrete enough to be taken seriously. Even more sinister in terms of what the Nazi New Order was going to be like was that the systematic murder of Europe's Jews and other "subhuman" minorities had begun, first in Poland and from the summer of 1941 onward in the Soviet Union. It was the "Holocaust in the villages" with mass shootings of men, women, and children that began before the extermination camps went into operation. Finally, as during the occupation of Western and Northern Europe in 1940, German corporate managers and other experts roamed the rear areas to tackle the economic integration of the new territories.[3]

When the news of what was happening in Eastern Europe reached London and Washington, Roosevelt felt confirmed in his earlier, increasingly pessimistic assessment of Axis aims that ultimately also threatened the Americas. Those businessmen who—as has been seen in chapter V—thought as late as 1941 that it was possible to preserve or restore peace and to lure Germany (and Japan and Italy) away from their conquests and the building of autarkic blocs back into the world economy had been proven terribly wrong. Now the U.S. president felt vindicated that from 1937 onward, he had laid the industrial foundations for a world war that would eventually turn the country into a belligerent. This time America was better prepared than in 1917 to participate in a world conflict that the Japanese and Hitler had forced upon a population that had believed for all too long that they were secure on a continent with the Atlantic on the one side and the Pacific on the other. They continued to believe that they could leave the fighting in the Far East to the Chinese and other East Asian nations, then exposed to Japanese expansionism, just as the war in Europe would be fought by the British. After Pearl Harbor and Hitler's declaration of war on the United States, Roosevelt was confident that an Allied victory could be expected sooner or later. The question was therefore bound to arise what the country would do with that victory.

2. Planning for Victory and Henry Luce's "American Century"

In February 1941—well before the official American entry into World War II—the prominent American businessman Henry Luce had published an article in one of his magazines, titled "The American Century."[4] It was not a piece that set out particularly specific peace aims. But it postulated in essence that, if the twentieth century had not been an American one in its first half, the United States should at least make every effort to realize this idea in its second half. Luce's piece fired the imagination of those who read and began to refer to it. Once the attempts to establish a *Pax Germanica,* a *Pax Nipponica,* and a *Pax Romana* had been thwarted, the United States would—rather belatedly and after two world wars—be in a position to shape a peace for the rest of the twentieth century that was based on American principles of sociopolitical and economic organization. Roosevelt had articulated this postwar vision in one of his fireside chats on 29 December 1940 when he spoke of "two worlds that stand opposed to each other" and proclaimed the United States to be the "great arsenal of democracy" politically, but in line with Hull's universalist concept of world order, also economically. A few weeks later, the American president discussed the Four Freedoms in his State of the Union address, that is, freedom of religion and of "speech and expression" as well as freedom from want and fear.[5]

The next step occurred—still before the American entry into the war, but as a confirmation of the support that Roosevelt was by then giving to Britain—in August 1941, when he met with Churchill onboard warships in Placentia Bay off the coast of Newfoundland. Although it is not entirely clear who first drafted the Atlantic Charter, its postulates could not have delineated more sharply to two worlds that the Axis powers, on the one hand, and the Anglo-American allies, on the other, were trying to create. For the latter it was a world without aggrandizement by force and without territorial changes not agreed upon by the people concerned. It was also a world in which citizens could freely choose their preferred government after the restoration of sovereign rights and self-government for those "who had been forcibly deprived of it."[6] The charter also laid down equal access to trade and raw materials "needed for economic prosperity," though "with due respect for . . . existing obligations." There was to be "fullest cooperation between all nations in the economic field with the object of securing for all improved labor standards, economic advancement and social security" as well as a life "in freedom from want and fear," enabling "all men to traverse the high seas and oceans without hindrance" and finally "abandonment of the use of force" and disarmament of nations that "threaten, or may threaten, aggression outside of their frontiers."

The meeting was not entirely harmonious and the main disagreement revolved (significantly enough also in light of later British-American quarrels) around the question of imperial possessions. Roosevelt felt that extracting raw materials from formal colonies without promoting their socioeconomic advancement was an outdated method that could no longer secure peace and stability. He added that he could not believe "that we can fight fascist slavery and at the same time not work to free people all over the world from backward colonial policy." Churchill was not pleased to hear this so that, for the sake of Allied harmony, in the end the clause relating to equal access to raw materials and trade became qualified by a vague reference that existing obligations should be respected.

If the Placentia Bay meeting alone made certain that the debate on the future of the British Empire and Commonwealth would not stop between Britain and the United States, Secretary of State Cordell Hull's favorite idea of establishing an Open Door multilateral world trading system merely exacerbated this difference of opinion. He had long been opposed to the closed, autarkic blocs that Germany, Japan, and Italy were erecting in the territories they had been conquering. And within those blocs, cartels and monopolies that were said to be dominating the Nazi economy were also anathema to Hull. After the war, liberal-capitalist market competition was to prevail, complemented by New Deal notions of social security. The trouble was that the British Empire and Commonwealth, while not sealed off from the rest of the world, had, at the Ottawa Conference in August 1932, increased preferential tariffs. This had in turn led to a massive redirection of British exports and re-exports to these protected regions. In Washington these preferences were deemed to be impediments to Free Trade once the war was over. Roosevelt was also unhappy that only two freedoms (from want and fear) had been mentioned at Placentia Bay, when his administration was envisioning two more, that is, freedom of religion and of information. In a speech before Congress on 21 August he reinserted the latter two. By 1942 articles appeared in such popular magazines as *Life* warning Britain not to have any illusions that the United States was fighting this war to keep the Empire together.

If the contours of Washington's peace aims were slowly emerging during 1941, the American entry into World War II triggered a flurry of activity in all ministries and agencies that were in one way or another involved in foreign policy making. In anticipation of victory, post-hostility committees and planning groups were formed from among the American experts on Europe. There were almost too many of them who were keen to make a contribution to an extensive debate that now set in. Many of these did not immediately focus on Germany and Italy. The bigger question was rather about what to do with Europe at large and how to rebuild it within the framework of the *Pax Americana*. At the same time the question of how to organize the world economy also raised the problem of what the inner-American structures of industry and finance should look like to facilitate effective international leadership via Washington and its business community.

As will be remembered from chapter V, sections of this business community, including powerful members of the banking world, had opposed the New Deal policies of the first Roosevelt administration. There was not merely the rejection of the social security system and the enhanced role of government. Manufacturing industry after all had always insisted on both its autonomy and on reductions of taxes. For the banking community the promulgation of the Glass-Steagall Act of 1933 that had built a firewall between investment banking and commercial and savings banks, to impede a repetition of the rampant speculation of 1927 to 1929, had been particularly objectionable. After his landslide victory in 1936 Roosevelt was more determined than before to strengthen compliance with the various rules on market organization that had been put on the statute book since the Sherman Act of 1890. While the decision to enforce "antitrust" was to some extent perhaps also intended as a punishment of corporations that had tried to undermine Roosevelt's presidency, the most important consideration was that, in slowly coming out of the Depression, industry itself needed to be made more efficient. The hope was that, by creating more jobs and offering cheaper consumer goods, the ordinary American's purchasing power would increase. The president also wanted industry to be capable of dealing with the eventuality of a major war and to be ready to compete in the future multilateral trading system that Hull was envisioning.

To some extent, these pressures on industry and banking had been helped by the isolationists in Congress through the constitution of a committee in 1935, chaired by Gerald P. Nye, the senator from North Dakota. Investigating business practices in World War I, it promptly found that many companies had been engaged in massive war profiteering. It was even alleged that corporate greed had been a prime reason why the country had been pushed into that earlier war. Nye and his supporters wanted to make certain that, as the international situation again pointed to war, this would not happen again. If the committee's findings put American big business into the limelight, Nye also gave the Roosevelt administration a reason to do something about the concentration of economic power. Accordingly, the prominent Yale Law School professor Thurman Arnold, who had written a number of influential books and articles, was put in charge of the Anti-trust Division of the Justice Department in early 1938.[7] The threat that he and his fellow academics had identified was not bigness, but the attempts by industry to form monopolies.

Apart from his best-known book *The Folklore of Capitalism*, *The Bottlenecks of Business* still provides many insights into how one might think about organizing the political economy of the United States.[8] Arnold began by reassuring his readers that he was not concerned with bigness as such, but rather with the Sherman Act and its subsequent revisions. "Anti-trust," Arnold continued, was not meant to destroy the efficiencies of mass production and mass consumption. His book did not propose to make radical changes to the country's economic structure. It was merely committed to maintaining the distribution of goods through free enterprise. This meant that "if Henry Ford has a more efficient method of transportation, he should be allowed to furnish it to the consumer, even though it destroys a lot of little automobile companies." Ultimately, the success of the system "depends upon the ability of the consumers . . . to use the instruments of government which they have at hand to get the maximum distribution of goods in a free market." Accordingly, the consumer could expect protection against price-fixing and inefficient, noncompetitive methods of distribution. If, Arnold added, many older studies on "anti-trust" had highlighted the "evil of bigness," size "in itself was not an evil, but it does give power to those who control it." That power must be constantly watched by an "adequate enforcement organization." Later on Arnold argued that, while the Anti-trust Division itself had a deterrent effect on big business to shy away from anticompetitive behavior, it had to look proactively for violations by individual companies.

If these were the well-worn arguments of the supporters of "anti-trust," what has often been overlooked is how Arnold linked what he called American "economic democracy" (secured by "antitrust") to the country's political democracy and, third, how he compared it to the Nazi political economy. To him economic and political democracy were complementary. Just as competition in the *political* marketplace was a basic principle of the American Constitution, so was competition in the *economic* marketplace. Where political democracy was on the wane, it would have a negative effect on "economic democracy." Conversely, a failure to secure competition in the economic marketplace would undermine political democracy.

These principles were also intended to draw a sharp contrast between the political- and economic-constitutional principles of the United States, on the one hand, and those of Europe and of Germany, on the other. After all, "there is nothing about European models that appeals to us." In fact what Arnold saw happening was the destruction of "domestic markets by private combinations, cartels and trade associations" in Germany in the 1930s. At the same time the Nazis had also abolished the political marketplace. Democracy had been replaced by a one-party dictatorship. Arnold concluded his book by asserting that just as the American political constitution was firmly rooted in the country, "the Sherman Act has become so woven into our habits of thought that it is today our economic common law."

Convinced that American big business had become inefficient, but also that the dictatorial systems in Europe and the Far East constituted a dangerous threat to America's political constitution, Arnold added many more lawyers to his Anti-trust Division. They became apostles of efficiency and the scourge of corporations suspected of being engaged in anticompetitive practices. Accordingly, the division by 1940 had initiated some 215 investigations and had filed over 3,400 complaints. Initially still satisfied with consent decrees by individual firms to stop their practices, Arnold soon began to start prosecutions industry-wide. Not surprisingly, this kind of activism became an enormous irritant to the business community as well as to the unions that were also caught Arnold's his antimonopoly dragnet. After the American entry into the war pressure mounted to get rid of him.[9] On 20 March 1942, Roosevelt ordered an end to all antitrust suits. Arnold resigned and was rewarded with a judgeship on the First Circuit Court of Appeals. Wendell Berge, his successor, had to operate under quite different conditions and became, significantly enough, involved in the investigations of *German* cartels and anticompetitive practices in Europe.

By this time all parts of the administration were engaged in postwar planning. Between 1942 and 1944 much of this preparatory work concentrated on the New Order in its broadest terms and the problem of monopoly and preferential tariffs abroad. Suspected foreign monopolies were recorded and classified. To begin with, there were the commercial policies adopted by the Axis powers together with those huge autarkic imperialist blocs that they so manifestly had begun to build with the help of corporations that had been producing the weapons for wars of aggression. But there was also the question of what to do with the British Empire and Commonwealth as a preferential tariff zone and the sterling bloc that had been in the cross-hairs of Wall Street since the end of World War I. As Sumner Welles put it in May 1943,[10] "Our victory must bring in its train the liberation of all peoples. Discrimination between peoples because of their race, creed or color must be abolished. The age of imperialism is ended." The contrast with Churchill's ideas about the Empire and Commonwealth could not be starker.

A further complication arose when the proposals of Washington's ministerial bureaucracy, including the Office of Strategic Services (OSS) as America's foreign intelligence arm, were augmented by those generated by a number of private associations, above all the Council on Foreign Relations (CFR) and the Committee for Economic Development (CED).[11] The CFR in particular, was divided into various subgroups often with academic experts. Some of them wrote papers on ways of eliminating all discriminations from international commerce. Others pondered the integration of Europe and made a number of proposals for putting the coal and steel industries under one umbrella that anticipated the later creation of the European Coal and Steel Community of 1951. While many of the CFR subcommittee reports were useful in clarifying an array of issues, it soon also became obvious that a sharper focus was needed, the more so since Britain had meanwhile also built up a committee structure and the two sides began to have joint meetings. In these latter contacts it quickly became clear that it was unwise to debate the future of the British Empire in terms of the points that Roosevelt had made at the Placentia Bay meeting. In fact the British committee members now insisted that this topic be excluded from their meetings.

3. Cartels and the "German Question"

There was another difficult issue, that is, how to deal with international cartels, cooperations, patent exchanges, and licenses in which American corporations had participated before the war.[12] There were suspicions that some of these agreements had not been cancelled when trading with the German enemy became treasonous in 1941. Especially the chemical industry, with its innumerable patent and license accords between I.G. Farben, Du Pont, Dow Chemicals, and others, proved very difficult to disentangle in the middle of the war, with Britain's ICI often also wrapped up in the packages and firms claiming that these were legally binding private contracts so that German patents could not simply be expropriated. There were also rumors that corporations with direct investments in Germany, such as GM and Ford, continued their links via Switzerland and ran other covert operations. Given that Roosevelt was dependent on the cooperation of the business community for winning the war and had asked a number of their top executives to serve on various postwar planning committees and boards, the Justice Department was told to put all probes on ice.[13] Those lawyers who were determined to prosecute wrongdoers demurred, but continued to gather and publish information in the expectation of an early Allied victory. The assumption was that once Germany had been defeated, the German side of the story of international cartels, patent agreements, and FDI could be reconstructed from captured German files. It was thought to be easier to get to the truth of this chapter of German-American business relations at that later point.

In the meantime the Teheran Conference of Roosevelt, Churchill, and Stalin at the end of November 1943 had revealed that, while it was difficult to agree on measures regarding the *reconstruction* of Germany, there was a general consensus among the Big Three on the Allies' "negative" aims: The defeated country was to be demilitarized, de-Nazified, and decartellized. With the scope of American planning for the New Economic Order having been reduced to these issues and the influence of the CFR and other private associations having been pushed back in the interest of the executive branch regaining tighter control, discussions in Washington, though organizationally simplified, became increasingly polarized. To some extent this seems to have been due to the fact that news about the horrors of the Nazi Holocaust had become more concrete.[14] As a result, the positions of government agencies on what to do with Germany also became more divided. On the one side were those who wanted to treat the Germans harshly. They clustered around the Justice and Commerce Departments, and Henry Morgenthau's Treasury Department; most prominently on the other side stood the War and State Departments. Supported—as will be seen later in this chapter—by the business community, they wanted to reconstruct the country and to reintegrate it as soon as possible into the community of nations and the projected international trading system. In this they were joined somewhat later by OSS.

A vigorous debate now ensued on whether and how far to deindustrialize defeated Germany. Partly because the Nazi regime painted a wildly exaggerated picture of Allied plans to unleash a horrific revenge on the German population, it has taken historical research some time to come to a more sober assessment of the proposals for a harsh treatment of Germany. These came to be encapsulated in the so-called Morgenthau Plan. As Bernd Greiner and others have shown, Germany was *not* to be converted into an agricultural society with all of its industries razed to the ground.[15] What the "Morgenthauians" were aiming at was to hit the war-making industrial capacities and hence the industries of the Ruhr region hard. They also envisaged a longer period when German living standards would remain below those of their European neighbors. The opposition to this plan was particularly strong among many American businessmen. These protagonists of a much milder treatment of the Germans pointed, on the one hand, to the dangers of a political radicalization of destitute populations. They harbored fears that people might turn to communism. There was also the problem that a starving population that could not feed itself would remain dependent on food imports and other aid that would burden the American tax payer. Furthermore, GIs, all of whom were straining to go home, would be required to stay to uphold law and order in occupied Germany. Yet another consideration on the minds of decision makers was the memory of the post-1918 period when the United States, instead of using its resources for European reconstruction, had withheld its support, at least until 1924–25. As a result, precious time had been lost and the recovery had been too weak to secure a more long-term upswing. Instead the Great Depression came that was now being viewed by many as the prelude to World War II.

However, this larger collective learning from the past that post-1945 historical research has retrieved from different archives should not lead to an underestimation of the drama that played out between the Americans and the British at the Quebec Conference in October 1944 where the Morgenthau Plan was presented.[16] This drama unfolded against the background of British resistance to American pressures not to try to preserve the Empire and Commonwealth as an economic bloc with preferential tariffs. Churchill had angrily opposed this suggestion at Placentia Bay as early as August 1941. But given its fixation on the Open Door, this did not prevent the State Department, backed by the business community, from raising it long before the end of the war. The lever that Washington used quite determinedly was the Lend-Lease Agreement. While Roosevelt's attitude was to postpone all questions of the New Economic Order until after victory, Cordell Hull's State Department wanted to nail down detailed Lend-Lease repayment provisions that the British were bound to be unhappy with. On top of this, Welles made another attempt to obtain a commitment from London by using the so-called "Wheat Talks" as a point of pressure, that is, the provision of grain to feed the British population. In these circumstances the interpretation of Article 7 of the Lend-Lease accord became a serious stumbling bloc. Although Churchill was in principle prepared to contemplate a liberalization of postwar trade, his cabinet colleagues refused to budge on Imperial preferences and opposed the wording of Article 7 because it would curtail Britain's economic relations with the Empire and Commonwealth.[17]

When the State Department signaled that it would agree to quite generous repayment terms for Lend-Lease, the Treasury Department under Henry Morgenthau appeared on the scene to cause difficulties with respect to the reserves that Britain would be allowed to keep. It also refused to accept a separate account for the gold that London had stored in South Africa. As all these negotiations continued, Congress, since the November 1942 elections again dominated by the Republicans, decided to investigate Lend-Lease. Furthermore, the Foreign Economic Administration presented the British with a detailed list of what had already been lent and leased. When American soldiers arrived in Britain in larger numbers in preparation of an eventual invasion of Hitler's Fortress Europe, the question became of how to deal with the dollars that the GIs were spending in the United Kingdom. Given these issues that the Americans were raising relentlessly, Keynes, one of the chief negotiators on the British side, and his colleagues became increasingly suspicious that their American counterparts had only one concern, that is, how to secure a dominant position for the United States in the postwar world. They had tried to replace Britain as the center of finance and industry before 1929, and now they were thought in London to be pushing for it again.

From the American perspective there was another consideration: Washington was also guided by memories of what had happened to its domestic economy after World War I. This time the reconversion of American industry to civilian production was to be buttressed by vigorous exports. Merely to rely on domestic demand, it was feared, would lead, as in 1919–20, to a straw fire followed by an early recession. Not surprisingly in light of their own experience in 1919–20, London was motivated by similar concerns and therefore anxious to preserve the preferences that the Empire and Commonwealth offered for British reconversion and exports after the war. To be sure, in principle Hull and his negotiators sympathized with the British quest to stabilize and expand their postwar economy. But Congress stood in the way once again. Its members, with their voters back home on their mind, similarly expected the country to have reconversion problems. And so, as the Allies entered 1944 with victory in sight, the State Department revived both the Lend-Lease repayment issue as well as British preferential tariffs, hoping that Whitehall would at least agree to a gradual reduction of preferences.

This time the British negotiators found an American ally who had a different agenda: Henry Morgenthau, whose department had meanwhile drawn up a plan to destroy Germany's war-making potential, and especially that of the Ruhr industrial region, once and for all. He also wanted to exclude the country for a longer period from postwar reconstruction and Europe's integration into the *Pax Americana*. When the details of the Morgenthau Plan were revealed to Churchill at the Quebec Conference, his first reaction was to call them "un-Christian [!]." At the same time, the British prime minister was inclined to treat the Germans harshly on the assumption that disarming German industry would offer Britain additional export opportunities worth some £400 million. Roosevelt echoed this idea in the hope that a reduction of Germany's industrial potential would keep "Britain from going into complete bankruptcy at the end of the war."[18] What also united the two men with Morgenthau was abhorrence at the news that the Nazis had been murdering millions of Jews and other European minorities in the occupied territories. With Roosevelt having given his general approval to the Morgenthau Plan, Churchill saw an opportunity to strike a bargain. If he supported Morgenthau's way of settling the "German Question," Germany's postwar weakness not only would aid a British recovery and exports, but also might facilitate a deal on Lend-Lease. After all, it was not merely a matter of getting favorable repayment terms for what had already been received, but also to obtain a postwar extension to help reconstruct an economically exhausted Britain.

The Quebec Conference was barely over when the Morgenthau Plan was leaked, unleashing a huge public debate and mobilizing both supporters of the plan as well as its opponents. As Greiner and others have shown, both Churchill and Roosevelt now began to distance themselves from the Plan.[19] The protagonists of reintegrating Germany into the community of nations and an American-dominated world economy won out against the "Morgenthauians." However, it was not a swift victory. With Allied forces entering Germany in the west, the directives that were sent out by the Joint Chiefs of Staff, and JCS 1067 in particular, contained many elements of how to treat the German population and the country's industries that were punitive rather than "reconstructionist."

Apart from de-Nazification and demilitarization, there was the economic question that came to be debated under the opaque label of "decartelization." For some this meant a radical deconcentration and even deindustrialization. For others it was merely a Sherman-style ban on cartels and syndicates and a dismantling of corporations deemed to be holding a monopoly position in the Nazi economy. Nor did it help that a U.S. senator, Harley Kilgore, had become active in this field.[20] After Thurman Arnold's efforts to enforce "antitrust" had been shelved in 1942, Kilgore tried to revive the debate on monopolies and cartels. But this time the first target was not American, but German industry. Like Roosevelt, the senator had also come to see a close link between the Nazi regime and the high degree of cartelization of German industry. As the U.S. president put it in 1944,[21]

> During that past half century, the United States has developed a tradition of opposition to private monopolies. The Sherman and Clayton Acts have become as much part of the American way of life as the Due Process clause of the Constitution. By protecting the consumer against monopoly these statutes guarantee him the benefits of competition. . . . Unfortunately, a number of foreign countries, particularly in continental Europe, do not possess such a tradition against cartels. On the contrary, cartels have received encouragement from these governments. Especially, this is true with respect to Germany. Moreover, cartels were utilized by the Nazis as governmental instrumentalities to achieve political ends. . . . Defeat of the Nazi armies will have to be followed by the eradication of these weapons of economic warfare. But more than elimination of the political activities of German cartels will be required. Cartel practices which restrict the free flow of goods in foreign commerce will have to be curbed.

How far the organization of industry and that of Germany (and of Japan's zaibatsu system) had become a focus of attention is reflected in the title of a book that Wendell Berge, Arnold's successor, published in 1944, entitled *Cartels: A Challenge to the Free World*. The author argued that, if the Sherman Act were ratified again in the United States, it should be called more appropriately "Anti-Cartel Act" rather than "Anti-Trust Act."[22] If this book was to reassure American corporations that size was not the issue as long as the market retained its oligopolistic organization, Kilgore's subcommittee on Monopoly and Cartel Practices undermined this approach. Having been elected as senator from West Virginia, he had supported Roosevelt's New Deal and was in principle also in agreement with the president's assessment of the Nazi-industry nexus in the Third Reich.

But the hearings that he held in Washington in 1944 and 1945 almost inevitably began to veer from German cartelization to American corporations that were suspected of having cooperated with German firms in the field of patents and licenses before the American entry into the war and, worse, after December 1941. The activities of I.G. Farben and its American and British partners therefore quickly moved to the center of Kilgore's investigations. The speeches that the senator made had the rings of the Nye Committee findings on profiteering in World War I and generated a good deal of heat inside the United States. As Mark Ruff put it,[23] "From 1944 onwards, Kilgore carried on a one-man crusade against cartels. He turned his Senate Subcommittee into a public forum from which to expose the prewar cartel alliances between American and German industry," ultimately hoping "to change the behavior of American business."

4. The Role of American Big Business in Postwar Planning

However, some parts of the American business community were not prepared to change, and with the prestige of industry greatly enhanced by the vital material contribution it was making to the war effort, they were even hoping to scale back the powers that the executive branch in Washington had accumulated since 1940. Many of them had also been either hostile to, or skeptical of, Roosevelt's New Deal and the expansion of workers' rights. But—as will also be recalled—there had been other industrialists who had welcomed the president's policies, even if they had cost them in terms of social benefit obligations and the spread of unionization. They also acknowledged that the president had been right about Axis preparations for war and about stimulating the economy by preparing the country's infrastructure for war production. Although there was some overlap between these industrialists and the study groups of the CFR that have been mentioned above, they had tended to be associated with the CED, constituted in 1942.

This body was to "become one of the nation's most important sources of new economic thought, both during and after the war and the bureaucratic home of such influential Keynesians as Beardsley Ruml and Herbert Stein."[24] Being in principle more concerned with advising business on how to respond positively and pragmatically to the economic policies of the Roosevelt administration, CED's research division in particular was supposed to publicize information that would "aid in 'bringing into being a climate more favorable to continued high employment.'" While this division relied on academic expertise, the CED's Research and Policy Committee was made up exclusively of businesspeople who were wedded to the idea that the modern manager needed not merely technological advice, but also the insights of the modern social sciences. The group's first chairman was Paul Hoffman, president of the Studebaker Corporation and a good example of the more progressive leaders of industry who worked not only for the modernization of the domestic economy, but also for the building of an Americanized postwar world and promoting the economic and techno-logical reconstruction of postwar Europe.[25]

More will be learned later in this chapter about Hoffman's role in the administration of the Marshall Plan in the later 1940s. During the war, he was speaking of free enterprise as an alternative to the Nazi system. He added his belief that monopoly was a public enemy and that any corporation that merely sought maximum profit would undermine free enterprise. While agreeing that postwar prosperity "depended mainly upon [an] expansion of the domestic market," he was also convinced that "America had to abandon isolationism and nationalism by encour-aging freer international trade."[26] For him "international trade was a two-way street that required imports" to the United States as well as American exports. Accordingly, he was happy to join CED, "with lead-ers of the National Association of Manufacturers, the U.S. Chamber of Commerce, and other business organizations," among which Chase National Bank's Winthrop Aldrich was also a key figure.

One of the most interesting CED publications, demonstrating that big questions, such as that of the treatment of Germany or of whether the wartime alliance with the Soviet Union would continue after Al-lied victory, were being widely debated, is Edward Mason's *Controlling World Trade*.[27] In it this prominent Harvard economist moved gingerly between the pre-1939 practices of American big business and a radical international ban on cartels. Thus he confirmed the legality of export as-sociations under the terms of the Webb-Pomerene Act and of American firms or their foreign subsidiaries participating in cartels abroad, pro-vided that they did not impede imports by American companies that were not members of the cartel concerned. At the same time, Mason ad-vocated a ban on international cartels that tried to regulate markets in third countries. Overall, he recommended "to project American policy toward international business agreements on the basis" of the follow-ing assumptions: "Firstly that state import and export monopolies will be both more numerous and more extensive in the postwar period" than before 1939. Second, "that a greater proportion of foreign trade will be conducted by state-supervised import and export associations," and, third, that "domestic trade in most countries, insofar as it is pri-vate, will be heavily cartelized." Finally, Mason wrote, "that interna-tional commodity and cartel agreements among exclusively producer interests will not be completely avoided by an international economic organization" and that "quantitative import controls will continue to exist for a long time after the war."

In making these points, Mason was grappling with the problem of how to include the Soviet Union in the postwar economic order. What he underestimated was the determination of the Roosevelt administration and of influential entrepreneurs to shape the postwar world much more in the image of the American industrial system. Against his vision stood not merely that of the Justice and the Treasury Departments, determined to destroy the Axis cartel system and thereby the German and Japanese economic potential to wage war; there were also key corporate members of the CED who, while aiming at a Sherman-style ban on cartels, did not want to push deconcentration too far. They envisioned a postwar economy driven by oligopolistic competition of quite large units that would act as engines of material reconstruction. Nor could they see a role for the Soviet Union with its state-run economy as part of this system.

Mason's book has been mentioned because it provides another window to American foreign economic policy making and to the unfolding American-British-German relationship. Confident of its superpower status, the country's political and economic elites were determined to establish an Open Door world trading system, but then found that other powers were resisting the implementation of this project. Not all obstacles that stood in the way of good relations could simply be removed in the interest of close cooperation. Thus the notion of integrating the Soviet Union and Eastern Europe into the New Economic Order was abandoned. Instead the emerging Soviet Bloc was built up as a dangerous enemy. Yet the beginning of the Cold War was not merely a struggle that the United States tried hard to decide in its favor by military and economic means. The East-West conflict also acted as a glue that kept together not only a diverse American society wedded to competitive politics, but also the Western Europeans. Many of the latter in both Western and Eastern Europe had emerged from World War II with the hope that it might be possible to find a "third way" between Soviet-style communism and American-style capitalism. When the growing tensions between the Soviet Union and the United States put a stop to these hopes, Eastern Europe became Sovietized, whereas Western Europe came under the hegemonic influence of the United States.

5. The Start of the Cold War and
Anglo-American Relations
in Occupied Germany

This is not the place to recount the scholarly debate on who unleashed the Cold War. It probably was a mix of deeply held beliefs about this conflict being a lethal struggle between two superpowers, on the one hand, and cool calculations concerning the integrating effects of this struggle upon domestic populations. The basic point to be made here is that whatever the structural and ideological determinants, without the East-West conflict the American quest to reconcile the Western Europeans with those Germans who ended up on the Western side of the Iron Curtain would have taken much longer.[28]

The wholesale cancellation of Lend-Lease by U.S. president Harry Truman soon after Roosevelt's death hit not only the exhausted Soviet Union hard. It also deeply disappointed and embittered the British government and population that had been severely weakened economically by Axis aggression. The British *Economist* thought it "aggravating to find that losing a quarter of our national wealth in the common cause is to pay tribute for half a century to those who have been enriched by the war."[29] However, the announcement of 21 August 1945 that no new orders could be placed under Lend-Lease did not come as a complete surprise. British-American negotiations on issues other than Lend-Lease, such as trade with Argentina and the future of the airplane industry in the winter of 1944–45, had been difficult. And there were the old tensions over multilateralism that Hull had never stopped agitating for. When he retired for reasons of his poor health, he was succeeded by Undersecretary Edward Stettinius, who had looked after Lend-Lease, but, as a former chairman of the board of U.S. Steel, was also not in favor of a continuation of imperial blocs.

Furthermore, although Truman did not have the same rapport with Churchill that Roosevelt had established since 1940, his decision was also guided by considerable popular pressures back home not only to bring "the boys" home but also to reduce the financial burdens of the war.[30] Many American taxpayers wanted to see the repayment of wartime debts before new credit was extended to Britain. For the business community it was not just a matter of reducing the role of government in the economy but also of a speedy reconversion of private industry to civilian production. Remembering the conversion difficulties after World War I, American manufacturers were looking toward a revival of exports to complement domestic consumption. Consequently, they developed, in their majority, a strong preference for Hull's vision of the Open Door and not for Morgenthau's. Where this Open Door strategy ran up against preferential tariff walls or even old-fashioned colonialism such practices were to be abolished.

Britain, no less concerned about how to move from military to civilian production and further weakened by the end of Lend-Lease, was in no mood to go for the Open Door. After Churchill had lost the national elections of 1945 to Labour, the Cabinet of Clement Attlee was even more firmly wedded to a policy of full employment and a realization of the social welfare policies, such as the National Health Service. Neither Truman nor the American business community could do much about the Attlee government's domestic priorities. The British population had been promised higher living standards and social reforms, and the costs of these—as will be seen in section 8 of this chapter—made fresh investments in the modernization of manufacturing industry more difficult. There was also no enthusiasm in Washington for Labour's plans to nationalize key industries, such as railroads, electricity, gas, airlines, and telecommunications, making up about 20 percent of British industries. In 1947 the nationalization of iron and steel was also being considered. These policies were based on the argument that creating public corporations was an efficient way of organizing enterprises that the Americans, wedded to the idea that efficiencies were the result of competition in the private marketplace, found impossible to accept.

The tensions that such differences produced soon spilled over into occupied Germany. Here Britain had been allocated, with the exception of the American seaport enclave of Bremerhaven, the northern and western provinces, while the United States had taken charge of Hesse and Bavaria. France had occupied the southwest. Absorbed by its own plans to boost industry through nationalization and by its commitment to improve the welfare of its own populations, London found it more and more difficult to keep the destitute populations of the Ruhr and Rhineland regions from starving.[31] Desperate attempts had been made to get production and especially the Ruhr mining industry going again. But despite rationing back home in Britain, they proved inadequate.

The United States, by contrast, had plenty of agricultural produce that Midwestern farmers and the region's big agribusiness corporations were keen to export. And so began what has been called the "politics of food,"[32] resulting in a deal that the Attlee government had no choice but to accept: In return for grain deliveries to the British zone, Washington demanded a say in the reconstruction and reorganization of the Rhenish industrial region. The creation of the Bi-Zone in January 1947 was part of a pretty blunt American policy to gain a decisive voice in the direction of the region's economy. While the Labour cabinet had been contemplating a nationalization of the Ruhr coal and steel trusts and had dismantled entire steel plants, the Americans, strictly opposed to such programs, had by then converted their reconstruction plans for West Germany into tangible projects designed not only to rebuild but also to *recast* the West German industrial system into an efficient engine of growth.

In the 1970s, William Harris-Burland, the Briton involved in the mobilization of coal production, was still angry at the "American steel people" who were arriving in Düsseldorf in 1947 to take charge, not of the further dismantling and reduction of the Ruhr heavy industries, but their revival.[33] By 1948, this strategic shift was in full swing, as the following quotations illustrate. The first one is by Albert Schäfer, a rubber manufacturer from Hamburg-Harburg. He had traveled west, inter alia, to inspect the synthetic rubber installations at Hüls in the Ruhr region. When he got back to Hamburg, he reported that "in the Ruhr region one can grasp with one's hands what a focus of world attention the Ruhr represents today." To witness "the dynamic of a city like Essen had been overwhelming (*ungeheuerlich*)" even for him.[34] In October 1949 *Fortune* had this to say about the situation:[35] "The central workshop of Europe—the industrial complex of the Rhine and Ruhr basins—is now pulsing, if not at its prewar capacity, certainly with enough vigor to make the future of Germany a prime concern" not merely for Europe but also for the United States. Although American corporations were stronger and bigger, the Ruhr region continued to be "the greatest concentration of economic power on the [European] Continent."

If the focus of American attention in this period was not on Britain with its Labour government, but on West Germany, the specific policies of reconstruction that Washington and the Office of U.S. Military Government (OMGUS) had worked out after the initial conflicts over whether to punish the Germans or to integrate them into the Western community of nations had been decided in favor of the latter faction. Perhaps the most concise statement was by Paul Hoffman, administrator of the Marshall Plan in Europe, when he appeared before a Senate subcommittee in Washington in May 1950. Decartelization, he said, filled him with the "greatest hopes for the restoration of competition in Western Europe via Germany."[36] The aim was to create the type of free competitive economy that existed in the United States. Once this had been done, the efficient West German economy would spread beyond the country because having to compete with a dynamic economy would also promote the introduction of competition in neighboring nations.

Although the British occupation authorities were not completely sidelined after the founding of the Bi-Zone and still had enough control over individual firms to continue to dismantle some of them against ever louder protests from German employers, workers, and politicians, the British opposition to Hoffman's reconstruction policies had been largely removed. This was in part because the Attlee government was by this time also finding it increasingly difficult to keep control of the Empire. In 1947, South Asia cut itself loose, resulting in the violent separation of Muslims from Hindus and the creation of India and Pakistan. In the Middle East, London resisted, unsuccessfully, the establishment of Israel as a Jewish state, which in turn triggered the expulsion and resettlement of millions of Palestinians in the West Bank, Jordan, Syria, and Lebanon. It also became clear that the age of formal empire and colonialism was coming to an end in parts of Africa and Southeast Asia. Washington abandoned the Philippines, acquired in a fit of imperialism from the Spanish in 1898. Only where nationalist independence movements threatened to be overwhelmed by Moscow-supported forces did the United States make an increasingly vigorous attempt to prevent the seizure of power by communists, as happened in China and later in French Indochina. In Latin America Washington faced similar challenges when it failed to prevent Fidel Castro's victory in Cuba.

This rough outline of the incipient process of decolonization and the global reach of American influence during the Cold War is meant to highlight the full dimensions of the political-military interests of the United States during the first two decades after World War II, with the big corporations usually not far behind or in some cases even in the lead. Still, whatever the upheavals elsewhere that were frequently related to the Cold War between the Soviet Union and the United States, in 1945–46 Europe had become (and remained) the main battlefield of the East-West conflict and hence of Washington's efforts to rebuild Western Europe. As far as Anglo-American relations were concerned, it is not that the wartime "special relationship" ended abruptly with the cancellation of Lend-Lease. Affinities continued but mainly at the political and military level, promoted on the British side primarily by the Conservative establishment and the Whitehall bureaucracy. Relations with the Labour government with its ambitious domestic programs of welfare and nationalization were much more difficult.

As Ursula Lehmkuhl has argued, something like a *Pax Anglo-Americana* was to persist among diplomats under which the supposedly deeper British knowledge of non-European societies inside and outside the Empire was offered to the new superpower across the Atlantic that had now fully thrust itself onto the international stage but often lacked knowledge about more far-flung parts of the world. Thus in 1944 the Foreign Office produced a memorandum that hoped "to help steer this great unwieldy barge, the United States of America, into the right harbour" and prevent it from wallowing "in the ocean, an isolated menace to navigation." The underlying idea was not to deploy the Commonwealth to oppose the United States, but rather to "use the power of the United States to preserve the Commonwealth and the Empire." This is not how the State Department viewed the world. On 15 August 1945, it wrote quite unceremoniously that "British empire preference trade controls and economic blocs such as the sterling area would have to be abolished completely or sharply modified."[37] For the same reason and in respect to Western Europe, some Washington insiders wanted Britain to take instead a leading role in the integration of that region. But London did not take this cue to shift gears.

As in the past, American big business played an important role. Whatever sentimental feelings persisted toward the past union of the English-speaking nations, few businessmen felt much loyalty. More than ever, Wall Street wanted to make certain that this time the City was relegated to the second rank as a factor in international finance, and both Morgenthau and Dexter White agreed. Even before 1945 they wanted to "use the leverage of aid to crack the sterling bloc in the British Empire and make the dollar supreme."[38] In the future there was to be no preferential trading bloc, and international commercial banking and insurance business was to flow first and foremost through Wall Street. As to manufacturing, there was recognition of Britain's no doubt impressive economic mobilization during the war. But the findings of the Strategic Bombing Survey and other investigations into how Albert Speer had boosted German war production looked much more promising for a concentration on West Germany.

This fascination extended to science and technology, and this time it was not just the patents held by the chemical industry, but also the breakthroughs in jet propulsion and other cutting-edge developments that attracted the Americans. At first there was simple plunder.[39] But in early 1946 the unorganized removal was stopped, not least because one discovered that just having some machines without instructions or people who knew how to run them was irrational. Moreover, several studies on German reparations have shown that even the more regulated dismantling of machinery was less valuable than the capturing and exploitation of technological knowledge and patents in documents and correspondences. Accordingly, up to June 1947 some "12,000 Allied specialists had combed almost 30,000 research establishments, institutions of learning, laboratories, factories and workshops in Germany" and had "copied or transferred to Allied countries thousands of tons of documents."[40] Drawing also on the earlier research of the American historian John Gimbel and others, this led British scholar Carl Glatt to claim that, even disregarding the removals by other countries such as the Soviet Union or France, "in all probability" the "joint British-American seizure of vast quantities of German scientific and technological data" constituted "the greatest transfer of knowledge ever attempted in so short a period of time."[41]

To these gains must be added the personnel who, unlike in the Soviet case, were voluntarily recruited to continue their earlier research and development for the Nazi regime in the United States and Britain. As the example of Wernher von Braun and other rocket scientists showed, the Americans were more successful than the British at making them

offers that these experts found difficult to refuse.[42] Still, even if the flow
of money, technologies, and ideas was by the late 1940s more from
West to East, the reparations that were taken out of occupied Germany
in terms of patents and research should not be underestimated, even
though the contemporary public debate and also much of the early
research focused on the removal of physical plant and machinery. In
some cases it took German companies, such as Beiersdorf in Hamburg,
the developers of the "Nivea" skin cream, decades after the war to get
their rights back. That the firm had been Jewish-owned before 1933
helped only in the long term.

6. The Politics of Decartelization

However, in focusing on German industrial reconstruction in the hope
that a modernized economy in West Germany would carry with it
beneficial spillover effects for the rest of Western Europe, American
"reconstructionists," such as Hoffman, encountered, apart from the
British, two further obstacles that had to be removed if his strategy
was to work. Even after the Morgenthau Plan had been dropped at
the Quebec Conference in September 1944, JCS 1067 still contained
some quite harsh policy prescriptions. A number of experts from the
Treasury and Justice Departments were sent to Germany to investigate
the involvement of German firms in war crimes and to find out what
links had continued to exist with U.S. industry after the American
entry into World War II. They were also delegated to make certain that
the postwar structures and operations of the big German corporations
were being decentralized so as to make the preparation of another war
impossible.

In line with Roosevelt's above-mentioned view of a direct link between cartels and the Nazi regime, "decartelization" became the order
of the day in OMGUS. But this concept had two quite different mean-
ings. When General Lucius D. Clay arrived in Germany as Dwight D.
Eisenhower's deputy, he came as a hard-liner determined to punish the
Germans.[43] As he began to tour the country and saw the bombed-out
cities and factories, he—being a southerner—seems to have been reminded of what he had learned in school about the devastation that the
Civil War had left behind in the American South. A starving population
and the difficulty of getting production going in the hope of relieving
the American taxpayer contributed to his change of mind. The shift was
described by one of his staff, Charles Kindleberger:[44] "From 1942–1945 I
was engaged in helping to take the German economy apart; from 1945–
1947, I was busy helping to put it back together again."

However, among Clay's staff there were a number of officers who had remained sympathetic to Morgenthau's ideas and for whom "decartelization" had a broader meaning. For them it was not just a question of implementing a Sherman-style ban on cartels, syndicates, and monopolies. It was also a tool they could wield to break up big corporations and to effect a far-reaching "industrial disarmament." At the same time, Clay was surrounded by members of the "reconstructionist" camp. They were complemented by corporate executives and other experts who arrived in the Western zones straightaway in 1945.

At first they came as individuals. Among the early visitors was an American economics professor who traveled in war-torn West Germany soon after the end of the war where he encountered the opinion "that the present catastrophic situation could be rapidly and fundamentally overcome."[45] On the one hand, he had inspected "several engineering shops and steel-works which can be completely written off"; on the other, "the three largest plants of I.G. Farben" were "almost undamaged." According to "officers of Rhine Coal Control . . . the Ruhr mines have hardly suffered any damage." A Krupp director had assured him that steel production could also be raised to levels of up to two-thirds of wartime production or more. Judging from "surprisingly good conditions of the Krupp plants in the centre of ruined Essen and in the suburb of Borbeck" he did not think that what he had heard and seen was an unrealistic estimate. Another individual visitor was Winthrop Aldrich of the Chase National Bank and president of the American Chamber of Commerce, who came back complaining that there existed no systematic program for the reintegration of the West German economy into Western Europe.

Faced with a chaotic situation, Clay began to look for advice from the American business community. In 1946, he asked Lewis H. Brown, the chairman of the Johns Manville Corporation, to spend "as much time as possible in Germany to get first-hand information as a basis for a report on what should be done to get German industry on its feet and off the backs of the American tax-payers as soon as possible."[46] Subsequently, Brown talked to dozens of business leaders and bureaucrats in the United States and in Europe, including twenty-five unnamed West German managers. In the end, he produced an entirely pragmatic report that first discussed historical aspects before offering a plan for reconstruction and a summary of recommendations. Brown pinpointed what he thought were the mistakes made at the Potsdam Conference in July and August 1945. He declared dismantling impracticable because it did not furnish know-how for operating machinery and argued that the Level of Industry Plan that listed plants earmarked for removal revealed "in inconsistencies."

Brown also highlighted the food and coal shortages that had led to starvation and a booming black market. He was quite critical of the all-too-long de-Nazification procedures that deprived the "economic machine of the Germany of the very leadership necessary for its revival." Industry, he wrote, "must be freed to export," before enumerating the obstacles that Stalin, but also the French and British had put in the path of recovery. Railing at the Level of Industry Plan, Brown concluded that pursuing it would "restore exactly those conditions which breed Nazi and Communist totalitarianism." It seems that this report helped to modify the Allied reparations program and to reorganize the Western zones of occupation in the face of the evident failure of continuing the wartime cooperation with the Soviet Union. Philip D. Reed (GE president) apparently came to Germany with a similar mandate from Averell Harriman, the secretary of commerce, to see if this particular department could help with Clay's economic plans.

The largest group of visitors consisted of those who wanted to inspect the extent of the destruction of installations that they had owned until the Nazis had taken them over during the war. One of them was Major H. Rand, Jr., whose actions give some insight into how various networks were being mobilized. He had received a letter from a German detailing "certain plans which Remington Rand had respecting their German subsidiaries."[47] It appeared "from the letter that Major Rand, acting in the name of his company (not the army), was very busy last April and May 1945 getting his company's business underway."

Meanwhile Ford managers had come over to help restart production at the corporation's Cologne plant. For various reasons GM waited until May 1948 to decide on a resumption of ownership and production at Rüsselsheim. In June 1946, a delegation of the National Association of Manufacturers came at the invitation of Clay. Up to April 1946, some two hundred Americans had visited factories in the American zone and West Berlin. By August 1946, the rising numbers so concerned Clay's office that it asked for some "agency in Washington or elsewhere which wants to assume responsibility for picking a few businessmen from among the throng."[48] OMGUS also wanted to be sure "that buyers be buyers and not tourists, carpet-beggars, investors, or investigators of international restitution questions." A quota of 500 visitors per month might be manageable, "with 250 allocated to US types of all sorts, and 250 divided among the British, French, Dutch, Swiss, Swedes etc. on some basis to be negotiated with the British (on a reciprocal basis) and capable of explanation." A group of some fourteen executives probably arrived under those new rules in April 1947.

Even if they did not report their impressions as extensively as Brown, they all came back with views on what should be done in Western

Germany. Thus, GM's Alfred Sloan told a no doubt less enthusiastic Bernard Baruch in November 1945 that no other European countries could match Germany's efficiency and skilled labor. These and other factors could lay the foundations of postwar industrial development and efficient production and the Ruhr region was still the powerhouse, to be used for European reconstruction at large.[49] By 1949, West German industrialists such as Otto Friedrich of Phoenix A.G. in Hamburg-Harburg were on their way to the United States to revive business contacts from the 1930s. In April of that year OMGUS organized an industrial exhibition in New York at which some five hundred West German companies displayed their wares.[50]

To be sure, few of the visitors wanted to go back to the industrial structures of the Weimar Republic. Like Paul Hoffman, Brown, and others they wanted to ban cartels and syndicates in the strict sense but also to preserve large industrial units as engines of growth, and not merely for West Germany, but also for stimulating competition in Western Europe more generally. With U.S. Steel's Stettinius as Hull's successor, other "dollar-a-year" men had been brought in, such as William Knudsen (GM), Donald Nelson (Sears, Roebuck & Co.), and Will Clayton (Anderson Clayton).

Hoffman's trusted advisors were Thomas K. Finletter of Coudert Bros., James Zellerbach of Crown Zellerbach, James G. Blaine, president of the New York Midland Trust, and David Bruce of Baltimore with ties to the Mellon family.[51] Other like-minded individuals came out of the Washington administration, such as Milton Katz and Richard Bissell, Jr. This kind of stacking of the deck with businessmen was bound to lead, sooner or later, to a showdown with the "Morgenthauians" clustered in Clay's office around Col. Bernard Bernstein. He pursued a more comprehensive decartelization policy, but quickly clashed with the "reconstructionists" who began to demand his removal. By the end of 1946, they had won and Bernstein went back to the United States. His successor was James S. Martin, who was put in charge of what was now called the OMGUS De-Cartelization Branch.[52] Martin also advocated a ban on cartels, but rejected a Bernsteinian "industrial disarmament." His approach was much more to the liking of William Draper, his superior as head of the OMGUS Economic Division.

In many ways, Draper is an even more fascinating player among the "reconstructionists" than Hoffman.[53] He had worked for Dillon Read & Co., the investment firm that had floated many American loans during the Weimar years. Although he had the elevated military rank of general, he was much more a thoroughbred businessman who tended to irritate Clay by constantly talking business. Draper, as Martin's superior, supported decartelization in the narrow sense and was therefore opposed to a far-reaching breakup of German trusts. Only when corporations had gained a monopoly position in a particular branch of industry was Draper disposed to wield the knife to impose (limited) deconcentration. Accordingly, it was I.G. Farben and Vereinigte Stahlwerke (VSt) that were earmarked for breakup. The former was eventually cut up into four units: Bayer Leverkusen, Farbwerke Hoechst, Badische Anilin- und Soda-Fabriken (BASF), and Casella.[54] VSt was similarly divided into smaller units so that in the end there were some twenty-three companies, of which thirteen formerly belonged to VSt.[55] The Thyssen Trust was the largest among them, with a market share of some 25 percent.

Other firms also appeared on Allied lists, including Bosch, the Stuttgart electrical engineering firm, that had a well-known anti-Nazi record but was charged with monopoly practices.[56] The investigations continued until the early 1950s before they were abandoned. Other companies had charges against them dropped more quickly, so that inevitably the question arose how far considerations of trying to help a former or future German partner rather than the prescriptions of Allied law were a factor. A number of other big German corporations, such as Siemens, escaped early plans for their breakup, and this also applied to the banking system and in particular to Deutsche Bank, the largest financial institution, among several others.[57]

The key point about the Draper era is that the Economic Division enjoyed the support of the American business community also because it was keen to thwart a renewal of the Arnoldian "antitrust" drive back home and further investigations into the involvement of American trusts in the international cartel movement of the interwar period with their contacts with German firms before and after the American entry into World War II. Members of the Justice Department had poked into these contacts in the early 1940s. Just a few years later, when the talk among businessmen was about the reconstruction of Germany and Europe and about boosting American exports, it was better to sweep these charges under the rug. The British government, with its own conglomerates pushing from behind, retreated for the same reasons. Only a few Ruhr enterprises remained on their dismantling list. After all, ICI had been founded on the I.G. Farben model in mid-1920s and had been involved in cooperations that had been so characteristic of relations in the chemical industry in all three countries during the interwar years all the way up to the Düsseldorf Agreement of March 1939 and beyond.

Thus a powerful business coalition had come into being in the United States that agreed with the "reconstructionists" around Hoffman and Draper based in Western Europe. They had joined the war effort to defeat Axis annexationism and autarkic bloc formation and to help establish the Open Door and the move toward an American-style oligopolistic competitive market capitalism. Cartel behavior, subject to prosecution in the United States since before 1914, became criminalized in occupied Germany. But the limited breakup of companies preserved large production units that, as Hoffman had explained to the Senate in 1950, were to act as powerful tractors in the reconstruction as well as the recasting of *European* industry. Some scholars have felt that German industry should have undergone a much more radical reform. What happened was, in their eyes, a conservative restoration of German capitalism, but they have missed the crucial *recasting* element in the American design.[58]

To be sure, the Western zones retained an economy based on the private ownership of the means of production and finance, in contrast to the socioeconomic revolution that was imposed by the Soviets in the East. Yet, in the conception of the Hoffmans and Drapers, reconstruction always meant an *Umbau* of the highly cartelized German capitalism of the interwar years. This capitalism was to be wrenched free from its old organizational moorings to be aligned with the American model of a competitive, oligopolistic regime to which the New Deal had added a number of major welfare-statist elements. Even if some of these elements were being modified by entrepreneurial lobbyism in the late 1940s, there was no return to the older liberal-capitalist ideologies and practices—at least not until the 1980s when Reaganomics and Margaret Thatcher came along. In other words, the bricks of the postwar West German industrial "house" would not be laid in the same way as before, but along the lines of the American industrial system so as to ensure its functionality within a multilateral world trading system that the United States had begun to build under the aegis of its corporate leaders.

Autarkic territorial blocs would be a thing of the past, and not least because of American pressure to adopt the new economic structures. In line with Arnold's arguments in *Bottlenecks of Business*, these structures were in harmony with those of a democratic *political* constitution. Because the West Germans saw the benefits, the Federal Republic came to be based on these latter principles in the Basic Law of 1949. They had existed, though without strong roots, in society during the Weimar years before the Nazis had eradicated them. Now a majority of the population welcomed and supported the new political constitution with its catalogue of fundamental rights.

Britain, whether under Churchill or Attlee, had considerably more leverage than occupied West Germany to resist the Open Door that American industry and Wall Street were pushing for as part of what might be called an International New Deal, offered to Europe, though not to the non-European world. Even if the age of colonialism was over both objectively and in the minds of American decision makers, the British Empire was too firmly rooted in the British Establishment and society to be abandoned in the hour of victory. Instead London attempted to salvage it as part of a preferential trading bloc. The United States urged the British government to join in the unification of Western Europe that Washington promoted as a larger market on the condition that it did not become yet another preferential tariff zone. But in 1950 London kept outside the embryonic framework of unity, the European Coal and Steel Community (ECSC). This—as will be discussed in a later section—greatly complicated the country's future role within the Commonwealth as well as its relationships with the United States and the ECSC, which was expanded into the European Economic Community (EEC) in 1957.

7. The Response of West German Industry to America's Recasting Efforts

Before returning to British-American economic relations, this is the point to examine a further obstacle that appeared in the way of the American "recasters" and that proved more formidable than they thought: West German managers and those of the Ruhr heavy industries in particular. Although this barricade was ultimately also removed, the German-American negotiations and conflicts in this field lasted well into the 1950s. A first major stumbling block was the opposition to the dismantling of machinery in the Western zones of occupation, which seemed quite irrational at a time when Secretary of State James Byrnes, in a major speech in Stuttgart in September 1946, had proclaimed that the West Germans would be reintegrated into the Atlantic community of nations and its trading system. But rumors persisted that the "Morgenthauians" were continuing their work. The belated arrest and internment of many managers in the autumn of 1945 as well as the de-Nazification procedures to which all adult Germans had to submit merely augmented feelings of resentment and injustice. Finally, there was little public support when prominent industrialists, such as Alfried Krupp, Friedrich Flick, and the entire board of I.G. Farben, were put in the dock at Nuremberg, however justified their indictments were in light of their involvement in the slave labor system and other Nazi crimes.[59]

It is against the background of these emotions that the structures and practices of German industry before 1933 did not seem so damnable in the eyes of most West German businessmen. After all, the cartels and syndicates had supposedly proven their worth in the *Kaiserreich* and the Weimar Republic. They had—so it was now claimed—merely been warped and abused by the Hitler dictatorship. The role of big business in the collapse of the Weimar Republic was played down, if not even denied. With the Ruhr region still the potential powerhouse of Western Europe, the British occupation authorities had to bear the brunt of the opposition to Allied occupations policies. The Labour government in London continued to talk about a nationalization of basic industries in the Ruhr region. No less objectionable, London, in alliance with the West German trade unions, had introduced *paritätische Mitbestimmung* in the coal and steel industries.[60] This system of codetermination had put union representatives on the supervisory board and, even more radically, had created the position of a "worker director" who sat with equal rights on the management board.

There was strong opposition to codetermination from the Ruhr managers, but it turned out to be a blessing in the long run in its subsequently modified form, that is, without "worker directors," but elected consultative employee "works councils." This fostered relative peace between the two sides of industry during the postwar decades. The irony was that the model was introduced with the help of the British whose labor relations were not reformed and, as in the 1920s, proved to be a major problem through the 1970s. Although Stafford Cripps had, as early as October 1946, "expressed the opinion that British industry controlled by the workers is at present an impossibility," Labour pursued its nationalization policies that never delivered the "efficiencies" that were promised to come from it.[61] Industrial strife continued, reaching new heights in the 1970s, until Prime Minister Margaret Thatcher came along and virtually destroyed the British labor unions in the 1980s. Her economic policies finalized the shift from manufacturing industry toward the City that boomed until the crisis of 2008 when it had to be rescued by the state.

Although the American "steel people" who appeared in Düsseldorf after the founding of the Bi-Zone did not like codetermination with its mixing of capital and labor, it was too late to stop it for Ruhr heavy industry. When in 1950 the trade unions wanted to extend this model to all large enterprises in all branches, the American business community was not unhappy that the resistance of West German industry was vigorous. The extension bill failed in the West German parliament, which, with the founding of the Federal Republic, had begun to convert Allied decrees into proper legislation, as laid down in the new parliamentary-democratic constitution, the Basic Law. What was put on the statute books instead was the Works Constitution Law that gave the unions rights of consultation and information in all enterprises over two thousand employees.

However, the Americans were quite determined to proscribe cartels and syndicates and to break up monopolies, such as VSt, though only to the degree that they became oligopolies. So, when cartels had at first been banned in Sherman-style fashion by Allied decree, German resistance, even outside the Ruhr region, was strong and raised American suspicions that cartels continued to exist covertly. The Bi-Partite Control Office (BICO) was supposed to police the bans and also to enlighten companies and their trade associations why it was to their ultimate benefit to accept the abolition of the old system.[62] When in early 1949 the rubber industries association was suspected of violating the ban and of engaging once again in restrictive practices, a delegation was invited to the BICO office for a discussion. Among the members was Otto A. Friedrich, soon to become a prominent figure in postwar German-American business networks. His biography and role in the larger picture of West German reconstruction will be discussed in a moment. Here his account of what went on at this meeting is of interest.[63] According to Friedrich, the BICO representative began by stressing that his agency was not opposed to industrial associations, but wanted to promote free and fair competition. Americans, he added, did not expect the Germans to share American attitudes toward competition completely as long as they moved in a similar direction. The German economy was to be freed from all restrictions.

During the subsequent discussion Friedrich got up to challenge BICO policies and engaged the American in a lively discussion on cartels. He had just returned from a trip to the United States, where he had resumed old contacts for a possible partnership between his company, Phoenix A.G., and B.F. Goodrich in Akron, Ohio; but he had also studied American "antitrust" legislation and enforcement. His interlocutor was probably surprised by the questioner's detailed knowledge of American law and practice and, while responding flexibly, held the line on what American decartelization was designed to accomplish in West Germany. Since he was himself in favor of building a competitive economy, Friedrich subsequently saw himself as a mediator and used internal meetings with his colleagues to persuade them accept the principle of competition.[64] He even mocked their timidity and the various "deeper reasons" that they gave for the retention of restrictive practices. At the same time and having worked in the German rubber cartel system in the 1930s, he could not feel but sympathy with his colleagues. The belief in this system, he acknowledged, was so ingrained in German business culture that it might take years of hard work to change long-standing habits.

However, he felt that practicing the new rules might help, the more so since from the American point of view time was running out on the special leverage that the United States had as an occupying power. The founding of the Federal Republic and the ratification of the Basic Law shifted the legislative balance toward a democratically elected West German parliament, with the Allies merely retaining certain residual powers of intervention in times of crisis. Accordingly, OMGUS and its successor, the U.S. High Commission, decided to concentrate on the "big fish" among the "cartelists" and to break up whatever anticompetitive practices still existed among the trusts in coal and steel, chemicals, and electrical engineering. In the end, some of the trusts in the Rhineland were simply ordered to get rid of restrictive agreements and to accept a limited breakup into oligopolies. Vertical integrations between coal and steel in the Ruhr as well as the *Deutscher Kohlenverkauf* (DKV), a sales syndicate, were dissolved against the will of the resentful Ruhr bosses. I.G. Farben—as has been mentioned above—was divided into four units.

Although these were the cases in which the Americans eventually put their foot down, they by and large adhered to patient persuasion. In this respect they adhered to a principle that Edward Mason, the Harvard economist and astute CED author, had formulated in his book in 1946:[65] "If any permanent anti-monopoly policy could be put into effect during the period of Allied occupation, the disruption and disorder incident to this application would count for little. Of all the institutions and policies known to history, however, those imposed by victors on a vanquished enemy are likely to be the most impermanent. The only lasting structural changes that can be made in the German economic and political system will have to be made, in the absence of continuous occupation, by the Germans themselves." These were no doubt wise words, and over the longer term this is what happened. The recasting occurred because the West Germans, supported by their political and economic elites, eventually wanted it themselves.

Furthermore, they were also prepared not only to put American reconstruction aid to good use, but also to join Hoffman's "Productivity Councils."[66] This was a program to provide intellectual support under the auspices of the Marshall Plan. It enabled industrialists, trade unionists, and also administrators, such as officers of Federal Railways, to visit the United States and its major industrial centers in Michigan, Ohio, and Pennsylvania to study technology, labor relations, management practices, and work organization. The hope was that they would come back having seen not only a Fordist production system, but also American living standards, including the many cars in the parking lots outside the factories. As Mason had suggested, this was seen as a more subtle way of changing a society and its industries than an Allied ruling from the top.

One of the consequences of the accelerated recasting of West German industry was that, once Allied decrees had to be replaced by parliamentary legislation, some very conservative and deeply resentful Ruhr bosses were able, through their lobbyism among the politicians, to delay until 1957 the Law for Securing Competition, which banned cartels and syndicates. It took economics minister Ludwig Erhard, the prime advocate of this law, almost ten years before he succeeded.[67] But before analyzing these developments and the role of American big business in them, it is time to turn to the reconstruction of British industry in the later 1940s and the fate of the Anglo-American wartime "special relationship."

8. Britain and the Difficulties of Economic Reconstruction

As has already been mentioned, the cancellation of Lend-Lease came as a great shock to the British. After all, with the help of American finance they had been hoping to convert their war industries to civilian production, to stimulate their exports, and to provide full employment for some 4.5 million members of His Majesty's victorious armed forces, together with increased social security benefits for all. Some 270,000 soldiers and 60,000 civilians had been killed. Just as after World War I, their families had to be supported and wartime promises of improvements in social welfare had to be fulfilled.

The problems that the country was facing were indeed enormous and—it should not be forgotten—they were in large part the result of Germany having started another world war and the American political and economic elites being determined to make certain that their vision of a multilateral, bloc-free world trading system would under their leadership emerge from the conflict. Aware of this strategy, a report prepared on the basis of consultations with British entrepreneurs for the War Cabinet's Reconstruction Committee by the Board of Trade, titled "Long-Term Prospects of British Industry," had warned as early as June 1944 that the country would have to "secure a substantial increase of export trade: an average increase of 50 per cent is being authoritatively mentioned."[68] Yet "for many industries the prospect of securing an expansion of exports is doubtful, *unless* there is an increase in their competitive power, together with increased prosperity in overseas markets and a decrease in the barriers hampering international trade." In making this latter point, the Board of Trade was apparently thinking of American import tariffs, whose continued existence was regarded as a case of American hypocrisy. Surely, when preaching the Open Door, this principle should also apply to the United States. However, as in other fields, Congress lay across the tracks of a change, even if the Truman administration had wanted it. Worse, the "Buy-American" campaigns also continued. Returning to Britain's own internal problems, the report concluded that, if there was no improvement of competitive power (or "'efficiency,' using the word in its widest sense to include production costs, style design, marketing methods etc."), performance would be more likely the same as in the sluggish 1930s.

There was also Britain's impoverishment due to the war that was reflected in several statistics. Thus consumption of basic food items was lower at the end of 1944 than before 1939, and it was clear that the rationing that had been introduced would have to continue. The external debt at the end of the conflict stood at £2,000 million or possibly even £3,000 million, despite the fact that many overseas assets had been used to pay for the military equipment and food that had to be imported.[69] Apart from the promised social reforms and nationalization plans, the Labour government was also struggling with the continuously high expenditures for defense. In 1946 they ran into some £300 million and included occupation costs in Germany. There was also the expensive program to develop a nuclear capability. Given all these burdens, it is small wonder that London was forced to agree to the creation of the Bi-Zone with the United States. On their own the British just did not have the wherewithal to get production in the Ruhr mining industry going and to feed the population for whose survival they were responsible under occupation law.

Theoretically, there was a way out of this crisis, that is, through increased export earnings. But this required an expansion of between 50 and 70 percent—a patently unrealistic goal. After all, not merely American industry was appearing on the world market in order to avert a 1921-style reconversion slump back home. The Western Europeans, including the West Germans, were doing the same, with Clay, Hoffman, and others working tirelessly to turn West Germany into the engine of growth of Western European reconstruction. The cancellation of Lend-Lease had in Keynes's words been a "financial Dunkirk"; in December 1945, Robert Bothby had spoken of an "economic Munich" while Hugh Dalton concluded that Britain was facing "total economic ruin."[70] To avoid such a disaster, negotiations took place in the autumn of 1945 for a fresh American loan. The Agreement that was finally signed was not ungenerous. To begin with, it reduced the Lend-Lease debt from around $2,000 million to $650 million. As to the new loan, the original request was for $6,000 million, which the British side then reduced to $4,000 million, having learned that the Americans were thinking of $3,500 million.[71] When the American negotiators insisted on their figure and negotiations became deadlocked, the case was finally put to Truman who split the difference and signed off on $3,750 million at 2 percent interest over fifty years.

The press was less than happy about this deal. The *Manchester Guardian* commented that the British had saved their freedom in the war "at a great price," whereas the Americans had "materially saved theirs at a profit."[72] What was even more horrifying, the paper added, had been to watch "the progress of the loan through Congress. Most people must often have felt they would like to withdraw the whole thing rather than be under obligation to a legislative body containing so many ignorant and ill-natured members." The *Economist* echoed the bitterness, writing that it was no longer possible to rely on Congress "to pursue with any consistency the policy of moderation and liberality without which the whole structure of the loan, of Bretton Woods and of non-discriminatory trade is built on sand."[73] *The Times of London* was more resigned, feeling that the country had no choice but to accept the loan, even if "with a heavy heart."[74] It was not the end of the ordeal. The American loan, as negotiated in the autumn of 1945, quickly proved inadequate. The next step came after the announcement of the Marshall Plan in June 1947: By 1948 its funds began to flow into Europe, with Britain receiving a major chunk. Again this support helped some—until the next crisis in 1949 that resulted in the humiliating devaluation of the pound.

This step showed that, like industry, the City was in not in good shape. By the end of the war, the value of income from foreign investments had fallen to below 40 percent of what it had been before 1939. With invisible earnings from abroad down, investment policies at home had reduced the banking system's lending capacity. During the war the clearing banks had taken on "large amounts of government securities" and Treasury Deposit Receipts (TDRs) in particular, and this as well as "general war controls constrained the private sector's ability to borrow; the share of advances fell sharply, reaching a record low of some 16 per cent of total deposits at the end of 1945."[75] There was a doubling of advances between 1946 and 1952 in absolute terms. But "the continuing importance of public securities and the retention of wartime controls" over banks and the private sector more generally "meant that in relative terms only a modest recovery" took place up to 1951. In assessing the situation, the Radcliffe Committee had pointed out that many of the commercial and industrial loans were short-term when more long-term finance was needed. There was also the old practice of British banks to provide no more than overdraft facilities that could be revoked at any time and made business planning even more precarious.[76]

To overcome such bottlenecks, the Bank of England together with the Scottish clearing banks now created the Industrial and Commercial Finance Corporation. It was designed to aid small and medium-sized firms whose "capital requirements were not large enough to justify raising funds on the stock market" and yet surpassed the lending capacity of ordinary banks.[77] In some ways, the corporation copied the Rooseveltian model of the 1930s, but its impact fell short of actual needs to stimulate production and to modernize machinery. It was certainly less successful than Jean Monnet's Modernization Plan in France and the solutions—to be discussed below—that West German industry found for its capital needs beyond the Marshall funds it had been receiving from Paul Hoffman.

Britain's difficulties were almost bound to lead to conflicts with the labor unions that, as in the 1920s, frequently disrupted production. In both 1945 and 1946 the number of stoppages reached over 2,200 with over two million workdays lost. There was a slight improvement between 1948 and 1953 when the figure hoverred around 1,700, before rising again to over 2,000 in the late 1950s and early 1960s. In 1962 strikes involved some 4.4 million workers, with a loss of around 5.7 million workdays. However, just as it would be wrong to put all responsibility for Britain's social and economic woes at the door of German military aggression in 1939 and American reluctance to rescue British industry and finance in 1945, it would also be too simple to put the blame for poor industrial relations at the door of militant unions, their shop stewards, and disgruntled workers whose living standards, notwithstanding many promises, barely rose above wartime scarcity. There was also the old problem of entrepreneurial and managerial attitudes. Thus, the ailing shipbuilding industry remained "imprisoned by History."[78] Textiles present an even better case in point. The cotton industry's structures dated back to the nineteenth century and were still run by all too many undercapitalized family firms.

Change was not easy to effect, when even the Department of Overseas Trade took the view that it was "better to use machinery, even if obsolete, to produce yarn at prices which at least cover the costs of using the machines" rather than keeping them idle—when there was no money to replace them.[79] After all, the department continued, even if "prices received do not cover the full interest and depreciation charges on the machinery at the value at which they happen to stand in the books of the firm . . . it is better that he [the spinner] should be permitted to produce and give employment to his labour and equipment to the benefit of the home consumer or the export trade." Accordingly, it was even thought "undesirable" that "amalgamations" be used to "enable obsolete machinery to be bought up or scrapped."[80] For "it withdraws production equipment which might still be capable of making some contribution to the relief of shortage." It also raised "operating costs of the purchase-for-scrap," and it weakened "the competitive position of the amalgamation." The sense of frustration that these realities engendered was well encapsulated in the verdict that the textile industry was "in the hands of old men, prone to take short views" who were thought to favor "price-fixing arrangements, state subsidies and increased levels of protection." A mere 6 percent of the weaving and 8 percent of the spinning machinery had been installed since 1945.[81] To call this "misdirected modernisation" is probably too mild a description of what was going on in the textile industry.[82]

The predicament of the British iron and steel industry was somewhat better, but it suffered from transitional problems when it was finally nationalized by Labour in 1949. Some investments, it is true, had been made in the 1930s that had increased capacity by another two million tons by 1939. But much of basic plant had become obsolete, "especially in the highly export dependent tin plate sector."[83] The greater efficiency that nationalization was supposed to bring about was not achieved. By contrast, chemicals, machine tools, motor vehicles, and electrical goods industries could look more optimistically into the future. The verdicts on textiles and steel are therefore not meant to say that the overall performance of the economy was unimpressive. And yet the larger underlying problem of insufficient modernization continued, and it is by making comparisons with other European countries that these weaknesses became visible. At the same time the sterling area's dollar deficit kept rising, putting pressure on the distribution of aid under the Marshall Plan. With Bank of England reserves rapidly dwindling, some in the Labour government were contemplating a further retreat into the Empire and Commonwealth. This being unacceptable to Washington, negotiations began to provide more Marshall funding. The way to stop the constant drain of sterling reserves was through a devaluation of the pound. This step, however humiliating, would, it was hoped, increase British exports to the United States. Britain's trade deficit began to disappear, and by June 1950 it achieved a trade surplus of $200 million, followed by steady growth into the late 1950s.

Still, the bad blood that all this left in Anglo-American relations, partly because of Cripps's stubbornness and his angry talk of a dollar dictatorship, partly because of growing frustrations on the American side, merely made the British cabinet more determined to rely on the Empire and Commonwealth. Meanwhile the Americans continued to push from two directions. In quite relentless pursuit of their larger economic strategy of the Open Door, they worked for the implementation of more global frameworks of multilateral trade, such as the

International Trade Organization (ITO) and the General Agreement on Tariffs and Trade (GATT), the grand plan, developed at Bretton Woods, New Hampshire, to lower tariffs throughout the Western international economy. The meeting was no less important in terms of the long-term American quest to make the dollar the dominant Western currency and to relegate sterling to the second rank.[84] To this extent it might be said that Wall Street had finally won out against the City, as would become abundantly clear after 1945 and in 1956 in particular.

At the same time, Washington nudged the Western Europeans to build a federation, designed to create a larger market but also as a bulwark against the Soviet Union, now that the Cold War had set in. The GATT and ITO negotiations were inevitably slowed down not just because of Britain's reluctance to lower tariff barriers and remove other impediments to the Open Door, but also because of other powers, such as France, with their own imperial possessions to defend. As to European integration, it became clear that while there were many Western Europeans who wished for a political "United States of Europe," the majority of the population did not want to embark upon such an experiment that included West Germany. A few years after the end of Nazi occupation people just could not envision close cooperation with a brutal former enemy.

With GATT negotiations dragging along and the *political* integration of Western Europe going nowhere, the Americans, in the face of an escalating conflict with Stalin, began to push for European economic union. Time and again Hoffman and his colleagues encouraged the Western Europeans to move toward a closer integration of their economies. This time they urged the French, who had been upset about the distribution of ECA funds and about being kept in the dark about the sterling devaluation, to take the lead. As Hoffman put it on 31 October 1949, Western Europe should "create a single large market within which qualitative restrictions on the movement of goods, money barriers to the flow of payments, and eventually all tariffs are permanently swept away." Without this integration, he added, bilateral barter might again become the pattern. His theme was an old but now more insistently heard one, as he kept rephrasing ideas that Dean Acheson at the State Department, for example, had articulated shortly before Marshall's speech at Harvard in June 1947 when he spoke of "the creation of an all-European organization designed to accelerate lagging reconstruction and to achieve greater long-run economic unity in Europe."[85]

The refusal of Britain to join this enterprise together with the structural and attitudinal conditions prevailing in its economy help explain why the political and economic elites of the country resisted American attempts to establish a larger and competitive European market as well as a multilateral world trading system. The Empire and Commonwealth were not to be voluntarily dismantled. Even if Britain's colonial possessions were crumbling in South Asia and the Middle East, tariff preferences were to be upheld. If competition became too strong in third markets, these were the regions of the world in which the mother country held commercial advantages that it was determined to defend. In 1942, Churchill had proclaimed that he had "not become the King's First Minister in order to preside over the liquidation of the British Empire."[86] Even if this was happening on the watch first of the Attlee government and then of his own (after Churchill regained power in 1951), colonialism was upheld, until Britain was stopped by the United States during the Suez Crisis. Significantly, it was also the point at which the reconstruction and recasting of West Germany had largely succeeded and the EEC, with its essentially open market, had been founded through the enlargement of the ECSC.

9. The Origins of the European Coal and Steel Community

The idea of creating a common market, starting with coal and steel, was being promoted by the Americans in the hope that it might appease the French, who had joined the Bi-Zone in April 1948 with their southwest German zonal territory.[87] Having been in the forefront of attempts to weaken German industrial power by dismantling plants in their zone, Paris assumed that the formation of the Tri-Zone entitled it to a voice in the Ruhr region's recasting and now advocated the creation of an International Ruhr Authority. Wedded to the reconstruction of West Germany under American leadership, the Truman administration refused to consider a French-led internationalization of the Ruhr. As has been mentioned above, Hoffman's idea was rather to harness West German production and management skills to the restructuring of Western Europe as a whole. When this sank in, Jean Monnet, after completing the modernization program of French industry, came up with a proposal that he submitted to Robert Schuman, the French Foreign Minister, in the spring of 1950. He recommended a pooling of French and West German coal and steel production. Certain activities going on at the time between the Ruhr and Lorrainean industries may have triggered this plan. At least there appeared, in early 1950, press reports, that the two industries were talking about a *private* coordination of their operations.[88] Alarmed that this might mean a revival of the international cartels of the interwar period, Monnet, while favoring the economic integration of the two regions, insisted that any such arrangement must be supervised by a powerful supranational office.

After its announcement in May 1950 and the inclusion of Italy and the Benelux countries, the Schuman Plan, as it came to be called, became the subject of protracted negotiations that ended with the initialing of the ECSC Treaty in April 1951. There are three aspects to this treaty that are relevant to the state of the European-American relationship in the early 1950s. After the State Department's Dean Acheson had been quite worried that the Western European coal and steel pool might be a 1920s-style international cartel in a different guise put forward to turn Europe into a closed trading bloc, "antitrust" clauses, to be enforced by a High Authority, were inserted into the ECSC treaty, which kept the door open to foreign trade.[89] Furthermore, in order to create a level playing field for international competitors, a resentful Ruhr industry was cajoled by U.S. High Commissioner John McCloy into accepting the dissolution of the DKV coal sales syndicate. The idea was to establish, within the projected ECSC, a rough balance of economic power between the Ruhr and Lorraine regions. As Sidney Willner, one of McCloy's assistants involved in the negotiations, explained, the American intervention was designed to reassure the French.[90] With Britain staying out of the pool, France was understandably nervous about facing the mighty Ruhr coal and steel corporations. To create a better industrial balance, the U.S. High Commission clipped the wings of the Ruhr trusts.

Following these American actions, the initialing of the ECSC Treaty hung in the balance until the spring of 1951, largely because of the obstructionism of some Ruhr operatives. Just as Otto A. Friedrich had found in 1949 when meeting with his colleagues in the rubber industry, the conservative coal and steel managers could not visualize a market economy without cartels and syndicates. But there were always other people who realized that the ECSC could not be allowed to fail. One of them was Günter Henle, Peter Klöckner's son-in-law, who, after the death of the latter, had taken charge of the Klöckner steel empire.[91] Another was Hans-Günter Sohl, who, learning from his experiences on the VSt management board, decided to streamline the Thyssen corporation into a "pure" steel trust along American lines by ridding it of the vertical integration with coal mining.[92] Sohl was certainly farsighted: with the rise of oil, the Ruhr coal industry soon lapsed into deep crisis, while steel thrived in the 1950s. It was only in the 1960s that Thyssen Steel also ran into trouble when new competitors, such as Japan, appeared on the world market.

Although the Ruhr industry was under considerable pressure from the U.S. High Commission in Germany to recast its organizations, there was an upside to American industrial policy that has often been forgotten. While the West German share of Marshall Plan funds was smaller than that of Britain or France, ultimately amounting to some $1,537 million, McCloy had another source of reconstruction funding that he alone was in charge of and did not have to submit to Congress for scrutiny.[93] This was a program called "Government Appropriations for Relief in Occupied Areas" (GARIOA) and contained special funds allocated to the Department of the Army for the administration of the American zone "to prevent disease and unrest." From July 1946 to March 1950, OMGUS and its successor, the U.S. High Commission, had distributed food, but also fertilizer, seeds, and gasoline to the tune of $1,620 million.[94] In fact, up to 70 percent of mostly GARIOA-funded deliveries to the Bi-Zone were in foodstuffs until 1948. While the comprehensive London Foreign Debt agreement that the Federal Republic negotiated in 1952–53 included the promise to repay $1,000 million of all GARIOA and ERP funds in installments until 1966, by 1949 the feeding of the West German population was no longer a priority and the unused funds were thenceforth deployed to pay for raw materials and vital industrial imports and credits.

As German industry was being rebuilt and recast and exports were still lower than imports, about half the German trade deficit was covered by GARIOA and ERP funds. Meanwhile the gains (counterpart funds) of these deliveries were put into a special account from which McCloy was able to offer investment credits on quite favorable terms to West German and West Berlin's commerce and industry. In this way the counterpart funds were used to provide medium-term and long-term loans for industries in which bottlenecks had developed. Once the Korean War had broken out, these bottlenecks affected the coal, steel, and electricity generating industries in particular. To facilitate the distribution of all these funds, BICO had approved in November 1948 the founding of a bank, the Kreditanstalt für Wiederaufbau (KfW, Credit Institution for Reconstruction) that by the end of 1950 had channeled some 3,200 million marks into the economy, of which three-quarters came from counterpart funds, the rest from a reviving private market.[95] Some of KfW's investments went into job creation programs; others to increase productivity.

However, the final distribution of loans took place under the auspices of the Investment Auxiliary Law (Investitionshilfegesetz, IHG) of 1952, another instrument that helped boost the West German economy.[96] Since it was calculable that the GARIOA/ERP funds would be running out, it was domestic industry and finance that devised yet another scheme to move credits where they were most needed. Thanks to the beginning boom in civilian goods, manufacturing was doing sufficiently well to agree to a kind of self-denying ordinance by which they would support with some of their own resources the modernization and expansion of coal and steel—two basic commodities on which manufacturing industry depended, including coal-fired electricity generation.

It should have become clear by now that, while West German industry was put under Allied pressure to restructure and to join the ECSC, relief came at the other end not only via Hoffman's ERP, but also via GARIOA, which the mighty U.S. Army was in charge of and whose funding policies politicians in Washington were in a weak position to challenge. Werner Abelshauser, in an article, has rightly termed the Marshall Plan "the practical basis of American policy in the Federal Republic of Germany" that ensured, as Hoffman had envisioned, that "West German reconstruction meshed closely with the aim of reconstruction of Western Europe." But there was another more covert accelerator of the reconstruction and recasting of industry: GARIOA, extended by the mechanism of the Investment Auxiliary Law. In other words, as Abelshauser wrote in his article, there was American "help," but also the "self-help" through industry and government action.[97]

10. American Big Business and Otto A. Friedrich

These larger structural shifts in coal and steel also took place in the heavy industries of Britain, but, as in the case of textiles, management reacted by and large very conservatively. The contrast is perhaps best demonstrated by returning to Friedrich and to how he responded to the changes in an increasingly American-dominated Western economy. In the 1920s, he had followed in his brother's footsteps by going to the United States.[98] While Carl Joachim had received a fellowship to go to Harvard and then stayed to become a very influential political scientist with many contacts into Washington politics, Otto, after abandoning his medical studies in Weimar Germany and veering toward business, took a lowly job with B.F. Goodrich in Ohio. Having caught the eye of his superiors, he rose to a managerial position and evidently came to like a by no means easy life and work in the United States. In the summer 1927, at the height of the American FDI boom, he accepted a position as "special factory representative" and liaison to Goodrich's German agency, the ATRAG car and tractor dealership, run by Dr. Bernhard. The plan was also to sell Goodrich's interests in the powerful Continental Gummiwerke in Hanover and to build up a sales organization of its own. But the Great Slump hit these plans hard. Friedrich eventually found a job first with the German rubber cartel organization before joining the Phoenix A.G. rubber firm in Hamburg-Harburg. For a long time he kept away from the Nazi Party, and, when he joined it in 1940, soon became unhappy with his decision. And yet, as so many other managers, he made his contribution to the war effort not only through Phoenix, but also as deputy coordinator for rubber production. In 1945, he returned to Harburg after surrender in order to get production going again in the war-damaged Phoenix factories.[99]

Surrounded by economic and political chaos and trying to reconnect with his wife and children, his mother, his brother in the United States, and his other siblings, he seems to have lapsed into a midlife crisis. Looking for a way out, he set new goals for himself in his professional and political life that his wife disliked intensely. Their marriage fell apart. He started an affair with his secretary, whom he later married and who loyally typed up a diary that he had begun to write at the end of the war. This source is in many ways a unique contemporary record not only of his personal struggles, but also of the professional path that he decided to take after the collapse of the Third Reich. He came to see himself not as a businessman who was narrowly focused on the reconstruction of the Phoenix corporation. He aspired to leadership in West German industry and began, as a person interested in ideas, to think quite deeply about the lessons to be learned from German history and about the future of Germany in the "American century." His years in the United States had widened his horizons and had, as he once put it, "dropped him between two continents." Widely read and a good speaker, he tried to carve out a reformist agenda between what he saw as a "modern" America and a to-be-modernized West Germany.

Accordingly, he went back to the United States as soon as possible not merely in search business opportunities for his company, but also to be able to report back firsthand on the business practices he had seen across the Atlantic and on what should be done in war-torn West Germany.[100] Once Carl Joachim had forgiven his wayward brother his association with the Nazi Party, he introduced Otto to his colleagues at Harvard and to people of influence in American business and politics. Friedrich also resumed contact with American colleagues whom he had known in the 1930s from meetings of the International Rubber Regulation Committee (IRRC). One of them was Albert Viles, who had been very pessimistic in the 1930s and, like Carl Joachim, at one point had tried to persuade Otto to return to the United States. In January 1947, Viles asked him to produce a longer report on the development of the German rubber industry since 1939. Friedrich was happy to respond, probably also in the hope that this might lead to an invitation to America. This first trip, facilitated by his brother, who arranged a large number of meetings for Otto, finally materialized in January 1949. Carl

Joachim had meanwhile learned that there existed reservations against his brother because of his activities in the Nazi wartime rubber industry.

The first encounter between Friedrich and Viles provides an intriguing glimpse into the post-Hitler world of German-American business relations that was probably not unique. Apparently the conversation made a slow start. Viles regretted what had happened since their last meeting at the IRRC in the 1930s and reminded him that he saw the catastrophe coming. When the question of American reservations toward Friedrich arose, Viles denied that there had been a campaign against Friedrich and quickly digressed into a disquisition of the new global role of the United States. He then pinpointed the "weak spots" around the world, such as China, Indochina, and Europe, as the United States grappled with the power position that the Soviet Union had built up against his country. With Friedrich still wondering about the attitudes of other businessmen whom he was hoping to see, Viles agreed to call John Collyer, the president of Goodrich, and P. W. Litchfield, the chairman of the Goodyear board. When he saw Viles again at the end of his trip, the latter reiterated that there had been no adverse publicity against Friedrich "as a main agent of Hitler," adding that this was also true with regard to colleagues in France with whom Friedrich had had contact during the Nazi occupation.

If Viles's responses made a more general point about German-American economic relations in the late 1940s, it seems that they tallied with the attitudes of "reconstructionists," such as Hoffman and Draper, and also with the poll that the CFR conducted in some twenty-two American cities in 1946–47:[101] Covering the continent as comprehensively as possible by region, it came to the general conclusion that "members of the same profession or occupation frequently tended to divide on an issue for more or less the same reasons and in more or less the same proportion, regardless of where they lived." Given this uniformity, the replies by those who were categorized as "business" people, 180 in all, are quite helpful for understanding what they wanted to see done with vanquished Germany. Thus some 81 percent approved of the idea that the country's demilitarization should be guaranteed for twenty-five years, with 9 percent opposed, 9 percent uncertain, and one who did not answer at all. At the same time some 84 percent voted in support of the notion that a unified, prosperous Germany was essential to the economic stability of Europe, with 13 percent answering with "no" and 3 percent being uncertain. On the question of whether it should be American policy to encourage the development of German industry to generate increased production for export as a means of financing imports, 87 percent approved, 9 percent disapproved, 3 percent were uncertain, and one who did not answer at all. When it came to the breakup of cartels as being essential to the political and economic stability of Europe, 68 percent replied with yes, followed by 16 percent who were uncertain and 15 percent opposed. As to whether Germany should be permitted to control the chemical and metallurgical industries of the Rhineland and Ruhr regions, no more than 53 percent thought this to be a good idea, while 37 percent voted against and 10 percent were uncertain. Some 73 percent thought that the country should continue to pay reparations, with the no responses at 24 percent and 3 percent being uncertain. Some 85 percent, however, were against taking these reparations by removing capital assets, with 10 percent in favor and 3 percent uncertain, and 2 percent giving no answer.

Taking both Friedrich's experiences during his visit and the above polls together, it is clear that the past was not forgotten. While supporting reconstruction, a recasting of the organization of German business was deemed necessary, if West Germany was to contribute to the economic stabilization of Western Europe. The occupation authorities were also spearheading an "economic re-education" to complement the Allies' political re-education program—soon to be renamed "reorientation." It is probably not too farfetched to conclude therefore that Viles's words of empathy for the situation in which German businessmen had found themselves under a despicable Nazi regime was more widespread. The latter were assumed to have tried their best to pull their enterprises through the crisis of the 1930s. Resistance, even of the more covert kind that Friedrich had engaged in during the war, for example, by hiding a member of the resistance whom the Gestapo hunted following the unsuccessful attempt on Hitler's life on 20 July 1944, was very dangerous and required a courage that not all of Friedrich's hosts during his 1949 trip might have plucked up themselves. Overall, it seems that business contacts were still not relaxed. The risks of FDI were carefully weighed, and it was only in December 1951 that a delegation of the Bundesverband der Deutschen Industrie (BDI), West German industry's peak association, attended an international meeting of industrialists in New York under the leadership of BDI president Fritz Berg.

11. Modernizing Phoenix A.G. and Erhard's Anti-Cartel Bill

Equipped with the information that Carl Joachim had given him in advance of his journey, Friedrich was perhaps rather less self-conscious than other German visitors when he talked to American colleagues. His English was fluent and he could discuss his experiences in Akron in the

1920s with enthusiasm. He also realized that, while German research and technology had fallen behind in many areas, openness toward what his American counterparts were doing was vital. He also took an interest in the organizational structures that they had created to secure what was then a competitive and dynamic rubber manufacturing sector. In the end, he came back to Harburg with two ideas. For one, he asked himself how and how far the technologies and practices that he had seen on his visit might be profitably applied in his own company. Second, he always wondered about the wider applicability of what he had witnessed in the United States and how these insights might be transmitted to West German industry and politics at large.

Thus, one day at the end of May 1949 when visiting one of the Phoenix workshops, he recorded disdainfully that the rolling machines could "be transferred to the German Museum [of Technology] in Munich," just as they were sitting there.[102] He also noted that one of the calanders "allegedly dated from before 1900" but was "still doing its work." Nor did he have a good impression of the rolling workshop that had been "rather provisionally rebuilt." Friedrich's reactions to these conditions in comparison to what he had seen in the United States were those of a technological modernizer who was keen to reap for his firm the benefits of American ideas on how to equip and organize a modern factory. He also decided that the most effective way of obtaining new technology was to form partnerships with American companies. What was more difficult to come by was FDI. For Friedrich the way forward was to get an American company to take a stake in Phoenix. This proved to be an arduous task. He negotiated with Goodyear for many months, in the end without success. Perhaps this was a blessing in disguise, as Harvey Firestone suddenly became interested in a deal with Phoenix. After further negotiations a link was forged that gave the Harburgers access to the Firestone Corporation's advances, such as the manufacture of tubeless tires.

Apart from modernizing his firm, Friedrich was also keenly interested in reforming West German industry at large, and not merely its organizational structures, but also its labor relations. After being proscribed and persecuted by the Nazis, the newly founded trade unions had to be reckoned with in a democratically organized West German society and its constitutionally guaranteed basic rights. Just as he had argued for a cartel-free economy, he also knew that a modern capitalist system had to have a social security infrastructure. A country in which there existed millions of war widows, orphans, ex-soldiers, and families who had lost everything in Allied bombing raids or on the trek to the West as refugees or expellees, simply could not do without a welfare net.[103] Their poverty and destitution had to be mitigated, not least because they were now voting citizens in a parliamentary democracy. If there was no hope of a better life ahead, they might rebel at the polls. To be sure, Germany had had a gradually widened system of social security since the days of Bismarck in the 1880s. But the social crisis of the late 1940s had more immediate roots in World War II, even though repeated references to Imperial and Weimar Germany reinforced dispositions that a welfare state capitalism was a sine qua non.

While broadly aware of these necessities, Friedrich again presents an interesting case of how this worked at company level. He gained an appreciation of some of the daily pressures on his workers through frank discussions with them and their representatives. His driver proved to be a particularly shrewd Social Democrat who not only scoffed at some of Friedrich's lingering misperceptions of what had allegedly been "good" about National Socialism and its labor policies, but also gave him thoughtful private tutorials in the realities of socioeconomic divisions by class in West Germany.[104] Here one encounters a "modernized" Otto Friedrich, in contrast to Albert Schäfer, his entrepreneurial mentor. He—as so many other managers of the older generation—just could not emancipate himself from his antilabor views and memories dating back to the Weimar Republic. The tensions that this produced between the two men did not stop Friedrich from introducing a system of welfare provision and employer-employee communication that was partly derived from indigenous traditions and partly adapted from American labor relations. In making this point of a blending of German and American business customs and practices it is important to remember that America's economy was no longer the kind of laissez-faire capitalism that had existed in the nineteenth century. It, too, had been tempered by the New Deal in the 1930s so that the distinctions between the two industrial systems had also been leveled, though not extinguished.

In line with his revamped belief system, Friedrich reached out beyond his company. He opened a dialogue with trade union leaders and Social Democrat politicians in Hamburg and Bonn. This happened at a time when his archconservative colleagues in the heavy industries of the Ruhr were still locked in confrontations with their workers and trade union representatives that were reminiscent of the Weimar years. Concerning his opposition to restrictive practices, he began to support Ludwig Erhard, whose ministry had gotten busy in the spring of 1949 to draft anti-cartel legislation to replace Allied decrees.[105] Few people would have expected in 1949 that it would take until 1957 for a Law for Securing Competition to be ratified by the Federal Parliament. Led by the powerful BDI and supported by various economists and journalists, the opposition to this law put so many obstacles in the way of its passage through the Bundesrat and Bundestag that the Americans, now

bereft of their once strong occupations rights of intervention, were beginning to wonder if West Germany would ever get an anti-cartel law.
As one critical observer predicted in *Fortune* magazine in May 1954 in
an article titled "The German Business Mind,"[106] should Erhard's competition bill be rejected altogether "West Germany may well slip back
into the economic authoritarianism of the old days, with repercussions
that no man can yet foresee." However, if the bill were ratified, "even
in modified form," this feat would "mean a major victory, perhaps the
greatest victory ever won in Europe for the principles of [a] dynamic
American-style capitalism."

Over time the power of the conservatives in the BDI began to
weaken. It was partly a generational question, as a cohort of older managers who had resumed their former positions soon after 1945 retired.
They were often replaced by younger colleagues who were more cos-
mopolitan in outlook and habitus and hence more open to American
ideas on how to shape a modern industrial economy. They also tended
not to have risen in the coal and steel industries but in those of electrical
engineering, chemicals, and machine manufacturing. While the older
industries continued to produce primarily for the domestic market, the
new industries were looking toward the world trading system that the
United States was trying to restore. Friedrich, born in 1902, was one of
the modernizers who fought his battles both in the presidium of the
BDI and in his many speeches.

What helped the reformers was the boom that the Federal Republic experienced in the 1950s and that also tipped the balance of power
against the conservatives. Gilbert Burck's hopes of May 1954 came true
more or less as Hoffman had outlined in 1949–50. Competition became
a more widely accepted principle in all of Western Europe and encouraged the progressive integration of a European common and yet open
market, except for parts of the retail trade with its small businesses and
agriculture that continued to be protected by tariffs, net price agreements for retailers, and, perhaps most important, subsidies from Brussels. But agriculture also constituted a special case in the United States.
To be sure, all this relates to the question of the "Americanization" of
Europe or—to refer back to Stead in chapter I—of the world and will
therefore be taken up again in the Conclusion.

12. The Reluctant Modernization
of British Industry

Britain, while also benefitting from the general postwar prosperity,
remained aloof from these developments on the European Continent.

The Anglo-American "special relationship" had for all practical purposes been badly damaged in 1945–46, when Truman and America's corporate leaders decided to make West Germany their main base of operation and to use the greater potential and perceived dynamism of its industries as an engine of growth but also of transformation of neighboring economies. Britain continued its preferential tariff system with a shrinking Empire as well as with the Commonwealth, some of whose members were fostering their trade with other countries. Meanwhile the City did not invest in domestic industry, but went overseas. Some of the reasons for the sidelining of British industry have already been mentioned, in particular those that were beyond the control of Britain's economic and political elites, such as the scrapping of the Morgenthau Plan that would have advantaged British industry, the cancellation of Lend-Lease, and the determination of both Wall Street and the big corporations to establish a *Pax Americana*.

But it was not all external circumstances or the Labour government that made things difficult for the British economy to benefit from the incipient postwar boom more fully. As far as its manufacturing industries were concerned, there was growth in the 1950s, but it was relatively slow. Taking of gross value added per person hour to manufacturing industry, it remained level in Britain between 1951 and 1964. In West Germany it rose from 78 points to 117, while in the United States it had seen a very slight decline from its high level of 254 points in 1951 to 253 in 1964. As before, Britain's performance also resulted from the country's inability to overcome the internal socioeconomic conflicts that had vexed it in the interwar period and to some extent even since the late nineteenth century. Car manufacturing, which was doing well in the United States and West Germany during the same postwar years and became a major engine of growth, offers a good case in point. Geoffrey Owen, who devoted a chapter to the British motor industry, speaks of "an avoidable disaster."[107] Jonathan Wood, the author of the most detailed study on the "rise and fall of the British motor industry" from the late nineteenth century to the 1980s, titled his book *Wheels of Misfortune*, to which one might add "of miscalculation" and a striking inability to adapt to a changing technological and international economic environment that was driven by competition.[108]

It has already been mentioned in chapter III that before 1914, when Ford was at the forefront of motorization in the United States, the British car industry remained fragmented into many small companies whose output and profits were low.[109] After the general slump in the early 1920s, it was especially the industry's leaders, such as Morris, who, having modernized their production, succeeded in increasing their sales. Morris outpaced both Ford, which had built its first British factory even before 1914, and GM, which had failed to acquire a participation in Morris and in 1925 had to make do with taking over the much weaker Vauxhall Company. In 1929, Morris, Austin, and Singer Cars held the first top places in Britain, not the Americans. In that year total production reached 182,347 vehicles of which some 75 percent were sold in the domestic market. As was true of the British economy more generally, the motor industry also experienced a less serious slump after 1929, followed by a recovery that was not a boom but was strong enough to avoid the second dip that the Americans went through in 1937.

With production of military vehicles having provided a further stimulus during the early 1940s, hopes were quite high that automobiles would be among the leading branches of postwar reconstruction and modernization. The Labour government tried to encourage this. Thus the president of the Board of Trade, Cripps, speaking at a dinner of the Society of Motor Manufacturers and Trades in November 1945, urged his audience that "we must provide a cheap, tough, good-looking car of decent size—not the sort of car we have hitherto produced for smooth roads and short journeys in this country—and we must produce them in sufficient quantities to get the benefits of mass production."[110] Export opportunities, he added, would suffer if the industry continued to offer as many models and makes as in the past. When he put forward the idea that exports should be at the level of 50 percent, there were grumbles in his audience. He was not alone in his criticism. From Canada came the comment a few years later that British cars were characterized by "narrow tracks, small luggage space, and [a] reputed inability to stand up to bad roads."[111] In September 1947, the Attlee government, possibly with the example of Volkswagen before its eyes, again exhorted the manufacturers to move to single model production. But a year later Austin's range of models was the largest in Europe.

Later, when the Marshall Plan was up and running, Hoffman also offered his British colleagues trips to the industrial centers of the United States under the auspices of the "Productivity Councils."[112] It was a program to convince them that in order to achieve productivity gains the two sides of industry had to change their habits and traditions of class confrontation and adapt to the American model of labor relations. Hoffman and other businessmen involved in European reconstruction and recasting pointed to higher productivity and wages across the Atlantic, thanks to which Americans had achieved a living standard that was now held up to the British. Terry Gourvish and Nick Tiratsoo have examined the exchanges between "missionaries and managers" and have concluded that "progress *was* made in the first two decades after World War Two, and many projects owed a great deal to American advances in productivity, technological change, and the training of managers."[113]

But they also point to the many "other actors in the play: politicians and government bureaucrats, with their own agendas; bodies representing the interests of employers; trade unions; and the educational establishment which was more often conservative in its attitude to business education than it was innovative and flexible."[114]

A very interesting article appeared in December 1949 in *Der Arbeitgeber*, the journal of the West German Employers' Federation.[115] It started with the observation that in the summer of 1948 the Americans had agreed to call the visiting program an exchange of experiences. The idea was to "treat British self-confidence gently" since the hosts had to reckon "with the reaction that, as far as industrial practice was concerned, hardly anyone had anything to teach the English and this applied even more to the Americans with their 'twisted standardization.'" The author added that this "first explosive response had in fact happened." But it was discovered and admitted later that further study was worthwhile, and so the rest of the article was at great pains to explain the lessons that might be learned.

The response to the Volkswagen had been the most striking example of British conservatism. The Wolfsburg VW complex had been run by the German Labor Front and was therefore a public company that became British occupation property in 1945. British engineers then organized the conversion from military *Kübelwagen* production to the "beetle"-shaped passenger car that—as has been mentioned in chapter V—had been designed in the 1930s for "Aryan" mass motorization. A British company could easily have acquired the entire factory complex, and it appears that the occupation authorities in the British zone offered it on a platter. A report of the British Intelligence Sub-Committee concluded that "compared with other automobile factories in Germany and visualizing the originally intended factory layout, the Volkswagen effort is outstanding and is the nearest approach to production as we know it."[116] It added that the plant was in good condition and that the machinery had been successfully operated for years. Accordingly, examples were sent "to practically every British car company for inspection."[117] None of them took an interest in this car with its rear-mounted, air-cooled boxer engine and its peculiar independent torsion-bar suspension. As the Rootes Group put it,[118] "We do not consider that the design represents any special brilliance." It was not "regarded as an example of first-class modern design to be copied by British industry." Yet, by March 1946, Wolfsburg had produced just over one thousand cars, and a few years later those same British manufacturers would complain about Volkswagen's competition in third markets. Not even Ford's British Anglia model, though "a steady domestic seller," became "the serious challenger to the VW Beetle that was initially expected."[119]

Of course, it was tempting to sit on one's hands in the 1950s after there had been some growth and rationalization. In 1952 Morris and Austin merged to establish the British Motor Corporation (BMC). But oddly enough very little rationalization took place, as "both firms retained their distributor and dealer networks."[120] Perhaps because British buyers were particularly loyal customers, there was a growing demand in the home market so that BMC "could initially afford this inefficient structure [of 400 distributors and 4,500 dealers] in a seller's market." Exports, mainly to the Commonwealth, were more volatile but also doing well overall, with 399,000 units in 1950, 373,000 in 1955, and 570,000 in 1960 . But "the merger had a disappointing effect on long-term productivity and profits." In 1958, BMC put out close to 450,000 vehicles and raked in a profit of £21 million. But in 1956 the profit per vehicle was only £35, compared to GM's Vauxhall Ltd. that had modernized its complex at Luton, reduced its output to three body styles, and had gains of £80 per vehicle. Still, it "always seemed a cosy, provincial sort of outfit," and Glatt even went so far as to speak of "old men prone to take short views."[121] Meanwhile Rootes had "no profit plan which fully spelled out how its objectives were to be achieved." There was merely "a broad target" for "an annual improvement."[122]

By comparison, Ford's Dagenham factories suffered from a lack of productivity but had profits of £45 per car. As John Barber, from 1962 onward Ford U.K.'s chief financial officer, concluded,[123] "When I joined Ford it was a fairly old-fashioned company and the finance department was full of little men in green eyeshades. At the time we had virtually no graduates." Barber tried to change this, but the 1960s saw little improvement. And this also applied to quality control. British cars were prone to breaking down, especially because of electrical troubles. Nor, in response to earlier Canadian criticisms about road worthiness, had they meanwhile been technologically updated for export to North America or West Germany, where long-distance travel on highways and autobahns at sustained high speeds put a strain on engines and cooling systems. Even with respect to the upmarket and no doubt attractively designed Jaguar with its expensive walnut-wood veneer dashboard there was the standing joke in this period that you really had to have two of these beautiful cars as one of them might well be in the workshop for repairs.

The development of the Mini by the Alec Issigonis was no doubt a technologically brilliant feat, but, though it was a best seller, its profitability was diminished because the company had badly miscalculated its pricing.[124] When British Leyland Motors (BLM) was forged in 1968, it had a 40.6 percent share of the market and respectable pretax profits. By 1975, the share had shrunken to 30.9 percent and the company was making a hefty loss of over £23 million. As a result, BLM was national-ized when the British government decided that it was too big to fail. But the new BL (British Leyland) did not do any better. When Margaret Thatcher became prime minister, she decided to put BL out of its mis-ery. At that time the average British family had to contribute some £200 to British Leyland's survival, and this clearly could not go on. It was the end of the British-owned motor industry and of Britain as a major car manufacturing country. Foreign companies picked up the pieces, among them American, German, and Japanese firms. A modernized version of the Mini is now being produced successfully at the former BMC plants in the Oxford suburb of Cowley by BMW.

While this gradual decline was to a considerable extent due to man-agement problems, the industry as a whole was, as in the 1920s, beset by another serious problem: poor labor relations.[125] As Ford U.K. ex-panded, its Dagenham complex became affected by tensions between management and the workforce. By contrast, the Ford factory in Co-logne, with its Fordist mass production, saw few serious labor troubles. Again in Britain this was in part because of a lack of qualified people on the management side. The *Economist* complained in 1959 that BMC was "short of good personnel to whom the top management could leave the handling of negotiations" with the workers' representatives.[126] And here it was not so much the power of the trade union movement overall, but that of the local shop stewards who were willing to trig-ger a spontaneous walkout or a longer strike the moment there was a minor dispute. To cut a distressing story short that existed in many parts of British industry, labor relations were as terrible as in the 1920s, when, among other factors, they had been a major drag on the post-1918 recovery.

It was no better with British engineering. For "despite its enormous ideological influence . . . the practical impact of the Americanization drive on British engineering remained surprisingly limited during the first postwar decade."[127] The push for modernization that followed from the mid-1950s proved no less dispiriting: "Far from reviving its competitive fortunes, . . . this putative Americanization of British engi-neering was associated instead with a rapid loss of market share both abroad and at home, resulting in a steep decline of domestic production and employment." An industry that had been a "world leader" before 1914 had become a "niche player" by the 1970s, resulting in "a process of specialization and internationalization as companies played to their strengths and searched for defensible positions in the world market."[128]

To put it all in a nutshell, there is the telling observation by an Ameri-can managing director of a subsidiary in Britain who, addressing col-leagues, remarked,[129] "There is a tremendous in-built hunger for the status quo in your society—how did they do things before, [and] then how can they keep things the way they are? The business leaders over here would love to have things stay just the same for the next ten years, then they wouldn't have any worries at all." Another American manager added,[130] "There is a lot of inertia here, the resistance to innovation almost defies belief. Even though they see a thing is logical and right, they still say they can't do it. So many of the people who run companies are skilled maintainers of the status quo."

However peculiar many West German business cultures and social customs and attitudes may have appeared in the eyes of American visitors and partners, they were deemed to be more dynamic, open to change, and prepared to integrate the economic ideas and practices that the postwar presence of the new hegemonic power of the West offered them. The plan of building an autarkic territorial bloc on the European Continent had been defeated, and they had no overseas colonies and empire to fall back on and to defend. Nor did British industry ever have the powerful associations that also shaped industrial policy in the Federal Republic. Compared to the BDI, the voice of its British equivalents—the Federation of British Industries and the later Confederation of British Industry—was weak.[131]

Thus, the British search for preserving the status quo may have been the deeper reason why, apart from feeling let down by the Americans in 1945 over Lend-Lease, Britain resisted the establishment of the Open Door and insisted on retaining their preferential tariff system to secure export markets. Betting on the continued existence of the Commonwealth link, the country refused to join the EEC, which, by the late 1950s, had begun to emerge as major trading area. The European Free Trade Zone (EFTA) of 1960 that the U.K. spearheaded in the late 1950s proved to be a poor substitute for direct access to the much larger market of the EEC. It was not only EFTA but a more general aversion to the British that caused French president Charles de Gaulle to reject the application when it was finally made in the 1960s. Only in the mid-1970s did Britain finally become part of the EEC. And here lies another reason for the country's continued relative decline: counting on the Empire and Commonwealth as a preferential trading zone for British goods turned out to be a miscalculation in the longer term, as the non-European parts of the world shifted toward other partners, most notably the Americans, the Germans, and the Japanese. In the early 1950s Britain was the largest exporter of cars. By 1987, she was in fifth place among the European car manufacturers behind Germany, France, Italy, and Spain, not to mention the Japanese, and increasingly also the South Koreans.

Although the Americans were to no small degree *indirectly* responsible for the British decision to maintain preferences after the end of

World War II, they were certainly irritated. The thorn was the persistence of the British imperial bloc when the era of empires was, in the eyes of Washington, supposed to be over. It was buttressed by the continuing, if weakened, position of the City as a financial hub. Here many major commercial and financial operations were still being transacted. American bankers wanted global finance to be threaded through Wall Street. The British clinging to formal colonial possessions in different parts of the world also required large military expenditures. These burdens were further increased by London's decision to become a nuclear power. By 1952, Britain had developed atomic weapons, four years later the hydrogen bomb, plus the requisite and notoriously expensive delivery systems. Although the defense review after the Suez adventure reduced the armed forces from 700,000 to 400,000 by 1962, this was still 7 percent in terms of GDP when West Germany spent only 4 percent.

After Suez, the new prime minister, Harold Macmillan, asked for an analysis of the costs and benefits of the country's overseas possessions. But the ruling Conservatives in Parliament were not in the mood to do the rational and cost-saving thing to accelerate the process of decolonization. Consequently, resources remained committed to defense and maintenance of the Empire that were lacking at home for the modernization of industry and for further improvements to Britain's social infrastructure, including the National Health Service. The importation of dismantled German machinery, much of it clapped-out due to round-the-clock production during the war, proved much less valuable than had been estimated.[132] It did not encourage technological modernization and the overdue move out of textiles and mining into chemicals, electrical engineering, and consumer durables. This leaves the question of whether Britain could have modernized more successfully under different international conditions. The answer may be that internal and external factors in Britain's economic woes were interacting with one another and hence are difficult to separate. No doubt the Americans wanted the Open Door and were hostile to the protectionism of the Empire and Commonwealth. Nor—as we have seen—did the election in 1945 of a Labour government make cooperation easier. But there were also the domestic obstacles to industrial modernization that had deep roots in British business culture, whether with respect to labor relations or managerial traditions.

13. America and the Suez Crisis

While the Germans, who, having unleashed two world wars, were also partly responsible for Britain's plight, successfully demilitarized and

concentrated on precisely this kind of modernization both of its manufacturing industry and its provision of social security, Britain, seeing
itself as a victor and therefore perhaps incapable of contemplating a
radically different approach to both its industrial and foreign policies,
failed to keep up. Worse, given the determination of the United States,
objectively the undisputed hegemonic power of the West, to build a
multilateral world trading system, Britain was sooner or later in for a
rude shock. It came at Suez in 1956. The background to the crisis is well
researched, and Jean Edward Smith has recently retold it with respect
to the key decision maker, U.S. president Dwight D. Eisenhower.

A crucial moment in a development that had for some time revolved
around the plans of the nationalist Egyptian regime of Col. Gamal
Abdel Nasser to build the Aswan Dam on the Nile River came when he
announced the nationalization of the Suez Canal.[133] Hearing that Britain was thinking of a military intervention to thwart Nasser's move,
Eisenhower warned Prime Minister Anthony Eden that he should not
even think of the use of force. Yet, by the end of October preparations
had been made for Britain to reoccupy the Canal Zone together with
the French and Israelis. When the Israelis opened the attack on 29 October 1956, the U.S. president, on his reelection campaign trail in Virginia,
went back to Washington to order John Foster Dulles to tell Jerusalem
that the United States would apply sanctions, go to the United Nations,
and "do everything there is" to halt "this thing."[134] When he learned
that the French and British would support the Israelis, Eisenhower re-
torted, "Nothing justifies double-crossing us. I don't care whether I am
re-elected or not. We must make good on our word, otherwise we are a
nation without honor."

But instead of de-escalating the crisis, London and Paris issued ul-
timatums to Egypt, followed by an Israeli one the next day to enable
their own forces to move into the Canal Zone under the pretext of need-
ing to protect international shipping. The flurry of diplomatic activity
that ensued in the first days of November in the face of the armada
of warships that Britain and France had assembled along the northern
coast of Egypt, ready to invade, culminated on 6 November when Eden
announced his willingness to withdraw. But what did the trick was not
American military pressure, although this was applied, too. Rather it
was the American threat to trigger the collapse of the pound and to create havoc in the City.

On 1 September 1956 British dollar reserves still stood at $2,276 mil-
lion. As Cole C. Kingseed put it,[135] "British gold and dollar reserves
had already dropped $141 million in October; by November these
losses doubled to $279 million." One reaction to this was to ask the
Americans for a postponement of British loan payments. But as Harold

Macmillan, the Chancellor of the Exchequer, found, they were being "very difficult."[136] All the while preparations for an invasion of Egypt continued, depleting reserves to a perilously low level of $2,000 million and threatening a run on the pound. On 5 November British and French troops began their assault on Egypt, following the Israelis, who had launched their attack on 29 October. On the following day Macmillan informed Prime Minister Anthony Eden that the run on sterling was getting very dangerous. In an attempt to support the currency, Macmillan "telephoned [U.S.] Treasury Secretary [George] Humphrey seeking assistance."[137] He was told "that he would be available only if Britain accepted a cease-fire." Although demonstrations in London and shortages of petrol also weighed on the Eden cabinet, it was Eisenhower's tough response that did the trick. His threat to impose economic sanctions and to block any British attempt to obtain loans from the World Bank together with the danger that American inaction would push the pound into the ground and, finally, the weakness of the British financial system to halt the pressure on sterling stopped the Suez adventure. As the president is said to have remarked, "If you don't get out of Port Said tomorrow, I'll cause a run on the pound and drive it down to zero."[138] It was clear that the age of European colonialism and of Empire and Commonwealth bloc preferences was definitely over.[139]

The year 1957 therefore seems to be a good moment to take stock of the Anglo-American and German-American "special relationships" after World War II. While Eisenhower and Eden exchanged polite reassurances of continued good diplomatic relations, Eden soon resigned. He was replaced by Harold Macmillan, who established a good rapport with the White House, especially during the 1958–59 Berlin crisis, but had a very tense relationship with president John F. Kennedy, with Britain now very clearly the junior partner at the political and military level and even more so at that of finance, trade, and industry. In fact, it is probably no exaggeration to say that, with the exception of a few companies, such as ICI, Unilever, and Shell, the Americans no longer saw British industry as a serious competitor and/or partner.

Relations with West German industry were by contrast quite different. By the mid-1950s, the West Germans had finally resolved their cartel debates and had stabilized their "social market economy" that, whatever the differences in detail, fitted well enough with the "commercial Keynesianism" that the United States had adopted after 1945. This resulted in many renewed cooperations, mutual licensing agreements, the settling of the war's legal legacies, and direct investments. American private investments, it is true, did not flow into the country in large numbers.[140] But West German industry and banks found a way out of their rapidly growing capital needs. When the GARIOA and

ERP funds began to run out, the Investment Auxiliary Act stepped into the breach and helped to modernize and boost coal, steel, and electricity production without which manufacturing industry could not have sought out export markets to earn exchange to pay for imports. Thus, the expansion of the economy that had begun with the currency reform of 1948 and the creation of a market for civilian goods could continue, unburdened by high military expenditure. After years of debate and delays, rearmament was finally approved by the Bundestag in 1956, after which it took several more years before the Bundeswehr was able to make its tangible contribution to NATO. All this took place in the shadow of the multilateral world trading system that the Americans had been planning to build after 1945 and under the protective umbrella of the armed forces of the United States in its Cold War against the other superpower, the Soviet Union.

If there was a more serious difference of opinion it was over commercial relations with the Soviet Bloc. Here it was especially the capital goods industries of the Ruhr that were straining to revive their interwar trading links, especially with the Soviet Union.[141] One reason for this may have been that many of the more conservative managers, remembering 1929, never stopped wondering if this second American attempt to establish the Open Door in the West might not run into trouble again. For this contingency it was obviously good to have the Soviet Union as an additional strut, as it had been in the 1920s. However, Washington demanded strict adherence to the Battle Act and other rules to prevent the export of goods that might have a military-strategic value to the Russians. These German-American tensions continued in the 1960s, for example over a West German pipeline deal with the Soviets, and into the 1970s when *Osthandel*, which the Adenauer government, out of loyalty to the Americans, had been reluctant to support, was complemented by chancellor Willy Brandt's *Ostpolitik*, which connected the two policies. The problem was that it revived bad memories among West Germany's allies in Washington and London of the Rapallo agreement between the Weimar Republic and Bolshevik Russia in 1922. It took some time to overcome them.

With reference to relations in the 1950s and 1960s, the balance of American business sentiment and activity between Britain and the United States, on the one hand, and between West Germany and America, on the other, was, as during the Weimar days, tilted in favor of a closer partnership with the latter rather than with Washington's wartime British ally. This is reflected in rich research that German business historians have undertaken, most of it accessible only in the German language.[142] In these studies, the question of the role of the United States in the reconstruction and recasting of the West German economy after 1945 is, directly or indirectly, being raised. Some authors have remained more skeptical of the Americanization paradigm, which is why the issue will be taken up again in the Conclusion.

Notes to Chapter VI

1. On Hitler's plans beyond the conquest of the Soviet Union, see Jochen Thies, *Hitler's Plans for Global Domination* (New York, 2012); Rolf-Dieter Müller, *Das Tor zur Weltmacht. Die Bedeutung der Sowjetunion für die deutsche Wirtschafts- und Rüstungspolitik zwischen den Weltkriegen* (Boppard, 1984).

2. *Hitler's Table Talks, 1941–1944*, with an introduction by Hugh Trevor-Roper (London, 1953), esp. the entries on 4–5 (for the night of 24/25 July 1941), 16 (for the night of 27 July 1941), 24 (for the night of 8/9 August 1941). This was the time when Hitler expected to have brought down the Soviet Union within weeks so that he was confidently mapping out his plans for the future.

3. Reinhard Opitz, ed., *Europastrategien des deutschen Kapitals, 1900–1945* (Cologne, 1977); Lothar Gruchmann, *Nationalsozialistische Grossraumordnung* (Stuttgart, 1962); John Gillingham, *Belgian Business in the Nazi New Order* (Ghent, 1977); Ludolf Herbst, *Der totale Krieg und die Ordnung der Wirtschaft* (Stuttgart, 1982); Arno Sölter, *Grossraumkartell* (Dresden, 1941); Werner Röhr and Brigitte Berlekam, eds., *Neuordnung Europas* (Berlin, 1996).

4. See above, pp. 2ff. See also Lawrence S. Kaplan, "Western Europe in the American Century," *Diplomatic History* 6 (Spring 1982): 111–23; D. W. White, "The American Century. The History of an Idea, 1941–1971" (PhD diss., New York University, 1979); Alan Brinkley, *The Publisher* (New York, 2010).

5. Quoted in Alan Brinkley, *The End of Reform* (New York, 1995), 143.

6. See, e.g., Frank Costigliola, *Roosevelt's Lost Alliances* (Princeton, 2012), 127ff., also for the following. See also Theodore Wilson, *The First Summit: Roosevelt and Churchill at Placentia Bay* (Lawrence, KS, 1991).

7. Brinkley, *End of Reform* (note 5), 117ff.; G. M. Gressley, "Thurman Arnold, Antitrust and the New Deal," *Business History Review* 38 (Summer 1964): 214–31; W. D. Miscamble, "Thurman Arnold Goes to Washington," *Business History Review* 56 (1982): 1–15.

8. Thurman Arnold, *The Bottlenecks of Business* (New York, 1940), with the following quotes passim. The argument that not the bigness of an enterprise was the problem to be feared and combated was also made by David E. Lilienthal, the chair of the Tennessee Valley Authority, in a book he published after the war: *Big Business. A New Era* (New York, 1952).

9. In his polemical *Trading with the Enemy* (New York, 1983), 46–47, Charles Higham pinpoints Standard Oil as one of the companies that were pushing back hard. But Henry Kaiser apparently also appeared in Arnold's crosshairs. He even took on the trade unions, suspecting them of antitrust violations. In the same category as Higham: Edwin Black, *Nazi Nexus* (Washington, DC, 2009).

10. Quoted in W. Roger Louis, *Imperialism at Bay: The United States and the Decolonization of the British Empire* (Oxford, 1978), 154–55.

11. On CFR, see, e.g., Michael Wala, *The Council on Foreign Relations and American Foreign Policy in the Early Cold War* (Providence, RI, 1994); on CED, Robert M. Collins, "American Corporatism: The Committee for Economic Development, 1942–1964," in Robert F. Himmelberg, ed., *Government-Business Cooperation, 1945–1964* (New York, 1994), 1–23.

12. See, e.g., Josiah E. Dubois, Jr., *Generals in Grey Suits* (London, 1953); Joseph Borkin and Charles A. Walsh, *Germany's Master Plan* (London, n.d. [1943?]); Joseph Borkin, *The Crime and Punishment of I.G. Farben* (New York, 1978). Harry Truman, who chaired a committee to investigate international business links in early 1942, thought that whatever was still going on "approaches treason." See Brinkley, *End of Reform* (note 5), 120–21. For "An Exposé of the Nazi-American Money Plot, 1933–1949" (subtitle), see Higham, *Trading with the Enemy* (note 9), covering a range of industries supposedly involved in illegalities. In the chemical industry these related to patents that corporations claimed could simply not be expropriated. For the British side, see H. Levy, *Monopolies, Cartels and Trusts in British Industry* (London, 1927). On the issues raised by patent laws, see Kees Gispen, "Hintergrund, Bedeutung und Entwicklung der Patentgesetzgebung in Deutschland 1877 bis heute," in R. Boch, ed., *Patentschutz und Innovation in Geschichte und Gegenwart* (Frankfurt, 1999).

13. See, e.g., Brinkley, *End of Reform* (note 5), 174, quoting praise by Henry Wallace of executives who are "oftentimes more interested in increasing production and thereby serving humanity than making money for money's sake." He added that "such men are in some ways the hope of America and the world."

14. There were by 1943 several channels through which news of the Holocaust reached the West, with some arriving via couriers and others because the British had succeeded in breaking the secret codes of the SS. See, e.g., Richard Breitman, *Official Secrets. What the Nazis Planned, What the British and Americans Knew* (New York, 1998).

15. See Bernd Greiner, *Die Morgenthau-Legende* (Hamburg, 1995); Wilfried Mausbach, *Zwischen Morgenthau und Marshall* (Düsseldorf, 1996); John Blum, *Roosevelt and Morgenthau* (Boston, 1972).

16. On the Quebec Conference, see the studies cited in note 15.

17. On the problems surrounding Article 7, see, e.g., Richard N. Gardner, *Sterling-Dollar Diplomacy in Current Perspective* (New York, 1980), 54ff., 110ff.; Alan P. Dobson, *The Politics of the Anglo-American Economic Special Relationship, 1940–1987* (New York, 1988), 29ff. On the "growing friction" between the two allies, ibid., 60ff.

18. Churchill quoted in Robert M. Hathaway, *Ambiguous Partnership, Britain and America, 1944–1947* (New York, 1981), 63. Roosevelt quoted in ibid., 64.

19. Greiner, *Die Morgenthau-Legende* (note 15). See also Robert Murphy, *Diplomat among Warriors* (Garden City, NJ, 1964); J. A. Schwarz, *The Speculator. Bernard M. Baruch in Washington, 1917–1965* (Chapel Hill, NC, 1981).

20. Mark E. Ruff, "Senator Harley Martin Kilgore and German Decartelization: The Workings of a Progressive Mindset" (paper, Brown University, 1992). See also below, note 86.

21. Quoted in J. Davidow, "The Seeking of a World Competition Code: Quixotic Quest?," in O. Schachter and R. Hellawell, eds., *Competition in International Business* (New York, 1981), 361–62.

22. Wendell Berge, *Cartels: A Challenge to the Free World* (Washington, 1944).

23. Ruff, "Senator Harley Martin Kilgore" (note 20), 13.

24. Brinkley, *End of Reform* (note 5), 173–74. See also Robert M. Collins, *The Business Response to Keynes, 1929–1964* (New York, 1981), esp. 142ff.

25. On Hoffmann and his career, see A. R. Raucher, *Paul G. Hoffman* (Lexington, KY, 1985).

26. Ibid., 59–60. See also C. L. Mee, Jr., *The Marshall Plan. The Launching of the Pax Americana* (New York, 1984).

27. Edward Mason, *Controlling World Trade. Cartels and Commodity Agreements* (New York, 1946), 67–68. See also Secretary of State James Byrnes, who said in October 1945 that the United States would "never join any groups" that were "in hostile intrigue against the Soviet Union." Quoted in Melvin Leffler, *The Preponderance of Power* (Stanford, 1992), 42.

28. Hathaway, *Ambiguous Partnership* (note 18), 79ff.

29. Quoted in Anne Orde, *The Eclipse of Great Britain. The United States and British Imperial Decline, 1895–1956* (New York, 1996), 161.

30. On Truman, see, e.g., Dobson, *Politics* (note 17), 76. Uneasy about Congress, he had also replaced the former U.S. Steel manager Stettinius with James Byrnes, a conservative from South Carolina, on 1 July 1945. On public opinion, see Astrid M. Eckert, *Feindbilder im Wandel. Ein Vergleich des Deutschland- und des Japanbildes in den US, 1945 und 1946* (Münster, 1999).

31. See John E. Farquharson, "Hilfe für den Feind. Die britische Debatte um Nahrungsmittellieferungen an Deutschland 1944 and 45," *Vierteljahrshefte für Zeitgeschichte* 2 (April 1989): 253–78; Mark Roseman, *Recasting the Ruhr, 1945–1958* (Providence, RI, 1992); C. Scharf and H.-J. Schröder, eds., *Die Deutschlandpolitik Grossbritanniens und die britische Zone, 1945–1949* (Wiesbaden, 1979).

32. John Farquharson, *The Western Allies, and the Politics of Food: Agrarian Management in Postwar Germany* (Leamington Spa, 1985); Paul Erker, *Ernährungskrise und Nachkriegsgesellschaft* (Stuttgart, 1990); Günter Trittel, *Hunger und Politik* (Frankfurt, 1991).

33. Interview with William Harris-Burland, 10 July 1978.

34. Otto A. Friedrich, diary, entry of 13 December 1948 (private access).

35. J. Davenport, "New Chance for Germany," *Fortune*, October 1949, 72.

36. Retranslated from *Industriekurier*, 9 May 1950. See also H. Mendershausen, "Fitting Germany into a Network of World Trade," *American Economic Review* 40 (1950): 548–67, an apt title in terms of American objectives.

37. Ursula Lehmkuhl, *Pax Anglo-Americana. Machtstrukturelle Grundlagen anglo-amerikanischer Asien- und Fernostpolitik in den 50er Jahren* (Munich, 1999). See also S. Croft, *The End of Superpower. British Foreign Office Concepts of a "Changing World," 1945–1951* (Aldershot, 1994).

38. Thus Alfred Eckes, Jr. and Thomas W. Zeiler, *Globalization and the American Century* (New York, 2002), 107. See also Dobson, *Politics* (note 17), 16, citing the *New York Herald Tribune* of 31 March 1946, when Morgenthau, ever conscious

of the Treasury's position in this picture, is supposed to have said to Truman that he was hoping to affect a shift from the City and Wall Street to "the responsible hands of the US Treasury."

39. On material reparations, see, e.g., Alan Kramer, *Die britische Demontagepolitik am Beispiel Hamburgs, 1945–1950* (Hamburg, 1991); O. Nübel, *Die amerikanische Reparationspolitik gegenüber Deutschland, 1941–1945* (Frankfurt, 1980); Jürgen Foschepoth, "Konflikte in der Reparationspolitik der Alliierten," in Foschepoth, *Kalter Krieg und deutsche Frage* (Göttingen, 1985), 175–97; Hanns D. Ahrens, *Demontage* (Munich, 1982). On patents, trademarks, research, and development, see John Gimbel, *Science, Technology, and Reparations. Exploitation and Plunder in Postwar Germany* (Stanford, 1990); Raymond Stokes, "Technology and the West German *Wirtschaftswunder,*" *Technology and Culture* 1 (January 1991): 10, mentions that the "economic think tank Ifo Institut pegged the loss of patents and trademarks for the chemical industry alone at $10 billion." See also Burghard Cisla and Matthias Judt, eds., *Technology Transfer out of Germany after 1945* (Amsterdam, 1996); Helmut Fiereder, "Demontagen in Deutschland nach 1945 unter besonderer Berücksichtigung der Montanindustrie," *Zeitschrift für Unternehmensgeschichte* 4 (1989): 209–39; Arnold Krammer, "Technology Transfer as War Booty: The U.S. Technical Oil Mission to Europe, 1945," *Technology and Culture* 22, no. 1 (1981): 68–103.

40. Carl Glatt, *Reparations and Transfer of Scientific and Industrial Technology from Germany,* 3 vols. (PhD thesis, European University Institute, Florence, 1994), 1:16.

41. Ibid.

42. See Christopher Simpson, *Blowback. American Recruitment of Nazis and Its Effects on the Cold War* (New York, 1988); Tom Bower, *The Paper Clip Conspiracy* (London, 1987).

43. Jean E. Smith, *Lucius D. Clay* (New York, 1990); Lucius D. Clay, *Decision in Germany* (Garden City, NJ, 1950); Harold Zink, *The United States in Germany, 1944–1955* (Princeton, 1957); F. M. Davis, *Come as Conqueror. The United States Army's Occupation of Germany, 1945–1949* (New York, 1967); Wolfgang Krieger, *General Lucius D. Clay und die amerikanische Deutschlandpolitik, 1945–1949* (Stuttgart, 1987).

44. Charles Kindleberger, *The German Economy, 1945–1947* (Westport, CT, 1989), ix (with Günter Bischof quoting Kindleberger in his introduction).

45. Quoted in Alan Kramer, *The West German Economy, 1945–1955* (Providence, RI, 1991), 25.

46. Lewis H. Brown, *A Report on Germany* (New York, 1947), v, thereafter passim.

47. Charles Kindleberger, *German Economy* (note 44), 39.

48. Ibid., 40.

49. See above, p. 297.

50. Werner Link, *Deutsche und amerikanische Gewerkschaften und Geschäftsleute, 1945–1975* (Düsseldorf, 1978), 104.

51. See Michael Hogan, *The Marshall Plan* (New York, 1987), 137–38.

52. James S. Martin, *All Honorable Men* (Boston, 1950).

53. See "Reminiscences of William H. Draper" (Columbia University Oral History Project, NXCP87-A824). Bernd Greiner called him the "Economic Tsar" for occupied Germany. Draper later moved to Japan, where he pursued the same decartelization and recasting policies for the zaibatsu system. It would be interesting to have a biography on him.

54. Raymond G. Stokes, *Divide and Prosper. The Heirs of I.G. Farben under Allied Authority, 1945–1951* (Berkeley, 1988); Hans-Dieter Kreikamp, "Die Entflechtung der I.G. Farbenindustrie A.G. und die Gründung der Nachfolgegesellschaften," *Vierteljahrshefte für Zeitgeschichte* 25 (1977): 220–51.

55. Gary Herrigel, "American Occupation, Market Order, and Democracy: Reconfiguring the Steel Industry of Japan and Germany after the Second World War," in Jonathan Zeitlin and Gary Herrigel, eds., *Americanization and Its Limits* (Oxford, 2000), 365.

56. Joachim Scholtyseck, *Robert Bosch und der liberale Widerstand gegen Hitler, 1933–1945* (Munich, 1999); Johannes Bähr and Paul Erker, *Bosch. Geschichte eines Weltunternehmens* (Munich 2013).

57. See, e.g., Lothar Gall, *Der Bankier. Hermann Josef Abs* (Munich, 2004); Theo Horstmann, *Die Alliierten und die deutschen Grossbanken* (Bonn, 1991); Harold James, *The Deutsche Bank and the Nazi Economic War against the Jews* (Cambridge, 2001).

58. For this view see, Carolyn Eisenberg, "US Policy in Post-War Germany: The Conservative Restoration," *Science and Society* 46, no. 1 (Spring 1982): 24–38; Eberhard Schmidt, *Die verhinderte Neuordnung, 1945–1952* (Frankfurt, 1970). See also Jutta Lange-Quassowski, *Neuordnung oder Restauration?* (Opladen, 1979).

59. See, e.g., Lothar Gall, ed., *Krupp im 20. Jahrhundert* (Berlin, 2002); Harold James, *Krupp. The History of a Legendary Firm* (Princeton, 2012); Norbert Frei et al., *Flick. Der Konzern, die Familie, die Macht* (Munich, 2009); Joseph Borkin, *The Crime and Punishment of I.G. Farben* (New York, 1978). On the more general situation of West German industry, see, above all, Jonathan Wiesen, *West German Industry and the Challenge of the Nazi Past, 1945–1955* (Chapel Hill, NC, 2001); Louis P. Lochner, *Tycoons and Tyrant. German Industry from Hitler to Adenauer* (Chicago, 1954).

60. See, e.g., W. M. Blumenthal, *Codetermination in the German Steel Industry* (Princeton, 1956); H. Thum, *Mitbestimmung in der Montanindustrie* (Stuttgart, 1982).

61. H. J. Spiro, *The Politics of German Codetermination* (Cambridge, MA, 1958); B. Muszynski, *Wirtschaftliche Mitbestimmung zwischen Konflikt- und Harmoniekonzeptionen* (Meisenheim, 1975); Karl Lauschke, "'Wir sind heute mehr Mensch als früher.' Unternehmenskultur in einem montanmitbestimmten Grossbetrieb der fünfziger Jahre," *Jahrbuch für Wirtschaftsgeschichte* 2 (1983): 137–57. On British plans in the Ruhr, see Horst Lademacher, "Die britische Sozialisierungspolitik im Rhein-Ruhr-Raum," in Joseph Foschepoth and Rolf Steininger, eds., *Britische Deutschland- und Besatzungspolitik, 1945–1949* (Paderborn, 1985), 101–17. On the Cripps quote, see *The Times*, 28 October 1946, quoted in K. Coates and A. J. Topham, *Industrial Democracy and Nationalisation* (Nottingham, 1975), 59–60.

62. Volker R. Berghahn, *The Americanisation of West German Industry, 1945–1973* (New York, 1986), 98–99, 103ff.

63. Volker R. Berghahn and Paul J. Friedrich, *Otto A. Friedrich. Ein politischer Unternehmer* (Frankfurt, 1993), 110.

64. Berghahn, *Americanisation of West German Industry* (note 62), 147ff.

65. Mason, *Controlling World Trade* (note 27), 132. This quote seems to come close to Geir Lundestad's concept of the United States being an "empire by invitation" that the defeated Germans integrated themselves into—not always, though, happily and with a good deal of direct pressure from Washington and the occupation authorities. See his "American Empire by Invitation," in Thomas G. Paterson and Robert J. McMahon, eds., *The Origins of the Cold War*, 3rd ed. (Lexington, MA, 1991), 110–18.

66. On German trips to the United States, see S. Jonathan Wiesen, "Bildungsreisen, Handelsmessen, Werbekampagnen: Begegnungen zwischen deutschen und amerikanischen Geschäftsleuten im Zeichen des Kalten Krieges," in Detlef Junker, ed., *Die USA und Deutschland im Zeitalter des Kalten Krieges* (Stuttgart, 2001), 870–88. See also Ernst Hickmann, *Produktivität durch "Management." Eindrücke von einer Studienreise in USA* (Bremen, 1955).

67. See, e.g., Peter Hüttenberger, "Wirtschaftsordnung und Interessenpolitik in der Kartellgesetzgebung der Bundesrepublik, 1949–1957," *Vierteljahrshefte für Zeitgeschichte*, no. 3 (1976): 287–307.

68. Quoted in Glatt, *Reparations and Transfer* (note 40), 40–41.

69. Hathaway, *Ambiguous Partnership* (note 18), 25.

70. Keynes in David Edgerton, *Britain's War Machine* (London, 2011), 297; Bothby in Gottfried Niethart, *Geschichte Englands im 19. und 20. Jahrhundert* (Munich, 1987), 186. Dalton in Hathaway, *Ambiguous Partnership* (note 18), 183.

71. See Kathleen Burk, *Old World, New World. Great Britain and America from the Beginning* (London, 2007), 567.

72. Quoted in Richard Gardner, *Sterling-Dollar Diplomacy in Current Perspective* (New York, 1980), 253.

73. Ibid. "Bretton Woods" is a reference to the international conference that was held in July 1944 at the Mount Washington Hotel, in Bretton Woods, New Hampshire. It was one of the most important attempts by the United States to reorder, in anticipation of an Allied victory, the world's financial and monetary system in pursuit of the Open Door. It united some forty-four nations who agreed to set up the International Bank for Reconstruction and Development (later World Bank), the International Monetary Fund (IMF), and the General Agreement on Tariffs and Trade (GATT). For Treasury Secretary Morgenthau the conference was to usher in the end of the economic nationalism of the previous decades. The Americans had prepared a framework for the IMF that became known as the (Dexter) White Plan, with Keynes having put forward an alternative proposal that was ultimately shelved in favor of White's. But as Benn Steil has shown in his *The Battle of Bretton Woods* (Princeton 2013), Washington's ulterior motive was to attain its objective, pursued since 1919, of replacing London as the financial center of the world. Bretton Woods was fundamental to the running of the postwar Western monetary system until it broke down in the context of the Vietnam War in 1971. However, both the IMF

and the World Bank continue to fulfill important roles in the world economy to this day. See also Marc Flandreau et al., eds., *International Financial History of the Twentieth Century* (Cambridge, 2003); Benjamin M. Rowland, "Preparing the American Ascendancy: The Transfer of Economic Power from Britain to the United States, 1933–1944," in Rowland, ed., *Balance of Power or Hegemony: The Interwar Monetary System* (New York, 1976), 193–224. See also below, note 84.

74. Quoted in Orde, *Eclipse of Great Britain* (note 29), 162.

75. Michael Collins, *Money and Banking in the UK: A History* (London, 1988), 439–40.

76. For a concise analysis of the British financial system, see, e.g., Karl Erich Born, *International Banking in the 19th and 20th Centuries* (New York, 1983), esp. 59ff., 160ff.

77. Collins, *Money and Banking* (note 75), 446.

78. Geoffrey Owen, *From Empire to Europe* (London, 1999), 90.

79. Glatt, *Reparations and Transfer* (note 40), 45.

80. Ibid.

81. Ibid., quoted from the Cabinet Papers 87/9, Committees on Post-War Reconstruction, 1941–1946, 2 September 1944.

82. Owen, *From Empire to Europe* (note 78), 57.

83. Glatt, *Reparations and Transfer* (note 40), 49.

84. On GATT and IMF, constituted at Bretton Woods (see note 73, above), see, e.g., Harold James, "The IMF and the Creation of the Bretton Woods System, 1944–1958," in Barry Eichengreen, ed., *Europe's Post-war Recovery* (Cambridge, 1993), 93–126; Douglas A. Irwin, "The GATT's Contribution to Economic Recovery in Post-war Western Europe," in Eichengreen, *Europe's Post-war Recovery*, 127–50.

85. Hoffman quote: Günter Bischof in his introduction to Kindleberger, *German Economy* (note 44), xvii. Acheson quote in Greg Behrman, *The Most Nobel Adventure* (New York, 2007), 264; A. Rappaport, "The United States and European Integration," *Diplomatic History* 5 (Spring 1981): 139–40.

86. Quoted in Hathaway, *Ambiguous Partnership* (note 18), 45. Of course, the Mau Mau Uprising in East Africa in 1954 demonstrated that supposedly vital parts of the Empire were held together by brute force. See also Richard Gott, *Britain's Empire* (London, 2011). On Churchill's attitudes and policies, see Richard Toye, *Churchill's Empire. The World That Made Him and the World He Made* (New York, 2010). That support for protectionism through cartels has continued to linger may be seen from the remarks that ICI chair Lord Harry McGowan made in the House of Lords in 1944. He believed that cartels, inter alia, promoted orderly production, curbed excessive competition, and helped stabilize prices. Wyatt Wells, *Antitrust and the Formation of the Postwar World* (New York, 2002), 10.

87. On the origins of the ECSC, see, e.g., John Gillingham, *Coal, Steel, and the Rebirth of Europe, 1945–1955* (Cambridge, 1991); William Diebold, *The Schuman Plan* (New York, 1959). Most recently and very detailed on ECSC origins: Behrman, *Most Noble Adventure* (note 85), 283ff.

88. See *Industriekurier*, 21 March 1950; *Industriekurier*, 31 March 1950; *Industriekurier*, 13 April 1950; *Industriekurier*, 11 May 1950. It seems that these initiatives,

if they were ever taken, harkened back to the efforts of the mid-1920s to create an entente between the Ruhr's coal and Lorrainian iron ore. See Eberhard von Vietsch, *Arnold Rechberg und das Problem der Westorientierung Deutschlands nach dem 1. Weltkrieg* (Boppard, 1958).

89. See, e.g., Secretary of State Dean Acheson's cable to John Foster Dulles in Washington, in *Foreign Relations of the United States*, vol. 3 (1950; Washington, DC, 1977), 694–95. See also Pierre Mélandri, *Les Etats Unis face a l'unification de l'Europe* (Paris, 1980); Holger Schröder, *Jean Monnet und die amerikanische Unterstützung für die europäische Integration, 1950–1957* (Frankfurt, 1994); Lawrence B. Krause, *European Economic Integration and the United States* (Washington, DC, 1968), esp. 141ff.; Geir Lundestad, *"Empire" by Integration: The United States and European Integration, 1945–1997* (Oxford, 1998); David Feldman et al., eds., *Post-War Reconstruction in Europe: International Perspectives, 1945–1949* (Oxford, 2010).

90. *Industriekurier*, 14 February 1951.

91. See Günter Henle, "Vom Ruhrstatut zur Montanunion," in D. Blumenwitz et al., eds., *Konrad Adenauer und seine Zeit* (Stuttgart, 1976), 1:566–90; Isabel Warner, *Steel and Sovereignty. The Deconcentration of West German Steel Industry, 1949–1956* (Mainz, 1996); Werner Bührer, *Ruhrstahl und Europa* (Munich, 1986). On the ECSC and Britain, see Behrman, *Most Nobel Adventure* (note 85), 290–91.

92. See Hans-Günther Sohl, *Notizen*, limited ed. (Bochum-Wattenscheid, 1985); Toni Pierenkemper, "Hans-Günther Sohl: Funktionale Effizienz und autoritäre Harmonie in der Eisen- und Stahlindustrie," in Pierenkemper and Paul Erker, eds., *Deutsche Unternehmer zwischen Kriegswirtschaft und Wiederaufbau* (Munich, 1999), 53–107.

93. On the Marshall Plan in Germany, see, e.g., Gerd Hardach, "Marshall Plan in Germany," *Journal of European Economic History* 16 (1987): 433–85. See also Stanley Hoffman and Charles S. Maier, eds., *The Marshall Plan* (Boulder, CO, 1984); Hogan, *Marshall Plan* (note 51).

94. See, e.g., Kramer, *West German Economy* (note 45), 148ff.; Manfred Knapp, "Wiederaufbau und Westintegration: Die Auswirkungen des Marshall-Plans auf Deutschland," in Willi Paul Adams and Knud Krakau, eds., *Deutschland und Amerika. Perzeption und historische Realität* (Berlin, 1985), 111–33.

95. See, e.g., Armin Grünbacher, *Reconstruction and Cold War in Germany. The Kreditanstalt für Wiederaufbau (1948–1961)* (Aldershot, 2004).

96. See Heiner Adamsen, *Investitionshilfe für die Ruhr. Wiederaufbau, Verbände und Soziale Marktwirtschaft, 1948–1951* (Wuppertal, 1981). Compared to what happened in the 1920s, these credits went almost exclusively into the modernization of private industry, not into infrastructure.

97. Werner Abelshauser, "Hilfe und Selbsthilfe. Zur Funktion des Marshallplans beim westdeutschen Wiederaufbau," *Vierteljahrshefte für Zeitgeschichte* 1 (1989): 85–113. See also Reinhard Neebe, "Technologie-Transfer und Aussenhandel in den Anfangsjahren der Bundesrepublik Deutschland," *Vierteljahrsschrift für Sozial- und Wirtschaftsgeschichte* 76 (1989): 54, with a graph showing a steep rise in investment-good outlays and a much more modest rise in investments in consumer goods industries.

98. See Berghahn and Friedrich, *Otto A. Friedrich* (note 63), 14ff.

99. Ibid., 27ff.

100. Ibid., 42ff., also for the following.

101. Joseph Barber, *American Policy Toward Germany. A Report on the Views of Community Leaders in Twenty-Two Cities, Council on Foreign Relations* (New York, 1947), 3, 9, 11, 14, 17, 19, 24, 25, 27.

102. Berghahn and Friedrich, *Otto A. Friedrich* (note 63), 48. The best study on the German and American rubber industry, both before and after 1945, is Paul Erker, *Vom nationalen zum globalen Wettbewerb* (Paderborn, 2005). It is 710 pages long. According to Raymond Stokes, "the role of technological change in the postwar West German economic miracle conformed by and large to German traditions of technological excellence tempered by the drag on the implementation of the latest technologies." German "concern for excellence combined with gradual, deliberate adoption of new [American] technologies determined the pace, success, and longevity of West Germany's economic miracle." See his article "Technology and the West German *Wirtschaftswunder*," *Technology and Culture* 1 (1991): 21–22. See also Deutsches Wirtschafts-Institut, ed., *Amerikanische Beteiligungen an westdeutschen Unternehmen* (Berlin, 1951).

103. See, e.g., Thomas Berger and Karl-Heinz Müller, *Lebenssituationen 1945–1948* (Hanover, 1983); Friedrich Prinz, *Trümmerzeit in München* (Munich, 1984); Doris Schubert, *Frauen in der deutschen Nachkriegsgeschichte*, vol. 1 (Düsseldorf, 1984); Wolfgang Benz, ed., *Zusammenbruch und Wiederaufbau* (Munich, 1985). The latter are the diaries of Ludwig Vaubel of Vereinigte Glanzstoff A.G. in Wuppertal, with rich detail on daily life, politics, and economic conditions in the later 1940s.

104. Berghahn and Friedrich, *Otto A. Friedrich* (note 63), 86.

105. Ibid., 97ff.

106. Gilbert Burck, "The German Business Mind," *Fortune* 49 (May 1954): 111–14, 218–22. See also Burck, "Can Germany Go Capitalist?," *Fortune* 49 (April 1954): 114–20, 247–56. See also Ralph Jessen and Lydia Langer, eds., *Transformations of Retailing in Europe after 1945* (Farnham, 2012).

107. For the gross value added figures, see B.W.E. Alford, *Britain in the World Economy since 1880* (London, 1996), 326. For the Owen quote, see Owen, *From Empire to Europe* (note 78), 208.

108. Jonathan Wood, *Wheels of Misfortune* (London, 1988).

109. Ibid., 30ff.

110. Ibid., 98.

111. Ibid., 99.

112. See, e.g., Charles S. Maier, "The Politics of Productivity: Foundations of American International Economic Policy after World War II," *International Organization* 31 (1977): 607–33; Bent Boel, "The European Productivity Agency: A Faithful Prophet of the American Model?," in Matthias Kipping and Ove Bjarnar, eds., *The Americanization of European Business, 1948–1960* (London, 1998). On the British visits and the European program more generally, see Behrman, *Most Nobel Adventure* (note 85), 311ff. On the German discussion of these topics in the journal of the West German Employers Federation, see "Die Proktivitäts-Verwaltung," *Der Arbeitgeber*, 1 October 1951, 10.

113. Terry Gourvish and Nick Tiratsoo, eds., *Managers and Missionaries, 1945–1960* (Manchester, 1998), 11.

114. Ibid, 11.

115. Edgar Gerwin, "England studiert Amerikas Produktivität," *Der Arbeit-geber*, 1 December 1949, 19–21. See also Stephen N. Broadberry, *Productivity Race* (Cambridge, 1997).

116. Quoted in Simon Reich, *The Fruits of Fascism. Postwar Prosperity in Historical Perspective* (Ithaca, NY, 1990), 172.

117. Wood, *Wheels of Misfortune* (note 108), 248; Simon Reich, *Fruits of Fascism* (note 116), 172, considers it a "popular myth that many British industrialists visited the Volkswagen plant and rejected both car and plant." But he also writes, "Representatives of the British car industry expressed reservations about the quality of the car and whether they could use the machinery effectively, but they did recognize the competitive threat the Volkswagenwerk would pose if it survived reparations."

118. Quoted in Wood, *Wheels of Misfortune* (note 117), 248. For further details on the British car industry's response, see Bernhard Rieger, *The People's Car. A Global History of the Volkswagen Beetle* (Cambridge, MA, 2013), 106–7.

119. See Reich, *Fruits of Fascism* (note 116), 96–97; see also Rieger, *People's Car* (note 118) on the initial difficulties to increase production and Wolfburg's eventual success.

120. Ibid., 240–41. There were some six thousand outlets worldwide.

121. Graham Turner, *Business in Britain* (London, 1969), 394. Glatt, *Reparations and Transfer* (note 40) I, p.45.

122. Turner, *Business in Britain* (note 121), 396.

123. Quoted in Wood, *Wheels of Misfortune* (note 117), 115.

124. Ibid. 134ff.

125. Reich, *Fruits of Fascism* (note 116), 218; he added (ibid., 243) that workers were often made the scapegoats for the larger problems of management and competence. See also Mike Richardson and Peter Nicholls, *A Business and Labour History of Britain* (New York, 2011); Bruce Collins and Keith Robbins, *British Culture and Economic Decline* (London, 1990).

126. Wood, *Wheels of Misfortune* (note 117), 112.

127. Jonathan Zeitlin, "Americanizing British Engineering? Strategic Debate, Selective Adaptation, and Hybrid Innovation in Post-War Reconstruction," in Zeitlin and Herrigel, *Americanization* (note 55), 152.

128. Owen, *From Empire to Europe* (note 78), 172.

129. Turner, *Business in Britain* (note 121), 431.

130. Ibid., 431–32. See also John Cockcroft, *Why England Sleeps* (London, 1971), with a comprehensive analysis of the problems besetting Britain in the 1950s and 1960s.

131. Stephen Blank, *Industry and Government in Britain. The Federation of British Industries in Politics, 1945–1965* (Farnborough, 1973); Wyn Grant and David Marsh, *The Confederation of British Industries* (London, 1977). Compare with, e.g., Gerard Braunthal, *The Federation of German Industry in Politics* (Ithaca, NY, 1965); Wiesen, *West German Industry* (note 59), esp. 129ff.

132. See Glatt, *Reparations and Transfer* (note 40), vol. 1, passim; ibid., vol., 3, 1010ff.

133. Jean E. Smith, *Eisenhower* (New York, 2012), 686ff.

134. Ibid., 697.

135. Cole C. Kingseed, *Eisenhower and the Suez Crisis of 1956* (Baton Rouge, LA 1995), 124; Herman Finer, *Dulles over Suez* (London, 1964).

136. Quoted in Diane B. Kunz, *The Economic Diplomacy of the Suez Crisis* (Chapel Hill, NC, 1991), 107. See also Nigel Ashton, *Eisenhower, Macmillan and the Problem of Nasser* (London, 1996).

137. Kingseed, *Eisenhower* (note 135), 124.

138. Quoted in Smith, *Eisenhower* (note 133), 704.

139. For more on the crisis and its context, including the complications stemming from the Soviet invasion of Hungary, as well as its aftermath, see also David A. Nichols, *Eisenhower 1956. The President's Year of Crisis: Suez and the Brink of War* (New York, 2011); S. W. Lucas, *Divided We Stand. Britain, the United States and the Suez Crisis* (London, 1991); Saki Dockrill, *Britain's Retreat from East of Suez. The Choice between Europe and the World?* (Basingstoke, 2002); Finer, *Dulles over Suez* (note 135).

140. Rudolf M. Christen, *Amerikanische Auslandsinvestitionen in der Nachkriegszeit* (Winterthur, 1966), 13–14; Lawrence B. Krause, *European Economic Integration* (note 89), 141ff.

141. On this subject, see, e.g., Robert Mark Spaulding, *Osthandel and Ostpolitik. German Foreign Trade Policies in Eastern Europe from Bismarck to Adenauer* (Providence, RI, 1997); Angela Stent, *From Embargo to Ostpolitik. The Political Economy of Soviet-West German Relations* (Cambridge, 1980); Peter Danylow and Ulrich S. Soénius, eds., *Otto Wolf. Ein Unternehmen zwischen Wirtschaft und Politik* (Munich, 2005); Karsten Rudolph, *Wirtschaftsdiplomatie im Kalten Krieg: Die Ostpolitik der deutschen Grossindustrie, 1945–1961* (Frankfurt, 2004); Ian Jackson, *The Economic Cold War: Britain and East-West Trade, 1948–1963* (Basingstoke, 2001); Claudia Wörmann, *Der Osthandel der Bundesrepublik Deutschland* (Frankfurt, 1982).

142. See, as a small selection, e.g., Reinhard Neebe, *Weichenstellung in die Globalisierung. Deutsche Weltmarktpolitik, Europa und Amerika in der Ära Ludwig Erhard* (Cologne, 2004); Jürgen Seidl, *Die Bayerischen Motorenwerke (BMW), 1945–1969* (Munich, 2002); Heidrun Edelmann, *Heinz Nordhoff und Volkswagen* (Göttingen, 2003); Richard Tilly, *Willy Schlieker. Aufstieg und Fall eines Unternehmers (1914–1980)* (Berlin, 2008); Susanne Hilger, *"Amerikanisierung" deutscher Unternehmen. Wettbewerbsstrategien und Unternehmenspolitik bei Henkel, Siemens und Daimler-Benz (1945/49–1975)* (Wiesbaden, 2004); Christopher Neumaier, *Dieselautos in Deutschland und den USA* (Stuttgart, 2010); Christian Kleinschmidt, *Der produktive Blick. Wahrnehmung amerikanischer und japanischer Management- und Produktionsmethoden durch deutsche Unternehmer, 1950–1985* (Berlin, 2002); Hartmut Berghoff, *Zwischen Kleinstadt und Weltmarkt. Hohner und die Harmonika, 1857–1961. Unternehmengeschichte als Gesellschaftsgeschichte* (Paderborn, 1997); Christopher Neumaier, *Dieselautos in Deutschland und den USA* (Stuttgart, 2010); Ute Jeck, *Amerikanische Tochtergesellschaften in der Bundesrepublik* (Frankfurt, 1962); Heinz Hartmann, *Amerikanische Firmen in Deutschland* (Cologne, 1963).

Conclusions

///

For the period up to World War I, it became clear that the elites of the United States, and its businessmen on the East and West Coasts in particular, saw their country as a highly dynamic and modern industrial and financial power. Based on the idea of a competitive capitalism, American big business, in the wake of the great merger wave of the late nineteenth century and congressional legislation that had banned the formation of cartels and monopolies, developed in the direction of an oligopolistic market organization. These developments shaped corporate attitudes and practices toward the domestic and international economy from 1900 onward. No less important, the emergence of the United States as a major industrial power stirred Britain and Germany into responses to the American challenge. Both countries began to debate more vigorously than before whether and how far the appearance on the stage of the new partner and competitor across the Atlantic might sooner or later lead to an "Americanization" of their own economies and societies, if not even—as William Stead had written—to an "Americanization of the World."

But a close reading of Stead's book, undertaken in chapter I, showed that it was in fact much more about how to forge a "special relationship" between Britain and the United States as a way of securing the survival of the British Empire, which many perceived to be a declining power, about to lose to America the hegemonic position it had held throughout the nineteenth century. However, there were also the Germans as the third player on the international stage and within the North Atlantic Triangle. They, too, saw themselves as a rising industrial power, and judging by their economic performance in the decades before 1914, they had high hopes of being counted among the top three or four nations of the twentieth century. It was only when some political and military leaders, including Wilhelm II and later Adolf Hitler, began to claim first place that reckless miscalculations occurred, seducing the German political leadership into unleashing two world wars in a struggle for hegemony against Britain and America.

For reasons that were partly related to the peculiarities of the German monarchical system and the eccentricities of Wilhelm II at its head, the Germans—as discussed in chapter II—were at first more confrontationist toward the other new industrial power across the Atlantic. But when this assertiveness, especially in Latin America, soured relations with Washington, Imperial Germany pursued a more flexible policy that enabled the German business community to expand earlier trading links with American enterprises. Cooperations and partnerships were reinforced or established. Americans, however cautiously, began to invest in Germany and to establish production facilities there. Even more gingerly, the Germans began to venture into the American market and a few companies, such as Stollwerck, built up a manufacturing base in the United States. Above all, the three countries engaged in an exchange of information on their industries and infrastructures. German entrepreneurs and engineers visited the industrial centers of the East Coast and the Midwest to study Taylorism and Fordism. American businessmen traveled to Germany to compare local business methods with their own practices. They were also keen to learn, for example, about the German system of education and training both of skilled workers and of managers and scientists involved in R&D at dynamic firms in chemical, electrical, and nonelectrical engineering.

All the while American visitors also stopped over in Britain, partly to foster existing business relations and partly to find out how their British counterparts were dealing with the burning issues of running a modern enterprise. But the impressions they came back with were often—as was shown in chapters II and III—that British industry had lost its drive. They were amazed at the conservatism and immobilism of many captains of industry who with their Oxbridge classics education had little understanding of the problems of modern production and marketing and of how to treat blue-collar workers and white-collar employees. They noted the influence of trade unions and their shop-floor representatives who were prone to call out their workers on strikes and to bring production to a halt. Time and again, American visitors returned home puzzled and disillusioned by what they had seen in Britain. By contrast, they tended to be impressed by their conversations with German businessmen and discovered attitudes toward modern production technology and organization that made it easier for them to decide on whether to strengthen whatever links that had already been established. In this respect the Vanderlip Papers proved to be a particularly insightful source.

The trouble was that German-American *political* relations began to deteriorate toward 1914 for reasons that were examined at the end of chapter II and at the beginning of chapter III. The more the specter of war appeared on the horizon, the more nervous the business communities of all three countries became. With few exceptions, they all believed that a great war between the major European powers would be a catastrophe, not merely because of the disruption it would cause for international trade that in previous decades had created so much prosperity on both sides of the Atlantic, but also because modern warfare would be an enormously wasteful drain on domestic resources and manpower and destroy the foundations of national wealth. The monarchs in Wilhelmine Germany and the Habsburg Empire had the exclusive constitutional powers to declare war and in exercising them relied primarily on their military advisers. It is now widely accepted that in the final analysis it was a small circle around Wilhelm II in Berlin and Franz Joseph I in Vienna that pushed Europe over the brink into the World War I. Prominent businessmen pleaded with them, but they were as powerless to preserve the peace as their colleagues in London and Washington and the ordinary people of Europe.

While Britain and Germany became deadly enemies in August 1914, the United States kept out of the war, at least until April 1917. At the same time and with their many prewar connections with Germany in tatters, the American business elites increasingly favored a victory of the Anglo-French-Russian alliance. In this sense, American relations with Britain once again grew more and more "special" until the two sides became formal allies with the belated American entry into the war. It was this entry that tipped the scales in favor of a victory of the Western Allies after Russia had been rocked by the Bolshevik Revolution and dropped out.

When the war finally ended with the defeat of the Central Powers in the autumn of 1918, the first question was what would happen to Anglo-American relations. The story that was told at the end of chapter III was not an uplifting one. Partly because of the immense domestic upheavals that the war had caused and partly because major strategic disagreements arose between London and Washington over what kind of peace to conclude with Germany, the wartime "special relationship" began to fray. One further reason for this was that Britain began to suspect, and rightly so, that the American business elites were determined not only to leave British industry to its own devices as it tried to reconvert to civilian production, but—no less alarming—also to undermine the primacy of the City as the financial hub of the world. Partly because the United States had been a debtor nation before 1914, Wall Street had not been able to become the main locus of international finance. With the positions of debt and credit between Britain and America reversed due to the war, the American banking community was quite blunt in the 1920s in its quest to replace the City.

As Anglo-American relations went downhill, the antagonistic wartime relations between the United States and Germany underwent a slow metamorphosis. Here the first surprise was that in 1919–20 key American bankers did in fact contemplate floating a huge international loan for the reconstruction of Europe's economies. And as Jan Smuts and Norman Davis had been arguing, this could be done only if German industry was the main target of this effort. However, it quickly turned out after visits from American experts and businessmen that, given the state of the societies and economies of Europe, the greatly strengthened banking system and Wall Street in particular were prepared to step forward only if Washington underwrote the initiative. Since it proved impossible to obtain the requisite majorities for this in Congress, where the representatives of noninvolvement or, worse, strict isolationism held sway, both the American administration in Washington and the business community took the backseat, notwithstanding the fact that the United States went through a reconversion crisis that some urged could be overcome by boosting American exports. Instead the nation witnessed how the French and the Germans, unable to get out of their own postwar depression, weakened each other to the point of financial and economic ruin over the question of German reparations payments. Even in retrospect, it is an amazing spectacle in polarization and mutual self-destruction that two democratic societies, unable to forge a consensus, went through.

After this collapse had taken place in 1923 in the wake of the French invasion of the Ruhr, the industrial heart of Germany, sobriety and rationality returned. Conscious of their responsibility and also their financial clout, American bankers now appeared on the scene to sort out the reparations mess by designing the Dawes Plan. This settlement gave a boost to an economic upswing that had begun in the United States in 1924 after several years of depression. This time Wall Street and the American business community showed more courage to make a commitment to European reconstruction. With Congress still persisting in a policy of noninvolvement, any help from the administration had to come through the back door, however much it knew that something had to be done after 1923. When American big business looked at the British economy in its continued sluggishness and racked by labor troubles, Britain did not seem to offer good prospects for investments. There was also the peculiar story of Britain's self-defeating return to the gold standard that industry warned against and that the Bank of England as well as the City promoted. Consequently, the Americans began to look toward Weimar Germany, as Davis had suggested as early as 1921. With its political system stabilizing, German industry seemed to be a more promising prospect for an engagement than rather undynamic Britain.

Chapter IV therefore examined in some detail both Anglo-American and German-American economic and political relations during the boom years of the mid-twenties up to 1929, when the speculative bubble burst in the United States. This unleashed a crisis that ricocheted around the globe, affecting Germany more deeply than Britain and leading to political radicalization and finally to the Nazi seizure of power in January 1933. Consequently, a considerable part of chapter V was devoted first to Hitler's foreign policy, rapid rearmament program and plans for using the weapons he had produced in a war of conquest, looting, and mass murder that he unleashed in September 1939. After all, Berlin had again become the center of European politics whose aims foreign statesmen and businesspeople tried rather desperately to make sense of.

In order to understand their responses to Nazi foreign policy and aggression, the first part of chapter V focused on Hitler's regime, though always also mindful of the simultaneous violent expansionism of Japan and Italy. Here the argument was that Roosevelt, who had felt a strong aversion to Hitler from the start, finally came out against Japan and Germany in his Quarantine Speech of October 1937. At the same time he began to lay the foundations of war industries that were to prove so much more productive in comparison to what the Axis powers succeeded in mobilizing. And to no small extent did these *preparations* contribute tangibly to the revival of the American economy and the reduction of unemployment following a second though milder depression in the United States in 1937. Above all, it moved a number of prominent business leaders to side with the president's economic and social policies, many of whom had opposed his New Deal during his first term. Now they put themselves at the disposal of the administration to help organize what Roosevelt had become convinced would be vital industrial foundations for a war in which the United States would sooner or later be directly involved.

The third section of chapter V moved back to Germany and focused on the policies of American big business when its leaders were confronted with the increasing political risk that the Nazi dictatorship posed, as it pushed ever more brutally for centralized control of the German economy. While many American firms withdrew from their investments, companies that had production facilities in the country found it more difficult to cut their losses and stayed. The dilemmas with which they were confronted were examined with reference to a range of companies, including entertainment and low-end retailing. More space was given to the manufacturing corporations and to Ford, GM, and IBM in particular. All three got dragged into Hitler's relentless preparations for war and did produce military or militarily significant goods. But, interestingly enough, some, such as GM's Mooney, also involved themselves in efforts to prevent the outbreak of war and, once war had begun, to pave the way well into 1941 for an early armistice. Meanwhile, others, such as his colleague Knudsen, responded to the call from the Roosevelt administration to work for the coordination of military production at home. This is how the question arose in the war whether some major American corporations had severed their connections with the enemy after Hitler had declared war on the United States in December 1941, at the same time as they were fulfilling, on a much larger scale, their patriotic duty to produce for the Allied war effort.

Chapter V, on the 1930s, also made clear that, while both Britain and the United States took an increasingly hard line toward Hitler's foreign and military policies, it could not be said that Anglo-American relations were particularly warm or even "special." London could not stop harboring suspicions that the American vision of wanting to overcome the Great Slump by rebuilding a multilateral Open Door world trading system was directed not only against the attempts by the Axis powers to create autarkic territorial blocs through violent expansion, but also against the British Empire and Commonwealth with its preferential tariff walls. The start of Hitler's wars against Britain and the nations of Western and Northern Europe in 1939–40 and the defeat of all of them on the Continent, including France, by June 1940, left Britain as the only power militarily still opposing Nazi conquests. The focus of Anglo-American relations shifted. With Churchill having replaced the Appeasers around Chamberlain and determined to fight the Germans on the beaches of the British Isles, London faced the question of how to pay for the enormous costs of military resistance. It seems that Churchill did his utmost to mobilize all resources of the country and also drew on those of the Empire and Commonwealth.

However, by the autumn of 1940 Britain was largely bankrupt and could no longer pay for American "cash-and-carry" deliveries of military hardware and food. For the moment this had been all that Roosevelt had been able to wrest from the congressional majority that, referring to the Neutrality Act, insisted on a continuation of "noninvolvement." When by November 1940 Churchill began to plead with Roosevelt to provide loans to pay for the resources needed to continue the war against Germany, the U.S. president was finally able to hold out to him the prospect of a Lend-Lease Agreement. If the British prime minister had been hoping that the Americans would offer generous terms, he was to be sorely disappointed: the funds had to be paid back, whereas the leases of territories to the Americans on British-Caribbean islands and in Newfoundland would be long-term.

British bitterness over this was reflected in the fact that negotiations over the Lend-Lease repayment terms continued into 1942. The issue resurfaced at the Quebec Conference of September 1944 when Churchill was lured into supporting the Morgenthau Plan that he had previously rejected. In return, Morgenthau apparently promised to support a peacetime extension of Lend-Lease. The calculation was also that a harsh treatment of Germany and a dismantling of its industries would enable British export industries to move into the gap. The gains would then contribute to making debt payments to the United States. Of course, the Quebec Conference was hardly over when both Roosevelt and Churchill distanced themselves from Morgenthau, whose plan had run into the vigorous opposition of the State and War Departments. They predicted chaos and revolution unless the United States helped the Germans get back on their feet and integrate themselves into Europe as part of their projected *Pax Americana.*

What further affected the never easy Anglo-American "special relationship" was that, however close Roosevelt and Churchill thought their personal rapport to be, when, after Roosevelt's death, Harry Truman became president, Washington cancelled Lend-Lease in a move that caused much anguish in Britain. Britain was left out in the cold and not surprisingly, though very much in contradiction to the American vision of the Open Door, continued its preferential tariff system with the Empire and Commonwealth. At the same time the City tried hard to buttress its position as the hub of the Sterling Bloc against the designs of the American banking community to become the unchallenged center of global finance. The City did not succeed, just as the Empire could not be salvaged. The hour of truth came in 1956 during the Suez Crisis, when, as discussed in chapter VI, Eisenhower threatened to trigger the collapse of the British currency and forced Eden to withdraw from Egypt.

Looking back over the decades since 1900, the British position in the world that had begun to weaken in the late nineteenth century was badly battered by the Germans when they twice in the twentieth century waged a war of aggression against the United Kingdom and badly depleted the country's wealth as it resisted defeat. However, the Germans do not have to shoulder all responsibility for this outcome. The United States and its business elites also acted as grave diggers by pursuing the diminution of both British industry and the City. They succeeded over time, while helping German industry to regain its strength after the two wars in which they had stood on opposite sides. There is a further irony to this tangled triangular relationship. On two occasions in the twentieth century, Germany tried to establish by military force a large territorial empire and closed economic bloc and failed, largely because of American opposition with its own vision of a multilateral world trading system that could accommodate *informal* imperial solutions, that is, the economic penetration of another society without its occupation and direct administration. At the end of the twentieth century, German big business, having always been in two minds about a formal empire, had command of an *informal*, though largely Open Door, sphere of influence, the European Union, without having fired a single shot.

In light of these developments that no one could possibly have predicted a century earlier, it would be tempting to extend the analysis into the end of the twentieth century. But this would require another book of how, following Britain's deindustrialization under Margaret Thatcher and her successors, the City had by the 1990s become an appendix of Wall Street. In this position it thrived for a while, partly by pushing the deregulation of the financial system even further than the Americans. The trouble was that the creation of almost unlimited speculative opportunities—in markets that operated largely outside the constitutional and institutional frameworks that had been established in the 1930s to regulate and enforce principles designed to prevent another wild investment boom and subsequent bust—produced yet another bubble that burst in 2007–8. There is now a rich literature that traces the roots, the workings, and the irresponsible behavior of economic and political elites—with those of the United States in the lead and the Europeans, with some exceptions, joining the exuberant party until the lights went out, just as they had in 1929.

The lessons of the interwar period were forgotten. The belief was that the secrets of permanent growth and prosperity had been found with the help of mathematical modeling and rational macroeconomic analysis and that the risks that capitalism had hitherto posed had disappeared. The crisis that followed bore many of the hallmarks of the 1930s. As far as Anglo-American economic relations were concerned the crisis proved even more fatal to Britain because this time it also caused havoc to the financial system. While Britain no longer had a manufacturing industry to speak of, the outsourcing policies of the multinationals also hit the American industrial sector hard. A sad example of this decline is a large area just north of the Tappan Zee Bridge across the Hudson River in New York. What had once been a large GM plant where Chevrolets and other cars had been assembled up to 1996 is now a *tabula rasa*. Faced with countless empty factory buildings and urban decay, Americans began to ask themselves after the failure of their financial sector what had happened to their manufacturing system, and since it had fallen so much behind whether it wasn't high time to *reindustrialize.*

It now turned out that the erstwhile German-American "special relationship" had in fact been abandoned because, unlike Washington, Berlin had refused not only to dismantle its postwar welfare system as radically as had happened in the United States, but also to abandon its manufacturing sector. Partly thanks to continued government support, this sector remained dynamic and innovative and did not have to be rebuilt from scratch to secure the country's prosperity and relative stability in highly competitive global markets. There Germany's large and medium-sized firms found the open markets that the United States had once determinedly shaped but now had to leave to others because they were not producing, as they had once done so successfully, "mass" and high value-added goods but merely generated purely speculative profits of no tangible and lasting value that lined the pockets of a very few. This outcome is perhaps the most unexpected balance sheet to emerge from the history of the North Atlantic triangle whose history has been at the center of this book.

Looking back across the twentieth century at American big business and its two "special relationships," there are other ironies and puzzles that deserve further research. Germany, whose politicians unleashed the havoc of two world wars upon its people and its business communities, suffered, like the rest of Europe, enormous losses in the first half of the century. But it then reemerged, with American help, as a more stable and prosperous country than Britain, the ally of the United States. And yet, West Germany's political and economic development after 1945 was not merely due to a stroke of good luck. The resurgence of West German industry and commerce was furthered not only by a greater willingness than existed in Britain to adopt and adapt to American ideas and practices of how to organize a modern market economy; nor was it merely the outbreak of the Cold War. Rather it was also the survival of traditions and institutions that dated back to the late nineteenth century: the support of manufacturing against the financial sector, the stress on high-quality work and education of both workers and managers, facilitated by cooperative labor relations, the capacity to export high value-added, reliable products. By contrast, Britain, already behind on all these counts before 1914, never marshaled the energies to catch up. Exceptions always granted, the manufacturing sector failed to modernize, labor relations and training remained poor, and the City expanded its influence, although it proved no match to the weight that Wall Street had consecutively gained in global international finance. In the end, London hitched its wagon to New York and, thanks to liberal regulation and lax enforcement, became a magnet for foreign investors who put their monies into hedge funds that operated outside the regulatory framework that had once upon a time been designed to control the power of the banks. Britain's decline was—as we have seen—partly self-inflicted, but it was accelerated by its former German foe as well as its former U.S. ally, with the American big business community leading the charge.

Beyond these tangible developments there is one final disciplinary point to be made that was first raised in the Introduction. While the quantitative aspects of the British and German economic experience under the *Pax Americana* are important, it is to be hoped that the comparative *qualitative* empirical material presented in this book will, on the one hand, persuade social and cultural historians to reintegrate the elements of business cultures and political economy in their research and teaching. On the other, it will perhaps convince economic historians not to look exclusively toward quantitative macroeconomics and mathematical modeling, but toward their colleagues in traditional departments of history. Finally, may this book contribute to the study not just of how the United States and its business community affected other societies, but also how they perceived and practiced their hegemony beyond the shores of the North American continent. There is still much work to be done in this latter field, and not just with respect to Britain and Germany but relating to the rest of Europe and the world.

ACKNOWLEDGMENTS

This book has gone through a long gestation period in the course of which I discussed its ideas and conceptualizations with more colleagues and friends than can be listed here. I would merely like to mention and thank explicitly those who read and commented upon individual chapters or the entire manuscript: Jeremy Adelman, Carole Fink, Walter Goldstein, Ira Katznelson, Jürgen Kocka, Gustav Schmidt, Anders Stephanson, Carl Wennerlind, Jonathan Wiesen, and three anonymous readers. I am also very grateful to Brigitta van Rheinberg and her staff at Princeton University Press for steering the manuscript through the review and production process, and to Joseph Dahm for his most careful copyediting. Marion, my wife, has—as on many previous occasions—not only been an indefatigable supporter of this project, its gentle critic, and my intellectual companion, but also shown great tolerance when over the past year or so my many notes, papers, and books on which this study is based wandered beyond my own four walls and cluttered up other parts of our apartment.

The book is dedicated to her and our three children.

INDEX

///

NB: Frequently recurring subjects, such as "Empire," "United States," and "Nazi," are not listed. German companies are identified as "A.G.," British ones as "Ltd." and American ones as "Co." or "Corp." Please also refer to the Table of Contents, whose many subheadings are designed to facilitate quicker reference to key concepts.

ACC (American Chamber of Commerce), 72, 243–44, 308

Adenauer, K., 189, 262, 280, 342, 347, 350, 353

AEG (Allgemeine Electricitäts-Gesellschaft), 62, 66, 98, 138, 170, 190, 192, 194, 199–200, 225

Afri-Cola (drink), 250

Agfa A.G., 67, 198, 259, 282

Aldrich, W., 300, 308

American Bridge Corp., 63

American Century (*see also* Luce, H.), 2–4, 18, 288, 327, 343, 345

American Manufacturers Export Association, 133

American Rubber Association, 185

American Ship and Commerce Company, 138

American Steel Export Association, 197

Americanization, 1–4, 12, 17–19, 31–32, 64, 185, 190, 195, 199, 332, 337, 343, 347, 351–52, 355

Angell, N., 88, 90–91, 103, 107, 153, 266

Anti-Americanism, 19, 34, 37, 45, 51, 70–71, 90, 100, 195, 240, 264

Anti-Semitism, 232, 241, 253–54, 257, 261, 265, 271, 273, 279, 283

Anti-Socialist Laws, 46

Antitrust, 83, 102, 196, 291–92, 298

Appeasement: American, 239–42, 250–54, 276, 283; British, 236–37, 241, 275–76

Arabia (ocean liner), 115

Arbeitgeber, Der, 335, 351–52

Army League, 87

Arnold, Th., 219, 247, 275, 291–92, 298, 312, 343, 346, 350

Asquith, H.H., 109

AT&T (American Telephone & Telegraph Company), 244, 247

Atlantic Charter of 1941, 20, 289

ATRAC A.G., 326

Attlee, C., 302–4, 312, 323, 334

Austin Motors Ltd., 263

Austria, 6, 30, 46, 59, 72, 76, 93, 97, 108–11, 126, 142, 150, 153, 235, 263

Autarky/autarkic, 7, 171, 285, 287, 289, 293, 311–12, 338, 360

Axis powers, 6, 163, 228, 250, 270, 283, 285–87, 289, 293, 299, 301–2, 311, 359–60

Babcock & Wilson Corp., 40
BAC (Business Advisory Council), 244
Baldwin, S., 167, 180, 184, 187, 238
Balfour, A., 53, 186
Balkan Crisis, 93
Ballin, A., 68–69, 78, 99, 106, 110–12, 154
Bank of England, 109, 182–83, 185, 187,
    215–16, 320–21
Baring Bank Ltd., 91
Barron's (magazine), 252–53, 279
Baruch, B., 242, 310, 344
BASF (Badische Anilin- und Sodafab-
    riken A.G.), 67–68, 99, 198, 311
Basic Law (of the Federal Republic of
    Germany), 312, 314, 316
Bayer A.G., 67, 99, 198, 311
BdA (German Employers Federation),
    335
BDI (Bundesverband der Deutschen
    Industrie), 329, 331–32, 338
Beaverbrook, Lord, 184
Bebel, A., 88
Beiersdorf A.G. (pharmaceuticals), 307
Benes, E., 152
Benthsen, A., 67
Berg, F., 329
Berge, W., 292, 298
Berliner Illustrirte Zeitung, 24, 62, 274
Bernstein, E., 310
Bethmann Hollweg, Th. von, 89, 106, 110,
    115–16, 122
BICO (Bi-Partite Control Office), 315, 325
Bilateralism, 234, 239–40
Bismarck, O. von, 9, 24–25, 35, 46, 56, 80,
    85–86, 222, 331, 353
Bissell, R., 310
Bi-Zone (British-American), 303–4, 314,
    318, 323, 325
BL (British Leyland Ltd.), 337
Bleichroeder Bank, 48
BLM (British Leyland Motors Ltd.),
    336–37
Blomberg, W. von, 251
BMC (British Motor Corporation), 336–37
BMW (Bayerische Motorenwerke A.G.),
    226, 337, 353
Boehringer, C.F. & Sons (chemicals), 198
Boeing Aircraft Corp., 246
Boer War, 22, 25
Bolsheviks, 124, 137, 146, 170

Borah, W., 167
Bosch A.G., 190, 192–94, 215, 255, 311, 347
Brandt, W., 342
Braun, O., 306
Bretton Woods (Conference and Agree-
    ment), 319, 322, 348–49
Briand, A., 146, 161, 168–70
Brown, Boveri & Cie., 66, 74
Brown, L.H., 308–10, 346
Brüning, H., 193, 207, 280
Brunner, Mond & Co. (chemicals), 67,
    198
Buchanan, F., 272
Bullitt, W.C., 269
Bülow, B. von, 29, 47, 52–53, 71, 78, 100
Burck, G., 332, 351
Burroughs Wellcome Ltd., 198
Business Week (magazine), 252–54, 279–80
Button Company, 60
Byrnes, J., 313, 345

Cannes Conference, 145–47, 158
Cartelization, 84, 102, 192, 197, 201, 217,
    298, 310
Cartels, 14, 43, 79–84, 87, 96, 102, 195–97,
    284, 289, 292–94, 298–301, 307–8
Case School of Applied Science (*see also*
    Education, Training), 38
Casella A.G. (chemicals), 67, 198, 311
CBI (Confederation of British Industry),
    338
CED (Committee for Economic Develop-
    ment), 110, 129, 293, 299–301, 316, 344
CFR (Council on Foreign Relations),
    293–94, 299, 328, 344
Chamberlain, J., 22, 28, 53, 84
Chamberlain, N., 235, 238–43, 246,
    267–68, 360
Charlottenburg Polytechnic, 38, 73
Chemical industries, 39, 66–68, 98–99,
    138–39, 175, 179, 187, 193, 198–99, 201,
    212, 259
Chemnitz Polytechnic (*see also* Technical
    High Schools), 26, 62, 73
Churchill, W., 7, 20, 111, 184, 221, 243,
    248–49, 277, 278, 293–97, 302, 312
Ciano, G., 270
City, The, pre-1914: 7–8, 10, 46, 48, 68; in
    World War I, 109, 114; in 1920s, 131,

133, 144, 146, 168, 170, 173, 182–89; in
  1930s, 215, 220, 240, 262, 276, 283–84;
  after World War II, 304, 306, 314, 319,
  322, 333, 339–40, 344, 346, 357–59,
  361–63
Clay, L.D., 307–10, 318, 346
Closed Space Economy (Grossraum-
  wirtschaft), 109, 114, 144, 196, 214, 234,
  264, 289, 324, 362
Coca-Cola Corp., 189, 228, 259, 272, 281
Codeterminantion (see also Works Coun-
  cils, Paritätische Mitbestimmung), 314,
  347
Collyer, J., 328
Columbian (magazine), 72
Communism, 151, 252, 269, 295, 301
Continental Gummi A.G., 65–66, 326
Coolidge, C., 177, 182
Cripps, S., 314, 321, 334, 347
Crossfields & Lever Bros. Ltd., 67, 198
Crowe, E., 186
CTR (Computing-Tabulating-Recording
  Co.), 272
Cunard (shipping line), 68–69, 73, 99

Dahlerus, B., 267
Daimler-Benz A.G., 41, 97, 264, 282, 284,
  353
Dalton, H., 318, 348
Darwinism, Social, 229, 264
Davis, N., 163–64, 346, 358–59
Dawes Plan, 168, 170–78, 183, 185–86,
  188, 194, 200, 203–7, 210, 358
DDP (Deutsche Demokratische Partei),
  168
De Gaulle, C., 338
De-cartellization, 294, 298, 304, 307–15,
  344, 347
Decolonization, 5, 305, 339, 343
De-Nazification, 294, 297, 309, 313
Deutsche Bank A.G., 48, 155, 311, 347
Dillon Read & Co., 200, 206, 224
Douglas Aircraft Corp., 246
Dow Chemicals Corp., 67, 176, 198, 294
Draper, W., 310–11, 328, 347
Dresel, E., 163–64
Duco Lackfabrik A.G., 198
Dürkopp A.G., 59
Düsseldorf Agreement, 167, 311

Dulles, J.F., 340, 350, 353
Dunlop Tyres Ltd. , 65–66
Dupont de Nemours (chemicals), 67
DVP (Deutsche Volkspartei), 168

Eberstadt, F., 206
ECA (European Cooperation Administra-
  tion), 322
Economist, The (magazine), 71, 300, 302,
  316, 319, 337
ECSC (European Coal and Steel Commu-
  nity), 313, 323–24, 326, 349–50
Eden, A., 340–41, 361
Edison, Th., 24, 78, 101
Education (and training), 31, 36–39, 45,
  55, 75, 87, 96, 100, 202, 232, 329, 335,
  356, 363
EFTA (European Free Trade Area), 338
Eisenhower, D.D., 307, 340–41
Entente Cordiale of 1904, 76, 89, 101
Erhard, L., 277, 317, 329, 311–32, 353
Eupen-Malmedy region, 169

Fabian Society (of Britain), 26
Fachhochschulen (see also for Education,
  Training), 76
Fachschulen (see also for Education,
  Training), 75
FBI (Federation of British Industry), 136,
  157, 184, 186, 266–67, 338
FDI (Foreign Direct Investment, by the
  U.S. in Europe), 15–17, 41–42, 44, 51,
  57, 60, 68, 95–98, 160, 174–75, 182, 187,
  192, 194–95
Federal Reserve Bank, 166, 168, 183, 211,
  214, 216, 221
Film (see also Hollywood), 224, 259, 281
Filmkontingenzgesetz, 189
Financial Times, 51, 56
Firestone Corp., 330
Firestone, H., 330
Flick, F., 313, 347
Forbes (magazine), 135, 138, 157, 178, 183,
  196–97, 220–21, 224–25, 252–53, 279
Forbes, B.C., 175
Ford, E., 247
Ford, H., 96, 223, 255, 261–62, 271–72,
  283, 291

Ford Motors, 16, 156, 191, 198, 215, 228, 261–64, 271, 282–83, 291, 294, 309, 333, 336–37, 360
Fordism (see also Mass production; Productivity), 55, 96, 192, 194, 282, 356
Fortune (magazine), 252–53, 304, 332, 345, 351
Fowlers Ltd., 73
Francis Joseph I, Austro-Hungarian emperor, 111, 357
Frederick II, king of Prussia, 9, 54–55, 71, 75
Free Corps, 137
Free Trade, 22, 28, 35, 84, 185, 289–91, 300, 338
Friedrich, C.J., 327–28
Friedrich, O.A., 315, 324, 326–32

Galbraith, J.K., 211–13, 225–26
GARIOA (Government Appropriations for Relief in Occupied Areas), 325–26, 341
GATT (General Agreement on Tariffs and Trade), 322, 348–49
Gavin Corp., 62
GE (General Electric), 66, 98, 168, 199–200, 210, 225, 244, 309
Generation (and generational change), 90, 98, 134, 163, 181, 211, 221, 256–57, 326, 331
Genoa Conference of 1922, 105, 124, 132, 145–46, 151–53, 158–59, 161–62, 170, 182, 217
Gilbert, P., 174, 188–89, 201–3, 205–11, 219, 276, 332, 351
Gladstone, W., 25
Glass-Steagall Act, 244, 290
Globalization, 14, 18, 345
GM (General Motors), 215, 244, 247–48, 259, 261–66, 268–72, 284, 294, 309–10, 334, 336, 360
Goebbels, J., 233, 265–69
Goldman Sachs Trading Corp., 212
Goodrich Corp., 65, 315, 326, 328
Goodyear Corp., 328. 330
Göring, H., 234, 265–69
Greater East Asia Co-prosperity Sphere, 228

Grey, A.S., 196, 207
Grey, E., 111
Guggenheim Corp., 139
Gwinner, A., 48

Haldane, R.B., 77–78, 111
Halder, F., 270
Halifax, E.L., 249, 269
Halske (Siemens A.G.), 66, 98
Hammond, J.H., 178–79, 181
HAPAG (Hamburg-Amerikanische Paket Aktien-Gesellschaft), 68–69, 99, 112, 138, 154
Harding, W., 161–62, 164, 177
Harriman, A., 309
Harriman, H., 244
Harris-Burland, W., 303, 345
Harvard University, 71, 300, 316, 322, 326–27
Heinrich, prince of Prussia, 70–71
Henle, G., 324, 350
Himmler, H., 230, 232, 271–72, 281
Hindenburg, P. von, 128, 201–2, 216, 225, 236–37, 250–51
Hitler, A.: 6, 15, 34, 56; and America, 239, 245–56; and British and American peace efforts, 266–74; and rearmament, 194, 257; rise and politics, 216, 225–36; and World War II, 287–89
Hoechst A.G. (chemicals), 67, 198, 311
Hoffman, P., 244, 299–300, 304, 307, 310–12, 316, 318, 320, 322–23, 326, 328, 332
Hollerith Corp., 200, 272–73
Hollywood (see also Film), 161, 189, 199, 258
Holocaust, 285, 287, 294
Hoover, H., 145, 162, 210, 216, 225, 248
Hossbach, F., 235, 241
Houghton, A.B., 176–77
House, E., 132
Housing, 26, 129, 136, 192
Hugenberg, A., 251–52
Hughes, C., 145, 162–65, 167, 176–77, 181, 218–19, 282
Hull, C., 239–43, 245, 264, 269, 273, 276, 288–89, 291, 295–96, 302, 310
Humphrey, A.L., 202–3
Humphrey, G., 341

ICI (Imperial Chemical Industries), 198, 294, 311, 341, 349
IG (Interessengemeinschaft), 198, 224, 282
IGE (International GE), 199–200
IH (International Harvester), 58–59, 94, 244
IHG (Investitionshilfe-Gesetz), 325
IMCC (Inter-Allied Military Control Commission), 169
IMMC (International Mercantile Marine Company), 68–69
IRA (International Ruhr Authority), 278, 365
IRG (Internationale Rohstahlgemein-schaft), 196–97
IRRC (International Rubber Regulation Committee), 327–28
Issigonis, A., 336
ITO (International Trade Organization), 322

Jagow, G. von, 107, 111–12
Japan, 6, 13; post-1918, 132, 142–43, 170; in 1930s, 227, 231, 235, 240–42, 245, 249; from 1941, 286–87, 289, 298, 324, 347, 359
Jaurès, J., 110–11
Jazmatzi (cigarettes), 61
JCS (Joint Chiefs of Staff), 297, 307
Johns Hopkins University, 75, 100
Junkers (Aircraft), 268

Kadett (Opel Cars), 263
Kahn, O., 216
Kaiser (see Wilhelm II)
Kaiser, H., 248–49, 343
Kalle A.G. (chemicals), 67, 198
Kapp Putsch of March 1920, 141
Katz, M., 310
Kayser Glove Corp., 60, 95
Kellogg-Briand Pact of 1928, 170
Keynes, J. M., 145, 161, 164, 181, 183, 217–18, 223, 279, 296, 318, 345, 348
Keynesianism, 194, 197, 223, 254, 341
KfW (Kreditanstalt für Wiederaufbau), 325
Kilgore, H., 298–99, 344–45
Klein, J., 175, 179

Klöckner, P., 324
Knudsen, W., 247–49, 266, 284, 310, 360
Kodak Corp., 259, 282
Kokswerke A.G., 198
Kreuz-Zeitung, 24, 29, 46, 53
Kronprinzessin Cecilie (ocean liner), 113
Krupp, A., 313
Krupp A.G., 39–40, 54, 63–65, 74, 97, 170, 308, 347
Kuhn, Loeb & Co., 92, 123, 216

Lamont, Th., 158, 165, 216, 225–26
Langer, W., 269, 284
Langnamverein (Ruhr Coal and Steel Association), 193
Laubfrosch (Opel Cars), 262–63
Laura Spelman Rockefeller Foundation, 244
Lausanne Agreement of 1932, 216
League of Nations, 87, 125–26, 144, 156, 166, 170, 178
Legge, A., 244
Lend-Lease Agreement, 243, 248–49, 278, 295–97, 302, 305, 317–18, 333, 338, 361
Lever Bros. Ltd., 67, 198
Liberals (in Britain), 28, 77, 84, 86, 101
Lindbergh, C., 249, 271, 283
Litchfield, P. W., 328
Lloyd George, D., 89, 118, 124, 144–48, 151–53, 158, 161, 163–64, 170, 218
Locarno Pact of 1925, 168–70, 202, 219
Loewe, L., 62
"Lost Generation," 181
Louise, queen of Prussia, 24
Lowell Institute, 38
Luce, H. (*see also* American Century), 2, 18, 244, 288
Ludendorff, E., 123, 201, 218
Lusitania (ocean liner), 115, 119, 122
Luther, M., 9

Macdonald, R., 180–81, 276
Macmillan, H., 156, 339, 341, 353
Macy's (department store), 244
Maginot Line, 169, 219
Mahan, A., 71
Maltzan, G.O. von, 202

Mandates (under League of Nations),
    125, 144, 156
Mantoux, E., 161, 217
Marshall Plan, 132, 157, 300, 304, 316,
    319–22, 325–26, 334, 344–45, 350
Martin, J., 310
Marx, W., 176
Mason, E., 281, 300–301, 316, 345, 348
Mass-consumption, 4, 11, 29, 60, 78, 80,
    83, 95–96, 160–61, 192, 194, 222, 228,
    230, 247, 257–63, 267, 281–82, 291, 302,
    318
Mass-production (see also Fordism; Ra-
    tionalization; Taylorism), 4, 11, 41, 60,
    80, 96, 160, 186, 194–97, 213, 261, 264,
    282–83, 291, 334, 337
McCloy, J.J., 324–25
McCormick Corp., 2, 18, 58, 94
Mellon, A., 167, 174, 212, 310
Mendelssohn, F. von, 48
Merchandise Stamp Act, 28
Merck A.G., 198
Merck, G., 198
Merck, G.W., 198
Merganthaler Corp., 60, 95
Metropolitan Vickers Electrical Company
    Ltd., 200, 202
MFN (Most Favored Nation) Trade
    Treaty, 240
Mini (Austin, later BMW car), 336–37
Minnesota Mining and Manufacturing
    Corp., 198
Moltke, H. von, the Elder, 24
Moltke, H. von, the Younger, 106–8,
    110–11, 153
Mond, A., 184
Monnet, J., 320, 323, 350
Monopoly, 21, 55, 60, 79–80, 82–83, 102,
    192, 195, 255, 293, 298, 300, 311, 316
Monroe Doctrine, 27, 35, 53, 240
Moody, J., 205–6
Moody's Investors Services, 205
Morgan, J.P., 109, 113
Morgan Bank, 58, 68–69, 121, 123, 157–58,
    165, 172–73, 177, 216, 220–21
Morgenthau, H., 239, 242–43, 245–47, 249,
    266, 277–78, 286, 294–97, 302, 306–8,
    361
Morgenthau Plan, 295–97, 302, 306–8,
    333, 344–45, 361
Morley, J., 111

Moroccan Crisis of 1905, 76
Moroccan Crisis of 1911, 89
Morris, H., 263
Morris Motors Ltd., 262–63, 333, 336
Motorization, 64–65, 96, 260, 282, 333,
    335
Müller, G.A. von, 105–6, 153
Müller, H., 209
Multilateralism, 239–40, 302
Munich Agreement, 238, 246, 267
Mussolini, B., 134, 171, 218, 228, 243,
    245–46, 250, 279, 287

NAM (National Association of Manufac-
    turers), 244
Napoleon I, 23–24
Nasser, G.A., 7, 340, 353
NCB (National City Bank), 30, 49, 53,
    91–92, 94, 109, 113–14, 118, 120, 123,
    126–28, 156
NCR (National Cash Register), 60, 139,
    272
New Deal, 190, 243, 247–48, 250, 253–55,
    277, 289–90, 298–99, 312, 331, 343, 359
New Order (American plans for), 293
New Order (Nazi plans for), 229–31, 237,
    274, 287, 343
NGL (North-German Lloyd), 68–69,
    112
NHS (National Health Service), 303
Niles Tools Corp., 42, 62, 96
Nobel Ltd., 67, 198
Norman, M., 88, 90, 103, 107, 141, 144,
    153, 158, 163, 183–86, 216, 266, 358
NRK (Nationale Registrier-Kassen), 60
Nye, G. P., 291
Nye Committee, 299
NYT (New York Times), 52–53, 60, 66,
    70–72, 75, 83, 155, 214, 251

Oerlikon Company of Switzerland, 74
Oligopoly, 14, 79, 82, 298, 301, 312,
    315–16, 355
OMGUS (Office of Military Government
    US), 304, 307, 309–10, 316, 325
Opel Cars, 60, 64–66, 215, 261–66, 268,
    282–84
Open Door (American plans for): 7,
    11–12, 25; pre-1914, 63, 71, 77, 81; in

1920s, 133, 143–44, 167, 171, 175, 182,
    185, 196, 207, 217; in 1930s, 239–40,
    257–58, 264; in World War II, 289, 295;
    after 1945, 301–2, 312, 318, 321–24, 332,
    338–39, 342, 348, 360–63
Osram A.G., 199
OSS (Office of Strategic Services), 293–94
Osthandel, 220, 342, 353
Ostpolitik, 220, 342, 353
Otis Elevators Corp., 61, 96, 139
Ottawa Conference of 1932, 215, 289
Ottoman Empire, 35, 125

Pan-German League, 87
Papen, F. von, 251
Paris Peace Conference of 1919, 124–25,
    132, 143, 163–64
Paritätische Mitbestimmung (see also
    Codetermination; Works Councils),
    314
Parliamentarization, 86
Patents, 28, 44, 199, 274, 293–94, 344
Pax Americana, 143, 245, 286–91, 297, 361,
    364
Pax Anglo-Americana, 7, 20, 181, 305
Pax Gallica, 169
Pax Germania, 286–91
Pax Nipponica, 288
Pax Romana, 288
Pearl Harbor (Japanese attack on, 1941),
    249, 274, 288
Pfaff A.G. (sewing machines), 59
Phoenix A.G., 310, 315, 327, 329–30
Poensgen, E., 197
Pogrom (Nazi in 1938), 265
Poincaré, R., 111, 146, 161–62, 167–68,
    185, 219
Poniatowski, (Prince and French banker),
    93, 104, 121–22, 156
Porsche, F., 260, 263–64, 284
Potsdam Conference of 1945, 308
Pound (see also Sterling), 182, 184–85, 215,
    319, 329–30
Pratt & Whitney Corp., 247
Procter & Gamble Corp., 198
Productivity (see also Fordism; Rationali-
    zation; Scientific Management; Taylor-
    ism), 21, 81, 120, 179–80, 191, 213, 222,
    325, 336
Productivity Councils, 316, 334

Qualitätsarbeit, 41, 54, 96, 363
Quality, 2, 11, 28, 41, 44, 62, 64, 127–28,
    336, 352, 363
Quarantine Speech of 1937, 241, 246, 254,
    359
Quebec Conference of 1944, 295, 297, 307,
    344, 361

R&D (Research & Development), 15, 44,
    64, 356
Rapallo Conference of 1922, 147, 150, 158,
    161, 217, 342
Rathenau, E., 66
Rathenau, W., 98, 138, 199
Rationalization (see also Taylorism, Ford-
    ism, Scientific Management, productiv-
    ity), 26, 43, 96, 180, 186, 190–92, 194–95,
    197, 260–61, 336
RCA (Radio City of America), 168, 199,
    212
RDI (Reichsverband der Deutschen
    Industrie), 193–94
Reagan, R., 7–8, 20
Red Army, 170, 250, 286
Red Star Line, 68
Redfield, W., 127
Reed, Ph., 309
Reich Court, 81, 102
Reichsbank, 110, 185, 202, 221, 233
Reichstag, 16, 29, 46–47, 70, 77–78, 86–87,
    89, 92, 176, 201, 209, 232, 252
Reichswehr, 170, 194, 220, 232–33, 250–51
Remington-Rand Corp., 309
Renault Cars, 137, 157, 284
Reusch, P., 193, 223
Revelstoke, Lord, 91, 104
Revere Corp., 60
Ribbentrop, J. von, 234, 267, 270, 275
Robertson, H.M., 204
Rockefeller, W., 53
Röhm, E., 232
Roosevelt, F.D., 235, 239, 241–50, 254–55,
    257, 264–66, 269–73, 276, 280, 284, 286–
    95, 297–99, 301–2, 307, 343–44, 359–61
Roosevelt, Th., 7, 20, 23, 34–35, 70–71, 76,
    100–101
Rootes Ltd., 335–36
Rothermere Press, 186
Rothschilds (bankers in France and Brit-
    ain), 109–110

Ruhr industrial region, 148–50, 152, 160, 162, 165–69, 172, 185, 193–97, 209, 218–19, 233, 256, 259, 295, 297, 303–4, 308, 310–11, 313–18, 323–24, 329, 331, 342, 345, 347, 350, 358
Ruhreisenstreit, 193, 197
Rukeyser, M.S., 183
Ruml, B., 244, 299
Rüsselsheim (Opel-GM factory), 60, 263, 265–66, 268, 284, 309

SA (Sturmabteilung of Nazi Party), 232, 237
Samoa Islands, 27
Sand, G., 24
Sarajevo, Crisis of July 1914, 94, 105–6
Sartorius von Waltershausen, A., 71–72
Saturday Evening Post (magazine), 271, 279
Schacht, H., 185, 202, 216, 233, 253
Schäfer, A., 304, 331
Schering A.G. (pharmaceuticals), 198, 224, 277
Schiff, J., 92, 104, 123
Schlieffen, A. von, 106
Schuckert (of Siemens A.G.), 41, 66, 203
Schuman, R., 323–24, 349
Schwabach, P., 111
Schwerin-Krosigk, L., 257, 280
Scientific Management (see also Fordism; Productivity; Rationalization; Taylorism), 55, 191
Sears & Roebuck Corp., 244, 310
Ségur, P. de, 34, 78, 102
Sherman, J., 80
Sherman Act, 14, 79–80, 96, 102, 133, 195, 290–92, 298, 301, 308, 315
Siemens A.G., 66, 98, 138, 170, 191–94, 200–201, 203, 220, 225, 256, 282–83, 311, 353
Singer Corp., 59–60, 95, 139
Skoda Works of Czechoslovakia, 111
Sloan, A., 114, 155, 244, 262–63, 283, 310
Smoot-Hawley Tariffs, 216
Smuts, J., 163–64, 218, 358
Society of Motor Manufacturers and Trades of Britain, 334
Sohl, H.-G., 324, 350
Spanish-American War, 23, 27, 52
SPD (Sozialdemokratische Partei Deutschlands), 24, 46–47, 88–89, 197, 209

Speer, A., 306
Speyer, J., 216
Sprenger, J., 265–66, 268
SS (Schutz-Staffel of Nazi Party), 232, 271–72
Stalin, J., 228, 235, 286, 294, 309, 322
Standard Oil Corp., 40, 53, 63, 82–83, 97, 102, 115, 138, 198, 244
Stead, W.T., 2, 6, 18, 30–37, 45, 50–52, 54, 57, 70, 199, 332, 355
Stein, H., 299
Sterling, 7, 48, 113, 180, 182–85, 215, 293, 305–6, 321–22, 341, 344, 348, 361
Stettinius, E.R., 246–47, 302, 310, 345
Stillman, J., 53, 90, 92–93, 103–4, 126–27, 155–56
Stresemann, G., 168–70, 176, 209, 218–19
Strikes, 47, 56, 74, 180, 186, 202, 320, 356
Strong, B., 183–85
Studebaker Corp., 156, 244, 300
Submarine warfare (in World War I), 115–17, 121, 123
Suez Crisis of 1956, 7, 11, 287, 323, 339–41, 353, 361
Suttner, B. von, 24
Swan Hunter Ltd., 73
Swope, G., 199, 244
Syndicates, 14, 43, 79–81, 195, 298, 308, 310, 314–15, 317, 324

Taft, W.H., 83
Tariffs, pre-1914: 22, 28–29, 44, 46–48, 52, 56, 64, 66, 68, 84; in 1920s, 144, 180, 197; in 1930s, 215–16, 240; post-1941, 290, 293, 295, 297, 318, 322, 332, 348
Taxation, 77–78, 208, 212
Taylor, F., 18, 55, 75, 99, 191, 244, 280
Taylorism (see also Fordism, productivity, rationalization, mass production, Scientific Management), 42, 55, 96, 191, 222, 260, 356
TDR (Treasury Deposit Receipts), 319
Teagle, W., 244
Technical High Schools (see also Education; Training), 38, 73
Teheran Conference of 1943, 294
Tennant, E.W., 267
Thatcher, M., 7–8, 20, 312, 314, 337, 362
Thoiry Conference of 1926, 169
Thyssen A.G., 311, 324
Thyssen, F., 195

Tietz (department stores), 61, 96
Time-Life Corp., 244
Tirpitz, A. von, 34, 37, 51–52, 54, 70, 77,
    89, 97, 101, 115, 155, 275
Tischbein, W., 65
Titanic (ocean liner), 54, 68, 99
Tocqueville, A. de, 85
Tolstoy, L., 25
Trade unions, 31, 47, 56, 120, 180, 190–92,
    209, 222, 232, 314, 316, 330–31, 335, 337,
    343, 356
Training (*see also* Education; Technical
    High Schools), 30–31
Tri-Zone (American-British-French), 323
Triple Entente of 1907, 89
Truman, H., 302–3, 318–19, 323, 333,
    344–46, 361
Trust: 5, 16–17; pre-1914, 48, 50, 79–80,
    82–83, 102, 111; in 1920s, 138, 146, 193,
    196, 199–200, 203; in 1930s, 259, 262;
    post-1941, 290–92, 298, 310–11, 324

Unilever Ltd., 341
Union Carbide Corp., 198
Union Electrical Corp., 41–42
Union Switch Corp., 202
United Alkali Corp., 67, 198
United Steel Works (*see also* Vereinigte
    Stahlwerke; VSt), 195–97, 255, 311, 315,
    324
Urbig, F., 48
U.S. Mail Steamship Co., 138
U.S. Navy, 35, 97, 249
U.S. Rubber Corp., 65–66
U.S. Steel Corp., 62–64, 94, 195, 197, 212,
    244, 246, 302, 310, 345

Vansittard, R., 269
Vauxhall Cars Ltd., 262–63, 334, 336
Venezuela Crisis of 1902, 23, 27, 52, 70
Verbundwirtschaft (vertical integration
    between coal and steel), 195
Verne, J., 112
Versailles Treaty of 1919, 125–26, 137,
    146–47, 162, 164, 169, 233
Vickers Armstrong Ltd., 200, 202
Viles, A., 327–29
Vögler, A., 195–97
Volkswagen Works, 236, 259–60, 263, 268,
    282, 334–35, 352–53

Vorwärts (Social Democrat newspaper),
    25, 53
Vossische Zeitung, 200
VSt (Vereinigte Stahlwerke), 195–97, 255,
    311, 315, 324

Warburg, M., 107–8
Warburg, P., 182–83, 202, 206
Washington System/Treaties of 1922, 13,
    142–44, 146
Watson, Th., 200, 272–74
Webb-Pomerene Act of 1918, 133, 196,
    300
Welles, S., 269–71
Weltpolitik, 13, 34–35, 70, 76, 94, 103, 154,
    226, 231, 275
Wertheim department stores, 61
Westinghouse Corp., 40, 42, 66, 74, 98,
    138, 202–3, 212, 214
Wharton School of Business, 38
White, D., 306
White Star Line, 68, 99
Wilhelm II, German emperor: 16; consti-
    tutional position, 45, 51, 54, 64, 70–72,
    76, 78, 87, 90; lessons from Wilhelmine
    foreign policy, 275, 356–57; role in
    outbreak of war and wartime, 94, 98,
    100–103, 106–8, 110–12, 123; role in
    politics, 22, 33–35, 37
Willner, S., 324
Wilson, W.B., 127
Wilson, W.W., 114, 116, 119, 124
Winter, J., 181
Wohlthat, H., 268–69, 284
Woolworth Corp., 61, 96, 228, 257–58,
    272, 280
Worchester Polytechnic, 38, 285
Works Councils (*see also* Codetermina-
    tion; Paritätische Mitbestimmung), 314
World Exhibitions and Expositions, 41,
    55, 58, 75, 94
Wright Aeronautics Corp., 212

"Yellow Peril," 13
Young, O.D., 168, 177–78, 182–83, 185,
    188, 199, 224
Young Plan of 1929, 200

Zimmermann Telegram of 1917, 116, 155